ANNUAL EGYPTOLOGICAL BIBLIOGRAPHY
BIBLIOGRAPHIE ÉGYPTOLOGIQUE ANNUELLE

INTERNATIONAL ASSOCIATION OF EGYPTOLOGISTS
ASSOCIATION INTERNATIONALE DES ÉGYPTOLOGUES

# ANNUAL EGYPTOLOGICAL BIBLIOGRAPHY

# BIBLIOGRAPHIE ÉGYPTOLOGIQUE ANNUELLE

## 1978

Compiled by / Composée par

**JAC. J. JANSSEN**

with the collaboration of / avec la collaboration de

**INGE HOFMANN**

and / et

**L. M. J. ZONHOVEN**

ARIS & PHILLIPS LTD

British Library Cataloguing in Publication Data

Annual Egyptological bibliography.—1978
  1. Egyptology—Bibliography—Periodicals
    016.932'007'2      DT60

  ISBN 0 85668 204 7

© Jac. J. Janssen 1982. All rights reserved. No part of this publication may be reproduced, stored in a retrieval system, or transmitted in any form by any means without the prior written permission of the publishers.

Printed and Published by ARIS & PHILLIPS LTD, Warminster, Wilts, England.

## TABLE OF CONTENTS

| | |
|---|---:|
| Acknowledgements | vi |
| List of Abbreviations | vii |
| Alphabetical List of Authors and Titles | 1 |
| Necrologies | 221 |

# ACKNOWLEDGEMENTS

The editor acknowledges the financial contribution for collecting the material for this volume by the following institutions:

Aegyptologisk Institut, Københavns Universitet,
Centre d'Études Orientales, Genève,
Deutsches Archäologisches Institut, Berlin-Cairo,
Durham University, Durham,
Egypt Exploration Society, London,
The Griffith Institute, Oxford,
Heidelberger Akademie der Wissenschaften, Heidelberg,
The Metropolitan Museum of Art, New York,
Museum of Fine Arts, Boston, Mass.,
Oosters Genootschap in Nederland, Leiden,
The Oriental Institute, The University of Chicago, Chicago, Ill.,
Royal Ontario Museum, Toronto,
Schweizersches Institut für Ägyptische Bauforschung und Altertumskunde, Kairo,
University of Liverpool, Liverpool,
The University Museum, The University of Pennsylvania, Philadelphia, Pa.,
Kon. Vitterhets-, Historie- och Antikvitetsakademien, Stockholm.

Adres van de redacteur / Editor's address
Adresse du rédacteur / Anschrift des Schriftleiters:

Dr. Jac. J. JANSSEN
Nederlands Instituut voor het Nabije Oosten
Noordeindsplein 4-6
LEIDEN 2311 AH

# LIST OF ABBREVIATIONS

1) *periodicals,* Festschriften *and serials:*

*Aegyptus:* Aegyptus. Rivista Italiana di Egittologia e di Papirologia, Milano 58 (1978).
*Address:* Università Cattolica (Scuola di Papirologia), Largo A. Gemelli 1, 20123 Milano, Italia.

*Aegyptus Antiquus:* Aegyptus Antiquus, Buenos Aires 3,1 (1978).
*Address:* Comité científico del Centro de Investigaciones Egiptológicas Buenos Aires (CIEBA), Canning 2194/3° "E", 1425 Buenos Aires, Argentina.

*AJA:* American Journal of Archaeology, [New York] 82 (1978).
*Address:* General Secretary, Archaeological Institute of America, 260 West Broadway, New York, N.Y. 10012, U.S.A.

*Antiquity:* Antiquity. A Quarterly Review of Archaeology, [Cambridge] 52 (1978).
*Address:* Heffers Printers Ltd, 104 Hills Road, Cambridge, CB2 1LW, Great Britain.

*Archaeology:* Archaeology. A Magazine Dealing with the Antiquity of the World, [New York] 31 (1978).
*Address:* Archaeology, 260 West Broadway, New York, N.Y. 10013, U.S.A.

*ASAE:* Annales du Service des Antiquités de l'Égypte, Le Caire.
*Address:* Service des Antiquités de l'Égypte, Le Caire, Egypte (R.A.U.).

*Atti del 1° Convegno Italiano sul Vicino Oriente Antico:* Atti del 1° Convegno Italiano sul Vicino Oriente Antico (Roma, 22-24 Aprile 1976), Roma, Centro per le Antichità e la Storia dell'Arte del Vicino Oriente, 1978 (20 x 28 cm; IX + 241 p., 36 fig. [many folding] on pl., 13 pl.) = Orientis Antiqui Collectio, 13.

*BASOR:* Bulletin of the American Schools of Oriental Research Number 229 (February, 1978), 230 (April 1978), 231 (October 1978) and 232 (Fall 1978).
*Address:* American Schools of Oriental Research, Publications Office, 126 Inman Str., Cambridge, Massachusetts 02139, U.S.A.

*BIFAO:* Bulletin de l'Institut français d'Archéologie orientale, Le Caire 78, fasc. 1-2 (1978).
*Address:* Imprimerie de l'Institut français d'Archéologie orientale, 37 Rue el Cheikh Aly Youssef (ex-rue Mounira), Le Caire, Égypte (R.A.U.).

*BiOr:* Bibliotheca Orientalis, Leiden 35 (1978).
*Address:* Noordeindsplein 4-6, Leiden, Nederland.

*BSFE:* Bulletin de la Société française d'Égyptologie. Réunions trimestrielles. Communications archéologiques No. 81 (mars 1978); No. 82 (juin 1978); No. 83 (octobre 1978).
*Address:* Mme. F. Le Corsu. Cabinet d'Égyptologie, Collège de France, 11 Place Marcelin-Berthelot, Paris 5^e, France.

*CdE:* Chronique d'Égypte. Bulletin périodique de la Fondation égyptologique Reine Elisabeth. Bruxelles LIII, Nos 105-106 (1978).
*Address:* Fondation égyptologique "Reine Elisabeth". Musées Royaux d'Art et d'Histoire, Parc du Cinquantenaire, B 1040 - Bruxelles, Belgique.

*Egitto e Vicino Oriente*: Egitto e Vicino Oriente. Rivista della sezione orientalistica dell' Istituto di Storia Antica Università degli Studi di Pisa, Pisa 1 (1978): rev. *Annali. Istituto Orientale di Napoli* 39 (N.S. 29)(1979), 345-347 (Giovanni Garbini).
*Address*: Giardini editori e stampatori de Pisa, Via Santa Bibbiana 28, 56100 Pisa, Italia.

*Enchoria*: Enchoria. Zeitschrift für Demotistik und Koptologie. Herausgegeben von E. Lüddeckens, H.-J. Thissen, K.-Th. Zauzich, in Kommission bei Otto Harrassowitz, Wiesbaden 8, Teil 1 (1978); 8, Teil 2 (1978); 8, Sonderband (1978).
[Lieferung I: 1. Internationales Demotisten-Colloquium. Berlin 26. - 28. September 1977; Lieferung II: 1. Internationaler Kongress für Koptologie. Kairo, o8. - 18. Dezember 1976].
*Address*: Otto Harrassowitz, Taunusstrasse 5, Postfach 349, 6200 Wiesbaden, Bundesrepublik Deutschland.

*Études nubiennes*: Études nubiennes. Colloque de Chantilly. 2-6 Juillet 1975, Le Caire, Institut français d'Archéologie orientale, [1978](20.4 x 27.7 cm; VII + 374 p., 60 pl. [2 folding], 3 maps, 5 fig.) = Bibliothèque d' Étude, 77; rev. *BiOr* 37 (1980), 57-58 (Inge Hofmann).

*Études et Travaux:* Études et Travaux, Warszawa 10 (1978).
*Address*: PWN-Éditions Scientifiques de Pologne, Warszawa, Pologne.

*GM*: Göttinger Miszellen. Beiträge zur ägyptologischen Diskussion, Göttingen Hefte 27-30 (1978) [Heft 28 = Hans Jakob Polotsky. Göttingen 25. Juli 1928].
*Address*: Seminar für Ägyptologie der Universität, 34 Göttingen, Prinzenstrasse 21, Bundesrepublik Deutschland.

*Hommages Vermaseren*: Hommages à Maarten J. Vermaseren. Recueil d'études offert par les auteurs de la Série Études Préliminaires aux religions orientales dans l'empire romain à Maarten J. Vermaseren à l'occasion de son soixantième anniversaire le 7 Avril 1978 édité par Margreet A. de Boer et T.A. Edridge, 3 vols, Leiden, E.J. Brill, 1978 (15.7 x 24.7 cm; Volume I: XVII + 500 p., colour frontispiece, pl. 1-96, 1 map; Volume II: XV + p.501-958, pl. 97-198; Volume III: XV + p.959-1387, pl. 199-275) = Études préliminaires aux religions orientales dans l'empire romain, 68, I-III; rev. *Acta archaeologica academiae scientiarum hungaricae* 31 (1979), 437-438 (L. Castiglione); *BiOr* 36 (1979), 181 (Herman de Meulenaere). Pr. fl. 960

*Immortal Egypt*: Immortal Egypt. Invited Lectures on the Middle East at the University of Texas at Austin. Edited by Denise Schmandt-Besserat, Malibu, Undena Publications, 1978 (22 x 29 cm; VIII + 62 p., portrait = frontispiece, 47 pl.); rev. *BiOr* 37 (1980), 25-26 (Ingrid Gamer-Wallert). Pr. $9.50/ $16

*JAOS*: Journal of the American Oriental Society, New Haven, Connecticut 98 (1978).
*Address*: American Oriental Society, 329 Sterling Memorial Library, Yale Station, New Haven, Connecticut 06250, U.S.A.

*JARCE*: Journal of the American Research Center in Egypt, Princeton, New Jersey 15 (1978).
*Address*: J.J. Augustin Publisher, Locust Valley, New York 11560, U.S.A.

*JEA*: The Journal of Egyptian Archaeology, London 64 (1978).
*Address*: Honorary Treasurer of the Egypt Exploration Society, 2-3 Doughty Mews, London WC1N 2PG, Great Britain.

*JEOL*: Jaarbericht van het Vooraziatisch-Egyptisch Genootschap Ex Oriente Lux, Leiden [VIII], No. 25 (1977-1978).
*Address*: Noordeindspl. 4-6, 2311 AH Leiden, Nederland.

*JNES*: Journal of Near Eastern Studies, Chicago, Illinois 37 (1978).
*Address*: University of Chicago Press, 5801 Ellis Avenue, Chicago, Illinois 60637, U.S.A.

*Journal Faculty of Archaeology*: The Journal of the Faculty of Archaeology Special Issue (= Book of the 50th Anniversary of Archaeological Studies in Cairo University. Part III), Cairo, Central Agency for University and School Books, 1978.

*JSSEA*: The SSEA Journal, Toronto 8 (1977-1978).
*Address*: The Society for the Study of Egyptian Antiquities, 30 Chestnut Park, Toronto, Ontario, M4W 1W6, Canada.

*MDAIK*: Mitteilungen des Deutschen Archäologischen Instituts Abteilung Kairo, Wiesbaden 34 (1978).
*Address*: Verlag Philipp von Zabern, P.O.B. 4065, Mainz/Rhein, Bundesrepublik Deutschland.

*MNL*: Meroitic Newsletter. Bulletin d'Informations meroitiques, [Paris] No. 19 (Juillet 1978).
*Address*: Jean Leclant, 77 rue Georges Lardennois, F-75019 Paris, France.

*Mundus*: Mundus. A Quarterly Review of German Research Contributions on Asia, Africa and Latin America. Arts and Science, Stuttgart.
*Address*: Wissenschaftliche Verlagsgesellschaft mbH, Postfach 40, 7000 Stuttgart 1, Bundesrepublik Deutschland.

*Newsletter ARCE*: Newsletter of the American Research Center in Egypt, Princeton, N.J. Nos 103 (Winter 1977/1978); 104 (Spring 1978); 105 (Summer 1978); 106 (Fall 1978).
*Address*: 20 Nassau Street, Princeton, N.J. 08540, U.S.A.

*OLZ*: Orientalistische Literaturzeitung, Berlin 73 (1978).
*Address:* Akademie-Verlag GmbH, Leipzigerstrasse 3-4, 108 Berlin.

*Oriens Antiquus*: Oriens Antiquus. Rivista del Centro per le Antichità e la Storia dell' Arte del Vicino Oriente, Roma 17 (1978).
*Address*: Centro per le Antichità e la Storia dell' Arte del Vicino Oriente, Via Caroncini 27, 00197 Roma, Italia.

*Orientalia*: Orientalia. Commentarii trimestres a facultate studiorum orientis antiqui pontificii instituti biblici in lucem editi in urbe, [Roma] Nova Series 47 (1978).
*Address*: Pontificium Institutum Biblicum, Piazza della Pilotta 35, 1-00187 Roma, Italia.

*Das ptolemaische Ägypten*: Das ptolemäische Ägypten. Akten des internationalen Symposions 27.-29. September 1976 in Berlin. Herausgegeben von Herwig Maehler und Volker Michael Strocka, Mainz am Rhein, Verlag Philipp von Zabern, 1978 (23 x 31 cm; XIV + 282 p., 1 plan, 13 fig., 49 pl.[1 folding]); at head of title: Deutsches Archäologisches Institut.

*RdE*: Revue d'Égyptologie, Paris 30 (1978).
*Address*: Librairie C. Klincksiek, 11 rue de Lille, Paris 7$^e$, France.

*Rivista*: Rivista degli Studi Orientali, Roma 52 (1978).
*Address*: Dott. Giovanni Bardi editore, Salita de crescenzi 16, Roma, Italia.

*SAK*: Studien zur Altägyptischen Kultur, Hamburg 6 (1978)[unter Mitarbeit von Winfried Barta = Festschrift Hans Wolfgang Müller (Professor Dr. Hans Wolfgang Müller zum 16. August 1977)].
*Address*: Helmut Buske Verlag, Hamburg, Bundesrepublik Deutschland.

*Serapis*: Serapis. The American Journal of Egyptology, Chicago 4 (1977-1978).
*Address*: The Editors of Serapis, 1155 E. 58th Street, Chicago, Illinois 60637, U.S.A.

ВДИ: Вестник Древней Истории, Москва 1 (143)-4(146), 1978.
*Address:* Москва В-36, ул. Дмитрия Ульнова. Д. 19, Комн. 237, Институт всеобщей Истории, АН СССР.

*WZKM*: Wiener Zeitschrift für die Kunde des Morgenlandes, Wien 70 (1978).
*Address*: Selbstverlag der Wiener Zeitschrift für die Kunde des Morgenlandes, Universitätsstrasse 7 V, A-1010 Wien 1, Österreich.

*ZÄS*: Zeitschrift für ägyptische Sprache und Altertumskunde, Berlin 105 (1978).
*Address*: Akademie-Verlag GmbH, Leipzigerstrasse 3-4, 108 Berlin.

*ZDMG*: Zeitschrift der Deutschen Morgenländischen Gesellschaft, Wiesbaden.
*Address*: Franz Steiner Verlag GmbH, Bahnhofstrasse 39, Postfach 743, 62 Wiesbaden, Bundesrepublik Deutschland.

2) *other abbreviations:*

| | | | |
|---|---|---|---|
| AEB: | Annual Egyptological Bibliography/Bibliographie égyptologique annuelle. | M.K.: | Middle Kingdom |
| | | N.K.: | New Kingdom |
| | | O.Eg.: | Old Egyptian |
| B.D.: | Book of the Dead | O.K.: | Old Kingdom |
| cfr: | *confer*, compare | O.T.: | Old Testament |
| cm: | centimetre(s) | p.: | page(s) |
| col.: | column | pl.: | plate(s) |
| C.T.: | Coffin Texts | pr.: | price |
| etc.: | *et cetera* | P.T.: | Pyramid Texts |
| fig.: | figure(s) | publ.: | publication(s) |
| F.I.P.: | First Intermediate Period | rev.: | review *or* summary |
| ill.: | illustration(s) | S.I.P. | Second Intermediate Period |
| km: | kilometre(s) | T.I.P.: | Third Intermediate Period |
| L.Eg.: | Late Egyptian | Urk.: | Urkunden |
| L.Z.: | L. Zonhoven | ⌒ | above a numeral, this hieroglyph indicates a monograph |
| m: | metre(s) | | |
| M.Eg.: | Middle Egyptian | | |

# ALPHABETICAL LIST OF AUTHORS AND TITLES

78001  ABD el-HALIM, Nabila Mohamed, The Problem of the Royal Placenta in Ancient Egypt, in: *Journal Faculty of Archaeology*, 83-90, with 7 ill.

After a medical explanation of the function of the placenta the author refers to the modern belief that it is the "second child". She then deals with the placenta-on-standard from the O.K., and summarizes the discussion about the name of the royal placenta (ẖ-nswt = "child of the king") and its relation to Khonsu.

78002  ABD er-RAZIQ, Mahmud, Eine Stele Nektanebos I., *MDAIK* 34 (1978), 111-115, with 1 fig. and 1 ill. on a pl.

Publication of a stela of Nectanebo I from Luxor. The main scene shows the King before Amon-Re, and behind him the goddess W3st. The text, of the year 10, mentions the construction of a girdle wall in Karnak. In this connection the author discusses Nectanebo's building activities on the border of the temenos of the temple.

78003  ABERCROMBIE, John R., Egyptian Papyri. The University Museum's Collection of Papyri and Related Materials, *Expedition*, Philadelphia, Penn. 20, No.2 (Winter 1978), 32-37, with 8 ill.

Short survey of the papyrus collection in the University Museum of the University of Pennsylvania, which comprises smaller collections of hieroglyphic, hieratic and demotic papyri.  *L.Z.*

ABOU-GHAZI, Dia', see our numbers 78565 and 78845.

el-ACHIRIE, Hassan, see our number 78390.

78004  [ADAMS, William Y.], Excavations at Qasr Ibrim, 1978, *Nyame Akuma*, Calgary No. 12 (1978), 18-20.

Fortsetzung unserer Nummer 76003.
Die befestigte Zitadelle, jetzt eine Insel, wurde spätestens in der 19. Dynastie gegründet und war bis zu Beginn des vorigen Jahrhunderts besiedelt, war als für Jahrtausende eines der wichtigsten politischen, religiösen und wirtschaftlichen Zentren Unternubiens. Die Festung und die Tempelüberreste sind unter Abfallhaufen begraben die nur von Siedlungen stammen können. Der Inhalt eines Abfallhaufens in der Festung stammt aus der römischen Zeit: ptolemäische und römische Münzen, Leinengewänder, römische Lampen und Geschirre, Ledersandalen, Stiefel römischen Typs und Fragmente von Lateinischen Papyri. Die Keramik ist ganz unähnlich der bisher aus Nubien bekannten Ware; das lässt die Vermutung zu, dass Qasr Ibrim im letzten Jahrtausend v. Chr. einer der wenigen bewohnten Vorposten in einer allgemein verwüsteten Region war.  *Inge Hofmann*

78005   ADAMS, W.Y., Varia Ceramica, *in*: *Études nubiennes*, 1-23.

Es werden eine Anzahl von Arbeiten vorgestellt, die sich mit nubischer Keramik von der pharaonischen bis zur gegenwärtigen Zeit beschaftigen. Abschliessend folgt ein Bericht über den gegenwärtigen Stand der Keramik-Studien des Verfassers; es wird darauf verwiesen, dass das Ergebnis von 15 Jahren Forschungsarbeit demnächt *in extenso* veröffentlicht werden wird. Eine Revision der Daten für die Keramik um etwa 50 bis 100 Jahre erscheint unerlässlich.

*Inge Hofmann*

ADAMS, William Y., see also our number 78008.

78006   Ägyptische Malerei. Das Grab des Nacht. Mit einer Einführung von Dietrich Wildung. Aufnahmen von Albert Burges, München-Zürich, R. Piper & Co. Verlag, [1978] (13.4 x 21.7 cm; 64 p., 16 colour pl. [= p. 17-48], colour ill. on cover).

The text of this booklet presents a general introduction to the Egyptian tomb and its function as well as to Egyptian art. Then follows a description of the scenes in the tomb of Nakht (Theban Tomb no. 52) referring to the colour plates, in which Wildung points out not only their artistic value but also, particularly on account of the fishing scene, the hidden erotic and politico-religious meaning.

78007   AFIFI BADAWI, Fathi, Die Grabung der ägyptischen Altertümerverwaltung in Merimde-Benisalâme im Oktober/November 1976, *MDAIK* 34 (1978), 43-51, with 1 map, 5 fig. and 1 pl.

Report on the excavations in one sector during the first campaign at Merimde-Benisalâme (see our number 78240). The various finds are described   The three main periods of the settlement appear to follow each other directly.

78008   Africa in Antiquity. The Arts of Ancient Nubia and the Sudan. I. The Essays. II. Steffen Wenig, The Catalogue, [New York], The Brooklyn Museum, [1978] (22 x 30.5 cm; [Vol. I:] 143 p., 9 maps, 5 plans, 60 ill., 40 colour ill., 9 fig., 1 table, colour frontispiece, 2 colour ill. on cover; [Vol. II:] 366 p., 10 plans, 350 ill., 42 colour ill., 2 tables, colour frontispiece, 2 colour ill. on cover).

This is the catalogue of an exhibition held in the Brooklyn Museum, New York, and in Seattle, New Orleans and the Hague, in 1978 and 1979.
The first volume contains a Foreword by the director of the Brooklyn Museum, Michael Botwinick, maps, a bibliography and nine chapters presenting an introduction to the history of Nubia. William Y. Adams deals with geography and population of the area; Bruce G. Trigger with the physical type of the inhabitants through the ages. Ahmed M. Ali Hakem presents a survey of the archaeological research down to the UNESCO campaign. David O'Connor describes the Nubian cultures up to the N.K.; Jean Leclant the Egyptian activities during the O., M. and N.K.; Karl-Heinze Priese the Napatan and Fritz Hintze the Meroitic Period. The Ballana Culture and the coming of Christianity are discussed by Trigger, and Medieval Nubia by Adams, who is also the author of the

chapter on ceramics.
All chapters are lavishly illustrated and present not only an up-to-date introduction for the visitors of the exhibition but also several scientifically important observations.
Volume II, by Steffen Wenig, consists of two parts. First (after i.a. a chronological chart and a list of the reigning kings and queens of Kush), in five chapters, an extensive and well illustrated survey of the art, architecture and minor arts of Nubia within the context of the development of the civilization. Each chapter is devoted to a particular period, ranging from the prehistoric times to the Christian era.
The catalogue proper consists of 295 numbers, objects lent by collections in Egypt and the Sudan and in various European and American countries. All objects are briefly described, technical data and bibliographical references are listed, and a commentary is added. Moreover, the descriptions are all accompanied by at least a small but adequate photograph, in many instances by a larger one (some in colour), while others have been depicted also in Vol. I.
At the end an extensive bibliography to both volumes, concordances and an index.

78009 AGAM, Y., Eine ägyptologische Privatbibliothek auf Mikrofilm, *GM* Heft 30 (1978), 9-12.

Es wird ausführlich beschrieben, mit Hilfe welcher Mittel und Gerätschaften ägyptologische Werke auf Mikrofilm aufgenommen werden können, um sich auf diese Weise eine Bibliothek zu beschaffen.   *Inge Hofmann*

78010 AHITUV, Shemuel, Economic Factors in the Egyptian Conquest of Canaan, *Israel Exploration Journal*, Jerusalem 28 (1978), 93-105.

Studying the question whether economic factors played a significant role in the Egyptian conquest of Canaan during the XVIIIth Dynasty the author successively discusses landownership, agricultural products, raw materials, industrial products and slaves. He concludes that the economic interest was very limited, the main economic reason for the conquest being the wish to control the commercial road leading to Mesopotamia. The collapse of Canaan in the period was not due to economic exploitation, but to frequent wars, internal strife and Egyptian mismanagement.

78011 ALBENDA, Pauline, Landscape Bas-Reliefs in the *Bīt-Ḫilāni* of Ashurbanipal, *BASOR* No. 225 (February, 1977), 29-48, with 22 ill.

The author attempts to demonstrate that the trophy objects present in the garden on the landscape reliefs from Ashurbanipal's palace at Niniveh were i.a. once possessed by the King of Egypt.   *L.Z.*

78012 ALDRED, Cyril, Tradition and Revolution in the Art of the XVIIIth Dynasty, in: *Immortal Egypt*, 51 - 62, with 1 fig. and 12 ill. on 9 pl.

In the first part of the paper the author argues that the art of the XVIIIth Dynasty, although reverting to the inspiration of the M.K. style, also shows a growing influence of the more cosmopolitan and sophisticated style of Lower Egypt. In religion this is seen in the increasing dominance of the sun-god, in art in the enhanced interest in the classical past of the O.K. Several examples are discussed.

The second part deals with the innovations of the Amarna Period: the new subject-matter and a new space-concept. The former is i.a. illustrated by the family scenes and the position of Nefertiti, the latter by the 'correct' representations of left and right feet and the management of space shown by figures of goddesses on the corners of Tutankhamun's sarcophagus and canopic chest.

78013 ALDRED, Cyril, Jean-Louis de CENIVAL, Fernand DEBONO, Christiane DESROCHES-NOBLECOURT, Jean-Philippe LAUER, Jean LECLANT, Jean VERCOUTTER, Le Temps des Pyramides. De la Préhistoire aux Hyksos (1560 av. J.-C.), [Paris], Gallimard, [1978] (21 x 28 cm; [VIII +] 355 p., 432 ill. [including 1 colour frontispiece; many in colour], fig., plans and maps) = Le monde égyptien, Les pharaons, [1] = L' univers des formes, [26] ; rev. Antike Welt 11, Heft 1 (1980), 63 (anonymous); Comptes rendus de l' Académie des Inscriptions et Belles-Lettres, 1979, 220-221 (Jean Leclant).

After a general introduction to the Egyptian civilization and a short sketch of the history of archaeology, there follows the first and main part of the book devoted to the arts and architecture from the Prehistoric Age to the end of the M.K.

Prehistory is dealt with by F. Debono, and Predynastic and Protohistory by J.-L. de Cenival. The following chapters are divided after themes and internally arranged in a chronological order. J.-P. Lauer discusses the royal and funerary architecture of the O.K., while only a small text portion is devoted to the religious, civil and military architecture of the M.K. J. Vercouttter discusses relief and painting, while the royal and private statuary is dealt with by C. Aldred. The last chapter, on the smaller arts, by C. Desroches-Noblecourt, is arranged after the various handicrafts and themes. Short concluding words by J. Leclant.

In the second part follows by means of illustrations an integrated arrangement of the above subjects after periods, while the third part contains the general documentation, such as plans and cross-sections with commentary, a chronological table listing i.a. the main achievements, and an extensive bibliography and index. The photographs are of high quality, some are of less well-known objects or from unusual viewpoints.                                       L.Z.

ALDRED, Cyril, see also our number 78612.

78014 el-ALFI, Mostafa, Two Egyptian Statuettes in the Museum of Cherchel in Algeria, GM Heft 30 (1978), 13 - 18 with 2 fig., and 2 ill. on 1 pl.

Es handelt sich um den unteren Teil einer Statuette Thutmosis' I. (Ausstellungsnummer 95 im Museum von Cherchel, ungefähr 100 km westlich von Algier) und eine Statuette des Petubastet (Ausstellungsnummer 24), der in die Zeit der Kleopatra VII. zu datieren ist. Beide Statuetten sind kurz erwähnt in Porter und Moss VII, 367 und 368.                          Inge Hofmann

ALI, Osman Suleiman Mohammed, see our numbers 78823 and 78824.

78015   ALLAM, Schafik, Le droit égyptien ancien. État de récherches et perspectives, *ZÄS* 105 (1978), 1-6.

L'Égypte ancienne a connu la codification, la jurisprudence (dans la pratique) et la théorie juridique (empirique). Les Égyptiens ont été les premiers à développer un système juridique, un système de structure familiale patrilinéaire et monogamique et une société de type individualiste. Le secteur du droit était en grande partie sécularisé déjà sous l'Ancien Empire
Les écrivains grecs et latins éprouvaient un grand respect pour le droit égyptien mais n'en ont pas transmis une description détaillée. Nos recherches dépendent des sources indigènes qui sont assez nombreuses.
*M.Heerma van Voss*

78016   ALLAM, S., Un droit pénal existait-il *stricto sensu* en Égypte pharaonique?, *JEA* 64 (1978), 65-68.

The article discusses whether the ancient Egyptians distinguished a penal and a civil aspect to their law. Using the Deir el Medîna texts it is clear that the local council of justice did not deal with crimes such as adultery or acts of violence committed by the inhabitants, but reserved these cases for the civil authorities. Although the use of the bastinado may have been the deciding measure as to whether the crime was civil or penal the matter is not certain.
For an abstract see *Revue historique de droit français et étranger* 56 (1978), 698. *E.P.Uphill*

78017   ALLEN, David, An Astronomer's Impressions of Ancient Egypt, *Sky and Telescope,* Cambridge, Mass. 54, No.1 (July 1977), 15 - 19, with 1 map, 1 fig. and 7 ill. (5 in colour).

The author makes several remarks on ancient Egyptian monuments from the astronomer's point of view, and is even sceptical as regards the issue of astronomy and the Great Pyramid. *L.Z.*

78018   ALMAGRO BASCH, Martín, Francisco PRESEDO VELO, María del Carmen PÉREZ DÍE, María José ALMAGRO GORBEA, La tumba de Nefertari, Madrid, Ministerio de Cultura. Direccion General del Patrimonio Artistico Archivos y Museos, 1978 (20.5 x 30 cm; 38 p., including 8 pl. [ 3 in colour], 2 colour ill. [ 1 on cover], 2 fig., 2 plans) = Museo Arqueologico Nacional. Monografías Arqueológicas, No.4.

After some introductory remarks on Nefertari and Ramses II, the authors offer a description of the tomb and a translation of the texts of the tomb, which correspond with the numbers on the situation plan of the texts. The last part, being the photographical reconstruction of the tomb, consists of partly black-and white, partly colour photographs of parts of the tomb decoration.
Cfr our number 71560. *L.Z.*

ALMAGRO BASCH, Martín, see also our number 78492.

ALMAGRO GORBEA, María José, see our number 78018.

78019 ALTENMÜLLER, Hartwig, Schenkelträger und Veterinär bei Seschemnefer III. in Gizeh, *GM* Heft 30 (1978), 19-26, with 2 fig.

Es wird die Bedeutung eines nachträglichen Eingriffes von "zweiter Hand" in eine Darstellung aus dem Grab Seschemnefers III. in Gizeh (G 5070) untersucht. Das Bild wurde zu einem unbekannten Zeitpunkt überarbeitet und zeigt nun einen Beamten, der sich bei den Schlachtungen der Westwand des Grabes als Veterinär betätigt. Die verbliebenen Spuren lassen aber erkennen, dass die Figur vor ihrer Überarbeitung einen mit einem Rinderschenkel beladenen Schlachtgehilfen darstellte. Die Beischrift gehörte zum ursprünglichen Bild des Schenkelträgers und dürfte, wie sich aus einem Vergleich mit ähnlichen Darstellungen ergab, gelautet haben: "gib dieses Herz!". Die Revision dürfte kurz nach der Fertigstellung der Grabdekoration erfolgt sein, um die logische Inkonsequenz zu bereinigen, dass der stehende Mann bereits einen Schenkel trägt, bevor dem auf dem Boden liegenden Rind das Vorderbein abgetrennt war. Die Beischrift wurde gelöscht.                *Inge Hofmann*

78020 ALTENMÜLLER, Hartwig, Vom Weiterleben ägyptischer Symbole in der abendländischen Kultur, *Mannheimer Forum,* Mannheim 77/78 (1978), 169 - 229, with 7 fig., 5 ill. and 9 colour ill.

In three sections the author discusses symbolism in Ancient Egypt and the survival of Egyptian symbols in the European civilization: first the early contacts between Egypt and Greece (e.g., the Bes-figure), Rome and Early Christianity (Physiologus); then crypto-Egyptian symbols in the Middle Ages (phoenix, pelican) and pseudo-Egyptian in the Renaissance (e.g. Dürer's baboon and Kircher's hieroglyphs); and, in the third section, the symbols as they were understood by the Egyptians themselves, in writing (e.g. *rhyt,* $^c$*nh* and *dd*) and myths (e.g., the representations of the sky, and the moon-eye).
In conclusion (p.224-228) the author states that from Early Christianity onwards Egyptian symbols have been reinterpreted, e.g. obelisks and pyramids. The article has no notes and only a very brief bibliography (p.229).

78021 ALTENMÜLLER, Hartwig, Zur Bedeutung der Harfnerlieder des Alten Reiches, *SAK* 6 (1978), 1 - 24, with 4 fig.

The author poses the question whether, as Lichtheim has demonstrated for the M.K. (*JNES* 4 [1945], 178-192) the harpers' songs of the O.K. also possessed a funerary or ritual character. He discusses and compares instances of the scenes in which harpers' songs occur in O.K. tombs, concluding that they represent a festival during which the dead returned temporarily to the world of the living. The return was caused by dances and music, constituting a ritual called "singing the *sn ntrw*", which may mean "to unite with him who became god". According to the songs it is Hathor who allows the return of the dead.

78022  ALTICK, Richard D., Snake was Fake but Egyptian Hall Wowed London [The Story of the Great Showman Who Wowed London Museum-Goers with Everything from Napoleon's Bullet-Proof Carriage to Mexican Loot in Egyptian Halls], *Smithsonian,* Washington, DC 9, No. 1 (April 1978), 68-77, with 8 ill.

Mention is made of Belzoni and the Egyptian Hall in London.  *L.Z.*

78023  ALTMAN, Amnon, Some Controversial Toponyms from the Amurru Region in the Amarna Archive, *Zeitschrift des Deutschen Palästina-Vereins,* Wiesbaden 94 (1978), 99-107.

The author attempts to identify certain problematic toponyms in the Amurru region, which are known from the el-Amarna archive.
In this connection he discusses Abdi-Ashirta's accusation in an Amarna letter that Šeḫlal, which is proposed to be located east of the Orontes, attacked Sumur, the Egyptian administrative centre in the area.  *L.Z.*

78024  ALVAREZ, Octavio, The Celestial Brides. The Visions of the Eastern Paradise Infiltrate the Mediterranean Afterlife. A Study in Mythology and Archaeology, Stockbridge, Mass., Herbert Reichner Publisher, [1978] (20 x 28 cm; XXIV + 275 p., 152 pl., numerous fig., ill. on title page).

The author's thesis is that lovemaking, which was an essential part in the Indian conception of the hereafter, gradually permeated the conceptions of the beyond in the Mediterranean world. In this connection three chapters are devoted to Ancient Egypt, called "Tefnut and Eleusis", "The Asiatic Influx in Egypt" and "Enigmas in the Pyramid Texts", while in the next chapter, on females in the beyond, the first section also deals with Egypt.
The author's point of view differs from that usual in Egyptology, as may appear from his summary of the chapter on the P.T. (p. 101). He there states, e.g., that "lovemaking became a major concern in Egypt's heaven"; that "the sombre death-god Osiris is eclipsed by Hathor, divinity of love and joy, as 'protectress' of the dead"; that "the Pharaoh wishes to reappear in the Beyond as an Asiatic puissant love-god, to unite with Hathor as his lover", and that he "is said to make love to several other divinities in the Above"; even "it is said that he can call up to him any earthly woman, even out of the arms of her husband". Unfortunately, "it is not possible to establish dates of that development" by which "the most advanced views concerning lovemaking appear as modernistic afterthoughts and appendix" and occur "between the main texts clinging to the archaic concepts of Osiris".

78025  AMIRAN, Ruth, The Date of the End of the EB II City of Arad. A Complementary Note to *Early Arad,* I, *Israel Exploration Journal,* Jerusalem 28 (1978), 182-184, with 2 tables and 1 fig.

A complementary note to our next number, which re-assesses the chronology of Bronze Age Arad as largely concurrent with the Protodynastic Period in Egypt. L.Z.

78026 AMIRAN, Ruth *et al.*, Early Arad. The Chalcolithic Settlement and Early Bronze City. I. First - Fifth Seasons of Excavations, 1962 - 1966, Jerusalem, The Israel Exploration Society, 1978 (24.5 x 31.5 cm; XIV + 138 p., 62 tables, 20 fig., 193 pl.); at head of title: The Israel Exploration Society. The Institute of Archaeology, The Hebrew University of Jerusalem, The Department of Antiquities and Museums, Ministry of Education and Culture. The Israel Museum; rev. *AJA* 84 (1980), 243 - 244 (Patty Gerstenblith); *JNES* 39 (1980), 315 - 322 (Leon Marfoe).

In part 4, conclusions and implications, conclusions in which ancient Egypt is involved are drawn: the finds of Egyptian vessels point to two-way trade relations between Arad and Egypt during the First Dynasty, although the actual trade routes are as yet unknown. L.Z.

78027 Ancient Egypt. Discovering it Splendors, Washington D.C., National Geographic Society, 1978 (26.5 x 35 cm; 256 p., numerous ill., mostly in colour, frontispiece, colour ill. on cover).

This is a book on the Egyptian civilization, intended for the general reader. Its main value lies in its illustration, which is of an unusually high quality, while its text has been written by a number of specialists.
Chapter 1 (by William H. Peck), called "The Constant Lure", deals with the history of Egyptology; chapter 2 (by Karl W. Butzer) with the land; chapter 3 (by I.E.S. Edwards) with the pyramids and their building methods; chapter 4 (by Barbara Mertz) with various aspects of daily life; chapter 5 (by William Kelly Simpson) with writing; chapter 6 (by Virginia Lee Davis) with religion; chapter 7 (by Edna R. Russmann), called "Change in a Changeless Land", with the Amarna Period; and chapter 8 (by Anthony J. Spalinger) with the N.K.
A large part of each chapter is devoted to the colour photographs and their extensive captions. At the end of the book an illustrated time chart (p. 241-249), relating Egyptian history to that of other civilizations, a bibliography, and indexes.

ANDERSON, Robert A., see our number 78320.

78028 ANDREU, Guillemette et Sylvie Cauville, Vocabulaire absent du *Wörterbuch* (II), *RdE* 30 (1978), 10 - 21.

Seconde liste de mots ne figurant jusqu' à présent dans aucun dictionnaire ou index développé (pour la liste des ouvrages non dépouillés, voir le premier article des auteurs, *RdE* 29 = notre No. 77028). *Ph. Derchain*

78029 ANDREWS, Carol A.R., A Family for Anhai ?, *JEA* 64 (1978), 88 - 98.

The Book of the Dead belonging to this priestess (BM 10472) gives quite a lot of details of her family. In addition to her father, possibly called Nebsumenu, her mother Neferiytu is shown. From this and using a considerable amount of evidence from Theban tomb paintings and references to the High Priests of Osiris a table of five generations is built up.   *E.P.Uphill*

ANDREWS, Carol A.R., see also our number 78340.

78030   Anonymous, Arbeiter der Totenstadt, *Antike Welt*, Feldmeilen 9, Heft 2 (1978), 60 - 61.

Very short note on Deir el-Medîna.

78031   Anonymous, Association Internationale des Égyptologues. Statuts, *Oriens Antiquus* 17 (1978), 297 - 298.

Publication of the articles of the International Association of Egyptologists.

78032   Anonymous, V.I. Avdiev (1898 - 1978 гг.), ВДИ 4 (146), 1978, 208.

Obituary notice. See our number 78895.

78033   Anonymous, The Berkeley Map of the Theban Necropolis. Preliminary Report 1978, *Newsletter ARCE* No. 105 (Summer 1978), 19-50, with 2 fig., 5 ill., 8 maps and 1 folding pl.

Since there exists no accurate and complete map of the Theban necropolis, the Berkeley Map Project plans to prepare a detailed archaeological map to be published in a library and a field edition, accompanied by a concordance and a catalogue of West Bank archaeological materials.
After a sketch of the history of Theban maps from before 1900 to after 1960, of the object of the new map which will be based on the baseline of the Karnak temple, and of the progress during 1978, the survey methods (both horizontal and vertical control) are described.
The anticipated publication order of the area maps is: 1. West Valley of the Kings; 2. Dra' Abû el-Naga'; 3. Valley of the Queens; 4. Deir el-Bahri, 'Asâsîf, Khôkha, Sheikh 'Abd el-Qurna; 5. Qurnet Mura'i, Deir el-Medîna, Ramesseum; 6. Medînet Habu; 7. Area North of Dra' Abû el-Naga' and the Sethōs temple, altogether amounting to approximately 230 map sheets.   *L.Z.*

78034   Anonymous, Egyptian Art, *Annual Report of the Museum of Fine Arts*, Boston 102 (1977 - 78), 26 - 27.

Notable acquisitions were a XVIIIth Dynasty blue faience bowl with a design (Inv. No. 1977.619), the lid of a double shawabti-chest from the same period (Inv. No. 1977.717), a M.K. royal head (Inv. No. 1978.54) and an O.K. painted relief with an agricultural scene (Inv. No. 1978.168).   *L.Z.*

78035   Anonymous, Fouilles de Hala Sultan Tekké (= Chronique des fouilles et découvertes archéologiques à Chypre en 1977, 5), *Bulletin de Correspondence Hellénique*, Athènes 102 (1978), 913 - 914, with 2 ill.

A faience pommel of a sceptre in papyrus form, with the cartouche of Horemheb, was found at Hala Sultan Tekke.   *L.Z.*

78036 Anonymous, Inauguratie van de tempel van Taffeh in het Rijksmuseum van Oudheden te Leiden, *Phoenix,* Leiden 24 (1978), 66 - 74.

On the inauguration of the Taffa temple in the Museum of Antiquities, Leiden, in 1979.
*L.Z.*

78037 Anonymous, Jahresbericht 1977 des Deutschen Archäologischen Instituts. Abteilung Kairo, *Archäologischer Anzeiger,* Berlin, 1978, 629 - 633.

Yearly report of the activities of the German Archaeological Institute, with short sections on the excavations at Elephantine, Thebes-West, el-Salamuni, Abydos, Qasr Sagha (Faiyûm), Dashûr, Saqqâra and Merimde.
*L.Z.*

78038 Anonymous, Charles Kuentz, *BSFE* No. 82 (Juin 1978), 4 - 5.

Obituary notice. Compare our number 78896.

78039 ARANOV, Maurice Moshe, The Biblical Threshing-Floor in the Light of the Ancient Near Eastern Evidence: Evolution of an Institution, *Dissertation Abstracts International,* Ann Arbor, Mich. 38, No. 10 (April 1978), 6179/80-A.

Abstract of a thesis New York University, 1977 (362 p.; order no. 7803060). The use of the threshing-floor for cultic-ritual purposes in Egypt is discussed.
*L.Z.*

78040 ARMAYOR, O. Kimball, Did Herodotus Ever Go to Egypt?, *JARCE* 15 (1978), 59 - 73.

The author seriously questions the authenticity of Herodotus' account (compare our number 70411), especially in the following cases: (a) the black colour of the Egyptians. They shared it with the Colchians, and in repeating this Greek tradition Herodotus adds circumcision as another correspondence. He improves on his logographic predecessors. (b) In view of the Egyptian xenophoby, it is doubtful whether Herodotus ever had access to priestly informers of whatever kind; he does not mention having used interpreters. Too many Greek traditions are reflected in these reports. (c) The profound syncretism in Herodotus' Egypt is unsupported by archeological vestiges; it cannot have been due to the (only limited) presence of Greek mercenaries. (d) The existence of Herodotus' city of Chemmis (near Neapolis, in the district of Thebes) with its chief god Perseus and its typically Greek customs cannot be authenticized from elsewhere.
Even if Herodotus ever went to Egypt, his narrative has too much of a good story-teller's; much of it goes back on existing Greek literary tradition.
*J.F.Borghouts*

ARNDT, Helmut, see our number 78202.

78041 ARNOLD, Dieter, Vom Pyramidenbezirk zum "Haus für Millionen Jahre", *MDAIK* 34 (1978), 1 - 8, with 3 plans.

Proceeding from his explanation of the outlay of the O.K. pyramid temple (see our number 77045) the author follows the change of the basic idea through the mortuary temples of Mentuhotep and Hatshepsut to those of the N.K. Instead of reflecting the position of kingship that has to be preserved in the hereafter the Theban tradition conceived the building as a place for the cult of king and gods together. The XIIth Dynasty attempted to return to the old Memphite style, but gradually this proved to be impossible, while Hatshepsut took up again the idea of Mentuhotep. The cult of the king was now moved from the sanctuary to the Upper Terrace, and the next step under Amenophis I was to divide tomb and temple completely. The essence of the mortuary temple is henceforth a combination of the cult of the king and that of Amen-Re.

ARNOLD, Dorothea, see our number 78546.

78042 The Art of Ancient Egypt. An Exhibition of Archaeological Works of Art Dating from Pre-Dynastic to Coptic Times. December 15 - April 1, New York, Safani Gallery, [1978] (21.7 x 28 cm; 12 p., 36 ill. [9 in colour]).

This catalogue presents a representative sample of an exhibition on the arts and crafts of ancient Egypt. The captions to the illustrations offer a description and a reference to similar works and the provenance of the piece, if known. *L.Z.*

78043 ASSAF, A. Abou—L. KHALLOUF, الشـام مسَارحملـة تحوتمس الثالث الثامنـة علی بــلاد . *Annales archéologiques arabes syriennes*, Damas 26 (1976), [1978], 167-192.

"L'itinéraire de Thutmès III [à travers la Syrie]."

78044 ASSMANN, Jan, Eine Traumoffenbarung der Göttin Hathor. Zeugnisse "Persönlicher Frömmigkeit" in thebanischen Privatgräbern der Ramessidenzeit, *RdE* 30 (1978), 22-50.

En règle générale, les textes de piété personnelle que l'on trouve dans quelques tombes ramessides consistent en hymnes adressés aux dieux entre les mains de qui le défunt remet son destin d'outre-tombe. L'inscription de Thothemheb (TT 194) publiée et commentée ici fait une exception, comme du reste celle de Samout dit Kiki (TT 409) étudiée dans le même tome de la *RdE* par P. Vernus (notre No. 78818). Elle fait dépendre l'attitude religieuse du défunt et ses espoirs funéraires d'une expérience survenue pendant sa vie, en l'occurrence un rêve que lui envoya la déesse Hathor pour lui indiquer l'emplacement de sa tombe.
L'inscription est conçue comme un discours tenu à la divinité qui formule à son tour une réponse. Ce dernier trait permet, malgré le type exceptionnel de composition, de rattacher l'inscription de Thothemheb à la catégorie examinée au début de l'article. *Ph. Derchain*

78045 Assuan. E. BRESCIANI, Il tempio tolemaico di Isi. S. PERNIGOTTI, I blocchi decorati e iscritti. Con un contributo di D. Foraboschi per le iscrizioni greche, Pisa, Giardini Editori e Stampatori, 1978 (22 x 29.5 cm; 323 p., 59

pl. [2 folding, 3 in colour], 1 plan, 391 fig., fig. on wrapper) = Biblioteca di Studi Antichi. Sezioni egittologia, 16; rev. *Aegyptus* 59 (1979), 272 - 273 (Lucia Criscuolo); *CdE* LIII, No. 106 (1978), 380 - 382 (Jean Bingen).
Pr. L.35,000

The book, in which the references to the plates are throughout in the margin, consists of two parts. The first part, by Edda Bresciani, is devoted to the Ptolemaic temple of Isis at Aswân. After introductory remarks on the antiquities of Aswân she deals with the following subjects: the Ptolemaic temple of Isis in general; its architectonic description; the southern part of the temple; aspects of the theology of the temple, dedicated to Isis-first-of-the-army (ḥ3t p3 mš˓); a toponymical problem: 𓉔 𓊖 and variants, read *Sḥḥ* as a name for Elephantine, which may be based on a play of the homophonous words *3bw* "Elephantine" and *ı͗b*, "heart"; the mural painting near the gate of the southern cella; four altars of Alexander the Great; the figured graffiti; the remains of the Christian paintings on the columns of the temple made during its use in the Christian Period. Then follows the largest section on the scenes and the hieroglyphic texts, with the drawings on the left hand page, and the translations of the legends and texts on the opposite page. The scenes show the kings Ptolemy III and IV offering before various gods. In section 11 the author studies the hieroglyphic and demotic inscriptions and sketches. In the last and short sections 12 and 13 of the first part D. Foraboschi and S. Pernigotti deal with two Greek proskynema texts and the Coptic graffiti. The second part of the book, by Sergio Pernigotti, is devoted to the decorated and inscribed blocks. After an introduction he presents the catalogue, with Inv. Nos., of the blocks including the libation basins, offering tables and various fragments. The catalogue is divided after the finds of the 1970 mission (234 pieces) and the 112 blocks from that of 1971. The dated blocks are dealt with first in a chronological order, followed by the undated ones. After a section on 12 Coptic decorated elements and Christian stelae follow his conclusions concerning the finds of the two missions, the 1970 one ranging from Nectanebo II to Nero, and that of 1971 with finds only from the time of Tiberius and Nero. The book concludes with the study of a Greek inscription from Aswân by D. Foraboschi, a bibliography and indexes on kings, deities, toponyms, private names and varia.
L.Z.

78046  D'AVILA VILELA, Jarbas, Mumificação e Medicina no Antigo Egipto, *Revista Paulista de Medicina,* São Paulo 89 (1977), 115 - 124, with 4 ill.

"Mummification and Medicine in Ancient Egypt". General article.

BADAWI, Fathi Afifi, see our number 78007.

78047  BADAWY, Alexander, Egyptian Tomb Sculpture, *The Illustrated London News,* London 266, No. 6964 (November 1978), 109 - 110, with 4 ill.

The author describes the tomb of Kagemni at Saqqâra, particularly its reliefs.
L.Z.

78048 BADAWY, Alexander, The Tomb of Nyhetep-Ptah at Giza and the Tomb of 'Ankhm'ahor at Saqqara, Berkeley-Los Angeles-London, University of California Press, 1978 (22.8 x 30.5 cm; X + 61p., 113 pl. [41 with plans and fig., 20 folding; 72 with ill., 2 folding]) = University of California Publications: Occasional Papers Number 11: Archaeology; rev. *BiOr* 36 (1979), 311 - 315 (Hartwig Altenmüller); *CdE* LV, No. 109 - 110 (1980), 145 - 148 (Naguib Kanawati); *Oriens Antiquus* 19 (1980), 320 - 322 (Antonio Loprieno); *Rivista* 53 (1979), 198 - 200 (Luisa Bongrani Fanfoni). Pr. $18

Publication of the results of fieldwork in 1974 by the author and two students (for the work of 1973, see our number 76044).
The first tomb dealt with is that of Nyhetep-Ptah at Gîza, formerly recorded by Lepsius (his number LG 25) and situated at the Northernmost edge of the West Field (now numbered G 2430; see Porter-Moss III, $1^2$, 94 -95). The author gives a description of the tomb chapel, its false door and wall scenes (with translations of the inscriptions), a short discusssion of their style and the names in the inscriptions.
The second, larger tomb is that of 'Ankhm'ahor in the "rue de tombeaux" at Saqqâra (see Porter-Moss, III, $2^2$, 512 - 515), famous for its circumcision scene. The various rooms of the tomb and their wall scenes are described, with translations of the texts and discussion of details. There follows a description of the burial apartment and its contents as found by Firth and Gunn, with comparative material from the tomb of Khentika. Then a short section mentioning that an attempt to interpret the measurements in terms of cubits did not yield satisfactory results; a section on the style of the decoration; and lists of the names and titles.
The plates mostly bear line-drawings and photographs of the wall-scenes.
Indexes on p. 59 - 61.

78049 BAGNALL, Roger S., Notes on Greek and Egyptian Ostraka, *Enchoria* 8, Teil 1 (1978), 143 - 150.

Some additional and/or correcting remarks on eight already published Greek and Demotic ostraca. O. Amst. 93 (149 - 150) is identified as being Coptic, not Greek. *W.Brunsch*

78050 BAKER, A.T., Ancient Glory in Manhattan [and] New Light on a Dark Kingdom. A Glittering Trove of Nubian Objects in Brooklyn, *Time* Europe, Amsterdam 112, No. 14 (October 2, 1978), 52 - 54, with 6 ill. (4 in colour).

Short report for the general reader on the temple of Dendur in the Metropolitan Museum of Art, and the exhibition Africa in Antiquity in Brooklyn.
*L.Z.*

78051 BAKIR, Abd el-Mohsen, An Introduction to the Study of the Egyptian Language. 'A Semitic Approach'. I. Middle Egyptian, [Cairo], General Egyptian Book Organisation, 1978 (17 x 24 cm; XVIII + 191 p.). Pr. P.T. 250

This book meant as a student's grammar is based on a translation and an elaboration of our number 3153. In the preface the author explains his aims,

his method and his Semitic approach. After a systematic and selective bibliography he presents the generalities about language and writing.
In the following three parts: noun, pronoun and numerals; the verbal semantic; and the particle (prepositions), the morphology is dealt with, while the syntax is studied in the part called "Sentences". Usually the various sections consist of the theory (paradigms, etc.), remarks, examples and explanations, concluded by an exercise in translating into English and Egyptian and the pertinent vocabulary.
The last part of the book is autographed by the author and contains four appendixes ( a short history of the decipherment; a selection from the sign categories including abbreviations; calligraphy; answers to the exercises), an index of the grammatical terminology in English, French, German and Arabic, an English-Egyptian vocabulary, and a concordance to some well-known grammars. *L.Z.*

78052 BAKIR, Abd el-Mohsen, Slavery in Pharaonic Egypt, [Le Caire], L'Organisation Égyptienne Générale du Livre, 1978 (20.5 x 28 cm; XX +128 p., 20 pl. [15 folding]) = Supplément aux Annales du Service des Antiquités de l'Égypte Cahier No. 18.                                                                                    Pr. P.T. 570

Reprint of our number 2188, to which is added one page with a very brief preface to this second edition and the titles of two reviews to the first edition as well as of some articles and a book on the subject.

78053 BAKIR, A.M., Some Remarks on Nominal Patterns in Middle Egyptian, *JEA* 64 (1978), 130 - 131.

The predicate of a nominal identity pattern with implicitly defined subject should be general, i.e. undefined. Should both have identical definitions or non definition, *pw* may be supplied to form a full nominal sentence if required.
*E.P.Uphill*

78054 BALOUT, Lionel, La momie de Ramses II, *Archeologia,* Paris No. 115 (février 1978), 32 - 46, with 24 ill. (4 in colour).

The author gives a detailed report of the preservation treatment of the mummy of Ramses II by French scientists.                                                                 *L.Z.*

78055 BALOUT, L. et C. ROUBET, L'opération Ramsès II. Contribution des laboratoires à l'égyptologie, *BSFE* No. 83 (Octobre 1978), 8-23, with 7 ill.

La momie de Ramsès II avait souffert de pollutions diverses. Arrivée à Paris en septembre 1976. elle passa sept mois et demi en climatisation, sujette à un double examen: état actuel et causes de détérioration. Dix-sept laboratoires ont collaboré à l'examen et au traitement de la momie. L'emploi de xéroradiographies et de chromo-densitographies a conduit à plusieurs découvertes. Les embaumeurs avaient redressé la tête, provoquant ainsi une fracture. Le nez remodelé contenait une phalange et des grains; ceux-ci, présents également dans la gorge et l'abdomen, se révélèrent être du poivre. Des endoscopies ont fait apparaître des tissus arachnéens à fils bleus et or. Le coeur reposait dans

le thorax, où les goudrons recèlent la présence de "nicotiana". Le pollen de camomille regorge dans un onguent. Le squelette accuse la spondylarthrose et l'artériosclérose. Des recherches particulières sur les cheveux y ont relevé un pigment rouge, méditerranéen. La radiostérilisation au cobalt 60 a permis de neutraliser les cryptogames, surtout les dangereux "daedalea biennis". Les bandelettes une fois enroulées avec art, Ramsès II repartit, soigneusement calé dans "son" antique cercueil de cèdre, le tout sous plastique gonflable. Sous sa vitrine, la ventilation constante est pourvue de filtres antibactériens.
*J. Custers*

BAQUÉS ESTAPÉ, Lorenzo, see our number 78595.

78056 Les barbus au Musée Bourdelle. Paris Juin-Septembre 1978, [Paris], Mairie de Paris, [1978] (16.7 x 21 cm; 28 [unnumbered] p., 40 pl., ill. on cover).

Catalogue of an exhibition of representations of bearded men in the art of various periods, among which a few from ancient Egypt.
An introduction to the subject as regards Egypt, by Mme Desroches-Noblecourt, is followed by a description of eight objects, by Christiane Ziegler. Two of them are razors; three are represented on the plates; a M.K. mummy mask, a Late Period statue of Osiris, and a relief representing Ramses II and Amon.

78057 BARGUET, Paul, Remarques sur quelques scènes de la salle du sarcophage de Ramsès VI, *RdE* (1978), 51 - 56, with 2 fig.

Explication du décor de la salle mentionnée dans le titre. L'auteur fait apparaître une répartie en deux parties, dont l'une évoque la renaissance du roi par la représentation d'un parcours solaire nocturne, commandé par la succession des heures, sans la moindre allusion à Osiris, l' autre par la génération d'un nouveau soleil équivalente à la procréation d'Horus. *Ph. Derchain*

78058 BARKLEY †, Marylynn S., Vertebral Arch Defects in Ancient Egyptian Populations, *Journal of Human Evolution*, London - New York - San Francisco 7 (1978), 553 - 557, with 3 tables and 2 pl.

Study of the incidence of vertebral arch defects in 98 Egyptian skeletons, from Naga-ed-Dêr and Gîza, now in the Lowie Museum of Anthropology, Berkeley, Calif. Spondylolysis was present in the skeletal remains from both places. The frequency of the defect at Naga ed-Dêr may indicate that an hereditary etiological factor was involved. *L.Z.*

BARNS, John W.B., see our number 78738.

78059 BAROCAS, Claudio, L'antico Egitto. Ideologia e lavoro nella terra dei faraoni, [Roma], Newton Compton editori, [1978] (12.2 x 19.3 cm; 253 p., 45 fig., 32 pl., colour ill. on cover); series: Paperbacks civiltà scomparsi, 20.

The book consists of an introduction, two parts devoted respectively to representations and texts, and a final chapter. The point of departure of the study

is the idea that labour means civilization and civilization means labour.
The first chapter proceeds from the representations of the battle of Kadesh and argues that they are the expression of the ideology of the period. Then the development of the tomb wall decoration from the O. to the N.K. is sketched in so far as it relates to labour. The differences between the periods reflect the changes in the society.
In the second part a number of texts from various periods are analysed as reflections of the ideology of the time in which they are written. The author stresses,for instance, the increasing importance of the king's political role during the N.K.
In the final chapter the author i.a. pleads for a close cooperation between historians and cultural anthropologists and a revision of the art-historical methods.

78060 BARTA, Winfried, Bemerkungen zur Etymologie und Semantik der Götternamen von Isis und Osiris, *MDAIK* 34 (1978), 9 - 13.

Rejecting Osing's thesis about the names of Isis and Osiris (see our number 74551, and also Kuhlmann, our number 75424) the author discusses various possible explanations. It may be that the usual explanation of Osiris as "seat of the Eye" is correct, although the suggestion that *iri* is one of its elements is also plausible. It may be that Isis means "she who belongs to the womb", and that originally the words were etymologically different. Their meaning and together with it the essence of the divinities appear to have been unaffected by these explanations.

78061 BARTA, Winfried, Das Schulbuch Kemit, *ZÄS* 105 (1978), 6 - 14.

Verfasser gibt eine Gesamtübersetzung, begleitet von einer metrisch gegliederten Transkription und einem knappen Kommentar. Er unterscheidet im Buch drei Hauptteile: Begrüssungsformeln, Erzählung und Sentenzen.

*M. Heerma van Voss*

78062 BARTA, Winfried, Die Sedfest-Darstellung Osorkons II. im Tempel von Bubastis, *SAK* 6 (1978), 25 - 42, with 1 fig. and 4 folding pl.

Studying the scenes of the Sed-portal in the temple of Bubastis the author first lists the six main parts of the ritual as known from older representations (Abû Ghurâb, Karnak and Soleb). He then attempts to ascribe the preserved blocks of the portal to each of these parts, which leads to a reconstruction that in many respects differs from that by Naville.

78063 BASCH, Lucien, Le navire *mnš* et autres notes de voyage en Égypte, *The Mariner's Mirror*, Greenwich 64 (1978), 99 - 123, with 33 fig. and ill.

The author first discusses the word *mnš*, particularly its determinative in the Poem of the Kadesh Battle on the Abydos temple, the only one clear enough to recognize its characteristics. He concludes that the *mnš* is Syrian in design, but that these ships were probably built in Egypt.

The other sections deal with the ship graffiti from the Khonsu temple at Karnak and from the Dendera temple, showing a greater complexity in the development of Egyptian shipping than expected, but not easily datable; the ship in the scene of the Horus ritual at Edfu with certain particularities of rigging; and a stone anchor in the temple of Karnak, of a Cypriote type.

78064 BAUD, Marcelle, Le caractère du dessin en Égypte ancienne, Paris, Librairie d'Amérique et d' Orient Adrien-Maisonneuve, 1978 (17.5 x 24 cm; 94 p., 3 fig., 24 colour pl., 95 pl.); rev. *BiOr* 37 (1980), 41 - 42 (William H. Peck); *CdE* LIV, No. 108 (1979), 265 - 266 (B. v.d. Walle). Pr. F.F. 80

This study, the introduction to which is dated between 1937 and 1939 (although a few among the rare notes refer to more recent publications), is an extension of the author's article that has been published under the same title in Mélanges Maspero I (= MIFAO 66, 1934), 13 - 20; see also the author's "Les dessins ébauchés de la nécropole thébaine" (= MIFAO 63, 1935). In this introduction Mme Baud formulates as her point of departure that cubism is the modern heir of the Egyptian art, enabling us to appreciate the art of Egypt by liberating us from the exigencies of perspective art.
The book is divided into eight chapters. After stating the generalities from which the rules have been developed chapters 2-4 deal each with one of these principles: the totality of the characteristics of a motif are expressed; the elements of the scenes are represented in relation to a moving spectator; the proportions exployed express the major idea of the scene depicted.
In four chapters the author discusses: the way space is depicted, the views of the face, the expression of efforts and sentiments, and the techniques of drawing.
The plates bear very fine colour drawings by the author, line drawings and a few photographs, all of scenes and, particularly, of details by which the argument is illustrated.

78065 von BECKERATH, Jürgen, Geschichtsüberlieferung im Alten Ägypten, *Saeculum,* Freiburg/München 29 (1978), 11 - 17.

After introductory remarks on Manetho whose basic source of information must have been a king list from probably a temple archive, and the problem of events absent in the official tradition, the author turns to the question of the tradition of history, which in Egypt is indissolubly connected with the conception of history. He discusses the development from the early annals, i.a. the Palermo Stone, which very seldom record historical events, but normally ritual acts maintaining the static cosmic order (Ma'at). The purpose of the royal inscriptions, considered by us as historical sources, was the realization of the cosmic order. Comparison of the events mentioned in the early annals and Manetho's knowledge in this respect make it probable that events, not mentioned in the official tradition, must have made a deep impression on the people. It is from this oral tradition that literary fixation took place, although the literary fixation through the instructions for the class of civil servants has the purpose to maintain the cosmic order.

The very frequently described motif of the emergency situation, from which the land is saved by the saviour king, goes essentially back to the dogma that the world is recreated at the accession of the new pharaoh and chaos exists, theoretically, before that. The motif, however, refers to real historical events in periods such as the F.I.P., the S.I.P., and the Amarna Period. The other stories in the works of Manetho and Herodotus, though in the last case through Greek mediators, must originate from the same background.
The knowledge of the Egyptians themselves comes from both sources, and that of ours owes a lot more to these accidental, unofficial stories, although not made for that purpose, than to the official tradition. *L.Z.*

78066  von BECKERATH, Jürgen, Nochmals die Regierungsdauer des Haremhab, *SAK* 6 (1978) 43 - 49.

Discussing the higher year dates recorded for Haremhab the author suggests that "year 59" (or 58?) in the Inscription of Mes is probably a mistake (for 28 or 29?); that "year 27" on a limestone fragment from Haremhab's mortuary temple refers to the arrival of his statue there; that the "year 16" in an inscription on a bowl (see Redford, our numbers 73596 and 73597) is very uncertain. A reign of 20 to 30 years looks in accordance with the Babylonian chronology.

78067  BEDINI, Alessandro and Federica CORDANO, L'ottavo secolo nel Lazio e l'inizio dell' orientalizzante antico. Alla luce di recenti scoperte nella necropoli di Castel di Decima (= Lazio arcaico e mondo greco, 3), *La parola del passato*, Napoli 32 (1977), 274-311, with 14 ill. and 1 folding fig.

A scarab was found in a tomb at Castel di Decima, Lazio, dating from the beginning of the 8th century B.C. *L.Z.*

BEDINI, Elsa, see our number 78122.

78068  BEINLICH, Horst, Ein ägyptischer Räucherarm in Heidelberg. Mit einem Exkurs von W. Brunsch, *MDAIK* 34 (1978), 15 - 31, with 11 fig. and 4 pl.

On account of an arm-shaped censer found in the temple of Sheshonq in el-Hîba and at present in the Egyptological Institute in Heidelberg (Inv. No. 2419), which is here published, the author studies this type of object and its variations, actual objects as well as representations. A development of the shape from the M.K. to the Late Period is suggested.
In the excursus Brunsch studies the Demotic inscription on the censer in the Brooklyn Museum (Acc. No. 72.8).

78069  BEINLICH, Horst, Horus-Schu im 10. o.äg. Gau?, *GM* Heft 29 (1978), 11, with 1 fig.

Antwort auf die Kritik Graefes (vgl. unsere Nr. 77 297) zu einer verbesserten Lesung des Gottesnamens bei Brugsch (Thes. 623) aus dem Tempel von Dendera: eine erneute Untersuchung an Ort und Stelle ergab, dass die Lesung bei Brugsch tatsächlich falsch war und die Schreibung des Gottesnamens der von Thes. 621 entspricht. *Inge Hofmann*

78070  BEIT-ARIEH, Itzhak, A Canaanite Site Near Sheikh Mukhsen. Recent Discoveries in Southern Sinai, *Expedition,* Philadelphia, Penn.20, No. 4 (Summer 1978), 8 - 11, with 7 ill., 1 map and 1 plan.

The author notes at the end that, since the Egyptian presence in the South of the coastal plain of Palestine did not prevent the Canaanites spreading out to Southern Sinai, this hints at economic co-existence between the two countries.
L.Z.

78071  BEIT ARIEH, Itzhaq, Investigations in Mine L (Explorations at Serâbît el-Khâdim -1977), *Tel Aviv,* Tel.Aviv 5 (1978), 175 - 182, with 4 fig. and 5 pl.

The author describes some stone objects discovered in Mine L at Serâbît el-Khâdim, i.e. a bellows bowl and a casting mould for axes.
Compare our number 78288. L.Z.

78072  BELL, L., Reconstruction of the Chronology of the High Priests of Amun, *JSSEA* 8 (1977- 1978), 71.

Abstract of a paper.

BELL, Lanny D., see also our number 78597.

78073  BELLET, Paulinus, Analecta Coptica, *The Catholic Biblical Quarterly,* Washington DC 40 (1978), 37 - 52.

The author publishes some Coptic texts: 1. A Sahidic fragment of Exodus (21: 17 - 35/23:5 - 21; Walters Art Gallery W. 739); 2. Subakhmimic fragments of the Epistles of St.Paul (Heb. 5: 5 - 7, 8 - 9/5: 11 - 12, 13 - 14; Philemon 6: 15-16, University Library, Cambridge England). L.Z.

78074  BELOVA, G.A., Титулатура "царских сыновей Куша" как источник для исследования их функций, ВДИ 2 (144), 1978, 153-175, with an English summary on p. 175.

"The Titulature of the 'King's Sons of Kush' as Source for the Research on the Functions".
The author discusses the origin and development of the institution of the "King's Son of Kush", the head of the administration apparatus for subjugated Nubia. She draws up a list of "King's Sons of Kush" arranged after the reigning N.K. Pharaohs and clarifies the meaning of certain titles given to them. This resulted in a clearer picture of their sphere of operation and specific characteristics. L.Z.

78075  BELTZ, Walter, Katalog der koptischen Handschriften der Papyrussammlung der Staatlichen Museen zu Berlin (Teil 1), *Archiv für Papyrusforschung und verwandte Gebiete,* Leipzig 26 (1978), 57 - 119.

This partial catalogue of the collection of Coptic documents in the Staatliche Museen in Berlin deals with 681 papyri, 69 manuscripts on paper, and 153 on parchment. The material is firstly arranged after material, and secondly after contents. Of each document the usual data and the first line are given. The article is continued in the same periodical 27 (1980), 121-222.   *L.Z.*

78076   BERGER, Catherine, Audran LABROUSSE, Jean LECLANT, Présentation préliminaire de la céramique recueillie par la MAFS au temple haut de Pépi Ier à Saqqarah. Campagnes 1974 - 1977, Paris, 1978 (21 x 29.5 cm; 24 p., 1 plan, 17 pl.) = Publications de l' U.R.A. No.4 du C.R.A. "Pyramides Memphites et Archéologie méroïtique". Cahiers No. 1.

Publication of pottery found by the Mission Archéologique Française de Saqqâra in the Pyramid Temple of Pepi I. Apart from introductory remarks the publication consists of drawings of the vessels, with inventory numbers, place of origin and material of each indicated on the opposite pages. Groups of these vessels either came from the tomb of Hemi or date from the M. and N.K. A second volume has been published in 1979.

78077   BERGMAN, J., Zum Zwei-Wege-Motiv. Religionsgeschichtliche und exegetische Bemerkungen, *Svensk Exegetisk Årsbok,* Uppsala 41- 42 (1976-1977), 27-56.

Within the framework of a broad study of the motif of the two ways the author devotes some remarks to the Egyptian Book of Two Ways.   *L.Z.*

78078   BERLANDINI, J., La pyramide "ruinée" de Sakkara-Nord et Menkaouhor, *BSFE* No.83 (Octobre 1978), 24-34, with 2 plans, 1 fig. and 3 ill.

*Ntrỉ -swt,* la pyramide de Menkaouhor, n'a pu être localisée. Plusieurs monuments du Nouvel Empire témoignent pourtant d'un culte vivace pour ce roi. Outre deux reliefs du Louvre, B 48 et 50, et Berlin N I 1116, le linteau Caire J.E. 33258 concourt à le prouver. Ce dernier, qui groupe quatre souverains, refléterait la topographie cultuelle d'un secteur de Sakkara. Certes, chercher là le complexe funéraire de Menkaouhor semblait exclu par le "Décret royal" de Pépi Ier. Cependant, il suffirait d'interpréter ses mots *ínt* et *r3 -š* comme "réquisitionner (le personnel d'un) domaine royal" pour lever la difficulté. Le plan donné par Lepsius portait une pyramide ruinée, près de celles de Teti et d'Ipout. Firth la fouilla rapidement en 1929, et son carnet de notes la signale comme munie de deux herses.

Dans la V$^e$ dynastie, seul Menkaouhor répondrait à ce critére de portée chronologique; le nom du monument oriente dans le même sens. Firth attribuait la pyramide au problématique Ity, que l'on a tendance à placer dans la VIII$^e$ dynastie. Mais Firth lui-même a relevé une empreinte de sceau quasi décisive: la jarre porteuse de deux noms royaux proviendrait des magasins du temple haut de Menkaouhor.   *J. Custers*

78079   BERLANDINI, Jocelyne, Une stèle de donation du dynaste libyen Roudamon, *BIFAO* 78 (1978), 147-163, with 1 fig. and 2 pl.

The donation stela here published has been found in the reserves of the IFAO and is said to come from Kôm Firîn. It is dated to the 30th year of an unment-

ioned king who may be Sheshonq V and is dedicated by the Great Chief of the Libu Rudamon (±378 B.C.).
The author presents the text in photograph and drawing, with a translation and epigraphic and textual notes. She also deals with the historical background, collecting the data for two other persons called Rudamon, one a Theban kinglet after Takelot III, the other from el-Hîba. The present Rudamon was probably a powerful man in the Western Delta.

78080 BERLEV, O.D., Общественные отношения в Египте эпохи среднего царства. Социальный слой "царских *ḥmww*", Москва, Издательство "Наука". Главная редакция восточной литературы, 1978 (14 x 20 cm; 367 p., 7 tables [= p. 352-358] ).  Pr. 2P. 40K.

"The communal relations in Egypt during the period of the Middle Kingdom. The social layer of the 'royal *ḥmw.w*'."
First an Introduction (p.5-8), then some additions to Berlev's earlier monograph on the Working Class (our number 72070 - p.9-16), mainly consisting of a treatment of the (unedited) Pap. Berlin 10048, rt. (following a transcription by É.Devaud).
Chapter 1 (17-34) contains an evaluation of certain basic sources; the O.K. inscriptions of *Ḥnmty* (Cairo, CG 1643) and *'Itw-ḫ3ḫ3* (or *Tf-ḫ3y*, *Tf-nn*; Cairo, JdE 56994), both compared to shawabti contracts; the subject and objective factors in the appointments of funerary personnel are discussed. The following chapters are lexically organized around certain relevant titles and contain a wealth of detail (including prosopography) on their bearers.
Chapter 2 (35-62) is a detailed treatment of non-standardized terms for 'personnel': *rmṯ, ḏt*; the terms *wp.t* 'register' and *rḫ.t*, 'list'; *ṯs.t*, 'troop', *ḫ3d.t* (only in Naga ed Deir stelae; ed. Dows Dunham, 78), *mḥty.w* 'northerners'; the expression *ḫ3 n dd rmṯ*, here interpreted as *ḫ3 n ꜥ.wy rmṯ*, 'hall of manual labourers', and *ḥw.t* 'domain'.
Chapter 3 (63-125) deals with terms indicating poor-people: the have-nots. One finds *šw3w, tw3w, m3rw, ḥwrw, šww* (a variety of words - i.a. Wb IV, 427.20), *nḏsw* (very extensively documented).
Chapter 4 (126-234) is devoted to the personnel connected with a house (*pr*): *imy-n-pr, ḥny-pr, pry, ḥry-pr* (and all its associated titles and epithets: very extensive), *ꜥḥꜥy.t, sḏ3wty(.t), šmsw(.t), nš.t* ('hairdresser'), *sš.t* ('female scribe'), *iry-ḥbsw, iry-ḥnw* ('jar-keeper') and *rḫty* ('washerman').
Chapter 5 (235-327) surveys those working in the *šnꜥw*: the *iry(.t)-ꜥ.t, ꜥky.t, wdpw(.t), wb3w(.t), ḥtt-pr, ꜥfty(.t)* ('brewer'), *ꜥtḫw, rtḫty, kfny, psw* ('cook'), *sftw, iḥms, šnꜥw*.
An appendix (329-334) contains a selection of illustrative material (iconography and hieroglyphic writings of some titles partly given on p. 352-355). Bibliography (336-349) and extensive subject-oriented contents (359-367) make this invaluable book easily accessible.  *J.F. Borghouts*

BESTE, Irmtraut, see our number 78176.

78081 BETRÒ, Maria Carmela, Ricerche su un tipo di terreno nei documenti demotici, *Egitto e Vicino Oriente* 1 (1978), 85-94.

The author discusses the Demotic word *wrḥ*, used for a particular type of land, arguing from the evidence of the Pathyris papyri that it was only partly equivalent to φιλὸς τόπος. Originally simply meaning "soil" it developed into designating "building-site" or "fallow-land", but also land planted with trees (not with cereals). The development of the term during the Ptolemaic Period is described and its connection with economic changes indicated.

BETRÒ, Maria Carmela, see also our number 78123.

78082   BIANCHI, Robert S., Augustus in Egypt. The Temple of Dendur is Rebuilt at the Metropolitan Museum of Art, *Archaeology* 31, No.5 (September/October 1978), [4-11], with 1 map, 1 plan and 8 ill. (1 in colour).

Article for the general public on the temple of Dendur in the Metropolitan Museum of Art, New York.
A fuller report on the various aspects of the temple was written by C.Aldred, *Bulletin of the Metropolitan Museum of Art* 36 (1978-1979), 1-64.        L.Z.

78083   BIANCHI, Robert S., Egyptian Art from the Bastis Collection, *Apollo*, London 108, No. 199 (September 1978), 153-155, with 9 ill.

The author describes pieces of the Christos G. Bastis Collection which has been on view in the Brooklyn Museum, mainly consisting of objects from the Late and Graeco-Roman Periods. Especially noteworthy are two bronze statuettes of King Taharqa and the God's wife Shepenupet II (?), from the XXVth Dynasty and some heads from the XXXth Dynasty and the Ptolemaic Period.   L.Z.

78084   BIANCHI, Robert S., Egyptological Seminar, *GM* Heft 30 (1978), 7.

Ankündigung eines ägyptologischen Seminars in New York, das siebenmal im Verlaufe eines akademischen Jahres stattfinden soll mit dem Ziel, einen Gedankenaustausch über alle Aspekte des Alten Ägyptens von der prähistorischen bis zur koptischen Zeit zu fördern.                                *Inge Hofmann*

78085   BIANCHI, Robert S., Nubian Exhibit at Brooklyn Museum, *Newsletter ARCE* No.106 (Fall 1978), 10-13, with 5 ill.

Short note on the international exhibition "Africa in Antiquity. The Arts of Ancient Nubia and the Sudan" (see our number 78008), consisting of over 250 objects on loan from 25 institutions and collectors.        L.Z.

78086   BIANCHI, Robert S., The Striding Draped Male Figure of Ptolemaic Egypt,*in: Das ptolemäische Ägypten*, 95-102, with 1 fig. and 18 ill.

Studying a group of statues from the Ptolemaic Period the author argues that the vitality of the native pharaonic tradition when confronted with the Greek art was strong enough to be preserved. He deals with three different garments that are all of Egyptian origin. No Greek influence can be detected in the techniques of the sculptors who fashioned these draped male figures. Compare our number 77087.

BIANCHI, Robert S., see also our numbers 78239 and 78549.

78087 BIERBRIER, M.L., The Date of the Destruction of Emar and Egyptian Chronology, *JEA* 64 (1978), 136-137.

The recent excavations at Mesken in Syria show that it was destroyed at the same time as Carcemish, and had one tablet in a house occupied immediately before this, which is dated to Year 2 of Melik-shipak or c.1187 B.C. As this destruction date can be equated with year 8 of Ramesses III the writer working backward believes that a lower date than 1304 B.C. for the accession of Ramesses II is almost certain. *E.P.Uphill*

78088 BIERBRIER, M.L. Notes on Deir el-Medina. I. The Dating of the Verso of O. DeM.621, *JSSEA* 8 (1977-1978), 35-38.

Against Krauss (see our number 76467) the author argues from the names of the workmen mentioned in it that O. DeM. 621 vs. dates from the reign of Merenptah (year 2).

78089 BIERBRIER, Morris, Notes on Deir el-Medina. II. The Career of Paneb, *JSSEA* 8 (1977-1978), 138-140.

The author relates what we know from ostraca about the chief workman Paneb (late XIXth to early XXth Dynasty), adding remarks about the career of his son Aapehti.

78090 BIETAK, Manfred und Elfriede REISER-HASLAUER, Das Grab des 'Ankh-Hor. Obersthofmeister der Gottesgemahlin Nitokris I. Mit einem Beitrag von Erhart Graefe und Relief- und Fundzeichnungen von Heinz Satzinger, Wien, Verlag der Österreichischen Akademie der Wissenschaften, 1978 (23.5 x 30.5 cm; 151 p., 63 fig. [8 folding] including plans, ill. on cover; in a separate portfolio 32 folding plates [plans and drawings ]) = Österreichische Akademie der Wissenschaften. Denkschriften der Gesamtakademie, Band VI = Untersuchungen der Zweigstelle Kairo des Österreichischen Archäologischen Instituts, Band IV; rev. *CdE* LV, No. 109 - 110 (1980), 150 - 153 (P.Vernus).

This first part of the publication of Theban Tomb No. 414, that has been discovered and excavated by the Austrian expedition between 1971 and 1977, consists of an introduction and four chapters.
Chapter 1 is devoted to the topography of 'Asâsîf before and in the Late Period and the position of 'Ankh-Hor's tomb in the area. The short chapter 2 gives a survey of the Austrian excavations and the general stratigraphy of the Eastern part of 'Asâsîf. In chapter 3 (by Graefe) functions, family, descent of 'Ankh-Hor are studied, while four appendices (the last one by Mrs Reiser) deal with particular titles and the combinations of titles.
Chapter 4, by far the longest (p.55-151), contains the description and study of the superstructure and the foremost part of the substructure of the tomb. Architecture and wall decoration are discussed and presented in drawing, the texts, including that of the stela of 'Ankh-Hor's daughter Merit-Neith, are given in hieroglyphs and translation.

Some sections contain remarks of a wider scope, e.g. those on the function of the substructure, the orientation and order of the B.D. chapters on the pillars of the court, and the comparison of the frieze inscriptions with those in the tombs of Pedihorresnet and Pabasa. At the end a list of finds from the court. On the plates plans and sections as well as drawings of the wall decoration. The back part of the substructure and general conclusions as regards artistic qualities etc. will appear in volume II (still unpublished).

78091   BIMSON, John J., Redating the Exodus and Conquest, Sheffield, [JSOT], 1978 (14.8 x 21 cm; 351 p.) = Journal for the Study of the Old Testament. Supplement Series, 5; rev. *Liber Annuus. Studium Biblicum Franciscanum* 30 (1980), 419 - 422 (S.Loffreda).

Proceeding from the assumption that the biblical traditions of the bondage in Egypt and of the Exodus have a firm historical basis, the author investigates the arguments for dating the Exodus and the Conquest. In part I he presents a critical examination of the usual thirteenth century date of the Exodus, in part 2 he presents the arguments for an earlier date, in the first half of the 15th century B.C. In both particularly the archaeological evidence is studied, leading to the conclusion that the end of the MBA Period is later than usually accepted. That means that the destructions at the end of that period coincide with the Exodus.
In the course of the study some evidence from Egypt is discussed, particularly the towns Raamses and Pithom (p. 35-48).

78092   BINGEN, Jean, Rapport des directeurs, *CdE* LIII, No. 105 (1978), 6 - 9.

BISHARA, Sadek Ibrahim, see our number 78843.

BLANC, Nicole, see our number 78614.

78093   BLUMENTHAL, Elke, Die Leipziger Reliefs aus Meroe, *ZÄS* 105 (1978), 85-93, with 3 fig. and 4 ill. on 2 pl.

Im Jahre 1906 wurde der Denkstein Sesostris III. von Uronarti gegen einige Reliefs von den Pyramiden von Meroe zwischen der Königlich Sächsischen Regierung und dem Sudan ausgetauscht. Es handelt sich um zwei Reliefs und Bruchstücke die während des Kriegs zerstört wurden: Inv. 1688 und die Bruchstücke 1690 - 94 aus der Kapelle der Pyramide Lepsius A 38 (= Beg.N 17; Hinkel: NE-36-O/3-J-1.17) und Inv. 1689 aus der Pyramidenkapelle Lepsius A 31 (= Beg.N 19; Hinkel: NE-36-0/3-J-1.19), d.h. von den Pyramidenkapellen der Könige Amanitenmomide bzw. Tarekeniwal. Von den Reliefs Inv. 1688 und 1689 sind Archivfotos publiziert, die jeweils eine Aufnahme im Museum und in situ wiedergeben. Die Darstellungen werden beschrieben. Inv. 1690 - 1694 gehören zur Südwand von Beg. N 17, die von Lepsius bis auf die herausgebrochenen Stücke, die dann nach Leipzig kamen, in das Berliner Ägyptischen Museum gebracht worden waren. Die Gesamtdarstellung der Wand wird rekonstruiert.
*Inge Hofmann*

78094 BLUMENTHAL, Elke, Zur Göttlichkeit des regierenden Königs in Ägypten, *OLZ* 73 (1978), 533 - 541.

Review article of Barta's study "Untersuchungen zur Göttlichkeit des regierenden Königs" (our number 75042).

78095 BOCKENHEIMER, S., U. EICKHOFF, E. METZEL and K. VOIGT, Radiologisch-äquidensitographische Untersuchungen der Kalottenverletzungen des Pharao Seqenenre, *Fortschritte auf dem Gebiete der Röntgenstrahlen und der Nuklearmedizin,* Stuttgart 128 (1978), 691 - 694, with 1 fig, and 4 ill.

Skull radiographs of the pharaoh Seqenenre-Ta'a II with special densitographic techniques have shown that he survived a perforating skull injury. The technique is described and its use in medical history and archaeology is discussed.
*Author's summary*

78096 von BODELSCHWING, Kristina, Masterworks of Old Egyptian Ceramics, *The Connoisseur,* London 199, No. 801 (November 1978), 209, with 1 ill.

Short report on an exhibition. For the catalogue, see our number 78546.

78097 BOGOSLOVSKAYA, I.V. and E.S. BOGOSLOVSKY, Сиро-палестинская богиня Кудшу в Древнем Египте, Палестинский Сборник, Ленинград 26 (89), 1978, 140 - 164, with 1 ill. and an English summary on p. 163-164.

"The Syro-Palestinian Goddess Qudshu in Ancient Egypt."
The authors present a summary of all known monuments of the goddess Qudshu in Egypt, listing the inscriptions dedicated to her (in hieroglyphs and translation) and studying the iconography of the goddess (influence of the image of Hathor on the representation of Qudshu) and the stylistic features of the stelae, as well as investigating the ethnic and social origin of the Egyptians erecting monuments in honour of the goddess. These people appear to be Egyptians, although some of them may be of foreign descent.

78098 BONGRANI FANFONI, Luisa, Due elementi lignei di sarcofagi di babbuini, *Oriens Antiquus* 17 (1978), 197–198.

Publication of two wooden pieces of baboon sarcophagi, most probably originating from Tûna el-Gebel, and now in the Museo del Vicino Oriente Antico dell' Università di Roma. The texts, with only minor differences from each other, are presented in hieroglyphs with a translation. *L.Z.*

78099 BONGRANI FANFONI, Luisa, Intorno uno strumento funerario arcaico: il *psš-kf, Studi classici e orientali,* Pisa 28 (1978), 133 - 138.

The author discusses material and function of the funerary instrument called *psš-kf.* She suggests that it is a flint object which, as a new translation of P.T.

Spell 37 suggests, was used to keep open the mouth of the deceased. For the *psš-kf*, see now also R. van Walsem, *OMRO* 59 - 60 (1978-1979), 193-249.

78100 BONGRANI FANFONI, Luisa, I sandali e il cammino dell' 'Aldila', *Vicino Oriente*, Roma 1 (1978), 1 - 3.

On account of some spells from the P.T. and the C.T., but also chapters from the B.D., a scene from the tomb of Ramses VI, and even the Narmer palette, the author argues that sandals in this context have a symbolic, protective meaning.

78101 BONGRANI FANFONI, Luisa, F. HAIKAL, G. NOLLI, Le sarcophage No. 22.954 du Musée Vatican, *Rivista* 52 (1978), 153 - 182, with 6 pl.

This is only the first part of the article, which will be continued in *Rivista*. In the first section the first author presents a detailed description of the exterior and interior of the sarcophagus of Hetepheres (No. 22.954) in the Museo Gregoriano Egizio. She dates the piece to the XXVth Dynasty.
The second and third sections are by the second author. She first gives the texts of the sarcophagus in a handwritten copy, then their translations. Almost all are spells of the B.D.

78102 BONHÊME, Marie-Ange, Les désignations de la «titulature» royale au Nouvel Empire, *BIFAO* 78 (1978), 347 - 387.

The author discusses the designations of the royal titulary used during the N.K., namely *nḫbt/nḫb(w)*, *rn wr*, *rn mȝˁ* (only for Hatshepsut) and *rn(w)*, noting for each the writings and the use with various verbs. Of them *nḫbt* indicates the five royal names together or the Horus name as *pars pro toto; rn wr* each name separately except for the personal birth-name, but also, in some instances in plural, the total of the four names; *rn mȝˁ* is a variant of the last use; *rn* is used for each name or for all five together.
In a table the author lists the divinities and man "acting" with regard to the titulature. A list of 69 documents on which the study has been based on p. 380-387.

BONNEAU, Danielle, see our number 78214.

78103 BONNET, Charles, Fouilles archéologiques à Kerma (Soudan). Rapport préliminaire de la campagne 1977 - 1978, *Genava*, Genève 26 (1978), 107 - 127, with 5 fig., 11 ill. and 3 plans (2 folding).

Kerma, das Zentrum eines grossen sudanesischen Reiches, liegt strategisch sehr günstig. In der Stadt wurde eine gewaltige Befestigungsmauer ausgegraben sowie einige Häuser. Die Oberbauten der entdeckten Strukturen im Stadtinnern lassen darauf schliessen, dass die Stadt lange besiedelt war. Die Struktur der Gräber, ihre Ausstattung und besonders die Keramik zeigen, dass jede Epoche der Kerma-Kultur belegt ist: das alte Kerma, das in das Ende des alten ägyptischen Reiches und die Erste Zwischenzeit datiert wird (KA), das mitt-

lere Kerma, das sich während des Mittleren Reiches bildete (KB), das klassische Kerma, das während der Zweiten Zwischenzeit blühte (KC) und das späte Kerma, das noch für die 18. Dynastie bezeugt ist (KD).
Weitere Untersuchungen betrafen die westliche Deffufa mit ihren Annexen, deren Funktionen nicht restlos geklärt ist. Die untersuchten Friedhöfe stammen aus dem Neuen Reich und der meroitischen Epoche. Der Friedhof aus dem Neuen Reich, dessen Gräber Skelette in zusammengekauerter Lage enthielten, zeigt, dass die Ägyptisierung noch nicht wie im Norden Fuss gefasst hatte. Die Grabausstattung zeigt eine Mischung von Gegenständen lokaler Herstellung und Import aus Ägypten. Die meroitische Nekropole enthielt oft Reste von Holzsarkophagen, meist anthropomorph, seltener rechteckig. Anhand der Funde kann sie in die ersten Jahrhunderte vor unserer Zeitrechnung datiert werden. Grab 10 wird eingehend beschrieben. *Inge Hofmann*

78104 BONNET, Ch., Nouveaux travaux archéologiques à Kerma (1973-1975), *in: Études nubiennes,* 25-34, with 2 fig., and 19 ill. on 12 pl.

In Kerma wurde ein grosser runder Komplex ausgegraben, der unter dem heutigen Bodenniveau liegt; auf der Nordseite führt eine Treppe in ihn hinunter. Bereits Lepsius hatte auf einen "gewaltigen Damm" aufmerksam gemacht, der jedoch Reisner bei seinen Arbeiten entgangen war. Er liegt im Süden der westlichen *Deffufa.* Ein Oberbau ist nicht mehr vorhanden; die Funde, u.a. Bruchstücke von wenigstens drei ägyptischen Statuetten sowie vor allem die Keramik verweisen den Komplex in die Kerma-Zeit. Seine Funktion konnte noch nicht eindeutig bestimmt werden, doch könnte er mit dem Bestattungswesen in Zusammenhang gestanden haben. *Inge Hofmann*

78105 BORGER, Rykle, Drei Klassizisten. Alma Tadema, Ebers, Vosmaer. Mit einer Bibliographie der Werke Alma Tadema's, Leiden, Ex Oriente Lux, 1978 (19.5 x 26.5 cm; [IV +] 48 p., frontispiece, 4 ill. [2 in colour] on 2 pl.) = Mededelingen en Verhandelingen van het Vooraziatisch-Egyptisch Genootschap "Ex Oriente Lux", 20.

This is a study by an Assyriologist of the work of the painter Lourens Alma Tadema (1836-1912) and his relations with the Dutch archaeologist Carel Vosmaer and the German Egyptologist Georg Ebers. The reason for this combination of persons in one study is the friendship between the painter and the two scholars, caused among other reasons by the painter's attempt to reproduce as carefully as possible a genuine classical or Egyptian atmosphere in his works so far as they had a historical setting. That he attained the end is demonstrated by the colour reproduction of two 'Egyptian' paintings on pl.1 (for a list of his "Egyptian" paintings, see p. 25-26).
The author describes the life and several works of Tadema (for his complete opus, see p. 5-18), but refrains from discussing their artistic value.

78106 BORGHOUTS, J.F., Ancient Egyptian Magical Texts. Translated, Leiden, E.J. Brill, 1978 (12.8 x 18.8 cm; XII + 125 p.) = Religious Texts Translation Series. Nisaba, 9. Pr. fl. 28

In the introduction the author provides background information to magical texts and presents his selection. Then he translates 146 magical texts, many of which for the first time: No.1: love charm; nos 2-5 and 12: against dangerous, mostly dead people, including the evil eye; 6-8: against alarming nightly visions; 9-11: against evil influences including various forms of death; 13-21: dangers during the epagomenal days; 22-27: against demons causing diseases; 28-64: against various diseases and accidents; 65-70: for children's protections; 71-81: spells accompanying the administration of medicines. Then follow those against dangerous animals: scorpions (84-123), crocodiles (124-135), snakes (136-143), and Apophis (144-146). Whenever a significant word in magic occurs in the translations, the original Egyptian is given in transliteration in between brackets.

The book is concluded by the notes, the sources and several indexes. *L.Z.*

78107 [BOSSE-GRIFFITHS, Kate], Pictures from the Wellcome Collection. No.1. Beadwork/Lluniau o Gasgliad Wellcome. Rhif 1. Gwaith Gleiniau, Swansea, University College/Abertawe, Coleg y Brifysgol, [1978] (21 x 14.6 cm; 16 p., 9 colour ill. [2 on covers], 1 ill., 1 fig).,

Description of ancient Egyptian beadwork in the Wellcome Collection at Swansea in both Welsh and English. *L.Z.*

78108 BOSSE-GRIFFITHS, Kate, Some Egyptian Bead-Work Faces in the Wellcome Collection at University College, Swansea, *JEA* 64 (1978), 99-106, with 2 pl.

Formerly in the Wellcome Collection these thirteen beadwork faces once belonged to Robert de Rustafjaell, nos W773-785. Three are described in detail of av. height and breadth 13.5 cm. An attempt seems to have been made to distinguish between male and female, the material being faience and shell and the colour green in general. Other features are shown in black, white and rust-red. Comparisons are made with those in other museums and the significance discussed. They are dated between 1000-500 B.C. and could have possibly come from Nubia. *E.P.Uphill*

78109 BOSWINKEL, E. et P.W. PESTMAN, Textes grecs, démotiques et bilingues (P.L. Bat. 19). Édités par divers auteurs et publiés, [Leiden], E.J. Brill, 1978 (22 x 28.5 cm; X + 287 p., 28 pl.) = Papyrologica Lugduno-Batava edidit Institutum Papyrologicum Universitatis Lugduno-Batavae moderantibus E. Boswinkel, M.David, B.A.van Groningen, P.W.Pestman, 19; rev. *BiOr* 37 (1980), 169-171 (W.Clarysse). Pr. fl. 240

In this collection of Demotic, Greek and bilingual texts, first the texts published in the first part of the book (p. 1-189) are listed, arranged after their material and period. Of the first group, texts on papyrus (Nos. 1-24), the nos 1-3 and 5, all dating from the Ptolemaic Period, are (partly) in Demotic, while the rest are in Greek. Documents 1 and 3, concerned with the lease of the same plot of land in a part of the Memnoneia, and document 2, a partition of landed property between a brother and a sister by which the sister is assigned the same plot of land that is leased in document 1, originate from the Memnoneia and are published by P.W.Pestman. Document 5, from Pathyris, contains the sale of a building site (published by P.W.Pestman).

All texts in group II, texts on pottery (Nos. 25-28), are in Demotic or bilingual and date from the Graeco-Roman Period. Document 25, the only bilingual one in this group and concerned with the partial payment of the land tax called the *artabieia,* is published by P.W.Pestman, while the publication of documents 26 and 27, both receipts for dyke tax, and 28, an account, is from the hand of A. el-H. Nur el-Din.

From group III, texts on linen, (Nos 29-39), all texts written on pieces of linen mummy cloth are bilingual (Nos. 29-32), but those on bands of linen (Nos 33-39) in Greek. They are published by M.Thieme and P.W.Pestman, who also treated the nature, provenance and date of these objects in two brief introductions to the respective sections.

In group IV, texts on wood (Nos 40-48), J.Quaegebeur first publishes three mummy labels and extensively comments upon their interconnections (No.40), while No.41 is discussed by R.L.Vos (all bilingual). Nos 42-48, published and introduced by A. el-H. Nur el-Din, R.L.Vos and P.W.Pestman, are Demotic mummy labels containing letters by embalmers to colleagues ordering (or permitting) to bury the mummies in question.

These 48 texts are mostly presented in hand-facsimile with transliteration, or in photograph, with bibliographical data, abstracts of contents, textual notes, translations and commentary, general as well as concerning more specific topics.

The second part (p.191-267) contains appendices (A-F), devoted to particular aspects of the texts meriting special attention and for the major part from the hand of P.W.Pestman (A-D; E in cooperation with A.Thieme). Appendix A is concerned with the plot of land referred to in documents 1-3 which come from the archives of a priest at the Memnoneia and deals primarily with the history, area and neighbours of the plot; appendix B with 14 *sꜥnḫ*-women (γυνή τροφῖτις) at Pathyris and Krokodilopolis and the families to which they belonged; and appendix C with the ἐγκύκλιον-tax at Pathyris and Krokodilopolis in the 2nd and 1st centuries B.C. Appendix E is devoted to the three types of inscribed mummy linen in the Roman Period, namely shrouds, bands and small linen "name-label" strips. Appendix F, by J.Quaegebeur, contains a detailed discussion of all kinds of aspects of mummy labels, such as appearance, contents, purpose, formal features, illustrations, date, provenance, etc. The last appendix G, by R.L.Vos, is concerned with texts Nos 42-48, containing the permission to bury addressed to one Titoês, a priest at Hermonthis. The book is concluded by two elaborate sets of indexes, one for the Demotic and the other for the Greek. *L.Z.*

78110 BOTHMER, Bernard V., On Photographing Egyptian Art, *SAK* 6 (1978), 51-53, with 12 pl.

An article on H.W.Müller as a gifted photographer of works of art, illustrated by photographs of little known objects of art or views of well-known objects seldom seen, made by the author. Each photograph is accompanied by technical data on the object and a brief comment.

BOTWINICK, Michael, see our numbers 78008 and 78239.

78111 du BOURGUET, Pierre, Bibliographie Copte. Suggestions, *Enchoria* 8, Sonderband (1978), 11* (57) - 12* (58).

Abstract of a paper read at the First International Congress of Coptology, held in Cairo, December 1976.
The author stresses the importance of an official Coptic Bibliography as a working base. *W. Brunsch*

du BOURGUET, Pierre, see also our number 78269.

BOURLARD-COLLIN, Simone, see our number 78581.

78112 BOURRIAU, Janine, Egyptian Antiquities Acquired in 1976 by Museums in the United Kingdom, *JEA* 64 (1978), 123-127, with 2 pl.

Lists 114 items from Palaeolithic times to the Coptic Period that have been acquired by five museums. *E.P.Uphill*

78113 BOWMAN, Charles Howard, The Goddess 'Anatu in the Ancient Near East, *Dissertation Abstracts International*, Ann Arbor, Mich. 39, No.3 (September 1978), 1527/8-A.

Abstract of a thesis Graduate Theological Union, 1978 (314 p.; order no. 7816218).
A large part of the dissertation is devoted to the Egyptian evidence concerning Anat in the XIXth Dynasty. *L.Z.*

78114 BRACKMAN, Arnold C., The Search for the Gold of Tutankhamen, London, Robert Hale Limited, [1978] (15.4 x 23.9 cm; IX + 197 p., 8 pl., 1 colour ill. on cover); rev. *Antike Welt* 9, Heft 4 (1978), 63 (anonymous). Pr. £ 5.50

This book, originally published in 1976 (not seen) claims to be the first one describing as well the search for and the discovery of the tomb of Tutankhamon as its aftermath. There is added an author's note containing used literature, the question of the find of papyri in the tomb, and remarks to various subjects among which popular problems such as Akhnaton.
There has also appeared a German edition: Sie fanden den goldenen Gott. Das Grab des Tutankhamun und seine Entdeckung, Bergisch Gladbach, Gustav Lübbe Verlag, 1978. *L.Z.*

BRACKMAN, Arnold C., see also our number 78524.

78115 BRADLEY, R., Meroe, *Nyame Akuma*, Calgary No.12 (1978), 43-44.

Die Publikation der Ausgrabungsergebnisse in Meroe wird in 2 Bänden in der Serie Meroitica erscheinen. Ein Korpus von meroitischen Wandmalereien soll geschaffen werden; sie wurden 1974/75 und 1975/76 bei der Ausgrabung einiger kleiner Tempel entdeckt. Sie waren über die Fussböden verstreut und teilweise verbrannt, als die Tempel zerstört wurden. Eine Rekonstruktion und Wiederaufrichtung der Wände ist geplant. *Inge Hofmann*

BRADLEY, R.J., see also our number 78678.

78116 de BRAGANÇA, Miguel, Ancient Egypt: God, King and Man. A Guide to the Exhibition. 10 December 1978 through 15 April 1979, [New Haven, Connecticut], Peabody Museum of Natural History, Yale University, [1978] (15.3 x 20.7 cm; 24 p., 12 ill., ill. on cover, map and table on endpapers).

After an introduction this guide presents descriptions and photographs of the 12 objects exhibited, all from the Peabody Museum and the Yale University Art Gallery. They range from Predynastic pottery to the bust of a Ptolemy and a mummy mask, and include i.a. a group statue, a stela and part of another one, and a lintel fragment from the XIXth Dynasty. All objects are of high quality.
Technical data and bibliographical references on p. 22-23.

78117 de BRAGANÇA, Miguel, Yale's Egyptian Collections, 1888-1978, *Discovery*, New York 13, No.2 (1978), 18-27, with 10 ill.

Yale's collections of Egyptian art are divided between the Peabody Museum and the Art Gallery. The author briefly describes the history of these collections, indicating which persons have mainly been responsible for their origin and growth.
On p. 24-25 a note to the exhibition "Ancient Egypt: God, King and Man", (see our preceding number) by Louise Laurentano DeMars.

78118 BRESCIANI, Edda, L'attività archeologica in Egitto dell' Università di Pisa: Saqqara 1974-1977, *Egitto e Vicino Oriente* 1 (1978), 1-40, with 3 plans, 10 fig. and 20 pl. (= p. 21-40).

Report of the excavations of the University of Pisa in Saqqâra between 1974 and 1977. During the investigations in the tomb of Bakenrenef, the vizier of Psammetichus I (Leps. 24) two unknown tombs were found immediately N. of it, numbered BN 1 and BN 2 (of $P^3$-šrỉ-$t^3$-ỉsw) dating from the XXXth Dynasty or shortly afterwards.
Each of the tombs and all objects discovered in them are carefully described. Although the major tomb has already been known for a long time its subterranean galleries with many side-rooms contained various interesting objects; for its plan, see our number 78576.

78119 BRESCIANI, Edda, Jean-François Champollion, Lettres à Zelmire. Presentées. Préface de Jean Leclant, [Paris], L'Asiathèque, 1978 (13.3 x 21.3 cm; II + 116 p., 4 pl.) = Champollion et son temps, 1; rev. *Annali. Istituto Orientale di Napoli* 40, N.S. 30 (1980), 179-182 (Claudio Barocas); *Comptes rendus de l'Académie des Inscriptions et Belles Lettres,* 1978, 666-667 (Jean Leclant).

After a preface by J.Leclant and an introduction by the author on the relation between Champollion and Angela Palli and the importance of the letters on account of the frequent allusions to his egyptological activities, the author publishes the 29 letters of Champollion (Zeid) to her (Zelmire), written in the period 1826-1829. Notes at the end of the book. *L.Z.*

78120  BRESCIANI, E., La prima lettera di Ippolito Rosellini dall' Egitto alla moglie nell' agosto 1828, in: *Journal Faculty of Archaeology*, 27-33, with an Arabic summary on p.33.

Publication with notes of a French letter by Rosellini to his wife Zenobia Cherubini, written 7-29 August 1828, begun in the port of Girgenti (Sicily) and continued in Alexandria on the first days of the Franco-Tuscan expedition headed by Champollion.

78121  BRESCIANI, Edda, La spedizione di Tolemeo II in Siria in un ostrakon demotico inedito da Karnak, in: *Das ptolemäische Ägypten*, 31-37, with 1 ill. on a pl.

The author deals with a (still unpublished) ostracon found during the excavations E. of the Sacred Lake at Karnak. The text is translated (for a photograph, see ill. 51a) without textual or philological comments. It contains a copy of a decree by Ptolemy II to carry out a complete census of the entire Egyptian territory on behalf of the financial interest of the state. The text is stated to have been made in year 28 when the king returned from Syria, and the formulation sheds light on the propaganda abilities of Philadelphus.

78122  BRESCIANI, Edda, Elsa BEDINI, Lucia PAOLINI, Flora SILVANO, Una rilettura dei Pap. dem. Bologna 3173 e 3171, *Egitto e Vicino Oriente* 1 (1978), 95-104.

Re-edition of the Demotic Papyri Bologna 3173 and 3171, published before by Kminek-Szedlo in 1895 and again by Botti in 1941.
The article presents a facsimile, transliteration and translation with commentary of both texts which relate dreams. A general commentary on p. 101-103.

78123  BRESCIANI, E., Sergio PERNIGOTTI, Maria Carmela BETRÒ, Ostraka demotici da Ossirinco, *Egitto e Vicino Oriente* 1 (1978) 61-84, with 7 pl. (= p. 78-84).

Sequel to our number 77110.
The present issue deals with 31 texts, one letter and various accounts and notices. They are all presented in photograph, facsimile, transliteration and translation with comments.

BRESCIANI, Edda, see also our number 78045.

78124  BREWER, Clifford, Horseisi son of Naspihimegori, *Annals of the Royal College of Surgeons of England,* London 60 (1978), 133-134.

On a mummy in the museum of the Royal College of Surgeons of England.

L.Z.

78125  BRINKS, Jürgen, Die Grabstele des *Nmtj.wj* und *Ḥpj* in Hildesheim, *GM* Heft 28 (1978), 25-33, with 1 fig. and 1 ill.

Die Grabstele des *Nmtj.wj* und seiner Gemahlin, Inventar-Nr. 1875, wurde aus dem Kunsthandel in Ägypten erworben. Dargestellt ist das Ehepaar vor dem Opfertisch; die Inschriften der Grabstele bestehen aus der Opferformel für den Grabherrn und seine Frau, der Weihinschrift, der Beischrift am Opfertisch und nochmals dem Namen der Frau. Die Stele ist recht gut erhalten; alle Farbtöne sind vorhanden, nur ist die Bemalungsschicht stellenweise abgeblättert. Die Hieroglyphenzeichen sind wahllos überwiegend monochrom grün oder blau ausgemalt. Der Herkunftsort der Stele dürfte Achmîm sein; aus orthographischen Gründen ist sie in die frühe Erste Zwischenzeit zu datieren.
*Inge Hoj*

BRISSAUD, Philippe, see our number 78883.

78126 BROADIE, A.– J. MacDONALD, The Concept of Cosmic Order in Ancient Egypt in Dynastic and Roman Times, *L'Antiquité Classique*, Bruxelles 47 (1978),106-128.

Proceeding from Philo of Alexandria's concept of the *logos* which expresses the universal order, the authors attempt to demonstrate that it is by no means accidental that the principles underlying it were essentially the same as those of the ancient Egyptian concept of Ma'at since he, having still firm roots in the Egyptian culture, inherited it from his Egyptian ancestors. Opinions of various Egyptological authors on the subject of Ma'at are quoted in this connection. Attention is also drawn to the fact that the Egyptian concept of universal order is not unique since the Sumerians also knew a similar concept, called *Me*.
*L.Z.*

78127 BROVARSKI, Edward J., Hor-aha and the Nubians, *Serapis* 4 (1977-1978), 1-2, with 1 fig.

Although there is evidence that Hor-aha and his successors penetrated Nubia the wooden tag from Abydos does not refer to this, as Emery suggested (our number 61210, p.51). The author reads the signs as "fashioning and opening the mouth of a statue of Anubis".

BROVARSKI, Edward J., see also our number 78177.

78128 BROWNE, Gerald M., Notes on Coptic Literary Texts, *Enchoria* 8, Sonderband (1978), 7*(53)-10*(56).

Abstract of a paper read at the First International Congress of Coptology, held in Cairo, December 1976.
The author gives some additional and/or correcting notes on "Constantini Episcopi urbis Siout encomia in Athanasium duo" (=our number 74545) and "The Martyrdom of Cyriacus and Julitta in Coptic" (Husselman, *JARCE* 4 [1965] = our number 65256).
*W.Brunsch*

78129 BROWNE, Gerald M., The Sahidic PPalau Rib. Gospel of Luke, *CdE* LIII, No. 105 (1978), 199-202.

Review article to our number 77625.

78130 BRUNNER, Hellmut, Zur Datierung der "Lehre eines Mannes an seinen Sohn", *JEA* 64 (1978), 142-143.

The writer discusses the date of the Teaching of a Man to his Son and suggests a date in the reign of Sesostris I rather than immediately after the shock of the murder of the father. *E.P.Uphill*

78131 BRUNNER-TRAUT, Emma, Altägyptische Literatur, *in*: Wolfgang Röllig, *Altorientalische Literaturen*, Wiesbaden, Akademische Verlagsanstalt Athenaion, [1978] (= Neues Handbuch der Literaturwissenschaft, 1), 25-99; rev. *Mundus* 17 (1981), 10-12 (Peter Munro).

In this important survey of ancient Egyptian literature, the author gives first in the Introduction her definition of literature, stresses the close relation between literary history and that of the human mind, and briefly discusses stylistic devices such as the thought couplet (parallelismus membrorum), which is typical of the aspective attitude of the ancient Egyptians. Then she deals with the various genres of which she discusses the most important items with many quotations illustrating her arguments, while she often draws parallels with other literatures.
The following sections are subsequently devoted to fairy and other popular tales including animal stories; the proverbial literature, complaints as well as instructions; autobiography, particularly the story of Sinuhe; and love poetry and harpers' songs. At the end of the study a short bibliography to the various genres, and notes. *L.Z.*

78132 BRUNNER-TRAUT, Emma [und] Vera HELL, Mit einem Beitrag von Renate JACOBI, Ägypten. Kunst- und Reiseführer mit Landeskunde. Dritte, erweiterte und verbesserte Auflage, Stuttgart - Berlin-Köln-Mainz, Verlag W.Kohlhammer, [1978] (12.8 x 17.8 cm; 784 p., 95 fig., 123 maps and plans, 2 coloured folded maps [on 1 loose sheet], coloured map on endpapers); rev. *Antike Welt* 9, Heft 4 (1978), 62 (anonymous); *BiOr* 35 (1978), 146 (anonymous).

Third, revised and enlarged edition of our number 62096.
That the total number of pages increased from 626 in the first edition to 784 in the present indicates how much has been added. That applies as well to the introductory part as to the guide proper. From the former we mention a new chapter on the Islâm (by Renate Jacobi, p. 232-250), a completely re-written chapter on land and people (by Frau Brunner) and on Coptic Christianity (by Vera Hell).
As an instance of revision and enlargement in the actual guide we may refer to the part on Aswân and its surrounding (1st edition: 520-541; 2nd edition: 653-704), where i.a. a description of the temples on Elephantine and the re-erected temples of Kalâbsha and Beit el-Wâli are new. On the pages on Saqqâra one now finds described the mastabas of Mehu, the double tomb of the queens Nebet and Khenut, the tombs along the causeway of Unas and that of Horemheb further south, showing that the recent discoveries are taken into account. The index (755-783) has also been enlarged.

78133　BRUNSCH, Wolfgang, Ein koptischer Bindezauber, *Enchoria* 8, Teil 1 (1978), 151-157, with 1 pl.

Publication of P.Würzburg inv. no.42 (10th century A.D., provenance unknown), a Sahidic charm for the mouth of a calumnious woman.　　*W.Brunsch*

78134　BRUNSCH, Wolfgang, Untersuchungen zu den griechischen Wiedergaben ägyptischer Personennamen, *Enchoria* 8, Teil 1 (1978), 1-142, with 1 fig.

This onomastic study, the author's dissertation, consists of two parts.
Part I (5-82) deals with the underlying linguistical phenomena and processes of language-interference as met with in the attempts of the Greek scribes and officials in Ptolemaic and Roman Egypt of rendering Egyptian proper names into Greek (phoneme- and grapheme-inventory of Egyptian and Greek; reconstruction of pre-Coptic dialects via Greek renderings of Egyptian proper names; proper names as accent units; prefixes of proper names).
Part II (83-120) exemplifies the results of part I on a group of proper names, namely, the proper names of the type of 'god (goddess) NN has come', including a list of bilingual (Demotic-Greek) theophoric proper names and of the various forms of the gods' names therein.
Two excursuses (on *Wp-w3.wt* and *Mwt*) and detailed indexes close the study (121-142).　　*W.Brunsch*

BRUNSCH, Wolfgang, see also our number 78068.

78135　BRYAN, Betsy M. and Edmund S. MELTZER, A Note on an Obscure Title, *t3y tnfyt pd(t) n nb t3wy, JSSEA* 8 (1977-1978), 60-65.

Studying the title *t3y tnfyt pd(t) n nb t3wy*, which occurs in Theban Tomb No. 22, the authors connect *tnfyt* with Dem. *dnf* and Copt. ⲬⲚⲞϤ (see Černý, Copt. Etym. Dict., 317). They argue that *tnf(y)t* is a container, particularly a "bag", which in the XVIIIth Dynasty represents a symbol of office. The title means "bearer of the bag and the bow for the Lord of the Two Lands".

78136　Bulletin de Liaison du Groupe International de la Céramique Égyptienne, Le Caire 3 (1978), 31 p.

Sequel to our number 77134.
In the preface Jean Vercoutter announces that the Bulletin henceforth will appear regularly thanks to the activity of Helen Jacquet-Gordon.
After an invitation to attend a special meeting during the congress at Grenoble (September 1979) there follows a list of brief reports on the pottery recently found in Egypt and Nubia, by the excavators themselves. Each report mentions the types of pottery found. Chapter 3 consists of some communications; chapter 4 of a list of recent publications on ceramics.

78137　BULLOCK, Ronald, The Story of Sinuhe. Containing Complete Collated Hieroglyphic Text with Interlinear Transliteration and Translation, plus Basic Grammatical Commentary on each Facing Page. Foreword by Professor H.S.Smith.

Second Edition Revised, London, Probsthain and Co., [1978] (21 x 30 cm; XII + 127 double pages). Pr. £6.50

After a foreword by H.S.Smith in which he explains that the book is a simple edition of a famous story intended for students without access to libraries, and an explanatory preface by the author, he presents the text of the story of Sinuhe in transcription, transliteration and translation on the left hand page, while on the right hand page appear the minimal commentary for understanding the text and a running translation. *L.Z.*

78138   BULTÉ, Jeanne, Les chaoubtis. Statuettes funéraires égyptiennes, *Connaissance des Arts*, Paris No. 312 (Fevrier 1978), 86-91(unnumbered), with 8 colour ill.

Within the framework of an Encyclopédie des Arts, sous François Duret-Robert, section: Égypte:chaoubtis 1-3, the author deals with various aspects of shawabtis. *L.Z.*

78139   BUNNENS, G., La Mission d' Ounamoun en Phénicie. Point de vue d' un non-égyptologue, *Rivista di Studi Fenici*, Roma 6 (1978), 1-16.

The author discusses the Report of Wenamun as a historical source for the situation in Phoenicia in the 11th century B.C. by taking into consideration the data contained in the el-Amarna Letters. He argues that Wenamun was sent out as a messenger bearing two letters, one of recommendation and one with the message proper, and not as a delegate. The status of a messenger is low and uncertain. Since Wenamun did not come to buy wood, but was carrying money with him for a present, according to the habit of reciprocal gifts between royal persons in the Amarna Letters, Zakerbaal refuses aid after the theft of the money. The relations turn only to normal after correspondence with Smendes and Tanutamun, although they did not give Wenamun his mandate but Herihor.
So, in fact, Wenamun only represents Upper Egypt, which did not have connections with Byblos as close as those of the rulers in Tanis. There seems to have existed an asylum right in Phoenician ports which prevented Zakerbaal surrendering Wenamun to the people of Dor, where probably one of his own crew had stolen the money. *L.Z.*

BURGES, Albert, see our number 78006.

78140   BURKHARDT, Adelheid, Philae-ein Reiseziel geht auf Reisen, *Das Altertum*, Berlin 24 (1978), 206-211, with 3 ill. and 2 fig.

General article on the temples of Philae and their transfer.

BURNEY, Ethel W., see our number 78640.

78141   [BURRI, Carla M.], Bollettino di Informazioni. Sezione archeologica. Istituto Italiana di Cultura per la R.A.E., No.45 (Novembre [1977] -Gennaio 1978),19 p.

Sequel to our number 77141.
The issue of the Bulletin contains i.a. reports on the Italian campaigns at Saqqâra and Antinoe and prehistoric researches in the Sudan, French works on the Pyramid of Pepi I and at Sedeinga, Polish activities in Alexandria, study of the reliefs of the Ramesseum by the Centre de Documentation, and a relatively long report on the Austrian excavations at Tell ed-Dab'a.

78142 [BURRI, Carla M.], Bollettino di Informazioni. Sezione archeologica. Istituto Italiano di Cultura per la R.A.E., No.46 (Febbraio-Marzo-Aprile 1978), 19 p.

Sequel to our preceding number.
Reports i.a. on the Italian-Egyptian mission at Maâdi, the Italian works in the Faiyûm, near Naqâda and Gebel Barkal, and the German and French campaigns in the Western Oases.

78143 [BURRI, Carla M.], Bollettino di Informazioni. Sezione archeologica. Istituto Italiano di Cultura per la R.A.E., No.47(Maggio-Giugnio-Luglio-Agosto 1978), 12 p.

Sequel to our preceding number.
Apart from a number of short notes the issue contains brief reports on the campaigns at Qasr Ibrîm and el-Kâb, work of the French-Egyptian Centre at Karnak, German activities in the monastery of Apa Jeremias at Saqqâra, and Polish ones in Deir el-Bahri and Old-Dongola.

78144 [BURRI, Carla M.], Bollettino di Informazioni. Sezione archeologica, Istituto Italiano di Cultura per la R.A.E., No.48 (Settembre-Ottobre-Novembre-Dicembre 1978), 22 p.

Sequel to our preceding number.
Reports i.a. on the Italian activities in Antinoe and Saqqâra, Finnish researches in the church of Deir Abu Hennis, and the Austrian campaign of autumn 1978 at Tell ed-Dab'a.

78145 BURRINI, Gabrielle, Profilo storico degli studi camito-semitico, *Annali Istituto Orientale di Napoli*, Napoli 38, N.S. 28 (1978), 113-153.

The author presents a historical survey of Hamito-Semitic studies in which, by its very nature, he often refers to Egyptologists. Continued in the volume of the same periodical of the next year.                                *L.Z.*

78146 BUTROS, Nabil Kamal, Coptic Music and its Relation to Pharaonic Music, *Enchoria* 8, Sonderband (1978), 67*(113)-69*(115).

Abstract of a paper read at the First International Congress of Coptology, held in Cairo, December 1976.
Brief summary of the author's Master of Arts thesis, wherein he studies the elements of Coptic music against its traditional (i.e.pharaonic) background.
*W.Brunsch*

78147 BUTZER, Karl W., Perspectives on Irrigation Civilization in Pharaonic Egypt, in: *Immortal Egypt,* 13-18.

The author presents a summary of his study "Early Hydraulic Civilization in Egypt" (our number 76132). He considers cultural ecology to be the study of the interrelationships of three independent variables, environment (including hydrology), technology and population (demographic structure and patterns of settlement) and one dependent, social organization and differentiation. Each of the variables are briefly discussed.

BUTZER, Karl W., see also our number 78027.

78148 CADOGAN, G., Dating the Aegean Bronze Age Without Radiocarbon, *Archaeometry*, Oxford 20 (1978), 209-214, with 1 table.

Short discussion of the main synchronisms between ancient Egypt and the Aegean dated without the use of radiocarbon, of the security of these dates and the help radiocarbon may provide in this respect.  *L.Z.*

78149 CALDERINI, Aristide, Dizionario dei nomi geografici e topografici dell' Egitto greco-romano. A cura di Sergio Daris. Volume terzo. Fascicolo primo. I - Κερεβω, [Milano], Cisalpino - Goliardica, [1978] (21.7 x 31.2 cm; 96 p.).

Sequel to our number 77144.

78150 CALLAWAY, Joseph A., New Perspectives on Early Bronze III in Canaan, in: *Archaeology in the Levant.* Essays for Kathleen Kenyon. Edited by Roger Moorey and Peter Parr, Warminster, Aris & Phillips Ltd, [1978], 46-58.

In a separate section the author discusses the Egyptian presence at Ai in the Early Bronze IIIA Age (ca. 2700-2550 B.C.). There is evidence that suggests Egyptian involvement in building Temple A on the acropolis. The author concludes to an Egyptian interest in controlling the city as a base for political and economic exploitation of interest in Canaan, and possibly as a first line of defence in securing the approaches to the East border of Egypt against encroachments from the North or from Trans-Jordan.  *L.Z.*

78151 CALLAWAY, Joseph A. and James M. WEINSTEIN, Radiocarbon Dating of Palestine in the Early Bronze Age, *BASOR* No.225 (February, 1977), 1-16, with 4 tables.

The authors compare the radiocarbon dates from EB Ic and EB II Palestine with the C-14 dates from the archaeologically contemporary Ist Dynasty in Egypt. Their conclusions support a higher chronology than the low chronology of Albright.  *L.Z.*

78152 CAMINOS, R.A., Ramesside Remains at Gebel es-Silsilah, *JSSEA* 8 (1977-1978), 72-73.

Abstract of a paper about the many Ramesside records on the W. bank at Gebel el-Silsila.

CAMINOS, Ricardo A., see also our number 78320.

78153 CARROTT, Richard G., The Egyptian Revival. Its Sources, Monuments and Meaning. 1808-1858, Berkeley-Los Angeles-London, University of California Press, [1978] (17.6 x 25.4 cm; XXII + 221 p., 136 ill. and fig. on 96 pl.).

The subject of this study is the Egyptian Revival in American architecture between A.D. 1808 and 1858, which "represents a significant pattern of early nineteenth-century formal and iconographic attitudes". During the period about eighty monuments have been built in the U.S.A. in this style, by thirty architects: synagogues and churches, bridges and prisons, cemetery gates and obelisks as monuments, etc.
In the introduction the author deals i.a. with eclecticism, stressing the essential difference between true Egyptian architecture and that of the Egyptianizing style. For instance, the pyramids were built neither in the proportions nor on the scale of the Egyptian models.
Chapter two discusses the background of the Egyptian Revival, dealing i.a.with Piranesi, the "Description", and the famous Egyptian Hall in Piccadilly, built by Robinson (1812). Chapter three is devoted to Egyptian architecture as it was understood in the U.S.A. The author argues that the style exemplified the ideals of Romantic Classicism, while, on the other hand, it served the purposes of the Picturesque.
Three other chapters deal with the formal development and the iconography of the Egyptian Revival in America. Conclusions on p. 130-137.
Two appendices list the obelisks and the major other monuments in this style in the U.S.A., while a third (p. 146-192) discusses the New York City Halls of Justice and House of Detention (the "Tombs"): the plans made for it and the building itself.
An extensive annotated bibliography on p. 193-205, followed by an index. On the plates numerous monuments in the Egyptianizing style, including some in Europe, presented in drawing and/or photograph.

78154 CASINI, Maria, Manufatti litici egiziani a coda di pesce, *Origini. Preistoria e protostoria delle civiltà antiche*, Roma 8 (1974), [1978], 203-228, with 5 ill. and an English summary on p.228.

The author studies silex "forked lances" or "fish-tails" from prehistoric Egypt. She distinguishes three types, one with a concave base, one with a bolder inward curve and a last one with a bold V-shaped curve, originating from various prehistoric places. She examines their morphological evolution and suggests a typology. The hypothesis of weapons is refuted and a new interpretation is suggested on account of the meaning of the *pesesh-kaf* in protodynastic times.
L.Z.

78155 CASTEL, Georges, Construction pour l'IFAO d'une maison de fouille à Balat (Oasis de Dakhla), *BIFAO* 78 (1978), 589-594, with 1 folding plan, 1 folding fig. and 4 pl.

Description of the building of an expedition house in the Oasis el-Dâkhla.

78156 CASTEL, Georges, Rapport préliminaire sur l'étude architecturale du mastaba de Khentika à Balat, *BIFAO* 78 (1978), 35-40, with 2 folding plans, 1 fig. and 2 pl.

Preliminary report on the mastaba M III of Khentika at Balât, el-Dâkhla Oasis, that had been previously researched by Fakhry in 1972. The structure has partly collapsed so that the caves are inaccessible. Since the excavation had not yet been completed in the campaign 1977-78 an interpretation is as yet impossible.

CASTEL, Georges, see also our number 78807.

78157 CASTIGLIONE, Ladislas — Tihamér SZENTLÉLEKY — Jean Georges SZILÁGYI, Art antique au Musée Déri de Debrecen et dans d'autres collections hongroises, *Bulletin du Musée Hongrois des Beaux-Arts*, Budapest 50 (1978), 3-34, with 34 ill.

Although the subject of the article is just outside the scope of the *AEB* we mention it because of the representations of Egyptian divinities (in Hellenistic style) such as Harpocrates and Serapis. The article describes extensively 4 stone sculptures, 23 terracotta figures, 4 faience statuettes, 6 vases and 2 lamps. Hungarian version on p. 135-151.

78158 CASTILLOS, Juan Josè, An Analysis of the Predynastic Cemeteries E and U and the First Dynasty Cemetery S at Abydos, *JSSEA* 8 (1977-1978), 86-98.

Continuing his analysis of cemeteries (see our numbers 76141 and 77152), the author studies the predynastic and dynastic tombs at Abydos excavated by Peet between 1909 and 1912 and by Habachi in 1939. He describes the methods applied and presents the results in tables (p. 87-97), followed by some conclusions concerning orientation of the bodies and wealth, sex and age of the buried persons.

CASTIONI, Christiane, see our number 78831.

CAUVILLE, Sylvie, see our number 78028.

78159 CAZEMIER †, L.J., Vrees in de Pyramideteksten, *JEOL* VIII, No.25 (1977-1978), 75-82.

Publication by M. Heerma van Voss of an incomplete manuscript found among the papers of the late Dr. Cazemier. It deals with some words for fear as they occur in the P.T., namely $šnḏ$, $š^ct$, $š3d$, $nr$ and $nwr$, indicating the context in which they are used.

78160 de CENIVAL, Françoise, La deuxième partie du P. dém. Lille 18: declaration de petit bétail (P. Inv. Sorbonne 1248), *Enchoria* 8, Teil 2 (1978), 1-3, with 2 pl. (1 folding).

Publication of P. Inv. Sorbonne 1248 which actually was a part of P. Dém. Lille 18 (its "écrit extérieur"), published by Sottas, P. Lille, Paris, 1921, 37. The text (provenance Ghoran, date 251 B.C.) is a declaration of small cattle of *Ḥr-wḏȝ*, son of *Ḥr-wḏȝ*, before Diogenes, the nomarch. *W.Brunsch*

de CENIVAL, Jean-Louis, see our number 78013.

78161 ČERNÝ, Jaroslav, Papyrus hiératiques de Deir el-Médineh. Tome I [Nos I-XVII]. Catalogue complété et édité par Georges Posener, [Le Caire], Publications de l'Institut français d' Archéologie orientale, [1978] (24.6 x 32 cm; VII + 27 p., 30 [double] pl.) = Documents de Fouilles, 8.

In the preface the editor relates the history of the publication, work on the text having begun by Černý, continued by Sauneron, and completed by himself. The transcriptions are basically those of Černý. The papyri have been found in 1928 S. of the chapel No. 1166 in the necropolis of Deir el-Medîna, together with two documents of Naunakhte (see *JEA* [1945], 36-39) and the Chester Beatty Papyri that had been stolen by workmen.
The most important of the seventeen papyri here published is no. I, with on its recto the Instruction of Ani and on its verso four magical texts. The other papyri bear letters and some accounts (Nos II, VII rt., XIII vs., and XVII). The description of the sheets is accompanied by a translation with comments of the magical texts and most of the letters. (Nos. VII, XV, XVI and XVII excluded). They are made by Černý and only enlarged and corrected by Posener. The letters are from a scribe Nakhtsobek (IV-VI) and from or to the carpenter Maanakhte (VII-XIII), while the others have been written and received by different persons.
The plates bear fine photographs with transcriptions on the opposite pages.

78162 ČERNÝ, Jaroslav and Sarah Israelit GROLL, assisted by Christopher EYRE, A Late Egyptian Grammar, 2nd Edition with additions, Rome, Biblical Institute Press, 1978 (19.3 x 27 cm; XLIV + 614 p.) = Studia Pohl: Series major. Dissertationes scientificae de rebus orientis antiqui, 4. Pr. L. 24,000/$30

Reprint of our number 75133, with the addition of two indexes: one of grammatical terms and one of Egyptian forms. *L.Z.*

78163 ČERVIČEK, Pavel, Felsbilder Oberägyptens und Nubiens, *in: Katalog Sahara. 10.000 Jahre zwischen Weide und Wüste. Ausstellung Kunsthalle Köln,* 1978, 279-285, with 9 ill. and 2 maps.

Die Felsbilder des oberägyptischen und nubischen Niltals, der westlichen und östlichen oberägyptischen Wüste sowie der südlich davon gelegenen Nubischen Wüste werden in chronologischer Reihenfolge betrachtet und an ihnen die Hauptepochen dieser Kunst in Oberägypten und Nubien aufgezeigt. Sie reichen von den Negade-Schiffen der Negade Kultur über Wildtiere, Menschen mit Rindern, ägyptischen Schiffen, Pferdereitern, Waffen schwingende Menschen, Kamelreitern bis zu Symbolen der byzantinisch-christlichen Kultur in Ägypten bzw. der X- und Tanqasi-Kultur im Sudan. *Inge Hofmann*

78164 ČERVIČEK, P., Notes on the Chronology of the Nubian Rock Art to the End of the Bronze Age (Mid 11th Cent. B.C.), in: *Études nubiennes*, 35-56, with 1 folding pl.

Aufgrund der Überlegung, dass Felsbilder als besondere Art von vorgeschichtlichen Kulturüberresten stilistisch und typologisch mit Darstellungen auf datierbaren Funden verglichen werden können, versucht der Verfasser, eine Chronologie nubischer Felsbilder von der A-Periode bis zur D-Epoche (entsprechend dem Neuen Reich) zu geben. Als Datierungskriterium für Bilder aus der A-Kultur werden Darstellungen aus der Naqada-Kultur verwendet; zur Datierung nubischer Schiffsdarstellungen wird gleichfalls auf Ägypten verwiesen. Bei den Tierdarstellungen wird, soweit möglich, die Einführung der jeweiligen Gattung nach Ägypten herangezogen. *Inge Hofmann*

CHAPMAN, Suzanne, see our number 78745.

78165 CHARLTON, Nial, The Tura Caves, *JEA* 64 (1978), 128.

Stresses the size of these and that they are quarries not of natural formation. Mentions also a block found in 1942 that was still resting on wooden rollers. *E.P. Uphill*

78166 CHASSINAT, É. et Fr. DAUMAS, Le Temple de Dendara. Tome huitième. [(Texte) et (Planches), Le Caire, Institut français d' Archéologie orientale], 1978 (24.4 x 34 cm; [Text] : X + 173 p., 4 plans, 8 fig. [6 on 3 folding pl.] ; [Plates] : 129 pl. [numbered DCXCIII - DCCCXXI] ); at head of title: Publications de l'Institut français d'Archéologie orientale du Caire.

Sequel to our number 72139.
In the introduction Fr. Daumas explains his slight alterations of Chassinat's original publication scheme with regard to the Hathor chapel on the roof, which, as regards its religious aspects, is related to those of the West staircase and the East corridor.
The first part of the text volume is devoted to this Hathor chapel (notation W') with its two gates and twelve columns. Next follow the Western staircase (notation X) and a jewellery chamber connected with it (X-R) and the Eastern corridor (Y).
The plates corresponding with each of the four parts are numbered: 692-737 (W'); 738-801 (X); 802-814 (X-R) and 815-821 (Y) and contain line drawings as well as photographs. *L.Z.*

78167 CLARK, J. Desmond, Interpretations of Prehistoric Technology from Ancient Egyptian and Other Sources. Part II: Prehistoric Arrow Forms in Africa as Shown by Surviving Examples of the Traditional Arrows of the San Bushmen, *Paléorient*, Paris 3 (1975-1976-1977), 127-150, with 6 ill., 1 fig. and 1 table.

Sequel to our number 75138.
The present article mainly deals with arrows of the San Bushmen. The author concludes that these reed and sometimes wooden shafted arrows are surviving variants of a very old traditional pattern, modifications of which also occur in ancient Egypt.

78168   CLARK, R.M., Bristlecone Pine and Ancient Egypt: a Re-appraisal, *Archaeometry*, Oxford 20 (1978), with 4 tables and 1 fig.

The author argues that the radiocarbon dates of tree-ring-dated bristlecone pine samples and those from historically-dated samples from Egyptian archaeological sites are compatible.   *L.Z.*

78169   CLARYSSE, W., Notes on Some Graeco-Demotic Suiety Contracts, *Enchoria* 8, Teil 2 (1978), 5-8.

In taking into account both the Demotic text on the recto and the Greek abstract on the verso of some of the already published P. Lille/P. Sorbonne (Sottas, de Cenival, Cadell), the author succeeds in shedding light on some hitherto unclear points:
1) In P. Lille Dem. II 96/P. Sorbonne 37 the name of the debtor's father is to be read Στοητιος (*St3.t̠=w-t3-wt*).
2) The royal scribe of this text is to be read *P3-dj-Ḫnsw*, son of *'Ij-m-ḥtp*, whose career can thus be completed.
3) Finally the author gives some additional corrections to the Greek P. Sorbonne 36 and 37.   *W.Brunsch*

78170   CLARYSSE, W., The Prosopographia Ptolemaica and Demotic Studies, *Enchoria* 8, Sonderband (1978), 7-9.

Abstract of a paper read at the First International Colloquium of Demotists, held in Berlin, September 1977.
The author, one of the collaborators of the Prosopographia Ptolemaica in Louvain, stresses the importance of the "enchoric evidence" for this huge research project.   *W.Brunsch*

78171   CLARYSSE, Willy, Prosopography and the Dating of Egyptian Monuments of the Ptolemaic Period, *in: Das ptolemäische Ägypten,* 239-244, with 2 ill. on a pl.

The author discusses various problems of dating private monuments from the Ptolemaic Period, presenting some examples from families of Theban priests.

CLARYSSE, Willy, see also our number 78555.

78172   CLERC, Gisèle, Isis-Sothis dans le monde romain, *in: Hommages Vermaseren*, 247-281, with 1 fig. and 5 pl.

In the first part of the article the author deals with the relations between Sothis (*Spdt*), the inundation and the calendar in Egypt, and her relations with Hathor, Satis, and, particularly, Isis. This means that Isis-Sothis was Mistress of the year's beginning and that she brought the inundation, that is, prosperity.
After discussing the iconography of Sothis in the Egyptian religious art the author turns to the Hellenistic aretalogies and the iconography of Isis-Sothis in Graeco-Roman art, which is the main subject of the study.

78173 CONDON, Virginia, Seven Royal Hymns of the Ramesside Period. Papyrus Turin CG 54031, München-Berlin, Deutscher Kunstverlag, 1978 (17 x 24 cm; [VIII] + 75 p., 6 pl.) = Münchner Ägyptologische Studien. Herausgegeben von Hans Wolfgang Müller, 37; rev. *BiOr* 36 (1979), 302-303 (Jesús López); *Orientalia* 48(1979), 417-418 (K.A.Kitchen). Pr. DM 25

After having described the three large fragments of Pap. Turin CG 54031, previously published in facsimile in Pleyte-Rossi, Papyrus de Turin on pl. 21-22 and 20 (=1886 rt. and vs.), 87-86 (1892 rt. and vs.) and 88-89 (1893 rt. and vs.) and containing royal hymns of the Ramesside Period, the author suggests the original compositions to date from the early XIXth Dynasty, although the present papyrus dates from the Late XXth Dynasty. Then she offers a transcription, a translation and a commentary to the seven hymns to Ramses VI and VII.

Although the subject of the hymns as a whole seems to be the coronation it is not quite certain where it must have taken place, up in the North at Heliopolis or in Thebes. The formal, stylistic and grammatical aspects are discussed in a short chapter.

The book ends with a chapter containing the conclusions, a selective bibliography of royal hymns, a bibliography, a palaeography and a glossary. *L.Z.*

78174 CONTI, Giovanni, Rapporti tra egiziano e semitico nel lessico egizio dell'agricultura, [Firenze], Istituto di linguistica e di lingue orientali. Università di Firenze, 1978 (17 x 24 cm; XII + 187 p.) = Quaderni di semitistica, 6; rev. *BiOr* 37 (1980), 308-310 (William A.Ward).

In the introduction the author presents a survey of the theories about the relationship between Egyptian and the Semitic languages leading to the gradual acceptance of a Hamito-Semitic (or Afroasiatic) family of languages. Accepting Garbini's theory of a Neolithic semitization of Egyptian, the author studies the Egyptian agricultural terms in order to establish whether they testify to that semitization and what they may teach us about its time. Since comparison of Egyptian and Semitic requires knowledge of the phonetic rules the author devotes to them a special section (see table on p. 29).

In five chapters the author then deals with Egyptian agricultural terms, for each of them discussing the possible or probable Semitic isoglosses: general terminology (*srd, rwd/rd, 3g* and *3kr*, etc.); agriculture with the hoe (*mr, iknw, b3*, etc.); agriculture with the plough (*hb, sk3 , 3zh, mhr*); cereals (*it, bdt, npr, šrt* and *šʿt*); viniculture (*i3rrt, k3nw/k3m, irp*).

The last chapter first presents the result in a tabulated form, and then deals with the question whether the terms or some of them testify to a common origin or are derived from Semitic. Conti attempts to distinguish between various levels (Chalcolithic, Sumerian, Accadian) and particularly for the agriculture with the plough he suggests Mesopotamian influence on Egypt. After discussing the possible Egyptian-Arabic, Egyptian-N.W. Semitic and Egyptian-Ethiopian isoglosses, as well as a Mediterranean substratum (on account of *i3rrt*) the conclusions are given on p. 165-166: two streams are to be distinguished, that developed from a "Proto-Euphratic" and "Mediterranean" substratum, recognizable in Sumerian, Accadian, and more recently, in N.W. Semitic and influencing Egyptian from Asia, and an independent development from a common base in Semitic and in Egyptian.

78175 COQUIN, René-Georges and Pierre-Henry LAFERRIÈRE, Les inscriptions pariétales de l'ancienne église du monastère de S. Antoine, dans le désert oriental, *BIFAO* 78 (1978), 267-321, with 1 plan and 6 pl.

Publication of the Coptic and Arabic inscriptions on the walls of the church in the monastery of St. Antonius in the Eastern Desert.

CORDANO, Federica, see our number 78067.

78176 Corpus antiquitatum aegyptiacarum. Lose-Blatt-Katalog ägyptischer Altertümer. Kestner-Museum. Hannover. Lieferung 1 = Irmtraut BESTE, Skarabäen. Teil 1, Mainz/Rhein, Verlag Philipp von Zabern, 1978 (21 x 30 cm; portfolio containing 5 + 176 loose p., 224 ill., 8 fig.). Pr. DM 68

In this first one of three fascicles devoted to the collection of scarabs and scaraboids from the Kestner Museum, Hannover, 77 pieces are published. The majority of the collection comes from the last century and was brought together by August Kestner himself. To them are added in 1976: a commemorative scarab of Amenophis III (not in this fascicle), a group of 55 pieces from Syria, and 23 pieces from the collection of the Duke of Northumberland.
Each object is described according to the rules of the CAA, with all technical data and extensive bibliographical references (our numbers 76387 and 77516 could not yet be consulted). The dating of the pieces had in several instances to be vague, particularly when neither text nor representation were present. Of most instances three photographs are given illustrating back, bottom and one side of the scarab. In a few instances (heart-scarabs) a facsimile of the text is added.
Several pieces bear royal names from the M.K. and N.K. We mention, for instance, a scarab of Tuthmosis III with a ring (No. 1965), and the representation of Ramses II on a chariot (No. 1982). Other pieces represent animal divinities. An important instance is the plaque No. 2040, with a stilling Isis on one side and four monkeys climbing a date palm on the other.

78177 Corpus antiquitatum aegyptiacarum. Loose-leaf Catalogue of Egyptian Antiquities. Museum of Fine Arts. Boston. Fascicle 1 = Edward BROVARSKI, Canopic Jars, Mainz/Rhein, Verlag Philipp von Zabern, 1978 (21 x 30 cm; portfolio containing booklet [16 p.] and 112 p., 89 pl.); rev. *BiOr* 36 (1979), 176-177 (Günther Vittmann); *CdE* LV, No. 109-110 (1980), 159 (Herman de Meulenaere). Pr. DM 68

Publication of 82 canopic jars or lids in the Museum of Fine Arts, Boston. In the introduction the author gives a survey of the history of the canopic jar, the changes in the material, shape and proportions between the O.K. and the Ptolemaic Period. There follow indexes.
The collection here published contains jars from the O.K., the M. K. (el-Bersheh), the XVIIIth Dynasty, the Ramesside Period (only 1 instance), and the Late Period. A large number comes from the pyramids of el-Kurru and Nuri and belonged to the royal family of the XXVth Dynasty (i.a. Taharqa and his wife) and later Ethiopian rulers. Far older is the set from the tomb of queen Meresankh (Saqqâra No. 7530 A), or a group from the tomb of Tuthmosis IV,

among which one inscribed with the name of prince Amenemhat. Others belonged to private persons. A few are dummy canopic jars.

The text presents technical data, a description, the inscription (if available) in facsimile and translation, a commentary and references to literature, while one or two photographs are given of each piece.

78178 Corpus antiquitatum aegyptiacarum. Lose-Blatt-Katalog ägyptischer Altertümer. Pelizaeus-Museum. Hildesheim, Lieferung 2 = Eva EGGEBRECHT, Spätantike und Koptische Textilien. Teil I, Mainz/Rhein, Verlag Philipp von Zabern, 1978 (21 x 30 cm; portfolio containing 113 loose p., 68 loose pl.); rev. *BiOr* 37 (1980), 184-185 (Dorothee Renner); *OLZ* 75 (1980), 432-435 (T.G.H. James). Pr. DM 68

Of the c. 300 fragments of textiles preserved in the Pelizaeus Museum this fascicle publishes 54 instances, with full technical data and a short discussion. Several pieces are here published for the first time, particularly those recently acquired. All date from the 4th to the 12th century A.D.

78179 Corpus antiquitatum aegyptiacarum. Lose-Blatt-Katalog ägyptischer Altertümer. Pelizaeus-Museum. Hildesheim. Lieferung 3 = Karl MARTIN, Reliefs des Alten Reiches, Teil 1, Mainz/Rhein, Verlag Philipp von Zabern, 1978 (21 x 30 cm; portfolio containing [IV+] 128 loose p. and 62 loose pl.); rev. *CdE* LV, No. 109-110 (1980), 159-161 (Naguib Kanawati). Pr. DM 68

This first fascicle on the O.K. relief (fragments) in the Pelizaeus-Museum, Hildesheim, contains about half the total. In it are described the acquisitions up to 1914 including the false door of *Wnšt*, found in 1914, but entered into the Museum in 1926, and the architrave fragments of the tomb of *Ḥm-iwnw*, given by Reisner, so as to present the parts of the tomb in the same fascicle. Some blocks still under restoration are excluded. The 50 (groups of) pieces consist on the one hand of architraves, (parts of) false doors, wall fragments, the offering table of *'Iwnw* and other parts of Gîza mastabas excavated by Steindorff, von Sieglin and, mostly, Junker. On the other hand, there are described many wall fragments from Sahure's funerary temple at Abûsîr, excavated by the Deutsche Orientgesellschaft in 1907, and Niuserre's sun temple at Abû Ghurâb, by von Bissing, 1898-1901. L.Z.

78180 Corpus antiquitatum aegyptiacarum. Lose-Blatt-Katalog ägyptischer Altertümer. Pelizaeus-Museum. Hildesheim. Lieferung 4 = Eva MARTIN-PARDEY, Plastik des Alten Reiches, Teil 2, Mainz/Rhein, Verlag Philipp von Zabern, 1978 (21 x 30 cm; portfolio containing booklet of 19p. and 85 loose p., 97 loose pl.). Pr. DM 68

This second fascicle on the O.K. statuary in the Pelizaeus-Museum, Hildesheim, continuing our number 77169, is at the same time the last. For that reason a booklet has been added containing, apart from instructions for the reader, indexes on inventory numbers, divine, royal, and private names, titles and epithets, groups of objects, materials and clothing attributes, and a general one comprising words not caught in the other sections. The index to place names refers, with only one exception, to Gîza.

The descriptions following the same system as in the first fascicle, this time 34 pieces are dealt with. They mainly originate from Junker's excavations, only a few from those of Steindorff. The objects, among which many bits of pieces comprise two reserve heads, a stone shrine, pieces of Chephren-diorite, and the peculiar statue of a nude man with closed legs. Apart from the wooden statues dealt with in the beginning nearly all other objects are of limestone. *L.Z.*

78181 Le CORSU, F., Bibliographie de Michel Malinine (1900-1977), *RdE* 30 (1978), 7-9.

78182 Le CORSU, France, Cléopatre-Isis, *BSFE* No.82 (Juin 1978), 22-32, with 4 ill. on 3 pl.

Quand Cléopâtre alla rejoindre à Tarse Antoine entré dans Ephèse sous la forme de Dionysos, le faste fut magnifique; Plutarque dépeint la reine à l'image d'Aphrodite. Mais l'historien ne fut pas témoin oculaire, et cette comparaison paraît erronée: il doit s'agir de la grande Isis. Depuis Arsinoé et les "dieux philadelphes", les Ptolémées s'identifièrent aux dieux, les rois surtout se faisant passer pour Sérapis; Philopator et Aulète s'assimilent à Dionysos, la forme d'Osiris qui sert de motif aux sarcophages dionysiaques.
L'épouse d'Osiris devait se considérer comme incarnant Isis. Une étude récente montre les souveraines sur les oenochoés: leur geste demeure invariable, le vêtement isiaque se précise. Dans les figurations de style égyptien, Cléopâtre porte les attributs d'Isis-Hathor. Isis et Dionysos: c'était là un couple attesté dans la tradition lagide. Antoine et Cléopâtre, rapporte Dion Cassius, se firent représenter en Osiris-Dionysos et Isis-Lune. Le motif de Cléopâtre Nea Isis "entourée d'amours" trouve alors une explication. La grande déesse fécondée par le Nil, c'est Isis, terre d'Égypte; une statue au Musée d'Alexandrie (24124) la montre, entourée de bambins, dans la même attitude que le génie du Nil.
*J.Custers*

CORTEGGIANI, Jean-Pierre, see our number 78705.

78183 COSTA, Pedro, The Frontal Sinuses of the Remains Purported to be Akhenaten, *JEA* 64 (1978), 76-79, with 2 tables and 2 fig.

The writer supports Harrison's conclusions against the theory of acromegaly suggested by Wells, and states that the remains are probably those of a man, although the parameters given do not differ significantly from those in women.
*E.P.Uphill*

78184 COULSON, William D.E. and Albert LEONARD, Jr., The Naukratis Project: 1978, *Newsletter ARCE* No.103 (Winter 1977/78), 13-26, with 1 map, 2 plans and 5 fig.

Naukratis, identified by Petrie with the area of Kôm Gi'eif and the site of excavations between 1884 and 1903, is the subject of a project of which the initial stage is here discussed. In the present century a lake has been formed covering most of the excavation area. The geography of the region is described as well as the Hellenistic and Roman pottery found by surface collection.

It appears that different areas were developed during the Greek and Roman Periods.

78185 COUROYER, B., *Brk* et les formules égyptiennes de salutation, *Revue Biblique*, Paris 85 (1978), 575-585.

The author points out that the meaning of the formula *brktk l* + god's name has to be sought in Egyptian correspondence, since the Egyptian-Aramaic epistolary formulae are parallel. *L.Z.*

COUVERT, M., see our number 78810.

COX, Charles F., see our number 78347.

CRISCUOLO, Lucia, see our number 78625.

78186 CROWFOOT PAYNE, Joan, A Hoard of Flint Knives from the Negev, in: *Archaeology in the Levant*. Essays for Kathleen Kenyon. Edited by Roger Moorey and Peter Parr, Warminster, Aris & Phillips Ltd, [1978], 19-21, with 1 pl.

Three prehistoric flint knives found at Tell Tuwail, Negev, are not Egyptian imports, but may well have been inspired by Egyptian models during a period of contact. *L.Z.*

78187 CRUZ-URIBE, Eugene, The Father of Ramses I: OI 11456, *JNES* 37 (1978), 237-244.

The monument described is a fragment of a grey limestone stela now in the O. I. Museum Chicago, showing three figures in a niche-panel. It belonged to the Troop Commander of the Lord of the Two Lands *Swty* (Seti). Other figures shown are his brother Khaemwast and his son, the stablemaster Ramose (or Ramses). *E.P. Uphill*

78188 CRUZ-URIBE, Eugene, Papyrus Libbey: a Re-examination, *Serapis* 4 (1977-1978), 3-9, with 1 pl.

The Demotic Pap. Libbey, first published by Spiegelberg in 1907, and now preserved in the Toledo Museum of Art, is here presented in photograph, transliteration and translation, with some comments. It dates from year 1 of Chababash and contains a marriage contract in which party A is female.

78189 CURTO, Silvio, Attività del Museo Egizio di Torino, in: *Atti del 1° Convegno Italiano sul Vicino Oriente Antico*, 109-110.

Short note on the activities of the Egyptian Museum in Turin. *L.Z.*

78190 CURTO, Silvio, In memoria di J. Omlin, V. Maragioglio e C. Rinaldi, *Aegyptus* 58 (1978), 222-224.

Obituary notices. Compare our numbers 78897, 78898 and 78899.

78191   CURTO, Silvio, Statua egittizante nel Museo delle Terme, *SAK* 6 (1978), 55-61, with 3 pl.

Publication of a granite statue of a standing male figure in Egyptianizing Hellenistic style, preserved in the Museo Nazionale Romano delle Terme. It is minutely described and compared with similar works of art from the Graeco-Roman Period, on account of which the author ascribed it to the Emperor Nero. It may date from the year A.D. 66.

78192   CURTO, Silvio, Il Torello Brancaccio, *in: Hommages Vermaseren*, 282-295, with 5 pl.

The author re-studies the so-called Torello Brancaccio, the black serpentine statue of a bull rediscovered in Rome in 1885, which has recently been discussed by several authors (see our numbers 69430, 72459, 72610 and 75385). The statue is at present exhibited in the Egyptian Museum, Turin.
The author deals with its classical and recent history, its date (late Ptolemaic or early Roman Period), the deity it represents (certainly Apis), and other problems.

CURTO, Silvio, see also our number 78498.

78193   DĄBROWSKA-SMEKTAŁA, Elżbieta, I międzynarodowy kongres egiptologiczny w Kairze, *Przegląd Orientalistyczny*, Warszawa No.1 (105), 1978, 68-69.

Short report on the First International Congress of Egyptology, held in Cairo, 1976.                                                                                                                                   *L.Z.*

78194   DAHOOD, M., Egyptian *ỉw*, "Island", in Jeremiah 10, 9 and Daniel 10, 5, *in*: *Atti del Secondo Congresso Internazionale di Linguistica Camito-Semitica*. Firenze, 16-19 aprile 1974. Raccolti da Pelio Fronzaroli, [Firenze], Istituto di linguistica e di lingue orientali. Università di Firenze, 1978 (= Quaderni di Semitistica, 5), 101-103.

Discussing the O.T. dislegomenon 'ûpāz/'īwē pāz "coast of fine gold" the author refers to Egyptian *ỉw*, "Island".                                                                                    *L.Z.*

78195   DANELIUS, Eva, Did Thutmose III Despoil the Temple in Jerusalem? A Critical Commentary to Chapter IV of "Ages in Chaos", *S.I.S. Review. Journal of the Society for Interdisciplinary Studies*, Elstree, Herts. 2, No.3, Special Issue (1977/78), 64-79.

After an explanation of the principles of Velikovsky's revised chronology the author first discards the name of the O.T. Shishak who conquered Jerusalem as untrustworthy and sketches the political situation in Israel-Judah in the 10th century B.C. Her main arguments against an identification of the city *My-k-ty* mentioned in the Annals of Tuthmosis III with Megiddo are the absence of Egyptian finds there and the greater plausibility of another route of the army which led to Jerusalem, one of whose names, Makdis, offers a good possibility

for its identiy with the city *My-k-ty* of the Annals. Her conclusion is that Jerusalem may very well have been the city which was captured by Tuthmosis III.
*L.Z.*

DARIS, Sergio, see our number 78149.

DAUMAS, François, see our number 78166.

DAVIES, W. Vivian, see our numbers 78320 and 78536.

DAVIS, Virginia Lee, see our number 78027.

78196  DAVIS, Whitney M., Dating Prehistoric Rock-Drawings in Upper-Egypt and Nubia, *Current Anthropology*, New York 19 (1978), 216-217.

Short report on the author's search for and classification of prehistoric rock-drawings in Upper Egypt and Nubia. *L.Z.*

78197  DAVIS, Whitney M., More on Prehistoric Rock-Drawings, *JSSEA* 8 (1977-1978), 84-85.

Addition to our following number.
The author discusses the correlation which may exist between the age of the rock-drawings and their elevation above sea-level, since it seems that generally high elevation is a feature of older drawings.

78198  DAVIS, Whitney M., Toward a Dating of Nile Valley Prehistoric Rock-Drawings, *JSSEA* 8 (1977-1978), 25-34.

After mentioning older and recent publications of rock-drawings in the Nile Valley the author presents preliminary remarks as to their chronology. The methods of dating by the degree of patination, superimposition or stratigraphical association can seldom apply. Hence the author attempts to classify the representations by trait-clusters (theme; technique; patina; type; quality and size of surfaces; station elevation; style); see the table on p.34. In order to test this method he studied some examples from the publication of Hellström (our number 70256). From these he concluded to a relative chronology, which then should be anchored to absolute dates. The present study presents some provisional results.

78199  DAVIS, Whitney, Two Compositional Tendencies in Amarna Reliefs, *AJA* 82 (1978), 387-394, with 1 ill. and 1 fig.

The author discusses two innovations in the composition of Amarna reliefs, the composition with a circular (adstrued on account of West Berlin Inv. No. 14145) and a triangular structure (the author lists 23 instances). *L.Z.*

78200  DAYTON, John, assisted by Ann DAYTON, Minerals, Metals, Glazing & Man, or Who Was Sesostris I ?, London, Harrap, [1978] (22 x 27.5 cm; 496 p., 31 maps, 32 colour pl., numerous fig., ill. and tables, maps on endpapers); rev. *Antiquity* 53 (1978), 154 (**P.R.S.** Moorey). Pr. £40

This extensive study dealing with an overwhelming amount of evidence from numerous civilizations started from a simple study of the evolution of glazing technology and leads through a discussion of the chronology of Ancient Near Eastern civilizations to startling conclusions, so startling that the author himself realizes that he "will no doubt be judged an idiot" (p.399).

In the preface the aims of the work are explained: to demonstrate that the usual interrelated chronology has been based on several mistakes (e.g., Petrie's high dates of the deposits in Abydos and Hierakonpolis) and to put it on the firm basis of geological facts and an analysis of archaeological data.

The study consists of three parts: "The Technical Problems" (on glass and glazes), "Geology, Metallurgy and Trade" (on copper) and "The Archaeological Evidence or It is better to be roughly right than precisely wrong" (on chronology). A surprising amount of archaeological evidence is discussed, illuminated by drawings and colour photographs: glass and glazes, faience, pottery, weapons and tools, etc., while numerous instances of chemical analysis presented in the form of tables constitute the backbone of the argument.

Throughout the work Egyptian material is amply used since it contains the key to the chronology of the entire Ancient Near East as well as the European Prehistory. As for examples we mention: a chapter on Egyptian blue and other pigments, and several chapters in part 3 on the dating of periods of Egyptian history, but also brief sections like that on gold mines (p.179, with a map on p.180).

In chapter 26 (398-433) the author draws up his general conclusions. Key problems are, for instance, the archaeological gaps at the end of the Early Bronze Age and in the S.I.P., as well as the absence in the Near East of tin, silver (although it occurs already in the tomb of Hetepheres), amber, antimony and lapis lazuli. The main conclusions are: that what is usually suggested to be Ist Dynasty faience and Early Bronze Age metallurgy actually belongs to the first half of the Second Millennium; and that there is ample evidence for a great upheaval throughout the Aegean and the Near East at about 2000 B.C., which came from Europe, bringing metallurgy from there to the Mediterranean. Thus the author partly reverses the theory of Childe that civilization came from the Fertile Crescent.

Nine appendices, dealing with various technical and other details, addenda, an epilogue, an extensive bibliography and indexes conclude this stimulating study.

DEBERGH, Jacques, see our number 78564.

DEBONO, Fernand, see our number 78013.

78201 DECKER, Wolfgang, Annotierte Bibliographie zum Sport im alten Ägypten, Sankt Augustin, Verlag Hans Richarz, [1978] (16.2 x 24.5 cm; 164 p. ); rev. *Aegyptus* 58 (1978), 289-290 (Sergio Pernigotti); *BiOr* 36 (1979), 166 (E.P. Uphill); *CdE* LV, No.109-110 (1980), 140-142 (Michel Malaise); *Oriens Antiquus* 19 (1980), 319-320 (M. Christina Guidotti); *Welt des Orients* 11 (1981), 144-146 (Waltraud Guglielmi). Pr. DM 49

In his introduction the author explains his wide use of the term "sport" since at present it is still hard to conceive of sport in a narrow sense in ancient Egypt, and he accounts for the bibliographical sources and the systematization. There then follows in a separate chapter a short history of the study of ancient Egyptian sport.

The annotated bibliography itself consists of six sections, each subdivided into various numbers of smaller units: general and introductory apparatus; general literature on the subject; royal sport; particular sporting activities such as archery, fighting sports, ball and other games, water sport, acrobatics, riding and hunting; and various themes such as sport in relation to literature, cult, cultural exchange, and hygiene.

The book ends with two indexes, one on authors and the other on persons and subjects. *L.Z.*

DECKER, Wolfgang, see also our number 78761.

DeMARS, Louise Laurentano, see our number 78117.

DEMUYNCK, M.A., see our number 78810.

78202 DENON, Vivant, Mit Napoleon in Ägypten. 1798-1799. Herausgegeben von Helmut Arndt, [Tübingen], Horst Erdmann Verlag, [1978] (12.6 x 20.6 cm; 374 p., frontispiece, 40 ill., maps on endpapers).

In 1802 Dominique Vivant Denon published an account of his journey through Egypt as member of the Commission during Napoleon's expedition, 1798-1799. In 1803 two German versions of the book have appeared. The present volume contains a new edition, illustrated by drawings of Denon himself and some contemporaries, and preceded by a preface of the editor who also added some notes. The preface gives a survey of the history of Egypt since the Turkish conquest in 1517, as well as of the French expedition and a brief biography of Denon. On p. 373-374 Denon's bibliography.

78203 DENTZER, Jean-Marie, Reliefs du banquet dans la moitié orientale de l'empire romain: iconographie hellénistique et traditions locales, *Revue archéologique*, Paris, 1978, 63-82, with 4 ill. and 1 fig.

Studying the motif of the banquet on Hellenistic reliefs, the author briefly discusses banquet scenes on Egyptian stelae mainly originating from Kom Abu Billu (Terenouthis). The presence of Egyptian figures and decorations on these stelae bear witness to the adaptation of a Greek motif to ancient Egyptian beliefs and funerary practices. *L.Z.*

78204 DERCHAIN, Philippe, "En l'an 363 de Sa Majesté le Roi de Haute et de Basse Égypte Râ-Harakhty vivant par-delà le Temps et l'Espace", *CdE* LIII, No.105 (1978), 48-56.

Le mythe d'Horus figurant sur la face interne du mur d'enceinte du temple d'Edfou peut se lire comme un doublet du mythe de la destruction des hommes dont il suit étroitement la structure, tout en en inversant point par point le signe. *Ph.Derchain*

78205 DERCHAIN, Philippe, Miettes (suite), *RdE* 30 (1978), 57-66, with 3 ill. and 1 fig.

Pour les miettes 1-5 voir notre No.74152
§6. Complément bibliographique à l'article "Sur le nom de Chou et sa fonction", *RdE* 27, 110-116 (Notre No. 75180).
§7. L'information de Chérémon selon laquelle les prêtres égyptiens auraient dormi sur des lits de nervures de palmier avec un chevet de bois pour oreiller décrit en fait un mode de coucher paysan qui n'a rien de particulièrement ascétique et est encore répandu dans la campagne égyptienne.
§8. La notice d'Horapollon I, 39 permet d'établir que le titre de ḥrỉ sšt₃ est à la basse époque un simple équivalent de Ḥrỉ ḥb dont il pourrait n'être qu'un substitut "valorisant", la fonction étant certainement très modeste.
§9. C.T. III 79b - 84b, éclairé par des représentations du Nouvel Empire dans lesquelles le mort s'abreuve à même une mare révèle une polémique entre deux conceptions de la survie.
§10. Un petit bronze de la collection Fouquet est l'occasion de débrouiller une combinaison de symboles qui évoquent tous l'idée de naissance et de fécondité.
*Ph.Derchain*

78206 DERCHAIN-URTEL, Maria-Theresia, Esna, Schrift und "Spiel", *GM* Heft 27 (1978), 11-21.

In die Texte aus dem Tempel von Esna wurden nicht nur durch die Schreiber eine Fülle von Neuerungen gebracht, sondern auch neue Ordnungsmerkmale in den Aufbau der religiösen Texte und besonders deutlich der Litaneien eingeführt. Anhand der Khnum-Litanei wird nun ein Aspekt dieser Neuerungen aufgezeigt. Jeder Vers wird zu einer kleinen, geschlossenen Einheit gemacht, indem eines der Zeichen zur Schreibung des Namens, ein "Leitzeichen", im nächsten Vers wieder aufgenommen wird. Noch andere Ordnungsmerkmale zeigen den Willen zur Geschlossenheit der kleinsten Aussageeinheit.
Berichtigung: *GM* Heft 29 (1978),7.
Mitteilung: *GM* Heft 29 (1978), 8. *Inge Hofmann*

78207 DERCHAIN-URTEL, Maria-Theresia, Zum besseren Verständnis eines Textes aus Esna, *GM* Heft 30 (1978), 27-34.

Westendorf machte darauf aufmerksam, dass der bisher nur mit der Bedeutung "frieren, Frost" belegte Stamm ḥsj auch "verbrennen" beinhalten könne (vgl. unsere Nummer 78855), wodurch sich ein besseres Verständnis für einen Vers einer Hymne an Chnum in Esna ergibt. Demzufolge lauten die Verse 28 und 29 folgendermassen: "Fürchtet Khnum, ihr, deren Körper erhitzt sind und die ihr zu ihm ruft; denn er wird wie eine angenehme Brise kommen und eure Körper durch den Wind kühlen; fürchtet Khnum, ihr, deren Knochen brennen, lasst nicht davon ab, ihm zu folgen; er wird (es) euch lohnen durch das, was aus seinem Gebiet kommt (=Wasser) und die seine Macht nicht kennen, sollen fern davon sein" (S.33). *Inge Hofmann*

78208 DESANGES, Jehan, Le littoral africain du Bab el-Mandeb d'après les sources grecques et latines, *Annales d'Éthiopie,* Paris 11 (1978), 83-101, with 1 map.

Eine Anzahl antiker Berichte aus drei Jahrhunderten, vom Periplus des Agatharchides bis zur Geographie des Ptolemaios, betreffen die afrikanische Küste am Bab el-Mandeb. Die griechischen oder lateinischen Zitate werden angeführt, ins Französische übersetzt und kommentiert. *Inge Hofmann*

78209 DESANGES, Jehan, Recherches sur l'activité des Mediterranéens aux confins de l'Afrique (VI$^e$ siècle avant J.-C.–IV$^e$ siècle après J.-C.), École Française de Rome, Palais Farnèse, 1978 (17 x 24.5 cm; XVIII + 467 p., 10 maps) = Collection de l'École Française de Rome, 38.

Der erste Teil der vorliegenden Untersuchung beschäftigt sich kritisch mit den verschiedenen Umschiffungen Libyens (Periplus des Ophelas, Periplus der phönikischen Seeleute zur Zeit Nechos, Periplus des Euthymenes, Periplus des Sataspes, die verschiedenen punischen Berichte zwischen 600 und 450 v.Chr., Periplus des Hanno, über Libyen im Periplus des Pseudo-Skylax, Periplus des Polybius, dem von L. Coelius Antipater berichteten Periplus und den Schiffahrten des Eudoxos von Kyzikus).

Im zweiten Teil werden die verschiedenen Sahara-Expeditionen, wie sie sich in antiken Berichten finden, vorgestellt: die Expedition der jungen Nasamonen, Archonides von Argos und Magon von Karthago und ihre Durchquerung der Wüste zur Ammons-Oase (während der sie trockenes Brot assen und nichts tranken), die Expedition des Cornelius Balbus gegen die Garamanten 21 oder 20 v.Chr. und die Expedition des Julius Maternus nach Agisymba.

Im dritten Teil kann man feststellen, dass die antiken Berichte über das nilotische und erythreische Afrika sehr viel reichhaltiger sind als die bisher vorgeführten über den Nord- und Nordwestteil Afrikas. In einem ersten Kapitel werden die Beziehungen der Saitendynastie zu Nubien bis zur Eroberung von Alexander untersucht. Im zweiten Kapitel handelt es sich um die Griechen im Niltalgebiet oder an der Küste des Roten Meeres von Alexander bis Kleopatra; das dritte Kapitel zeigt die Römer von Augustus bis Theodosius I. in demselben Gebiet. Nach einer Zusammenfassung folgt ein Appendix mit den Texten, die sich auf die libyschen Umschiffungen beziehen (griechisch bzw. lateinisch mit französischer Übersetzung). Ein ausführlicher Index und zehn Karten schliessen das überaus gründliche Werk ab. *Inge Hofmann*

78210 DESANGES, Jehan et Serge LANCEL, Bibliographie analytique de l'Afrique Antique X (1973-1974), Paris, E. de Boccard, 1978 (21 x 27 cm; 44 p.).

Zu den für unser Gebiet in Frage kommenden bibliographischen Angaben der vorliegenden analytischen Bibliographie des antiken Afrika vgl. Nr. 50 = unsere Nummer 73353 und Nr. 51 = unsere Nummer 74349 und Nr. 74: J. Ferron, Horus l'enfant sur les stèles votives de Carthage, *Rev. de l'Inst. des B.-L. arabes*, 36, no. 131 (1973), 79-92 and 4 pl. = p. 93-96. *Inge Hofmann*

78211 DESCHÊNES, Gisèle, Isis Thermouthis: À propos d'une statuette dans la collection du Professeur M.J. Vermaseren, *in: Hommages Vermaseren*, 305-315, with 7 pl.

Proceeding from a terracotta statuette (h. 9 cm) of a female figure with a body ending in a snake in the collection Vermaseren the author deals with this representation of Isis Thermuthis. She lists 11 other similar instances and discusses origin and iconography of the goddess, who was popular in the Roman Period and particularly connected with the Faiyûm.

78212 DESROCHES NOBLECOURT, Christiane, Une exceptionnelle décoration pour "la Nourrice qui devint reine", *La Revue du Louvre et des Musées de France*, Paris 28 (1978), 20-27, with 2 maps, 3 fig. and 5 ill. (1 in colour).

The author publishes an Amarna relief recently acquired by the Louvre (Inv. No. E 27.150) and originating from Roeder's excavations at Hermopolis. In contrast to Roeder's explanation of the fragment she argues that this relief belongs to an exceptional series in which the Lady Tiy, the later queen of king Eye, is represented as being present at the same rewarding scene of which she is the subject on the walls of her tomb at Amarna. *L.Z.*

DESROCHES NOBLECOURT, Christiane, see also our numbers 78013, 78056, 78581 and 78821.

78213 DEVAUCHELLE, Didier, À propos du papyrus de Genève D 229, *Enchoria* 8, Teil 2 (1978), 73-75.

Publication of a short Demotic inscription (name of the owner with filiation) of the hieratic papyrus D 229 (Book of the Dead) of the collection of the Musée d'Art et d'Histoire in Geneva. *W.Brunsch*

78214 DEVAUCHELLE, Didier, Un cautionnement démotique: P. dém. Leconte 1, *RdE* 30 (1978), 67-77, with 1 pl.

Publication d'un acte de cautionnement daté d'Athyr de l'an 5 de Ptolémée V (201-200), témoignant de la gravité de l'inflation à cette époque. Photographie, transcription, traduction et commentaire. La souscription grecque fait l'objet d'une note de Danielle Bonneau (p. 74-77). *Ph. Derchain*

78215 DEVAUCHELLE, D. and M. PEZIN, Un papyrus médical démotique, *CdE* LIII, No. 105 (1978), 57-66.

Article de critique sévère de E.A.E. Reymond, A Medical Book from Crocodilopolis (notre No. 76668).
Les auteurs analysent en particulier la liste des drogues reprises dans l'index de ce livre et proposent sept pages de corrections, soit de lecture du texte démotique même, soit d'identification. *Ph. Derchain*

78216 DEVOS, Paul, Le "chant" copte "de la vigne" dans deux feuillets de Berlin. Abraham et Lazare, *Analecta Bollandiana*, Bruxelles 95 (1977), 275-290.

The author publishes two Coptic sheets, Berlin 1606, 7-8, which are connected with Abraham and Lazarus as the prototypes of the rich and the poor man.
The contents are part of the Coptic Song of the Vine.
The commentary concentrates on only a few points. *L.Z.*

78217 DINKLER, E., Der Salomonische Knoten in der nubischen Kunst und die Geschichte des Motivs, in: Etudes nubiennes, 73-86, with 24 ill. on 8 pl.

Der sogenannte Salomonische Knoten kommt auf einer Scherbe aus Ghazali und auf Fresken in Faras vor; nach einer kurzen Abhandlung zur Frühgeschichte des Ornaments im Mittelmeerraum und seiner geographischen Ausbreitung wird betont, dass die nubische Kunst der südlichste Ausläufer der Kunst des Mittelmeerraumes ist. *Inge Hofmann*

DÖRNER, Friedrich Karl, see our number 78550.

78218 DOLL, Susan Kay, Texts and Decoration on the Napatan Sarcophagi of Anlamani and Aspelta, *Dissertation Abstracts International*, Ann Arbor, Mich. 39, No. 5 (November 1978), 2913-A.

Abstract of a thesis Brandeis University, 1978 (393 p.: order no. 7819935). Extensive study, philological as well as religious, of the funerary texts on the sarcophagi of Anlamani and Aspelta ($\pm$ 623-568 B.C.) from Nuri. Also the decorations are studied. *L.Z.*

78219 DOLZANI, Claudia, Il culto del dio Sobek e della dea Renenut nei testi del tempio di Medinet el-Ma'di, in: *Atti del I° Convegno Italiano nel Vicino Oriente Antico*, 95-100.

The author studies the relations between the deities Sobek and Renenut as they occur in the texts of the M.K. temple of Medinet Maadi. In her opinion the texts testify to a theological-political agreement between Renenut, to whom the temple is dedicated, and Sobek, the original and locally venerated god. *L.Z.*

78220 DONADONI, Sergio, Il "cenotafio" di Sankh-ka-Ra Mentuhotep a Qurna, in: *Journal Faculty of Archaeology*, 99-104, with an Arabic translation on p. 102-104.

The author, discussing the so-called cenotaph of Sankh-ka-Re Mentuhotep N. of the entrance to the Valley of the Kings, presents first a survey of its interpretation by several scholars. He argues that it was a temple of Horus and another divinity. A second building near it was a station of the desert police.

78221 DONADONI, Sergio, [Jebel Barkal], *Nyame Akuma*, Calgary No. 13 (1978), 39-40.

In der Kampagne vom 7. März bis 15. April 1978 wurde das Gebiet zwischen dem "Palast" und dem Tempel 1300 freigelegt; die kleinen Gebäude zeigen, dass das Gebiet ständig bewohnt war. Weitere Ausgrabungen zeigten, dass wenigstens eine, wenn nicht sogar mehrere Siedlungen in dem Gebiet lagen, in dem Natakamani den Tempel 1400, wahrscheinlich auch 1300, baute. Eine Gebäudekomplex, der provisorisch als Tempel 1500 bezeichnet wurde, besitzt eine Reihe von viereckigen Säulenbasen. Es scheint sich bei diesem Komplex um einen Kiosk gehandelt zu haben. Eine Besonderheit stellen Fragmente von emaillierten Terrakotta-Ziegeln dar, die blau und grün gefärbt sind. Einige zeigen

komplizierte Reliefs, zum Teil geradezu plastische Elemente, die in einigen
Fällen Lebewesen repräsentieren. *Inge Hofmann*

78222   DONADONI, Sergio, Ricordo di Michela Giorgini, *Oriens Antiquus* 17 (1978), 299-300.

Obituary notice. Compare our number 78900.

78223   DONOHUE, V.A., *Pr-nfr*, *JEA* 64 (1978), 143-148, with 1 fig.

Equates the term with the $w^cbt$ or place of purification or embalmment, and suggests a good rendering would be 'house of rejuvenation'. *E.P. Uphill*

DRAPPIER, D., see our number 78811.

DRENKHAHN, Rosemarie, see our number 78488.

78224   DUMA, G. and Cs. RAVASZ, Farbstoffe aus Tell-el-Amarna, *Acta antiqua academiae scientiarum hungaricae*, Budapest 26 (1978), 255-268, with 6 ill. and fig., and 1 table.

The authors present a chemical investigation of nine dyes, natural as well as artificial, originating from the German excavations at Tell el-Amarna. *L.Z.*

78225   DUNHAM, Dows, Zawiyet el-Aryan. The Cemeteries Adjacent to the Layer Pyramid, Boston, Department of Egyptian and Ancient Near Eastern Art, Museum of Fine Arts, 1978 (26.7 x 34.6 cm; XVII + 79 p., 1 plan, 8 + 20 ill., numerous fig., 37 pl. containing 59 ill.).

In the introduction there is provided some information on the minor excavation at Zawiyet el-Aryan from about 1911, carried out by Reisner and Clarence Fisher, which was never fully published. From the diaries, tomb cards and photographs on about 300 graves the present author has selected only 72 for final publication. In an added note he states that it is impossible for him at the age of 87 to judge the value of the conclusions of Maragioglio and Rinaldi (our number 63343).
After a plan of the Layer Pyramid and survey photographs of the site follow sections on the burials adjacent to the pyramid: 28 Early Dynastic graves, one of the Third Dynasty, 41 of the New Kingdom, and two of the Roman Period. Of almost all graves are given the measurements, the burial, a plan and/or a photograph, the objects and the findings in the debris, with photographs and drawings of the vessels and some interesting details. The Third Dynasty Grave yielded a rich harvest of vessels. Most objects could be traced in the Museum of Fine Arts, Boston. *L.Z.*

78226   DUPONT-SOMMER, André, Les dieux et les hommes en l'île d'Élefantine, près d'Assouan, au temps de l'empire des Perses, *Comptes rendus de l'Académie des Inscriptions & Belles-Lettres*, Paris, 1978, 756-772.

In this article on the Jewish colony at Elephantine during the Persian domination the author devotes some attention to the attitude of the Jews towards the local god Khnum and the Egyptians, and the relation between their god Yaho and Khnum. *L.Z.*

78227 DZIERŻYKRAY-ROGALSKI, Tadeusz, Badania antropologiczne w Oazie Dakhla prowadzone w 1977 r., *Przegląd Antropologiczny*, Warsawa-Poznan 44, Zeszyt 2 (1978), 353-359, with 4 ill., 1 table and an English summary on p.359.

"Anthropological Investigations in the Dakhla Oasis in 1977".
The author presents his work in the field of physical anthropology carried out in the Dakhla expedition by the IFAO. So far he only investigated skeletal remains from the Ptolemaic Period found in an old mastaba.
See also our number 78231. *L.Z.*

78228 DZIERŻYKRAY-ROGALSKI, T., Études préliminaires des ossements humains des IV$^e$-III$^e$ millénaires av. J.-C. à Kadero (Soudan), *in*: *Études nubiennes*, 87-90, with 4 ill. on 2 pl.

Der neolithische Fundort von Kadero gehört gemäss seines eruierten Materials in der Epoche des Neolithikums von Khartum und ist später als Esh Shaheinab anzusetzen. Bisher wurden 40 Gräber gefunden: die Skelette lagen in Hockerstellung auf einer Seite. Von den untersuchten Skeletten hatten die 11 Männer das Durchschnittsalter von 38.1 Jahren erreicht, die 8 Frauen dasjenige von 30.8 Jahren und die 9 Kinder das von 6.5 Jahren. Ein Vergleich zeigt, dass die Lebensbedingungen der neolithischen Bevölkerung von Kadero günstiger waren als die anderer Bevölkerungsgruppen zur gleichen Zeit in Europa. Die Schädel sind gekennzeichnet durch Prognathismus; heute wird dieser Rassentyp wesentlich weiter im Süden gefunden und wurde wahrscheinlich durch eine Bevölkerung aus dem Norden abgedrängt. *Inge Hofmann*

78229 DZIERŻYKRAY-ROGALSKI, Tadeusz, Neolithic Skeletons from Kadero, Sudan, *Current Anthropology*, New York 18, No.3 (September 1977), 585-586, with 2 ill.

Short note on Neolithic skeletons found at Kadero, Sudan. *L.Z.*

78230 DZIERŻYKRAY-ROGALSKI, T., On the Black Variety at Kadero, Sudan, *Current Anthropology*, New York 19 (1978), 406-407.

The author contests the opinion expressed in our number 78678. *L.Z.*

78231 DZIERŻYKRAY-ROGALSKI, Tadeusz, Rapport sur les recherches anthropologiques menées dans l'oasis de Dakhleh en 1977 (IFAO-Balat), *BIFAO* 78 (1978), 141-145.

The author studied human remains of 71 individuals found during the excavations at Balât. From the high average age (for the 14 women identified: 43.1 years) the author concludes that either the situation was economically favourable or that it was a privileged group. He also has found traces of lepra. The anthropological study will be continued.

78232  DZIERŻYKRAY-ROGALSKI, Tadeusz, Sur l' infirmité du pharaon Siptah (XIX$^e$ dynastie), *Études et Travaux* 10 (1978), 121-131, with 1 fig. and 9 ill.

The author studies the mummy of King Siptah, paying particular attention to the deformed left foot. The cause of the deformation is uncertain.

78233  DZIERŻYKRAY-ROGALSKI, T. et E. PROMIŃSKA, Tombeaux de deux dignitaires chrétiens dans l'Église Cruciforme de Dongola, in: *Études nubiennes*, 91-93, with 6 ill. on 3 pl.

Zwei Männerskelette werden untersucht; einer war zwischen 35 und 40 Jahre alt und mass 184.1 cm; der andere zwischen 60 und 65 Jahre und 168.2 cm gross. Es handelte sich bei ihnen um hohe kirchliche Würdenträger, die der lokalen nubischen Bevölkerung entstammten.                                *Inge Hofmann*

78234  EDEL, Elmar, Amasis und Nebukadrezar II., *GM* Heft 29 (1978), 13-20.

Die Amasisstele der Kairener Museums nennt das 1. und das 4. Regierungsjahr des Amasis. Der Inhalt umfasst die Schilderung einer kombinierten Land- und Seeoperation gegen Ägypten, die von Nebukadrezar II. geleitet wird. Während auf der Seite des Amasis ausser jonischen und karischen Söldnern Bundesgenossen aus "der Stadt Putujam" (Kyrene) genannt werden, befindet sich unter den asiatischen Truppen der entthronte Pharao Apries, den der Verfasser mit dem in der Amasisstele genannten "Überheblichen" identifiziert. Dieser muss demnach an den babylonischen Herrscherhof geflüchtet sein; der historische Teil der Amasisstele wird in Übersetzung gegeben.                  *Inge Hofmann*

78235  EDEL, Elmar, Der Brief des ägyptischen Wesirs Pašijara an den Hethitenkönig Ḫattušili und verwandte Keilschriftbriefe, Göttingen, Vandenhoeck & Ruprecht, [1978] (17 x 25 cm; 42 p., 4 pl.) = Nachrichten der Akademie der Wissenschaften in Göttingen.    Philologisch-historische Klasse. Jahrgang 1978, Nr. 4, p. 117-158.                                                                  Pr.DM 12

Publication in photograph, transliteration and translation with comments of the cuneiform text Bo 69/608 + 301/u, a letter from the vizier *P3-sr* and other officials to the Hittite king Ḫattušili, which mentions the sending of presents among which small golden boxes and garments.
This letter may be part of a group of letters, all sent in year 21, of which here also are discussed KUB III, 70, from crown-prince *Sth-ḥr-ḥpš.f* to the king, and KBo I, 29 - KBo IX, 43, from queen Nefertari to queen Puduḥepa. They probably were combined with KUB III, 52, a fragmentary letter of Ramses II to the king, and carried by the same man. The correspondence dates from year 21 of Ramses II, just after the treaty.
In an appendix the author studies the indication for the quality of cloth *p3kt* (= *šm't nfrt*).
There follow corrections to the author's article in *SAK* 1 (our number 74176) and indexes.

78236  EDEL, Elmar, A Comment on Professor Giveon's Reading of the New Sahureʻ Inscription, *BASOR* No. 232 (Fall 1978), 77-78.

The author proposes a rearrangement of the signs in the drawing published in our number 78285.
L.Z.

78237 EDEL, Elmar, Noch einmal zum Kult des Tetrodon Fahaka als Bringer der Überschwemmung im Elefantengau, *GM* Heft 30 (1978), 35-37.

Bezugnehmend auf einen Artikel von Helck (vgl. unsere Nummer 78355), bekräftigt der Verfasser noch einmal seine Auffassung, dass die Mugiliden als Bringer der Überschwemmung zu den "Hallen des Kugelfisches" nach Elephantine wallfahren, wobei auch der Fahaka in der gleichen Frühjahrszeit von den steigenden Wassern des Nil aus dem Süden herangeschwemmt wurde. Fortsetzung der Diskussion in *GM* Heft 36 (1979), 31-36 und *GM* Heft 41 (1980), 33-41.
Inge Hofmann

78238 EDWARDS, I.E.S., The Pyramids of Egypt. Edited with Notes by Fumio Sasaki, Tokyo, The Eihōsha Ltd, [1978] (13 x 18.6 cm; 110 p., 1 map, 2 ill., 5 fig.).

After a preface in Japanese there follows an abbreviated version of our numbers 92 and 61201, containing the chapters called "The Pyramid Age" and "Construction and Purpose". At the end a list of the major pyramids and explanatory notes again in Japanese.
L.Z.

EDWARDS, I.E.S., see also our number 78027.

EGGEBRECHT, Eva, see our number 78178.

78239 Egyptian Treasures from the Collection of The Brooklyn Museum. Photographs by Seth Joel. Introduction by Michael Botwinick. Commentaries by Robert S. Bianchi, New York, Harry N. Abrams, Inc., Publishers, [1978] (29.2 x 40.5 cm; 61 unnumbered pages, 28 colour pl., 2 colour ill. on cover).

After an introdcution by Michael Botwinick, the 28 full colour large size plates are presented, the data and the description being on the facing pages. Some of the objects shown in this representative selection are less well known. Much attention is paid to fine small pieces.
L.Z.

EICKHOFF, U., see our number 78095.

78240 EIWANGER, Josef, Erster Vorbericht über die Wiederaufnahme der Grabungen in der neolitischen Siedlung Merimde-Benisalâme, *MDAIK* 34 (1978), 33-42, with 2 fig. and 3 pl.

Preliminary report on the continuation of Junker's excavations at Merimde-Benisalâme. The first campaign was intended to get an impression of the site and to establish the most promising areas for further research. The author gives a description of the entire site and its stratigraphy, and describes the finds of this campaign. It appears that the major part of the prehistoric settlement is still undisturbed.

78241 ELAT, Moshe, The Economic Relations of the Neo-Assyrian Empire with Egypt, *JAOS* 98 (1978), 20-34.

The first section deals with the direct economic relations between Assyria and Egypt in the eighth and seventh centuries B.C. Among the "tribute" to Assyria are particularly animals native in Egypt, such as crocodiles, hippopotamuses and a rhinoceros (see our number 77730, 297-302). In a note (p.21) the author discusses the various lands called *Muṣru/i* in Assyrian texts.
The second section deals i.a. with the *kāru* established by Sargon near the Egyptian border. Then the Assyrian policy toward the Arabs in S. Palestine and N. Sinai is discussed, upon whose cooperation the connections with Egypt were dependent, as well as the Philistine trade with Egypt, through which Egyptian products reached Assyria.
A summary on p. 34.

78242 EMMEL, Stephen, The Nag Hammadi Codices Editing Project: A Final Report, *Newsletter ARCE* No. 103 (Winter/Spring 1977/78), 10-32, with 10 fig.

In this general survey of the Nag Hammadi Codices Editing Project the author deals with the reconstruction, conservation and publication of the papyri. The three appendices contain a table of texts in the codices, remarks on the scribes, and an inventory of pages and fragments in the Codices. At the end of the article a list of references.                                                                                     L.Z.

78243 ENDESFELDER, Erika, Fragen der kulturellen Entwicklung Unternubiens vom 2. Jahrtausend v.u.Z. bis zum 6. Jahrhundert u.Z. Kolloquium, Berlin 1977, *Ethnographisch-archäologische Zeitschrift*, Berlin 19 (1978), 517.

Short note on a colloquium on the problems of the cultural development of Lower Nubia, held in Berlin, March 1977.                                                                                     L.Z.

78244 ENGLUND, Gertie, Akh—Une notion religieuse dans l' Égypte pharaonique, Uppsala, [Gustavianum], 1978 (18.5 x 26.5 cm; 227 p., 3 fig.) = Boreas. Acta Universitatis Upsaliensis: Uppsala Studies in Ancient Mediterranean and Near Eastern Civilizations, 11.

The author analyses the concept *3ḫ* as it occurs in religious texts of the successive periods of Egyptian history, and its development through the ages. Consequently, the study is divided in four chapters, devoted to: the P.T., the C.T., the B.D., and the N.K. books of the Netherworld (Amduat, Book of the Adoration of Re in the West, Book of the Gates, Book of the Caverns, Book of the Creation of the Sun Disk).
Each chapter follows the same pattern: orthography and grammatical use of *3ḫ*; relations with divinities and other entities, and with places and spheres (e.g. the funerary sphere, the netherworld, heaven, etc.); how to become or be an *3ḫ*; various circumstances and effects (living and dying, birth and rejuvenation, participation in the life hereafter, etc.). The sections begin each with a catalogue of the sources, relevant passages in the texts in translation, while each of the four chapters is concluded by a summary.
General conclusions are given on p. 201-211, where the author compares the four groups of texts and presents a circumscription of the concept *3ḫ*, delimitating it against related concepts such as *b3*. One of her essential conclusions is given on p. 211: "*3ḫ* relie ce qui est fixé, figé, statique et stable et ce qui est

mobile, changeant et dynamique car le statique est virtuellement dynamique et le dynamique est la manifestation de l' inertie statique, chargée de potentialités. *3ḥ* est l'énergie incluse dans les ténèbres et l'énergie qui se fait jour à tout niveau où ce phénomène se passe."
Bibliography on p. 213-220; indexes p. 221-227.

78245   EPH'AL, I., The Western Minorities in Babylonia in the 6th-5th Centuries B.C.: Maintenance and Cohesion, *Orientalia* 47 (1978), 74-90.

The first section after the introduction is devoted to Egyptians in the cities of Babylonia. Several persons are listed and several professions mentioned, demonstrating that they were mostly civilians and not prisoners of war. They seem to have been organized in an institution called "assembly of the Egyptians' elders", which existed in Babylon, and probably also in other cities.

78246   [The exhibition of the Treasures of Great Kings and Queens of Ancient Egypt], Tokyo, The Yomiuri Shimbun, 1978 (24.8 x 24.5 cm; unnumbered p., 48 pl. [many in colour], 9 ill., 3 maps, 37 fig., 2 colour ill. on covers).

This is the catalogue in Japanese of an exhibition of 60 objects from the Cairo Museum which was shown in four Japanese cities. The writers are: Dia' Abou-Ghazi, Ibrahim el-Nawawi, Mohamed Ahmed Mohssen, Mohamed Abdel-Latif el-Tanbouli, Sania Abd-el-Al, Itsuji Yoshikawa, Teisuke Yakata.
The catalogue shows a very exquisite selection of well-known objects, all represented by a colour photograph, and all provided with a description.
At the end of the catalogue a glossary with drawings of gods, a bibliography in English, and the data of the 60 objects in English.                     L.Z.

EYRE, Christopher, see our number 78162.

78247   FARAG, Sami, Gamal WAHBA, and Adel FARID, Reused Blocks of Nectanebo I Found at Philae Island (Notizie da File, II), *Oriens Antiquus* 17 (1978), 147-152, with 8 pl.

The authors publish 21 reused blocks of a temple of Nectanebo I found during the dismantling operations of the Second Pylon and the Hypostyle Hall of the Isis temple at Philae, together with blocks bearing the name of king Amasis of the XXVIth Dynasty. They reconstitute five scenes of the king offering to various gods from 19 blocks. The other two probably belong to his porch, which led them to the observations that its actual site is not the original and that it had collapsed to some extent before its re-erection by Ptolemy II.       L.Z.

78248   FARID, Adel, The Stela of Adikhalamani Found at Philae, *MDAIK* 34 (1978), 53-56, with 1 fig. and 1 pl.

Under the pavement of the hypostyle hall of the Philae temple the upper part of a stela has been found. It represents the Meroitic king Adikhalamani, the contemporary of Ptolemy IV Philopator and Ptolemy V Epiphanes, offering before various gods, among whom the falcon-headed god called *p3 nty m p3 iw-wʿb*, "The one of the Abaton". The inscriptions are here given in transcription and translation.

FARID, Adel, see also our number 7824 /.

78249   FATTOVICH, Rodolfo, The Predynastic Decorated Vases from Hammamiya (Upper Egypt)(Scavi nel Museo di Torino, IX),*Oriens Antiquus* 17 (1978), 199-202, with 2 folding fig. and 2 pl.

The author publishes two predynastic vessels found in a Naqâda cemetery near Hammâmîya by Schiaparelli and Paribeni and now exhibited in the Museo Egizio (Inv. Nos S 4699 and S 4749). The first bears the rare representation of a running man or woman with a long skirt in between two boats, while the second shows a hunting scene.                                                                     *L.Z.*

78250   FAULKNER, R.O., The Ancient Egyptian Coffin Texts. Volume III. Spells 788-1185 & Indexes, Warminster, Aris & Phillips Ltd., [1978] (17 x 24.5 cm; VII + 204 p.); rev. *CdE* LIV, No. 107 (1979), 74-76 (Ph. Derchain); *Liber Annuus. Studium Biblicum Franciscanum* 30 (1980), 454-456 (A.Niccacci).
Pr. £10
Sequel to our number 77226.
This last volume of the series begins with a short preface in which the author points out some aspects of the C.T. and their philology.
The volume mainly consists of the translation with notes of spells 788-1185 (= de Buck's edition, vol. VII). This means that one here finds i.a. the translation of the "Book of Two Ways" (Spells 1029-1130); cfr Lesko's study, our number 72429.
At the end (p. 191-204) indexes to divinities, localities, celestial bodies, and selected words discussed in the notes, as well as a catalogue of component parts of boats and gear.

78251   FAULKNER, R.O.,'Liaison' *n* between -*n* and *wỉ*, *JEA* (1978), 129.

Refers to Gardiner's Notes on the Story of Sinuhe and the phenomenon of this *n* before the dependent pronoun, quoting twelve instances in support. Although the function is not clear, as it appears in all but one case after the final -*n* of a plural suffix, it may therefore have formed a speech strengthening liaison with the weak radical *w* following.                               *E.P. Uphill*

78252   FAZZINI, Richard, Tutankhamun and the African Heritage. A View of Society in the Time of the Boy King, [New York, The Metropolitan Museum of Art, 1978] (18.6 x 27.6 cm; 16 unnumbered p., 1 map, 1 table, 10 ill. [8 in colour], 2 fig.).

This amply illustrated booklet for the general reader deals with the racial composition of ancient Egyptian society.                                                      *L.Z.*

78253   FECHT, Gerhard, Schicksalsgöttinnen und König in der "Lehre eines Mannes für seinen Sohn", *ZÄS* 105 (1978), 14-42.

Verfasser gibt Umschrift und Übersetzung (mit Kommentar) der betreffenden Textteile. Meschenet hat dort die Aufgabe, "Luft festzusetzen" bei der Geburt, nachdrücklich nicht die der Prädestination. Die Funktion der Renenet ist wich-

tiger. Sie bestimmt die Länge der Lebenszeit, hat jedoch explizit keinen Einfluss auf deren Gestaltung. In der frühen 12. Dynastie hat man Schicksalsvorstellungen bekämpft, die der Rolle des Königs in Bezug auf die Lebenszeit seiner Untertanen widersprachen.
Zum Schluss vergleicht Fecht die Gliederung mit der des zweiten Teiles der *Loyalistischen Lehre*.                             M. Heerma van Voss

78254   FEUCHT, Erika, Zwei Reliefs Scheschonqs I. aus el-Hibeh, *SAK* 6 (1978), 69-77, with 2 pl. and 1 fig.

Publication of two relief blocks from a pillar in the temple of Sheshonq I in el-Hîba, at present in the Egyptological Institute in Heidelberg (Inv. Nos. 562 and 922). One represents the king before Isis, the other the king before the Moon-god Shepes. The fine pieces are minutely described and compared with similar older reliefs. Their style suggests that of Sethi I.

FILLIOL, René, see our numbers 78823 and 78824.

78255   FINNESTAD, R. Bjerre, The Meaning and Purpose of *Opening the Mouth* in Mortuary Contexts, *Numen*, Leiden 25 (1978), 118-134.

The author discusses the meaning and purpose of the ritual of Opening the Mouth, by seeking it not in its origin (whether it was applied to the statue or to the mummy), but by investigating its actual performance during the N.K. as it appears from representations. He argues that the fundamental idea was to make the object operative in a cultic sense: the statue as a medium of communication of the living people with the beyond; the mummy as the pre-condition of the dead man's Osirian cult relevance; the coffin in its function of guaranteeing the duration of the mummy. Hence the ritual was repeated for the statue, not for the mummy or the coffin.
Although from the mythical and theological point of view the ritual refers to the dead man, for the ritual it is the object itself that is the point of reference, and, therefore, it influences the meaning of the ritual. This is thus not simply a "rite de passage", but differs in connection with the object it is applied to.

78256   FISCHER, Henry G., Another Example of the Verb *nh* 'shelter', *JEA* 64 (1978), 131-132.

The writer links the verb with the noun *nht* 'shelter' and also points out the relationship with the sycamore tree whose shade was much prized in Egyptian gardens.                             E.P. Uphill

78257   FISCHER, Henry George, Five Inscriptions of the Old Kingdom, *ZÄS* 105 (1978), 42-59, with 8 fig. and 1 pl.

1. Sportive allusions to personal names.
2. The request of a wife to her husband: an unusual expression of asseveration.
3. An Overseer of Dwarfs (with Excursus).

4. Enigmatic epithets of a master butcher.
5. The reading zš iryw i'ḥ.
Addenda concerning 2, 3 and the Excursus are given by the author in ZÄS 107 (1980), 86-87. *M. Heerma van Voss*

78258 FISCHER, Henry G., Notes on Sticks and Staves in Ancient Egypt, *Metropolitan Museum Journal*, New York 13 (1978), 5-32, with 40 fig. and 9 ill.

The article is intended to be a supplement to Ali Hassan's study (our number 76343; see also Fischer's review, *JEA* 64 [1978], 158-162), giving a wealth of additional material. The following subjects are discussed: imyt-r staves (see also our number 77694); curved staves (type of Sign S 39 with variants); the O.K. procedure to straighten staves and the verb ḫnd, "to bend"; sceptre-like batons; forked staves; batons for leisure; sticks for policing; wooden staffs carved as imitations of reed staffs; some adaptations of the divine wȝs-staff and the royal mks; dummy staves composed of parts fitted together with pegs; the characteristic N.K. staff with a small curved projection at the top, called ʿwnt (perhaps "cherry-wood"); three N.K. staves in the MMA collections, two of them with inscriptions.

78259 FISCHER, Henry G., Quelques prétendues antiquités de l'Ancien Empire, *RdE* 30 (1978), 78-95, with 5 pl., 1 fig. and 1 ill.

Trois notes à propos de monuments dont l'auteur met en doute l'authenticité: Berlin 12547; Metropolitan Mus. Art 25.9; id. 1970.263; id. 26.7.1391 (provenant de la collection Carnarvon) et id. 58.107, 1 et 2. *Ph. Derchain*

78260 FITCHEN, John, Building Cheops' Pyramid, *Journal of the Society of Architectural Historians*, Philadelphia 37 (1978), 3-12, with 5 fig.

After having surveyed ancient Egyptian construction methods the author concentrates on the possibility of the rocker as a device employed for building the Great Pyramid. *L.Z.*

FORABOSCHI, Daniele, see our number 78045.

78261 FÓTI, L., Menes in Diodorus I. 89, *Oikumene*, Budapest 2 (1978), 113-126.

Rejecting the historicity of Menes, the author explains the story about him as related by Diodorus by arguing that the toponym Šdt, which seems to occur as the name of a place in the Faiyûm in the Archaic Period, was understood as "escaped", "saved". He then suggests that both the names Menes and Moiris developed during the XIIth Dynasty, being connected with Imeni and Amun; thus Imeni-Menes was associated with Amenemhat III-Moiris.

78262 FOUDA, Refaat, "What are the Americans Trying to Find in the Ground at Maskhuta?", *Newsletter ARCE* No. 105 (Summer 1978), 13-16.

Translation of an article for the general reader on Tell el-Maskhûta. *L.Z.*

FOUQUET, Alain, see our numbers 78823 and 78824.

78263 FRANDSEN, Paul John, A Fragmentary Letter of the Early Middle Kingdom, *JARCE* 15 (1978), 25-31, with 4 pl.

The letter (datable to the late XIth Dynasty on palaeographical grounds), preserved in the Klassisk Filologi Institut at Copenhagen (pap. Havn. Inv. No. Hierat. 1) perhaps came from Gebelein or thereabouts. The subject matter i.a. touches on stone transport.
Extensive note on *s3t* (*Wb.* III, 412,14); palaeographical tables added.
*J.F.Borghouts*

78264 FRANKFORT, Henri, Kingship and the Gods. A Study of Ancient Near Eastern Religion as the Integration of Society & Nature. With a New Preface by Samuel Noah Kramer, Chicago & London, The University of Chicago Press, [1978] (15 x 23 cm; XXV + 444 p., frontispiece, 52 ill. and fig. on 42 pl.) = An Oriental Institute Essay.   Pr. $7.95

Reprint of our number 462, with a preface to the present edition by Kramer (p. V-VIII) in which the contents are summarized.

78265 FREYDANK, Helmut, Walter F. REINEKE, Maria SCHETELICH, Thomas THILO, Der Alte Orient in Stichworten, Leipzig, Koehler & Amelang, 1978 (14.5 x 21.5 cm; 494 p., 4 maps [2 folding], numerous fig. including plans); rev. *BiOr* 37 (1980), 132-133 (M.J. Mulder).   Pr. M 25

This lexicon comprises the entire ancient East, from Egypt to China, and contains lemmata on names as well as on general concepts. In many of the latter the first part after some introductory words is devoted to Egypt. As an illustration we mention the lemmata under the letter R that deal with Egypt: Ramesseum, Ramessidenzeit, Ramose, Ramses, Ramsesstadt, Re, Rechmire, Recht(1), Rechtsprechung(1), Reichseinigung(1), Reichsheiligtümer (1), Rind (1), Rosette-Stein.
The lemmata are in some instances illustrated by drawings. No literature is mentioned since the book is more intended for the general public than scholars.

78266 FUHS, Hans F., Sehen und Schauen. Die Wurzel ḥzh im alten Orient und im Alten Testament. Ein Beitrag zum prophetischen Offenbarungsempfang, [Würzburg], Echter Verlag, [1978] (15.4 x 23.4 cm; XV + 378 p.) = Forschung zur Bibel, 32.

In this study of the root ḥzh used to indicate prophetic capacity the author also considers the Egyptian parallels: *ḥs3* ,"fierce (of face)", *ḥd*, "be white" and derivatives, and the loanword *ʿdd* as the possible hieroglyphic equivalent of the word *ḥzh/i*.
Compare our numbers 76217, 77277, and Cody, *JEA* 65 (1979), 99-106.   *L.Z.*

78267 FUNK, Wolf-Peter, Toward a Synchronic Morphology of Coptic, *in: The Future of Coptic Studies*. Edited by R. McL. Wilson, Leiden, E.J. Brill, 1978 (= Coptic Studies, 1), 104-124.

Stressing the importance of a synchronic systematic approach for the elucidation of the structure of Coptic, the diachronic method failing to tell about the language as a whole and leaving dialectology and phonology apart, the author demonstrates by way of some examples some points pertaining to inflectional or paradigmatic morphology, i.a. the relative converter ⲈⲦ- the analysis of word-formative patterns, and the active and passive meaning of Coptic verbs.
For other studies in the volume, see our number 78269. *L.Z.*

78268 FUNK, Wolf-Peter, Zur Syntax des koptischen Qualitativs. Fortsetzung. II. Die koptischen Präverbale und ihr Gebrauch beim Qualitativ, *ZÄS* 105 (1978), 94-114.

Fortsetzung unserer Nummer 77241.
Verfasser beschäftigt sich hier mit den Präverbalen und ihrem Gebrauch beim Qualitativ. Er bespricht ihre Funktion, Gesichtspunkte zu ihrer Definition und ihre Syntax. *M. Heerma van Voss*

FUNK, Wolf-Peter, see also our number 78397.

78269 *The Future of Coptic Studies*. Edited by R. McL. Wilson. Leiden, E.J.Brill, 1978 (15.5 x 24.5 cm; XII + 253 p.) = Coptic Studies, 1.

In the introduction the editor states that most of the main papers read at the First International Congress of Coptology, Cairo, December 1976, are included in this volume, except for those on Nag Hammadi (to be published elsewhere), those listed as to appear in a Sonderheft to *Enchoria* 8, 1978, and those on minor subjects, of the authors of which are given name and address. We mention: M. Krause, Die Disziplin Koptologie; J.M. Robinson, The Future of Papyrus Codicology; G. Mink, Allgemeine Sprachwissenschaft und Koptologie; W.-P. Funk, Toward a Synchronic Morphology of Coptic, which is separately abstracted in our number 78267; A.Y. Sidarus, Coptic Lexicography in the Middle Ages; T. Orlandi, The Future of Studies in Coptic Biblical and Ecclesiastical Literature; H. Quecke, Zukunftschancen bei der Erforschung der koptischen Liturgie; E. Lüddeckens, Die koptischen Inschriften des Koptischen Museums in Kairo; A. Guillaumont, Les fouilles françaises des Kellia, 1964-1969; R. Kasser, Fouilles Suisses aux Kellia; P. du Bourguet, Avenir de l'étude des tissus coptes; J. Gillespie, Coptic Chant.
The volume is concluded by indexes on museum collections etc., sites, persons, modern authors and general matters. *L.Z.*

78270 GALE, N.H. and S. STÓS-FERTNER, Lead Isotope Composition of Egyptian Artifacts, *MASCA Journal*, Philadelphia 1, [No. 1] (December 1978). 19-21, with 2 fig.

There is no evidence for ancient Egyptian silver coming from an internal source. Although lead was present as a raw material in Egypt, the Egyptians possibly went to Laurion to fetch the metals. *L.Z.*

78271  GALLERY, Leslie Mesnick, The Garden of Ancient Egypt, *in*: *Immortal Egypt*, 43-49, with 9 ill., 3 plans and 27 fig. on 28 pl.

After remarks about the setting of Egyptian monuments in the landscape and the architectural elements whose form is derived from plants the author deals with Egyptian gardens on account of their representations in tombs. The plants there depicted are mentioned. There is also a description of the garden laid out in front of Deir el-Bahri. Some remarks on Egyptian religion are slightly unusual.

78272  GAMER-WALLERT, Ingrid, Ägyptische und ägyptisierende Funde von der Iberischen Halbinsel, Wiesbaden, Dr. Ludwig Reichert Verlag, 1978 (20 x 27.5 cm; 313 p., 120 fig., 3 maps, 71 pl.) = Beihefte zum Tübinger Atlas des Vorderen Orients. Reihe B (Geisteswissenschaften), Nr.21.

In the preface the author enumerates studies on aegyptiaca that have been found in various countries round the Mediterranean, stating that the Iberian Peninsula has remained in this respect one of the blank spaces on the map. She also briefly presents a survey of the aims and contents of the present work, explaining that she only deals with objects found on the peninsula, excluding recent acquisitions of Egyptian collections.
However, many egyptianizing objects are included since the line of division is still hard to draw, particularly since most objects date from the last mill. B.C. from which not sufficient is known about the types of objects.
The study is divided into four parts. The largest, part I (p. 19-219), discusses the relevant finds within their archaeological contexts, arranged into four geographical groups: the Phoenician settlements at the S. and S.W. coasts, the native hinterland, the oriental and native settlements along the E. coast, and the Greek emporium Ampurias. The objects are described and extensively discussed, with many drawings and copies of the texts, while an attempt is made to date them.
Part II presents a synopsis of the material in three chapters. First the various types of objects are discussed: statues (mostly bronze), alabaster and canopic vessels, shawabtis and scarabs, etc. Then the question of the time gap between the manufacture of the objects in Egypt and their burial in an Iberian tomb, and the origin and destination of them; whether they travelled as legally exported objects or came from robberies of temples and tombs. The last chapter contains critical remarks to the map in Ibis II (see our number 74440), which, although mainly concerned with Isiaca from the Roman Empire which are omitted from the present study, also shows a certain degree of overlapping with the material here discussed.
In part III indexes (253-255) and two maps; in part IV (261-313) the catalogue of the objects arranged after the collections in which they are preserved, with mention of technical data and bibliography. Many of them are represented by photographs on the plates.

GAMER-WALLERT, Ingrid, see also our number 78792.

78273  GARBINI, G., L'egiziano e le lingue semitiche, *in*: *Atti del Secondo Congresso*

*Internazionale di Linguistica Camito-Semitica.* Firenze, 16-19 aprile 1974. Raccolti da Pelio Fronzaroli, [Firenze], Istituto di linguistica e di lingue orientali. Università di Firenze, 1978 (= Quaderni di Semitistica, 5), 45-54.

After introductory remarks on the problems of the relationship of ancient Egyptian and the Semitic languages the author briefly discusses the Semitic share of ancient Egyptian, draws a comparison of various Semitic languages on account of 16 isoglosses, and makes short concluding remarks on the classification of ancient Egyptian. *L.Z.*

GASCOU, Jean, see our number 78705.

GAUDIN, Elisabeth, see our number 78831.

GAUTHIER, A., see our number 78810.

GEHRIG, Ulrich, see our number 78832.

78274  GEORGE, Beate, Hathor, Herrin der Sistren, *Medelhavsmuseet Bulletin*, Stockholm 13 (1978), 25-31, with 1 fig. and 7 ill.

Proceeding from a hymn to Hathor from the Dendera temple the author discusses types and function of sistra. In this connection she publishes four fragments of sistra, two of faience and two of wood, preserved in the Medelhavsmuseet.

78275  Geschenk des Nils. Aegyptische Kunstwerke aus Schweizer Besitz. Archäologische Sammlung der Universität Zürich—Historisches Museum Bern— Kunstmuseum Luzern—Musée d'art et d'histoire Genève. Eine Ausstellung des ägyptologischen Seminars der Universität Basel. In Zusammenarbeit mit dem Schweizerischen Bankverein, [Basel, 1978] (21 x 27 cm; 112 p., 1 map, 3 ill., 9 fig., 114 pl. [with 394 ill.], ill. on cover ); rev. *BiOr* 37 (1980), 44-45 (Robert S. Bianchi).

This is the catalogue of an exhibition of aegyptiaca from several public and private Swiss collections, held in the Egyptological Institute at Basel. The catalogue is edited by Hermann Schlögl and prefaced by Erik Hornung. The exhibition comprises 394 objects of the most varied kinds and from all periods of the Egyptian history (until the beginning of the Roman Period).
After an introduction by the editor called "Von der bleibenden Wirkung Ägyptens" (p. 9-13) the catalogue itself consists of five chapters, each devoted to a particular period (Pre- and Proto-Dynastic Periods = nos 1-105; O.K. and F.I.P. = nos 106-128; M.K. and S.I.P. = nos 129-155; N.K. and T.I.P. = nos 156-279; Late and Post-Dynastic Periods = nos 280-394). The chapters and some particular sections, e. g. that on seals, amulets and scarabs of the N.K. and the T.I.P. (p. 73-82), begin with a general introduction.
All objects are carefully described, with important scientific remarks on style and representation, etc., while the descriptions are accompanied by technical data (museum number, material, measurements and date) and full bibliographical references. Some descriptions are signed with the initials of one of the

eight collaborators, those not signed being from the hand of the editor. All objects are represented by at least one and in some cases by several photographs on the plates.
Several of the pieces here studied are of outstanding quality and importance; many have been published previously, but a few appear here for the first time. A chronological table (with some royal names in hieroglyphs within cartouches) on p. 104-107, a glossary on p. 118-110.
There has also appeared a French edition entitled: Le don du Nil. Art égyptien dans les collections suisses. Archäologische Sammlung der Universität Zürich, Historisches Museum Bern, Kunstmuseum Luzern, Musée d' Art et d'Histoire Genève. Une exposition du Séminaire d'Égyptologie de l'Université de Bâle, Société de Banque Suisse, 1978.

78276 GESSLER-LÖHR, Beatrix, Hans Wolfgang Müller. Verzeichnis seiner Schriften 1933-1977, zusammengestellt, *SAK* 6 (1978), IX-XVI.

Bibliography of Hans Wolfgang Müller, consisting of 86 numbers. Added a list of publications of his pupils which appeared under his guidance.

78277 GEUS, Fr., Fouilles à Sai, in: *Études nubiennes*, 97-105, with 5 fig., and 11 ill. on 5 pl.

Es wurde an mehreren bedeutsamen Stellen gegraben: in der pharaonischen Stadt, der grossen Nekropole des Neuen Reiches, dem Tumulus-Friedhof beim Fort Adu und der Kerma-Nekropole. Im Stadtbereich wurde ein sehr schöner Kopf aus Serpentin einer Königin des Neuen Reiches gefunden. Auf dem grossen Friedhof des Neuen Reiches waren einige Gräber bis zu 8 m tief angelegt; von den Oberbauten ist nichts mehr vorhanden. Das in ihnen gefundene Material ist zum Teil abgebildet. Der Friedhof im Südosten des Forts gehört in die X-Periode. Die Ausgrabungen auf dem Kerma-Friedhof erweitern die Kenntnisse über diese Kultur: es können vier Perioden unterschieden werden, gekennzeichnet durch die Form der Gräber, die Beigaben und die Bestattungssitten.   *Inge Hofmann*

78278 GEUS, Francis, Rapport annuel d'activité 1976-1977. Sudan Antiquities Service, French Archaeological Research Unit, Khartoum, 1978 (20 x 26.5 cm; 44p., 57 fig., 1 map).

Bericht über die Forschungsarbeit im Jahre 1976-1977: die Ausgrabungen in el-Kadada wurden fortgeführt; die Niederlassung mit den Gräbern stammt aus neolithischer Zeit, liegt jedoch später als die neolithische Phase von Shaheinab und scheint zeitgleich oder wenig früher als die A-Kultur in Unternubien zu sein. Besonders zu beachten ist eine weibliche steatopyge Statuette mit Tatauierungsmerkmalen. Die meroitischen Gräber gehen bis in die Napata-Zeit zurück, reichen aber bis ins 3. nachchristliche Jahrhundert. Sie sind die ersten bekannten meroitischen Gräber, die im Herzen des meroitischen Reiches ausserhalb der Reichweite der Stadt Meroe gefunden wurden.
In der Umgebung von el-Kadada wurden in Hillat Hasaballa ein meroitischer Friedhof, bei Qerqur und Sara el-Suqur neolithische Siedlungen und zwischen el-Kadada und Qerqur zahlreiche Tumuli gefunden, die möglicherweise aus der

nachmeroitischen Zeit stammen. Im Khartum-Gebiet wurden bei Gebel Aulia Steinäxte und bei Baqeir el-Quddami neolithische Überreste entdeckt.
*Inge Hofmann*

GIJSELINGS, G., see our number 78811.

78279 GILBERT, Pierre, Le petit temple du Clitumne et la colonne-palmier de Tutankhamon, *Bulletin de la Classe des Beaux-Arts. Académie Royale de Belgique*, Bruxelles, 5e série, 60 (1978), 116-127, with 14 ill.

Within the context of a study of a Roman temple the author pays attention to palm column decoration, referring i.a. to a pen case from Tutankhamun's tomb in the shape of a palm tree column and to the palm tree in Egypt as a symbol of resurrection.

GILLESPIE, J., see our number 78269.

78280 GILLINGS, R.J., Response to "Some Comments on R.J. Gillings' Analysis of the 2/n Table in the Rhind Papyrus, *Historia Mathematica*, New York and London 5, No. 2 (May 1978), 221-227.

A reply to our number 77117.

78281 GILULA, Mordechai, *Hirtengeschichte* 17-22 = *CT* VII 36 m-r, *GM* Heft 29 (1978), 21-22.

Die Hirtengeschichte enthält einen "Wasser-Spruch", der wohl gegen Krokodile verwendet wurde, wenn die Hirten den Fluss durchqueren mussten. Dieser Spruch wurde nun unter den Sargtexten C.T.VII 36 m-r (Spruch 836) gefunden, wo er sich als Spruch innerhalb eines Spruches findet. Es handelt sich um den ersten Beleg dafür, dass ein Spruch in dieser und der jenseitigen Welt benutzt wurde.
*Inge Hofmann*

78282 GILULA, M., Peasant B 141-145, *JEA* 64 (1978), 129-130.

The writer disagrees with the usually accepted translation of 'waste lands' for this passage and prefers 'and builds the destroyed mounds', citing the Coffin Texts in support of the reading.
*E.P. Uphill*

78283 GILULA, Mordechai, *Pyr.* 604 c-d and *Westcar* 7/17-19, *JEA* 64 (1978), 45-51.

The writer differs from Faulkner and Sethe on the meaning of $ḥr$ in this passage, rejecting the idea that it is a preposition and favouring that of a particle or better an independent statement $ḥr$ + noun in extra-position + negatived subjectless nominal sentence.
*E.P. Uphill*

78284 GITTON, Michel, Variation sur le thème des titulatures de reines, *BIFAO* 78 (1978), 389-403.

After dealing with the formulae $rt-p^ct$, $wrt\ ḥst$, $wrt\ ḥts$, that introduce the epithets of queens and princesses, the author discusses five titularies, those of Hatshepsut before she seized power; Ankhesenamon, wife of Tutankhamon; Satre, mother of Sethi I; Nefertari, wife of Ramses II; Amenirdis the Elder. They show a wide variety of details, but also bear common traits. There is a parallel between the queens and the Divine Consorts; in both instances there is a theogamy, though the first is political, the other liturgical; but there is also a clear distinction due to the connection with the king or with Amon.

78285   GIVEON, Raphael, Corrected Drawings of the Sahure' and Sesostris I Inscriptions from the Wadi Kharig, *BASOR* No. 232 (Fall 1978), 76, with 2 fig.

A correction to the drawings published in our number 77268.
Cfr also our number 78236.                                                                                    L.Z.

78286   GIVEON, Raphaël, Fouilles et travaux de l'Université de Tel-Aviv. Découvertes égyptiennes récentes, *BSFE* No. 81 (Mars 1978), 6-17, with 25 ill. on 6 pl.

Lachish et Apheq constituent les principaux chantiers de fouilles de l'Université; un autre s'ouvre, assez prometteur, à Tell Michal. Le petit site d'En Besor a produit des empreintes de cylindres et, au niveau III, quantité de poteries (fin de la Ire dynastie) qui témoigneraient d'un habitat égyptien. A Lachish, les scarabées hyksos portent des entrelacs, spirales et sujets floraux, ou de multiples hiéroglyphes, notamment l'inhabituel *akhet*. Des empreintes du Bronze Moyen II indiqueraient une exportation régulière vers l'Égypte. Sur une feuille d'or du Bronze Récent apparaît, debout sur un cheval caparaçonné, une déesse nue coiffée de l'*atef* et tenant un lotus dans chaque main. Ce motif marquerait la transition entre les aspects cananéen et égyptien d'Astarté. Pharaon chasseur de lion décore un sceau du Nouvel Empire. Une statuette patèque (Age du Fer) porte la mention de Sekhmet. Apheq, riche en textes, livre des empreintes et des scarabées significatifs. L'auteur compte republier à part la plaque aux noms de Ramsès II et d'Isis, témoin d'une probable fondation de temple en Canaan, ainsi que la bague en faïence bleue à profession de foi amonienne.                                                                              *J. Custers*

78287   GIVEON, Raphael, The Impact of Egypt on Canaan. Iconographical and Related Studies, Freiburg Schweiz, Universitätsverlag/Göttingen, Vandenhoeck & Ruprecht, 1978 (15.6 x 23.6 cm; 132 p., 3 plans, and 70 fig. and ill. on 30 pl.); rev. *BiOr* 37 (1980), 324-325 (Manfred Görg); *CdE* LIII, No. 106 (1978), 272-274 (K.A. Kitchen); *JNES* 39 (1980), 167-168 (Siegfried H. Horn); *Orientalia* 49 (1980), 422-423 (P. Vernus); *Palestine Exploration Quarterly* 111 (1979), 67-68 (K.A. Kitchen); *Welt des Orients* 11 (1981), 150-151 (Jürgen Ebach).
Pr. Sw.Fr. 33

Under this title are collected articles by Giveon, mostly previously published in English and Hebrew, which are now translated into English, and all dealing with contacts between Egypt and Canaan. Of the articles published for the first time the introduction (p. 9-14) deals with a general setting of the contacts between Canaan and Egypt; "Ancient Egyptian Mining Centres in South Sinai" (51-60) with the Wâdi Maghârah, the Wâdi Kharig and Serabît el-Khâdim through history, but also new discoveries are mentioned: Hathor as a cow, prisoner scenes,

the stela of Sennufer (Tuthmosis III), the inscription of two chief charioteers, probably two sons of Ramses II or III, a purification scene and an inscription of Tuthmosis IV; "Pharaoh Killing Oryx and Rhinoceros" (81-84) with two scarabs found in Canaan, depicting pharaoh slaying an oryx, resp. a rhinoceros, both Sethian animals; and "A Cylinder-Seal from Tell Zaphit" (97-98) with a seal in Syrian style, depicting not only Seth, but also his hieroglyphic epithet. The chapter "Determinatives in the Hieroglyphic Writing of Canaanite Names" is based on our number 74229, but is now greatly changed and enlarged.
The following chapters appeared first in Hebrew and were translated for this volume into English: "An Egyptian Statuette from the Region of Ayn Hashophet", see our number 63185; "The Samarian Ivories" in: *Shomron. A Collection of Source Material and Essays*, Tel Aviv, 1971 (not included in the AEB); "Ivories from Nimrud and Palestine", *Bulletin of the Israel Exploration Society* 22 (1958), 55-61 (not in the AEB); "Lady of the Turquoise", see our number 75265; "Hathor as Goddess of Music in Sinai", see our number 72256; "The Scarabs from Ginnosar", see our number 74233; "A Plaque from Tell Nagila", *Teva Waaretz* 3 (1959), 137, 140 (not in the AEB); and an "Ancient Mondscheinsonate", *Tazlil* 9 (1976) (not in the AEB).
The following papers were originally published in English: "Egyptian Temples in Canaan", our number 72254; "King or God on the Sarcophagus of Ahiram", *Israel Exploration Journal* 9 (1959), 57-59; "Royal Seals from the XIIth Dynasty from Western Asia", our number 67218; "Ptah and Astarte on a Seal from Accho", our number 67217; "Egyptian Seals in the Maritime Museum, Haifa", our number 68230; "A Monogram Scarab from Tel Masos", our number 74232; "Two New Hebrew Seals and their Iconographic Background", *Palestine Exploration Quarterly* 93 (1961), 38-42 (not in AEB); and "Seals and Seal-Impressions of the XXVth Egyptian Dynasty in Western Asia", see our number 76288. The book ends with a list of sources, and indexes, a general one as well as one on Biblical passages and Egyptian words.         L.Z.

78288  GIVEON, Raphael, A Long-Lost Inscription of Thutmosis IV (Explorations at Serâbît el-Khadîm - 1977), *Tel Aviv*, Tel Aviv 5 (1978), 170-174, with 1 fig., 1 map and 1 pl.

The author publishes the Sinai Inscription No. 60, of which the exact position was as yet not located. It is a royal inscription from year 7 of Tuthmosis IV dedicated to the princess Wadjet, with an additional private text underneath it. Compare our number 78071.          L.Z.

78289  GIVEON, Raphael, The XIIIth Dynasty in Asia, *RdE* 30 (1978), 163-167, with 6 fig. and 6 ill.

Inventaire des objets (scarabées et sceaux) mentionnant des souverains de la XIIIe dynastie découverts en Palestine.          Ph. Derchain

78290  GIVEON, Raphael, Two Unique Egyptian Inscriptions from Tel Aphek, *Tel Aviv*, Tel Aviv 5 (1978), 188-191, with 3 ill. on a pl.

The author publishes a foundation deposit tablet which was possibly destined for an Egyptian temple for Isis there in the Ramesside Period, and a finger-ring with a praise of Amon. *L.Z.*

78291 Glass at the Fitzwilliam Museum, Cambridge, Cambridge University Press, [1978] (19 x 24.8 cm; 127 p., frontispiece, 212 ill. [2 on covers]).

After some introductory words on Egyptian glass the catalogue of the Egyptian objects is presented, arranged after periods and types (p. 12-18; nos 3-30). The descriptions and data are very short; many objects are illustrated. *L.Z.*

78292 GODLEWSKI, W., Some Problems Connected with Nubian Baptisteries, *in*: *Études nubiennes*, 107-117, with 2 fig.

Es werden einige Probleme bezüglich von Taufkapellen und Taufbecken aufgeworfen. Baptisterien innerhalb von Kirchen finden sich zumeist in Gebieten, die der Jurisdiktion des alexandrinischen Patriarchats unterstanden. Die Taufkapellen sind entweder viereckig oder rechteckig; an Taufbecken werden 7 Typen unterschieden. *Inge Hofmann*

78293 GOEDICKE, Hans, Another Remark about the Byblos Cylinder Seal, *GM* Heft 29 (1978), 23-24.

Fortsetzung unserer Nummern 77527 und 76292.
Der Name des Besitzers des Siegelzylinders aus Byblos lautet *ilu-m-l-g* und gestattet eine Identifizierung mit Ilumilki (= Elimelech), der anscheinend in der syrisch-palästinensischen Region einheimisch war. *Inge Hofmann*

78294 GOEDICKE, Hans, The Waning of the Ramessides, *JSSEA* 8 (1977-1978), 74-80.

The author discusses the reasons for the decline of the N.K. at the end of the XXth Dynasty. Several alleged causes pass the review: the wars with the Sea Peoples and the Libyans, inflation and economic collapse, corrupt bureaucracy and a breakdown of the central administration, but no one appears to be decisive.
Goedicke suggests a long-time strife between the rank-and-file Theban priesthood and the kings supported by their high-priests, of which the reign of Amenmesse, the assassination of Ramses III and the temporary ousting of high-priest Amenhotep II could be facets. The definite break came with the appearance of Hrihor leading to the autonomy of the Thebais. But actually the role of pharaoh as sovereign of the Levant was already lost at the end of the XIXth Dynasty.

78295 GÖRG, Manfred, Beobachtungen zur Basis *ḤṬB*, *Biblische Notizen*, Bamberg Heft 5 (1978), 7-11, with 1 fig.

Discussing the Semitic root *ḥṭb*, the author draws attention to the possible connections with the Egyptian words *mḥtbt* (Urk. IV 38, 15; 39, 3; 40, 16; 41,1) and *mḫt* (P. An. I 26,7; IV 26, 12) which both probably bear the connotation of "adorning". *L.Z.*

78296   GÖRG, Manfred, Die Funktion der Serafen bei Jesaja, *Biblische Notizen*, Bamberg Heft 5 (1978), 28-39.

Discussing the O.T. *śrpym*, "serafim", the author mentions the M. Eg. word *sfr*, "a winged desert animal, griffon", spelt *sfrr* and *srrf* in the Graeco-Roman Period, which last metathesis may have been caused by association with *srf*, "heat, fever, burn". Next the connections of the *srp* conceived in the O.T. as a winged snake, probably a cobra, with the Egyptian winged sun disk and the uraeus are investigated. L.Z.

78297   GÖRG, Manfred, Machtrag zu כִּפְרֵת, *Biblische Notizen*, Bamberg Heft 5 (1978), 12.

Addition to our number 77285.

78298   GÖRG, Manfred, Namenstudien I: Frühe Moabitische Ortsnamen, *Biblische Notizen*, Bamberg Heft 7 (1978), 7-14, with 2 ill. and fig.

Discussion of Moabite geographical names; mainly *bwtrt* (cfr our number 76294). L.Z.

78299   GÖRG, Manfred, Namenstudien II: Syrisch-Mesopotamische Toponyme, *Biblische Notizen*, Bamberg Heft 7 (1978), 15-21, with 2 ill. and 2 fig.

The author discusses some fragmentary Asiatic geographical names on a list found in the vicinity of the Hatshepsut obelisk at Karnak. L.Z.

78300   GÖRG, Manfred, *qmḥ* und *qm* in den Arad Ostraka, *Biblische Notizen*, Bamberg Heft 6 (1978), 7-11.

When dealing with the word *qmḥ* and *qm* in the ostraca from Tel Arad the author draws attention to the Egyptian words *ḳmḥ* and *ḳmȝ* occurring as a combination in the Egyptian offering lists as words for bread or the preparation thereof. L.Z.

78301   GÖRG, Manfred, Eine Variante von Mitanni, *GM* Heft 29 (1978), 25-26.

Es handelt sich um die Schreibungen der jeweils ersten Listennamen auf der Königsstatue Kairo Mus. CG 42192, die zuletzt von Giveon behandelt wurden (vgl. unsere Nr. 77269). Während die Schreibung des afrikanischen Namens eine Verschreibung ist, wobei eine Verlesung aus einer hieratischen Vorlage glaubhaft gemacht werden kann, bietet das asiatische Toponym ein Problem, da bei der Fehlschreibung für Mitanni die Endung (*n*)*ni* zu fehlen scheint. Doch findet sich auch in keilschriftlichen Schreibungen die Kurzform *mi-it-ta* bzw. *me-ta*. Die hieroglyphische Schreibung veranlasst die vorsichtige Frage, ob Mitanni sprachlich gesehen nichts anderes ist als das hurritische Gegenstück zum offenbar semitischen Naharina "Flussland". *Inge Hofmann*

78302   GÖRG, Manfred, Eine Weitere Geschenkbezeichnung in EA 14, *GM* Heft 27 (1978), 25-26.

Das hieroglyphische Äquivalent für die Schreibung *bu-a-ti* möchte Verfasser in der Nisbebildung zu *bj3jt* sehen; die Form würde zu den Nisben zu zählen sein, die "nach der Zugehörigkeit des Grundwortes zu ihnen bezeichnet sind". Bei dem Geschenk müsste es sich dann um einen Gegenstand handeln, für den ein Schmuckbesatz charakteristisch ist.
*Inge Hofmann*

78303 GÖRG, Manfred, Zur Bezeichnung *brjt* (pAnast. II 8,2), *GM* Heft 27 (1978), 23-24.

Verfasser legt dar, dass der in Pap.Anast. II 8,2 verwendete Begriff *brjt* eine Variante des seit dem A.R. bekannten *mrt* (Wb II 106) darstellen könnte. Damit entfiele eine Beschränkung des Ausdruckes *mrt* auf "Kriegsgefangene" im N.R. sowie die Ausschliesslichkeit der jedoch immer noch vertretbaren Annahme, es handle sich um ein semitisches Fremdwort. Möglich wäre eine "semantische Überlappung" eines einheimischen und eines fremden Wortes mit lautlicher Affinität.
*Inge Hofmann*

78304 GÖRG, Manfred, Zur Westpolitik der babylonischen Kassiten, *Ugarit-Forschungen*, Kevelaer/Neukirchen-Vluyn 10 (1978), 79-82.

On account of the twofold occurrence of the toponym Dur-Kurigalzu before Babylon on geographical lists from the time of Amenophis III the author attempts to evaluate the political significance of its possible promotion to capital.
*L.Z.*

78305 Götter. Pharaonen, [München, Ausstellungsleitung Haus der Kunst München E.V. 1978] (20.8 x 22.7 cm; 326 p., 2 maps, 212 ill. [46 in colour], colour frontispiece, 2 ill. on endpapers, colour ill. on cover).

This is the catalogue of an exhibition in Munich which also went to Essen, Rotterdam and Hildesheim and comprised 175 objects from the museums of Cairo and Alexandria, belonging to the Pharaonic and Graeco-Roman Periods, but not to Coptic art. The catalogue has been composed by Dietrich Wildung and Günter Grimm.
After a short introduction to religion and art of the two periods and a chronological survey the catalogue proper presents a description of each single object indicating its artistic and historical importance. Technical data such as museum number, material, measurements, provenance and bibliographical references are added. Moreover, of each item there is at least one photograph, generally of outstanding quality.
The choice of objects covers the entire field of Egyptian and Hellenistic art: statuary, reliefs, vessels, drawings, jewellery, coins, lamps, etc. Most objects are well known, a few seldom published. Among these we mention a F.I.P. stela from the tomb of Keti (no. 13), the sarcophagus of a cat from the time of Amenophis III (no. 28), and a statue of Amon from the Karnak cachette, dating from the late XVIIIth Dynasty (no. 49). The latter has not been published before.

78306  GÖTTLICHER, Arvid, Materialien für ein Corpus der Schiffsmodelle im Altertum, Mainz, Verlag Philipp von Zabern, [1978] (22.6 x 32 cm; [V +] 128 p., 56 pl.).　　　　　　　　　　　　　　　　　　　　　Pr. DM 115

In the introduction the author discusses the various aspects of ancient ship models, such as their technical evaluation, their function in the funerary cult and magic, as votive objects, in profane use, as works of art. He devotes also attention to references to ship models in literature. After explanatory words on the catalogue he presents the catalogue itself, giving a short description, museum inventory numbers, and a bibliography if present. Egypt occupies the numbers 270-303, most of which are represented by a photograph on the plates. Nos 304-305 are from Kerma, Sudan.　　　　　　　　　　L.Z.

78307  GOHARY, S.G., Minor Ramesside Works at Memphis, *Oriens Antiquus* 17 (1978), 193-196, with 1 pl.

Publication of two pillar-bases from a building of Merenptah and a statue of Ramses IV, now both in the vicinity of the colossus of Ramses II at Memphis. The hieroglyphic texts are provided with a translation and a short commentary.
　　　　　　　　　　　　　　　　　　　　　　　　　　　　　　L.Z.

78308  GOLOVINA, V.A., Аренда типа ḳdb в Египте эпохи Среднего Царства. Вестник Московского Университета. Серия 8: История, Москва No. 1/1978, 65-74.

"The Type of ḳdb Rent in Egypt in the Middle Kingdom Period."
The author particularly discusses the term ḳdb in the Hekanakhte Papers. Although generally meaning "lease", the author points out that Hekanakhte rented the land in the spring and that the rent was calculated after the area, not in accordance with the quantity of the harvest, as usually in Egypt (share-cropping). She concludes that ḳdb was a particular type of lease. By leasing the land before the inundation and receiving the sum immediately the leaser restricted his risks in this period of famines, whereas the lessee Hekanakhte acted as a speculator. This presents a capitalistic picture of the M.K. economy.

GOMAÀ, Farouk, see our number 78791.

78309  GOPHNA, Ram, 'En-Besor. An Egyptian First Dynasty Staging Post, *Expedition*, Philadelphia, Penn. 20, No. 4 (Summer 1978), 5-7, with 6 ill., 1 plan and 1 fig.

Stratum III of 'En Besor represents an Egyptian settlement from the Ist Dynasty near the 'En Besor springs.　　　　　　　　　　　　　　　L.Z.

78310  GOTTSCHALK, Herbert, Sonnengötter und Vampire, Berlin, Safari-Verlag, [1978] (17 x 34 cm; 376 p., 9 maps, 168 ill.) = Bebildertes Lexikon der Mythologie; II: Aussereuropa.

The first chapter of this volume (p. 17-50) is devoted to ancient Egypt, presenting a general introduction and some lemmata. In the introduction a number of subjects are briefly mentioned, e.g. ancient tourism, cults, hieroglyphs, land-people-history, while particular sections present summaries of the doctrines of Heliopolis, Memphis, Hermopolis, Thebes, other places, and the Osiris myth. The lemmata i.a. deal with Osiris and Isis, the judgement of the dead, the true name and the eye of Osiris, Thoth and Nun, etc. Vampires are absent in this chapter.

78311 GOYON, Georges, Les ranges d' assises de la grande pyramide, *BIFAO* 78 (1978), 405-413, with 2 fig. and 1 table.

The 201 remaining layers of the great pyramid are not all of the same height. Measuring them all (total height 138.745 m), the author found that roughly their height diminishes from the foot to the top, but not regularly. This is explained by the use of various layers of limestone in the quarry, of different thickness. The author describes how he conceives to have been the process in the quarry.

78312 GOYON, Jean-Claude, La fête de Sokaris à Edfou à la lumière d'un texte liturgique remontant au Nouvel Empire, *BIFAO* 78 (1978), 415-438, with 1 plan.

The author first studies a text from the Forecourt of the Edfu temple accompanying an offering scene before Osiris-Sokaris. He lists five earlier versions (Pap. Berlin 58030, 7, 1-2; Pap. Ch. Beatty IX, 4, 4-6; Pap. BM 10554 = Pap. Greenfield, where it is an appendix to B.D. chapter 142; Serapeum stela 34; Pap. BM 10209), presenting them in hieroglyphs with translation. He then gives a translation of the Edfu text, which is connected with the ceremony of the early morning procession of Sokaris on the 26th Khoiak. On account of the scenes and their captions in the Forecourt of Edfu the author presents his reconstruction of the route and the nine episodes of the procession.

78313 GOYON, Jean-Claude, *Hededyt*: Isis-Scorpion et Isis au Scorpion. En marge du papyrus de Brooklyn 47.218.50 - III, *BIFAO* 78 (1978), 439-458, 5 fig.

Sequel to our number 74257.
Proceeding from the epithet of Isis *Ḥddyt*, that is, "Scorpion", in the text called Confirmation du Pouvoir (Pap. Brooklyn Mus. 47.218.50; cfr our number 72269), IX, 7, the author studies the relations between Isis and the scorpion. In several scenes, particularly from Nubia, Isis occurs with a scorpion on her head. Actually one has to distinguish between two figures, an Upper-Egyptian Isis-*Ḥddyt* and a Lower-Egyptian Isis -*Wḥ ͨt* from Tell Tebilla (Onouphis). The author discusses some references to the latter, but particularly those to the former. She had her own cult, i.a. in the Apollonite nome and in Edfu, and protects the Sun against his enemies. The word *ḥddyt* may be derived from *ḥḏ* "white". In the late popular belief several figures of Isis, either with a scorpion on her head or even as a scorpion with a female head, may represent Isis-Scorpion, not Selkis.

GRAEFE, Erhart, see our number 78090.

78314   GRAHAM, Daniel, The Mummy at Glasgow Kelvingrove Art Galleries and Museum, *Radiography*, London 43 (1977), 218-222, with 9 ill.

Short report on the investigation of a mummy, possibly from the Ptolemaic Period, in the Kelvingrove Museum, Glasgow.                                                    L.Z.

78315   GRATIEN, Brigitte, Les cultures Kerma. Essai de classification, [Villeneuve-d'Ascq], Publications de l'Université de Lille III, [1978] (16 x 34 cm; 361 p., 5 maps, 5 plans, 63 ill. and fig., 14 tables); rev. *BiOr* 37 (1980), 326-329 (David O'Connor).

Reisner's thesis in his publication of the excavations at Kerma (1923) that the population of that town consisted of Egyptian artisans protected by an Egyptian garrison and ruled by an Egyptian governor has since been disputed by several scholars (see, e.g., our number 77007, not yet known to Mme Gratien). In this book the author proves the Kerma culture to be genuinely Nubian, and she studies its development and extension.
In the first part (p. 17-130) the material is presented. All sites with Kerma remains, mostly tombs, are briefly discussed, from the S. (4th cataract) to the N., the last three sites in Egypt itself (Qurna, Abâdîya and Abydos). The longest sections are devoted to the settlements and necropoleis of Sai and Kerma itself, probably the capital of the realm. Each section is preceded by bibliographical notes and accompanied by plans, photographs and drawings.
Part 2 (131-270) deals with the development of the Kerma culture and its characteristics. First each of its stages is studied: K.A. (=ancient), K.M. (= middle), K.C. (=classical) and K.R. (= recent), the period of egyptianization during the XVIIIth Dynasty. There are sections on settlements, tombs and their contents and dates. A summary on p. 222-223.
The next chapter discusses the characteristics of the civilization, their permanence and development, with particular attention to the ware and its decoration, but also sections on weapons and tools, dress, agriculture and cattle breeding (very important), social and political structures, etc.
In part 3 (271-331) three points are discussed: the limits of the Kerma territory during the four periods and its population; the contacts with Egypt, including its Egyptian name (probably "Kush"); the relations between Kerma and the other Nubian civilizations: the A-group (very close to K.A.), the C-group (contemporaneous with and related to K.M., but different from it), and the Pan-Graves People (closer to the C-group, but possibly from the E. desert). Conclusions on p. 319-323.
Extensive bibliography on p. 333-348; index p. 349-353.

78316   GREEN, Alberto R., Solomon and Siamun: A Synchronism between Early Dynastic Israel and the Twenty-First Dynasty of Egypt, *Journal of Biblical Literature*, Missoula 97 (1978), 353-367.

The author argues that the Pharaoh mentioned I Kings 9:16, who had given the conquered city of Gezer to his daughter, the wife of Solomon, must be Siamun. First he rules out the possibility of Psusennes II or Sheshonq I, and then sets forth the primary reasons for his identification: Siamun is the only pharaoh identifiable with I Kings 11:14-22 and 9:16 and whose regnal period synchronizes closely with the important first third of Solomon's reign; a fragmentary relief in Tanis, on which a crescentic-ax or a shield held by Siamun, must be associated with Palestine, the only region where Siamun could have campaigned. L.Z.

78317 GREENHALGH, M., European Interest in the Non-European: the Sixteenth Century and Pre-Columbian Art and Architecture, in: *Art in Society. Studies in Style, Culture and Aesthetics*. Edited by Michael Greenhalgh and Vincent Megaw, [London], Duckworth, [1978], 89-103, with 5 ill.

The author discusses Athanasius Kircher, who argued in his Oedipus Aegyptiacus the Mexican pyramidal form to be the link between the Old and New Worlds.
L.Z.

78318 GRENIER, Jean-Claude, L'Anubis cavalier du Musée du Louvre, in: *Hommages Vermaseren*, 405-408, with 1 pl.

Publication of a small bronze figure from the Roman Period (Louvre E 17410) representing Anubis, clad as imperator and riding a horse. It symbolizes victory over death.

78319 GRENIER, Jean-Claude, L' autel funéraire isiaque de Fabia Stratonice, Leiden, E.J. Brill, 1978 (15.6 x 24.5 cm; XIII + 34 p., frontispiece, 16 pl. ) = Édition spéciale des Études préliminaires aux réligions orientales dans l'empire romain à l'occasion du 60-ième anniversaire de Maarten J. Vermaseren publiée par Margreet B. de Boer et T.A. Edridge, 71; rev. *CdE* LIII, No.106 (1978), 391-392 (J. Gwyn Griffiths). Pr. fl. 46

The book deals with the funerary altar of Fabia Stratonice, at present in the Badisches Landesmuseum at Karlsruhe (Inv. No. 67/134), which is carefully described and commented upon.
Although it is not known whether the owner was a priestess of Isis, the representations of a sistrum and a situla next to that of the woman are indicative of her having taken part in the Isis ceremonies and processions. The sides of the altar show on the right the figure of Anubis, in Alexandrian religion functioning as guide and intermediary instead of as god of mummification, and on the left a figure, represented in the Egyptian way, who may be Antinoos, here not chosen for political reasons (the altar probably dates from the time of Hadrian), but for religious reasons, since he, unlike Osiris, was not murdered, dismembered or even mummified. L.Z.

78320 [GRIFFITHS, J. Gwyn], Editorial Foreword, *JEA* 64 (1978), 1-4.

The editorial foreword contains the following short reports:
H.S. Smith, North Saqqara (1977-8); Geoffrey T. Martin, The Memphite Tomb of Ḥoremḥeb; Robert Anderson, Qasr Ibrîm; W.V. Davies, Saqqâra Epigraphic Survey; Barry J. Kemp, El-'Amarna; R.A. Caminos, Gebel es-Silsilah. L.Z.

78321 GRIFFITHS, J. Gwyn, Isis in the Metamorphoses of Apuleius, in: *Aspects of Apuleius' Golden Ass*. Edited by B.L. Hijmans, Jr. and R. Th. van der Paardt,

Groningen, Bouma's Boekhuis, 1978, 141-166.

In this discussion of the theme of Isis and the Isis-cult in Apuleius' Metamorphoses, the author in some instances refers to Egyptian elements, e.g. the ritual of the Opening of the Mouth and P.T. 626d-627a. *L.Z.*

GRIMM, Günter, see our number 78305.

GROLL, Sarah Israelit, see our number 78162.

78322 GRUNERT, Stefan, Zum Eherecht im ptolemäischen Ägypten nach den demotischen Papyri, *ZÄS* 105 (1978), 114-122.

Grunert erörtert Eheverträge mit der direkten, bzw. der indirekten Scheidungsklausel. Mit Rücksicht auf den Hauptunterschied zwischen diesen beiden untersucht er die "Frauensachen". Sie besitzen im persönlichen Eigentum der Frau einen Sonderstatus neben Frauengabe und Alimentationskapital und haben sich als Institution eigenständig entwickelt. *M. Heerma van Voss*

78323 GRZYBEK, Erhard, Pharao Caesar in einer demotischen Grabschrift aus Memphis, *Museum Helveticum*. Schweizerische Zeitschrift für klassische Altertumswissenschaft, Basel/Stuttgart 35 (1978), 149-158.

The author discusses the date in the Demotic inscription on the Serapeum stela Louvre 335 (year 5, II šm 23). This day is said to be the festival of Isis, otherwise the birthday of Pharaoh Caesar. Usually it is suggested that this is Caesarion, but that cannot be correct. Actually the birthday of Augustus is meant.

78324 GUIDOTTI, M. Christina, A proposito dei vasi con decorazione hathorica, *Egitto e Vicino Oriente* 1 (1978), 105-118, with 20 fig. and 1 pl. (= p. 118).

The author discusses vessels decorated with a Hathor face, which all seem to come from the Theban West Bank where the cult of the goddess was popular. Particularly in Deir el-Medîna, from where several of these vessels come. In some instances the Hathor face is connected with the Bes figure, or with representations of leopards and panthers. The author suggests that the vessels may have contained milk and were used for cultic purposes, also in the houses. Where they were made is uncertain.
At the end one example and a fragment of another are published, both from the Egyptian collection in Florence (Nos. 3365 and 3285).

GUILLAUMONT, Antoine, see our number 78269.

78325 GUILMOT, Max, The Initiatory Process in Ancient Egypt, San Jose, California, A Rosicrucian Egyptian Museum Publication, [1978] (15 x 23 cm; 28 p., 1 map, 1 fig., 9 ill., colour ill. on cover) = Rosicrucian Library, 35.

Summary of our number 77307, dealing with the phases of existence, the Osireion of Abydos and the initiations there, the "preparation for the Holy Night", and the illumination.

78326 GUILMOT, Max, Une stèle inédite de Neb-Imen, ZÄS 105 (1978), 160, with 1 ill.

La stèle publiée ici par l'auteur et se trouvant dans sa collections est originaire de Thèbes Ouest. Elle montre Amon, Maât et un prêtre de cette déesse, Neb-'Imen, faisant l' adoration. Calcaire, hauteur 24.5 cm, fin de la XIXe dynastie.
*M. Heerma van Voss*

78327 GUKSCH, Heike, Das Grab des Benja, gen. Paheqamen. Theben No. 343. Photographien von D. Johannes, Mainz am Rhein, Verlag Philipp von Zabern, [1978] (26.5 x 35.5 cm; 51 p., 3 plans, 42 fig., 26 pl., 2 colour pl., colour frontispiece) = Deutsches Archäologisches Institut. Abteilung Kairo. Archäologische Veröffentlichungen, 7.

The publication of Theban tomb No. 343, of the foreigner Benia, called Pahekamen, begins by an introduction describing the site of the tomb and its present condition. Its occurrences in Egyptological literature are mentioned on p. 10.
Then a careful description is given of the elements of the tomb and their decoration, with the texts in facsimile and translation with notes. A separate section deals with the quickly sketched female figures, in red paint, that occur on some free spots of the walls. On account of stylistic arguments the author dates them between Tuthmosis IV and Amenophis IV, possibly to the time of Amenophis III. A section on finds from the tomb mentions only two funerary cones. Three possible occurrences of the owner's name outside the tomb are listed: on an ostracon from Deir- el-Bahri, in a letter (see Glanville, *JEA* 14 [1928], 297-302) and on a stela (Urk. IV, 1480, 13).
The third chapter is devoted to the conclusions: the date of the tomb (the reign of Tuthmosis III), the owner's names, his (foreign) parents, his titles (particularly *imy-r k3wt*), his close connections with the king, and some remarks to divinities mentioned in the tomb.
Then a list of the hieroglyphs is given, each one with indication of its colours. There is no index and only a brief bibliography. The plates represent the entire wall decoration in black-and-white photographs, a few details in colour photographs (by Dieter Johannes).

GULLENTOPS, F., see our number 78810.

78328 GUPTA, Tapan Kumar Das, Die alt-ägyptische Sammlung im Hamburgischen Museum für Völkerkunde, *Mitteilungen aus dem Museum für Völkerkunde, Hamburg* 8 (1978), 89-115, with 3 fig.

After introductions on the history of the Egyptian collection in the museum in Hamburg and on the publications of some of its pieces the author presents the inventory of the objects, with the exception of prehistoric artifacts and certain forgeries and imitations. The article is concluded by a bibliography to the objects in the collection, and a specimen of the stela of Kheruef (Inv. No. 13.37:1) with the transcription and annotations by Möller.          *L.Z.*

78329   GURALNICK, Eleanor, The Proportions of Kouroi, *AJA* 82 (1978), 461-472, with 7 fig.

Study of the proportions of kouroi with the help of the computer has shown that the kouroi which are most like the Egyptian second canon proportions date from the late seventh to late sixth centuries B.C. and originate from various workshops. Therefore the canonic principles must have been widely known, but were only followed by some sculptors.
Cfr our numbers 76323 and 77310.                                          *L.Z.*

78330   GUTBUB, Adolphe, Éléments ptolémaïques préfigurant le relief cultuel de Kom Ombo, *in: Das ptolemäische Ägypten*, 165-176, with 1 plan and 11 ill. (1 folding).

Discussing the question whether the development of the Egyptian religion shows a break between the Ptolemaic and Roman Periods because the Romans were not interested in the Egyptian religion, the author studies a relief in the Kôm Ombo temple. It is situated at the head of the temple, on the outer face of the 1st enclosure wall (cfr Porter-Moss VI, 197, No. 227) and dates from the reign of Trajanus. The author calls it a "relief cultuel" since it was an object of veneration, as, for example, the hymn in the lowest register demonstrates. The relief is extensively discussed, with various possible precursors. The conclusion is that it testifies to a new trend in the religion that originates from the reign of Trajanus.

78331   HAALAND, Randi, The Seasonal Interconnection between Zakiab and Kadero: Two Neolithic Sites in the Central Sudan, *Nyame Akuma*, Calgary No. 13 (1978), 31-35, with 1 fig.

Die Ausgrabungen der neolithischen Siedlung von Kadero zeigten, dass die Bewohner vor allem domestizierte Rinder und Sorghum besassen, dagegen fehlen Spuren, die auf das Betreiben von Fischerei hinweisen. Der Verfasser vermutet, dass die Bewohner von Kadero während der trockenen Jahreszeit dem zurücktretenden Nil folgten und sich in kleineren Fischerlagern niederliessen. Um diese Hypothese zu prüfen, wurde Zakiab, das an dem alten Flussufer lag, ausgegraben. Die Ausgrabungsergebnisse zeigten, dass Zakiab eine Art "Aussenposten" Kaderos für ein bis zwei Monate während der heissen Jahreszeit war. Für die jeweils nur kurzfristige Benutzung des Camps weist auch das Fehlen jeglicher Gräber der neolithischen Epoche hin (es wurden nur meroitische Gräber gefunden). Die Feldarbeiten sollen fortgeführt werden. *Inge Hofmann*

78332   HAARMANN, Ulrich, Die Sphinx. Synkretistische Volksreligiosität in spätmittelalterlichen islamischen Ägypten, *Saeculum*, München 29 (1978), 367-384.

The author discusses the image of ancient Egypt in the medieval Islamic world, in particular the themes and motifs relating to the Sphinx.                     *L.Z.*

78333 HABACHI, Labib, King Amenmesse and Viziers Amenmose and Kha'emtore: Their Monuments and Place in History, *MDAIK* 34 (1978), 57-67, with 5 fig. and 3 pl.

Proceeding from Helck's list of monuments of the vizier Amenmose (see Verwaltung = our number 58284, p. 459) and Černý's review of it (*BiOr* 19 [1962], 140-144) the author publishes three of these documents, as well as the relief block Or. Inst. Chicago 10816, in which the name Pra'emheb is superimposed upon that of vizier Kha'emtore. He then discusses the date of Amenmesse's reign, concluding that he preceded Sethi II who usurped some of his monuments. The viziers Amenmose and Kha'emtore belong to Amenmesse's reign.
In an addendum the author i.a. rejects Krauss' identification of Amenmesse with the viceroy Messuy (see our numbers 76467 and 77438).

78334 HABACHI, Labib, New Light on Objects of Unknown Provenance (II). A Group of Statues in Roemer-Pelizaeus Museum Hildesheim, *GM* Heft 27 (1978), 27-31, with 2 fig. on 1 pl.

Fortsetzung unserer Nummer 77313.
Es handelt sich um die Statuengruppe No. 1871, die aus einem Grab bei Theben kommt. Erhalten sind die Namen der Mutter (Renutet) und der Töchter (Takha und Tazeseret). Die Gruppe stammt aus dem Grab No. 50; sie repräsentiert Neferhotep und seine Familie, die während der Herrschaft des Haremheb lebte.
*Inge Hofmann*

78335 HABACHI, Labib, The Obelisks of Egypt, Skyscrapers of the Past. Edited by Charles C. van Siclen III, London-Toronto-Melbourne, J.M. Dent Ltd, [1978] (15 x 23.5 cm; XVI + 203 p., 51 ill. [2 on cover], 18 ill., 4 plans, 5 maps); rev. *Antiquaries Journal* 59 (1979), 132-133 (Peter A. Clayton); *Antiquity* 53 (1979), 74 (Paul Jordan); *BiOr* 36 (1979), 28-29 (Ulrich Luft); *CdE* LIV, No. 108 (1979), 267-268 (Agnes Rammant-Peeters); *JARCE* 15 (1978), 135-136 (David Lorton); *JSSEA* 8, No. 2 (1977-1978), 65-67 (Edmund S. Meltzer).
Pr. £ 5.95

In this book intended for the general public Labib Habachi relates in his usual lively way the story of the obelisks. The first chapter, meant as an introduction to the obelisk, deals with gods associated with them, the places where the major ones have been found, their inscriptions which commemorate victory or show a connection with the Sed-festival, and the orientation of the inscriptions. In the second chapter he describes the whole operation from the quarrying, the transport to the embankment, the voyage to the final erection, and includes remarks on polishing, decoration and the finishing with hieroglyphs. Especially the theories of Engelbach and Chevrier receive ample attention.
The following three chapters (3-5) are devoted, more or less in a historical order, to the obelisks of the O.K. and M.K., including the sun temples, to those of the XVIIIth Dynasty, mainly concentrated at Thebes, and to those

of the later periods up to the Graeco-Roman Period. In the chapters 3-4 much attention is paid to the inscriptions of the responsible officials, sometimes even to the observations of Arabic writers. The fifth chapter deals with a variety of towns, such as Piramesse, Heliopolis, Tanis, Luxor and Philae. In the sixth chapter are described in detail the vicissitudes of the thirteen obelisks of Rome and the one in Istanbul which were brought to Europe before recent times. The story of the three obelisks in Paris, London and New York is told in the last chapter.
At the end of the book the notes, chronological tables, suggestions for further reading and the index.
The original, American edition was published in 1977 by Charles Scribner's Sons at New York ($12.95). *L.Z.*

78336 HABACHI, Labib, The So-Called Hyksos Monuments Reconsidered. Apropos of the Discovery of a Dyad of Sphinxes, *SAK* 6 (1978), 79-92, with 4 pl. and 3 fig.

The author first presents a survey of the various theories about the date of the so-called Hyksos sphinxes of Tanis. In this connection he publishes the remaining sphinx of a dyad found by him in Tell Basta (Cairo JE 87082), much similar to the Tanis ones but smaller. He suggests that the "Hyksos sphinxes" too were originally carved as dyads, being split by Ramses II, and that they represent Sesostris III and his coregent Amenemhat III.

HAIKAL, Fayza M.H., see our number 78101.

78337 HAINSWORTH, Michael et Jean LECLANT, Introduction au Répertoire d'Épigraphie Méroitique (REM), = *MNL* No 19 (Juillet 1978), [VI] + 44 p.

Im vorliegenden Heft wird ein Führer zur Benutzung des Répertoire d'Epigraphie Méroitique (REM) gegeben: in 10 Kapiteln werden die Anordnung der einzelnen Dokumente, eine Einführung in die Registrierung der Texte, eine Einführung in den Index der topographischen Lokalisierung (mit einer Tabelle der verwendeten Abkürzungen), eine Einführung in den beschreibenden Korpus, eine Einführung in den bibliographischen Teil, ein Index der Fundorte der jeweiligen REM-Nummern, ein Index der meroitischen Texte nach dem Ort ihrer Aufbewahrung mit einem Überblick über die Dokumente, die sich noch *in situ* befinden, ein REM-Index der Toponyme, ein REM-Index der Himmelsrichtungen und ein REM-Index der Götternamen dargelegt. *Inge Hofmann*

78338 HAINSWORTH, M. et J. LECLANT, Le Point Actuel de Répertoire d'Épigraphie Méroïtique, *in*: *Études nubiennes*, 119-120.

Es wird ein Überblick über den Stand der Arbeiten am REM gegeben; vgl. unsere vorhergehende Nummer. *Inge Hofmann*

HAKEM, Ahmed M. Ali, see our number 78008.

78339 HALÉN, Harry, Handbook of Oriental Collections in Finland. Manuscripts, xylographs, inscriptions and Russian minority literature, [London and Malmö], Curzon Press, [1978] (15 x 22.3 cm; IV + 296 p.) = Scandinavian Institute of Asian Studies. Monograph Series, 31.

Part 1, section 10, nos. 395-460 (p. 110-118) is devoted to Egypt. The collection contains mostly Demotic and Coptic papyri and ostraca (almost all Demotic documents originate from the collection Wångstedt), but also funerary cones, some stelae, statuettes and shawabtis. The descriptions are very short.
L.Z.

78340 HAMILTON-PATERSON, James and Carol ANDREWS, Mummies. Death and Life in Ancient Egypt, London, Collins, in association with British Museum Publications Ltd., [1978] (15.5 x 24.2 cm; 224 p., 73 ill., 2 colour ill. on cover, frontispiece = time-table); rev. Sarapis 5, No. 2 (1980), 63-64 (Emily Teeter).
Pr. £5.95

After an introductory chapter with special attention to aspects of death in ancient Egypt, the authors deal with mummification, amply described in chapter 2; with funerary equipment, particularly shabtis, amulets and scarabs in chapter 3; with funeral and tomb, including religious texts and tomb scenes, and e.g. the contracts of Hapidjefa in chapter 4. The next three chapters are respectively devoted to tomb robbers (Hetepheres, the Tomb-Robberies Papyri), to Tutankhamon, Akhnaton and Amarna, as well as the royal tombs at Tanis, and to mummies and medicine, in which there is dealt with i.a. modern mummy investigations, dental attrition, the stature of the ancient Egyptians as to be drawn from mummies, but also with pyramidiotry.
Glossary of names and words, suggestions for further reading, and index at the end of the book.
There has also appeared a paperback edition: New York, Penguin Books, 1978.
L.Z.

78341 HANFMANN, George M.A. and David Gordon MITTEN, The Art of Classical Antiquity, *Apollo*, London 107, No. 195 (May 1978), 363-369, with 10 ill.

The collection of the Fogg Art Museum, Harvard, possesses some Egyptian pieces, among which an Amarna relief representing charioteers. L.Z.

78342 HANKE, Rainer, Amarna-Reliefs aus Hermopolis. Neue Veröffentlichungen und Studien, Hildesheim, Gerstenberg Verlag, 1978 (16.8 x 23.9 cm; X + 273 p., 61 pl. [= p. 213-273] with ill. and fig. [2 folding]) = Hildesheimer Ägyptologische Beiträge herausgegeben von Arne Eggebrecht, 2; rev. *BiOr* 37 (1980), 47-50 (William J. Murnane). Pr. DM 46

This study consists of three parts. Part I contains the publication of 52 Amarna reliefs from Hermopolis, at present in private collections, of which photographs

were found among the papers of Keimer in the German Institute in Cairo. They come in addition to those published by Roeder (see our number 69520, nos. PC 1-316). Each of them is described and discussed; photographs on pl. 1-23).
Part 2 deals with the reconstruction of the scenes to which the Hermopolis blocks belong. With Roeder the author argues that they came from el-Amarna, but they are probably from various buildings in the great Aton-temple. The building methods (normalized blocks, thickness of the walls) and the demolition of the original buildings are discussed. Then the author attempts to reconstruct the original walls and even some entire buildings on account of photographs taken by Karig, all under the same angle and from the same distance.
A summary of the results on p. 121-125. There follows a reconstruction of what the author calls "shrines" that stood in the first courts of the Gem-Aton. A summary on p. 130-132.
Part 3 is devoted to the changes in representations and inscriptions which were made during the Amarna Period, as well as with the conclusions to be drawn from them. They relate to Meritaton and Ankhesenpaaton and their daughters, and to the king himself. Hanke attempts to reconstruct the original texts (165-170), arguing that in at least seven of the texts the original name was that of Kiya, called wife of the king and mother of a royal daughter. In an excursus (171-174) he argues that her name also originally occurred on the coffin found in Theban tomb 55 (cfr our number 61223). The alterations in the figures also mostly relate to Kiya, particularly to her hairdress.
The author studies what is known about Kiya: her titles, her daughter, her rank (the same as that of Nefertiti ) and the date of the alterations. In the conclusion (196) he states that it is uncertain whether Kiya was the name of Nefertiti, or a second wife of the king; the latter looks less probable. As regards the reasons for the alterations, Hanke suggests that Akhenaton married both his daughters since he wanted a son, but they gave him only (grand)daughters. Then he made Meritaton heir to the throne and even reigning queen. It was she who wrote the letter to the Hittite king after Akhenaton's death, and afterwards married Smenkhkare, while she soon died.
A list of monuments used in the study on p. 205-211; and index of persons on p. 211-213.

78343   HANKE, Rainer, Bildhauerwerkstätten in Tell el-Amarna, *Mitteilungen der Deutschen Orient-Gesellschaft zu Berlin*, Berlin 110 (1978), 43-48, with 2 ill.

After posing the question whether the Amarna naturalistic plaster masks were only a realistic, individual point of departure for a more idealized head, the author draws attention to the plaster head Berlin Nr. 21350, generally called the portrait of an unknown, old person. This head with marked individual traits is compared with the head of Akhnaton bearing Inv. No. 21351. On account of certain correction lines in red ink on the former head, the author draws attention to the possibility that it might be a naturalistic representation of Akhnaton himself.                                                                              *L.Z.*

HARDEN, D.B., see our number 78738.

78344 HARI, Robert, Une statue du généralissime Sobekhotep, *Genava*, Genève 26 (1978), 135-139, with 3 ill.

The author discusses the N.K. block statue of a royal scribe and general Sobekhotep from the collection of Martin Bodmer, Cologny (Switzerland). He tries to identify the owner of the statue which probably originates from Abydos and cautiously suggests two possibilities of important Sobekhoteps from the time of Amenhotep II-III.
See also Málek, *GM* Heft 32 (1979), 75-76.                                    L.Z.

78345 HARI, Robert, La succession de Toutankhamon, *BSFE* No. 82 (Juin 1978), 8-21, with 2 ill. and 3 fig.

Toutankhamon, roi à six ans, mort à seize ou dix-sept, n'a guère pu gouverner. Aï, frère et père de reine, aurait-il régné "avec" l'enfant? Rentré quelque temps dans l'ombre, Aï reparait aux obsèques: imaginerions-nous, au tombeau d'Aï (réutilisé pour Toutankhamon, selon Engelbach) un corégent différent, Kheperourê? Comme aux jours d'Hatshepsout, autre "usurpatrice" exclue des listes royales, l' Égypte aurait-elle donc connu deux souverains simultanés?
A admettre cette hypothèse, plusieurs anomalies deviendraient compréhensibles. Les deux titulatures superposées (Aï au-dessus, effacé après coup) décoraient des architraves, réutilisées au IIe Pylône de Karnak. La tradition manéthonienne s'accorde pour relever un sixième monarque amarnien: Achêrês, Chebrès ou Achenchêrès, que Josèphe qualifiait de "heteros"; cet adjectif laisse supposer un prédécesseur à nom semblable. Kheperourê, le nom modifié lors des obsèques, rappellerait la transformation de l'ancien nom de Menkheper(ka)rê, quand ce roi devint seul souverain. Une corégence cadrerait mal avec la lettre d'Ankhesenamon à Soupilouliouma. Les feuilles d'or où figurent Toutankhamon et Aï, celui-ci tantôt en pharaon, tantôt en simple particulier et sans cartouche, s'expliqueraient également dans l'hypothèse d'un effacement volontaire. Verser au dossier: Hari, *Aegyptus* 59 (1979), 3-7.       *J. Custers*

HARI, Robert, see also our number 78831.

78346 HARIF, Amos, Middle Kingdom Architectural Elements in Middle Bronze Age Megiddo, *Zeitschrift des Deutschen Palästina-Vereins*, Wiesbaden 94 (1978), 24-31, with 4 plans.

The author first points out the resemblance between the fortifications at Megiddo and the Nubian M.K. fortresses. The find of a statuette of the Egyptian official Thothhotep at Megiddo and its architectural features point to close links between Egypt and Palestine during the reign of Sesostris III. Since Egypt was primarily interested in control over the trade routes in Palestine Egyptian strongholds had to be established in strategical places such as Megiddo, where most likely an Egyptian garrison was stationed for that purpose.       *L.Z.*

HARLÉ, Diane, see our number 78821.

78347  HARRIS, James E., Edward F. WENTE, Charles F. COX, Ibrahim el-NAWAWAY, Charles J. KOWALSKI, Arthur T. STOREY, William R. RUSSELL, Paul V. PONITZ and Geoffrey F. WALKER, Mummy of the "Elder Lady" in the Tomb of Amenhotep II: Egyptian Museum Catalog Number 61070, *Science*, Washington 200, No. 4346 (9 June, 1978), 1149-1151, with 5 fig. and ill.

The unknown female mummy from the cache in the tomb of Amenophis II is identified as Queen Tiye, on account of examination from Egyptological and natural sciences viewpoints.  *L.Z.*

78348  HARRISON, R.M., A Romano-Egyptian Portrait Head (= Museum Notes, 4), *Archaeologica Aeliana*, Newcastle upon Tyne, 5th series, 6 (1978), 171-172, with 1 pl.

Short description of an Egyptian head from the Roman Period, which is on loan from the Hatton Gallery of the Department of Fine Art of the University of Newcastle to the Museum of Antiquities there (acc. no. 1975.4).  *L.Z.*

78349  HART, E.G., I. KVAS and M. SOOTS, Blood Group Testing of Ancient Material with Particular Reference to the Mummy Nakht, *Transfusion*, Philadelphia 18, No. 4 (1978), 474-478.

Another investigation of the mummy of the weaver Nakht in the Royal Ontario Museum, Toronto. Compare our number 77537.  *L.Z.*

78350  HASSAN, [Ausgrabungsbericht], *Nyame Akuma*, Calgary No. 13 (1978), 6.

Die Feldforschungen in der Oase Sîwa ergaben, dass diese während der Feuchtphase von etwa 7500 bis 4500 von Sammler- und Jägergruppen besiedelt war. Das gleiche gilt für die Oase Baharîa. Die lithische Technologie ist ähnlich der der Isna-Industrie des Niltales. Die Untersuchungen der vordynastischen Siedlungen der Nagâda-Khattara-Region werden weiter vorangetrieben.
*Inge Hofmann*

HAYCOCK, Bryan G., see our number 78738.

78351  HAYNES, Joyce L., The Development of Women's Hairstyles in Dynasty Eighteen, *JSSEA* 8 (1977-1978), 18-24, with 15 fig.

Utilizing for this study securely dated two- and three-dimensional representations of upper-class, non-royal women, the author discusses the development of the coiffure during the XVIIIth Dynasty. There are two basic types, the tripartite and the enveloping style, with an intermediate form here called partial tripartite.
The tripartite coiffure is the older fashion; it almost disappears under Amenophis II but reappears under Horemheb. Elaboration of details such as curls, braids, fillets and flowers and the length of the locks enable us to identify the chronological development.

78352 HEERMA VAN VOSS, M.S.H.G., Ein ägyptischer Beter in Otterlo, *in: Hommages Vermaseren*, 478-482, with 4 pl.

The author describes a stelophorous statue of Neferhebef, from the XVIIIth Dynasty, at present in the Kröller-Müller Museum at Otterlo, the Netherlands (Inv. No. 196-B-00; see also AEB 66320, nr. 65). The stela contains a short sun hymn. *L.Z.*

78353 HEERMA VAN VOSS, M., Anoebis en de demonen. Voordracht gehouden bij het negende lustrum van het Vooraziatisch-Egyptisch Genootschap Ex Oriente Lux op 10 juni 1978, Leiden, E.J. Brill, 1978 (14 x 21.5 cm;[IV +] 12 p., frontispiece, ill. on cover).

Reconstruction of a new spell from the *Book of the Dead*, as found in *Papyrus Leiden T 3*, sh. 18-19 (Dyn. XXI; our no. 71260). The composition deals with the fourth and final examination in the judgement ot the dead. The court consists of seven demons, with Anubis as their "magistrate" (vignette). In case of a positive conclusion, the deceased is allowed to leave the hall of judgement. The author offers translation and commentary. *M. Heerma van Voss*

HEERMA VAN VOSS, M., see also our number 78159.

78354 HELCK, Wolfgang, Ägypten und die Ägäis im 16. Jahrhundert v. Chr. Chronologisches und Archäologisches, *Jahresbericht des Instituts für Vorgeschichte der Universität Frankfurt a.M.*, München 1977, (1978), 7-20, with 3 ill.

After pointing out that some of the allegedly fixed dates in the Egyptian chronology are still uncertain the author discusses the Egyptian evidence for the dating of Minoan and Mycenaean history, e.g. the lid of Khian's vessel from Knossos and the change of the Minoan into Mycenaean dress in the tomb of Rekhmire. It is fairly certain that the dagger of Apophis and the one from the tomb of Ahhotep are made by Cretans. More proof for close contacts between both countries in the early XVIIIth Dynasty, e.g. tapestry, are mentioned.
In the last part the author argues that horse and chariot indeed have been introduced by the Hyksos. The warrior-class which originated from this introduction, parallel to the *marjanina*, proves the close contacts in this period with Asia. See now also Helck's "Die Beziehungen Ägyptens und Vorderasiens zur Ägäis bis ins 7. Jahrhundert v. Chr." (Darmstadt, Wissenschaftliche Buchgesellschaft, 1979).

78355 HELCK, W., Der angebliche Kugelfischkult in Elephantine, *GM* Heft 29 (1978), 27-31, with 1 fig.

Es werden Bedenken geäussert gegen die von Edel konstruierte kultische Verehrung des Kugelfisches in "Zelten" (vgl. unsere Nr. 76220). In dem herangezogenen Text aus Kom Ombo wird nicht vom Kugelfisch gesprochen, die Blöcke

aus dem Satistempel von Elephantine zeigen keine Verehrer des Fisches, sondern sich reinigende Priester: dargestellt war der Beginn eines Besuches des Königs im Satistempel und die Reinigung der Priester vor dem Betreten des Heiligtums. Der beistehende Text hat sicher nur das "Beseitigen des Ärgers" der Satis genannt. Die topographische Angabe der "Hallen des Kugelfisches" auf dem Weltkammer-Relief im Sonnenheiligtum des Neuserre dürfte eine topographische Bezeichnung ohne kultischen Hintergrund sein.
Siehe auch unsere Nummer 78237, und die Fortsetzung der Diskussion in *GM* Heft 36 (1979), 31-36 und *GM* Heft 41 (1980), 33-41.     *Inge Hofmann*

78356 HELCK, W., Ein indirekter Beleg für die Benutzung des leichten Streitwagens in Ägypten zu Ende der 13. Dynastie, *JNES* 37 (1978), 337-340, with 2 fig.

Citing the Buhen horse skeleton of M.K. context and the ed-Dab'a excavations for Hyksos animals as evidence against the view of Van Seters that the Egyptians first encountered chariots in battle during the N.K. Asiatic wars, it is suggested here that as gloves in the N.K. scenes denote a connection with horsemanship, the appearance of these in the XIIIth Dynasty tomb of a commander at Edfu could indicate the same. Significantly this man lived in the reign of King *Ddw-msw* under whom traditionally the Hyksos invaded Egypt.     *E.P. Uphill*

78357 HELCK, Wolfgang, Die Weihinschrift Sesostris' I. am Satet-Tempel von Elephantine, *MDAIK* 34 (1978), 69-78, with 5 fig.

Studying the fragmentary inscription from the Satet temple on Elephantine recently published by Schenkel (our number 75665) the author attempts a reconstruction of the texts, which are actually two inscriptions. He presents also a translation with comments.

78358 HELCK, W., '200 Persea-Bäume im Ptahtempel von Memphis'?, *JEA* 64 (1978), 137-138.

This article follows up the inscription published by Gaballa in *JEA* 59 (1973), 113 (our number 73254) with three columns of text carved on a left sandstone doorpost mentioning Ramesses III and 200 persea trees. The king is described as being in Per-Ramesses whereas the post was found in Memphis, the king having gone there afterwards. Helck suggests the emended reading, "His Majesty proceeded to Memphis, he reached the house of Ramesses Ruler of Heliopolis", for the end of column two.     *E.P.Uphill*

HELCK, Wolfgang, see also our number 78488.

HELL, Vera, see our number 78132.

78359 HEYER, R., Ein archäologischer Beitrag zum Text KTU 1.4 I 23-43, *Ugarit-Forschungen*, Kevelaer/Neukirchen-Vluyn 10 (1978), 93-109, with 5 fig. and 25 ill.

Discussing the work and artifacts of the god of metal working in an Ugaritic text, the author often refers to furniture and suchlike objects in Egyptian representations which amply illustrate the article. *L.Z.*

78360 HILLERS, Delbert, A Study of Psalm 148, *Catholic Biblical Quarterly*, Washington DC 40 (1978), 323-334.

Studying Psalm 148 the author refutes the view that the psalm has its roots in the encyclopaedic tradition and has Egyptian forerunners in the Ramesseum and Amenope Onomastica. Its place in a hymnical tradition is stressed. *L.Z.*

78361 HINKEL, F.W., The Archaeological Map of the Sudan. Survey of the State of Progress, *in*: *Études nubiennes*, 121-128, with 1 fig. and 1 map.

Plan und bisherige Arbeiten an der "Archaeological Map of the Sudan" werden dargelegt. Es handelt sich darum, alle verfügbaren Daten über archäologische Stätten im Sudan zu registrieren und jedem Interessierten zugänglich zu machen. Letztes Ziel ist die Herstellung einer vollständigen Verbreitungskarte für jede bekannte Kultur des alten Sudan. Zur Bezifferung der archäologischen Stätten vgl. unsere Nr. 61001 und 61003; die Karteneinteilung wird dem System folgen, das bereits in Nubien verwendet wurde und das auf einer Serie von Karten basiert, die vom Sudan Government Survey Department im Massstab 1 : 250.000 herausgegeben wurde. Das Manuskript zu einem Führer für die archäologische Karte is bereits fertiggestellt.
Der erste Band (Band II) ist erschienen in 1979. *Inge Hofmann*

78362 HINKEL, Friedrich W., Auszug aus Nubien, Berlin, Akademie-Verlag, [1978] (24 x 30 cm; 104 p., 13 maps, 15 plans, 34 fig., 130 pl., 21 colour pl., map and chronological table on endpapers, fig. on cover); rev.*BiOr* 37 (1980), 168-169 (Inge Hofmann). Pr. M 34

The text of this lavishly illustrated book mainly consists of a vivid description of the demolition, removal and reconstruction of the monuments in Sudanese Nubia in which the author took a large part.
Chapter 1, "Abundance and Thirst", presents a description of the Nubian landscape and people, the history of the Nubian Salvage Campaign, an account of the resettlement of the inhabitants and a survey of Nubian history. Chapter 2, "Exodus from Nubia", deals with the demolition and removal to Khartûm of the monuments; chapter 3, "Nubia's Inheritance", with the new museum in Khartûm where they have been reconstructed.
The photographs not only depict the monuments, they also pay much attention to the Nubian people.

HINTZE, Fritz, see our number 78008.

78363 HOCHFIELD, Sylvia, Egypt Signs a Treaty—with the Brooklyn Museum, *Art News*, New York 77, No. 4 (April 1978), 62-64, with 2 ill.

On the appointment of the Brooklyn Museum as the Egyptian government's consultant for all museum projects. L.Z.

78364 HOCHFIELD, Sylvia, Egyptomania in New York, *Art News*, New York 77, No. 10 (December 1978), 44-49, with 9 ill. (4 in colour).

On the publication of our number 78380, the Tutankhamun and Africa in Antiquity exhibitions and the inauguration of the temple of Dendur in the Metropolitan Museum of Art, events which all happened around the same time in New York. L.Z.

78365 HOCHFIELD, Sylvia, The Mansoor Collection: An Insoluble Controversy?, *Art News*, New York 77, No.6 (Summer 1978), 50-57, with 24 ill.

The author aptly summarizes the arguments pro and contra the genuineness of the Mansoor collection of Amarna sculptures (see our numbers 71387 and 75046), concluding that a definitive solution of the controversy can not (yet?) be reached.

78366 HODJASH, S.I., Царские скарабеи, скарабеоиды и печати 1 тыс. до н. э. из собраний ГМИИ им. А. С. Пушкина и государственного Эрмитажа, ВДИ 3 (145), 1978, 60-65, with 1 pl. and an English summary on p. 65.

"Royal Scarabs, Scaraboids and Seals of the 1st Millennium B.C. in the Pushkin Museum of Fine Arts and the Hermitage".
Sequel to our numbers 73340 and 76373.
The author publishes only royal scarabs from the Late Period of which she has established beyond doubt that they are contemporaneous with the reign of the Pharaoh mentioned. Some of the scarabs published here are of historical or artistic interest.
Also one seal of Aspelta III is published. L.Z.

78367 HÖLBL, Günther, Zeugnisse ägyptischer Religionsvorstellungen für Ephesus, Leiden, E.J. Brill, 1978 (15.6 x 24.5 cm; XII + 93 p., 16 pl.) = Édition spéciale des Études préliminaires aux religions orientales dans l' empire romain à l' occasion du 60-ième anniversaire de Maarten J. Vermaseren, publiée par Margreet B. de Boer et T.A. Edridge, 73; rev. *BiOr* 36 (1979), 322-323 (Ladislav Vidman); *CdE* LIV, No. 108 (1979), 268-270 (Michel Malaise). Pr. fl. 92

In the first chapter the author gives a general survey of the pre-Hellenistic aegyptiaca, originating almost completely from the bases of the early archaic Artemisium of Ephesus and entered into the deposit around 600 B.C. Since the actual objects cannot be located all in the Archaeological Museum in Istanbul, the study is based on the records of Hogarth, who excavated Ephesus in 1904-5.
The second chapter deals with the history of the Egyptians in Ephesus, the temples and the inscriptions pertaining to Egyptian cults. Then follows the descrip-

tion of the objects: the Egyptian and Roman sculptures, the terracottas, the lamps, the coins and gems, and a marble relief. The author concludes with a discussion of some Greek stories from the 2nd century A.D., in which Ephesus and the Egyptian religion play an important role. At the end of the book extensive indexes on classical authors, papyri and inscriptions, museum numbers and a general index.  *L.Z.*

78368   HOFMANN, Inge, Apedemakverehrung im Norden des meroitischen Reiches?, *GM* Heft 29 (1978), 33-36.

Die von Žabkar (unsere Nr. 75819) angeführten Belege für eine Apedemak-Verehrung im Norden des meroitischen Reiches erscheinen nicht genügend beweiskräftig: die dekorativen Elemente auf dem Ledergewand aus Semma-Süd zeigen wahrscheinlich ein Löwinnenkopf auf einem Schlangenleib, die Straussenfedern stehen auf der Kartusche und haben nichts mit der *hmhm*-Krone des Apedemak zu tun. Die *trtekes-leb* des Apedemak, zu denen Männer aus Arminna-West in einem noch ungeklärten Verhältnis stehen (REM 1064 B, 7; 1063, 12), sind kein Beweis dafür, dass die Funktionäre des Apedemak gleichfalls im Norden des Reiches beschäftigt waren. Der Gott *P3 jr mkj* "der Schützer" aus der Kapelle des Adikhalamani in Dabod, der in ägyptischen Hieroglyphen im meroitischen Reich *Iprmk* geschrieben und "meroitisiert" zu Apedemak wurde, scheint in Namen und Wesen ursprünglich ägyptische Züge zu enthalten und nicht primär ein genuin meroitischer Gott zu sein.  *Inge Hofmann*

78369   HOFMANN, Inge, Beiträge zur meroitischen Chronologie, St. Augustin bei Bonn, Verlag des Anthropos-Instituts, 1978 (15 x 23 cm; 248 p., 75 fig.) = Studia Instituti Anthropos, 31; rev.*BiOr* 36 (1979), 317-318 (Bruce G. Trigger).

Es wurde versucht, anhand des vorliegenden Materials die meroitische Chronologie neu durchzuarbeiten. Als bisher nicht beachtetes Hilfsmittel wurden die Opfertafeln herangezogen, deren Texte im Benediktionsteil Opferformeln verwenden, die für Herrscher anders lauten als für Privatpersonen. Von diesem Unterscheidungskriterium ausgehend, wurden alle Personennamen der Opfertafeln mit der königlichen Benediktionsformel in die Liste der meroitischen Herrscher eingereiht, auch wenn sie auf dem nichtköniglichen Westfriedhof von Begarawîyah gefunden worden waren. Andererseits wurden alle die angeblichen Herrscher gestrichen, deren Namen nur als Vatersnamen auf den Opfertafeln von Königen bekannt sind. Da wir hinsichtlich der absoluten Chronologie über nur zwei wirkliche Fixdaten verfügen, wurde bewusst auf die Festlegung der Herrscher nach Jahren verzichtet.
In einem Exkurs wurde versucht, die Importware aus den meroitischen Gräbern mit Hilfe ihrer Entsprechungen in anderen Teilen der römisch-hellenistisch beeinflussten Welt zu datieren, um von daher Rückschlüsse auf eine Einordnung der meroitischen Grabanlagen zu gewinnen.  *Inge Hofmann*

78370   HOFMANN, Inge, Getreidesträusse in der meroitischen Ikonographie, *GM* Heft 29 (1978), 37-43, with 10 fig.

Es wird das Vorkommen von Getreidesträussen in der meroitischen Ikonographie untersucht und festgestellt, dass die meisten Beispiele aus der Welt der

verstorbenen Herrscher stammen; aber auch lebende Könige und Götter trugen sie und nicht nur Apedemak, wie vielfach angenommen wird. So wurde denn auch der Gott mit Nimbus und Strahlenkrone auf dem sogenannten Siegesdenkmal des Shorkaror, der dem Heerführer einen Hirsestrauss überreicht, als Erscheinungsform des Apedemak angesehen. Von daher wiederum wurde der *in situ* gefundene Hirsestrauss in Qasr Ibrîm mit Apedemak in Verbindung gebracht, doch bietet auch dieser Fund kein Indiz für eine Verehrung des Gottes im Nordteil des meroitischen Reiches.
*Inge Hofmann*

78371  HOFMANN, Inge, Die Gottheiten in der Invokationsformel der meroitischen Totentexte, *Marburger Studien zur Afrika-und Asienkunde*, Serie A: Afrika. Struktur und Wandel afrikanischer Sprachen, Berlin 17 (1978), 104-120.

In den weitaus häufigsten Fällen werden in der Invokationsformel der Totentexte lediglich Isis und Osiris angerufen. Allerdings kann Osiris durch Amun ersetzt werden; es wird vermutet, dass der in einigen Inschriften angerufene /maka-laẖa-li/ mit Amun identisch ist, da dieser der einzige Gott ist, der in meroitischen Texten das Beiwort "gross" /laẖa/ trägt. Die Beiwörter zu den Gottesnamen der sogenannten feierlichen Invokation sind wohl keine "Adjektive", sondern Nominalkomplexe, die wie Titel behandelt werden.
*Inge Hofmann*

78372  HOFMANN, Inge, Übersetzungsvarianten der Suffixe -s und -te im Meroitischen, *Afrika und Übersee*, Berlin 61 (1978), 265-278.

Die Grundbedeutung des meroitischen Suffixes -s umfasst zweifellos einen Ausdruck der Zugehörigkeit, so dass die bisherige Übersetzung mit "des" durchaus richtig ist, aber auch eine Übersetzung mit "bei, beim" zulässt. Ebenso drückt der Lokativ -te nicht nur ein Wohnen "in" einer Ortschaft, sondern auch ein Hingehen "zu" und "nach" und ein Herkommen "von" einer solchen aus.
*Inge Hofmann*

78373  HOFMANN, Inge, Welches Tier lieferte die biblischen Tachash-Felle?, *Anthropos*, Freiburg 73 (1978), 49-68.

In this article on the identification of the takhash-animal mentioned several times in the Bible, which the author argues to be the seal, Egypt is only briefly referred to in connection with the country of Tahsi, which may have practised seal hunting or may have acted as mediator and which thus may have lent its name to the skin.
*L.Z.*

HOLDEN, Lynn, see our number 78745.

78374  HOOD, S., Discrepancies in 14C Dating as Illustrated From the Egyptian New and Middle Kingdoms and From the Aegean Bronze Age and Neolithic, *Archaeometry*, Oxford 20 (1978), 197-199.

Short comparative study of C 14 dates available from certain samples from the M. and N.K. in Egypt and from the Bronze Age and the Neolithic in the Aegean.
*L.Z.*

78375 HOPE, Colin, Excavations at Malkata and the Birket Habu 1971-1974 under the Direction of David B. O'Connor and Barry J. Kemp. The University Museum, University of Pennsylvania Egyptian Expedition. Jar Sealings and Amphorae of the 18th Dynasty: A Technological Study, Warminster, Aris & Phillips Ltd., [1978] (21 x 29.5 cm; VI+80 p., 10 fig., 6 ill., 1 plan, fig. on cover)= Egyptology Today. No.2, Vol. V.

This is a technological study of the jar sealings from Malkata and, in part 2, of the amphorae bearing hieratic or painted labels (see our number 78472). In the introduction to part 1 the author states that the 361 sealings are studied in order to find an answer to two questions: 1) how were they made and applied to the vessel, and does the variation in their shapes correspond with the commodities the jars contained; 2) what sort of mud was used for them. The sealings are either hand-made or mould-made, while there occur a few instances of double sealings and of re-use of the jars. Six types of mud used for the sealings are distinguished. Before being sealed a stopper of reed, pottery or mud was placed over the mouth of the jar, while the sealings themselves received frequently a painted decoration. All these elements are discussed in four sections, as well as, in others, the amphora-types so far as the necks are still found in the sealings, and the contents of the jars in connection with the sealings. A survey of the results on p. 26-28. Two appendices follow, one about representations of jar sealings in tomb reliefs, the other describing an analysis of the reed stoppers. Then follow the tabulated catalogue of the jar sealings here studied (p. 47-58) and some other tables.
Part 2, on the amphorae with hieratic labels, begins with an introduction, mainly about the date of the jars. Then follow sections on their fabrics and styles (that is, their surface treatments), a general preliminary discussion of the sources of Egyptian clays, and a study of the occurrence of foreign elements amongst the material. Tables to this part on p. 76-79.

78376 HORN, Jürgen, Daten zur Geschichte der Ägyptologie in Göttingen, *GM* Heft 28 (1978), 11-19, with 1 table and 1 pl.

1867 wurde der ägyptologische Lehrstuhl errichtet, den zunächst H. Brugsch innehatte. Ihm folgten Sethe, Kees, Schott und Westendorf als ordentliche Professoren für Ägyptologie. Die kleine Studie verfolgt die Geschichte der Ägyptologie und des Ägyptologischen Seminars in Göttingen mit einer Übersicht über die Entstehung der Göttinger orientalistischen Universitätsinstitute.
*Inge Hofmann*

78377 HORNUNG, Erik, Grundzüge der ägyptischen Geschichte. [2., überarbeitete und erweiterte Auflage], Darmstadt, Wissenschaftliche Buchgesellschaft, 1978 (12.7 x 19.5 cm; VI + 167 p., 1 folding map) = Grundzüge, 3.

Second, revised and augmented edition of our number 65248.
Apart from additions and alterations due to recent developments in Egyptology which occur on many pages, the main difference between this and the first edition is that the footnotes are now replaced by extensive references to the literature at the end of the book (p. 135-158), while also a chronological table has been added (159-165).

BIBLIOGRAPHIE ÉGYPTOLOGIQUE 1978 97

78378 HORNUNG, Erik, Meisterwerke altägyptischer Dichtung, [Zürich und München], Artemis, [1978] (10.2 x 17.3 cm; 99 p., ill. on cover); series: Lebendige Antike; rev. *BiOr* 34 (1977), 330 (anonymous); *CdE* LV, No. 109-110 (1980), 105-106 (Michel Malaise). Pr. Sw. Fr. 12.80

The author presents translations of some "evergreens" of Egyptian literature for the general public. They are divided into four categories: narratives (The Eloquent Peasant, Sinuhe and Wenamun), the Instructions of Ptahhotep, religious poetry (P.T. Sp. 273/4; C.T. Sp. 1130; B.D. Ch. 125; the Sun-Hymn of Akhenaton) and examples of lyric poetry (the Dispute of a Man and his *Ba*; the harper's song of Antef; some N.K. love songs). All texts are completely translated, so far as possible. Notes to the text on p. 85-97.

78379 HORNUNG, Erik, Struktur und Entwicklung der Gräber im Tal der Könige, *ZÄS* 105 (1978), 59-66, with 1 table.

Von Amenophis II. an werden in königlichen Gräbern für Breite und Höhe der Korridore und für die Breite der Türdurchgänge feste Elle-Masse angestrebt, bzw. verwirklicht, die im Laufe des Neuen Reiches stufenweise vergrössert werden. Mit dieser Abstufung erhält man auch ein Datierungskriterium für undekorierte Königsgräber. Anschliessend gibt Verfasser noch sieben Elemente, die ein königliches Grab charakterisieren in Gegensatz zu allen anderen Grabanlagen.
Hornung bespricht dann Merkmale der Gräber von Angehörigen des Königshauses, der Mehrfach-Gräber (Polytaphe) und der Schachtgräber (pit tombs). Schliesslich erörtert er das Prinzip der Erweiterung und Vervielfachung des Bestehenden. Der ganze Prozess von Planung und Ausführung und die systematische Entwicklung der Gesamtkonzeption lassen sich für die thebanischen Königsgräber weitgehend rekonstruieren. *M. Heerma van Voss*

HORNUNG, Erik, see also our number 78275.

78380 HOVING, Thomas, Tutankhamun. The Untold Story, New York, Simon and Schuster, [1978] (15.3 x 24.4 cm; 384 p., 2 maps, 1 plan on endpapers, frontispiece, 32 pl. containing ill. [many in colour], fig. and 1 plan); rev. *New York Times Book Review* (Nov. 12, 1978), 51-52 (T.G.H. James). Pr. $12.95

On account of publications, but particularly of an extensive dossier with letters and documents preserved in the Metropolitan Museum of Art, New York, and discovered by him at an unusual place, the author relates the history of the discovery of Tutankhamon's tomb and the removal of its contents. Various points, some new, are stressed, e.g.: the close relations between Lord Carnarvon and Carter and the staff of the M.M.A.; the (until at present officially unknown) entering into the tomb by Carter, Carnarvon and two others in the night after the clearance of the doorway; the story of the jewellery from the Tomb of the Three Princesses and how they reached the M.M.A., an event in which Carter played an important part; the attempts to label the tomb as defiled so that Lord Carnarvon would receive his share of its contents; the problems with the press, and the endless struggles of Carter with the Egyptian authorities in the following years; the suggestion that a certain number of objects

secretly did leave Egypt through Carter and Carnarvon.
The book is written in a vivid style, with many quotations from letters and official documents, while the author presents his interpretation of the characters of the main actors.
There are no notes, but at the end a list of sources to the various chapters and indexes.
There has also appeared an English edition: London, Hamish Hamilton, 1979 (£7.95); a German version: "Der Goldene Pharao. Tut-anch-Amun. Die I. authentische Darstellung der grössten archäologischen Entdeckung aller Zeiten", Bern-München, Scherz, 1978 (DM 34); a French version: "Tout-Ankh-Amon. Histoire secrète d'une découverte", Paris, 1979.

78381   HRDY, Daniel B., Analysis of Hair Samples of Mummies from Semna South (Sudanese Nubia), *American Journal of Physical Anthropology*, Philadelphia 49 (1978), 277-282.

Hair samples from 76 Meroitic and X-group burials at Semna South were examined with the help of a variety of techniques.                                              L.Z.

78382   HUGHES, George R., John Albert Wilson. September 12, 1899 — August 30, 1976. The Andrew MacLeish Distinguished Service Professor Emeritus of Egyptology, University of Chicago, *in*: *Immortal Egypt*, 2-4, with portrait.

Obituary article. Compare our number 76870.

78383   HUMMEL, Siegbert, Ägyptische Miszellen, *Almogaren*, Graz 8 (1977), 1978, 87-95, with 2 fig.

The author attempts to understand certain enigmatic phenomena of megalithic cultures through motifs of the ancient Egyptian culture, between which cultures he recognizes connections. In this way he connects the *mnw*, "monument", but also "obelisk" (see our number 77201) with the Etruscan word manim, "monument" and the element men- in the word menhir; he compares the Egyptian causeway with the aligned rows of stones in megalithic cultures, and the various coffins, sarcophagi and shrines with the megalithic motif of concentric circles as symbol of water (=life and death). Small menhirs in tombs of the megalithic culture in Brittany are meant to provide the dead with endurance, the same notion of steadiness being present in the Egyptian root *mn*. At the end of the article some thoughts about the words for eternity, *nḥḥ* and *ḏt*.                                                                                                                        L.Z.

78384   HUMPHREYS, W. Lee, The Motif of the Wise Courtier in the Book of Proverbs, *in*: *Israelite Wisdom*. Theological and Literary Essays in Honor of Samuel Terrien. Edited by John G. Gammie, Walter A. Brueggemann, W. Lee Humphreys, James M.Ward, [New York], Scholars Press for Union Theological Seminary, New York, [1978], 177-190.

In order to test Proverbs 10-29 for its assumed didactic purport in educational training of future court officials the author examines the motif of the wise courtier in Egyptian Wisdom literature (Ptahhotep, Kagemni, Ani, Amenemope) in terms of salient features, literary function and theological potential. The conclusion is that this motif played only a limited role in Proverbs 10-29, and that there is hardly any influence from Egyptian instructions. *L.Z.*

78385 HYPHER, R.P., The Value of $\pi$ and the Pyramids of Egypt. Intentional or Accident ?, *JSSEA* 8 (1977-1978), 143-147, with 3 pl.

The author reaches two conclusions: the value of $\pi$ appearing in the relationship of height to peripheral base length of the pyramids is likely to be coincidental, and the coincidence of due East and due West elevations of the sun at the summer solstice at 30° N. and the elevation of some pyramids is not fortuitous.

78386 IBRAHIM, Mohiy Eldin, Some Ptolemaic Words Not Mentioned in the Wörterbuch, *in*: *Journal Faculty of Archaeology*, 79-82.

The author lists eight words occurring in the texts of the Edfu temple that are not mentioned in the *WB*. They are: *ir ḫt* ="partake"; *wdn-3t*= "long life"; *bỉ3(t)* = "evil, disloyalty"; *m3* = "progenitor"; *mꜥmꜥ* = "to kill"; *ḥ3ty* = "heart" (written with two wings); *sḥn-rḥyt* = "necropolis"; *kn* = "altar".

78387 IRVIN, Dorothy, Mytharion. The Comparison of Tales from the Old Testament and the Ancient Near East, Kevelaer, Verlag Butzon & Bercker/Neukirchen-Vluyn, Neukirchener Verlag, 1978 (20.9 x 30.3 cm; XV + 135 p., 3 pl. containing a table) = Alter Orient und Altes Testament. Veröffentlichungen zur Kultur und Geschichte des Alten Orients und des Alten Testaments, 32; rev. *Orientalia* 50 (1981), 112-116 (Dennis J. McCarthy).

Of interest to Egyptologists is a separate section (p. 82-90) in which the author investigates some motifs in various Egyptian tales (including the Birth of the Divine King) on account of Stith Thompson's Motif Index of Folk Literature. *L.Z.*

JACOBI, Renate, see our number 78132.

78388 JACQUET, Gérard, Au coeur du Sahara libyen d' étranges gravures rupestres, *Archeologia*, Paris No. 123 (Octobre 1978), 40-51, with 2 maps, 11 ill. (7 in colour, 1 on cover) and 3 fig.

In this article on prehistoric rock drawings found in the Fezzan, Libyan Sahara, the author briefly touches upon Egyptian influence. *L.Z.*

78389 JACQUET, Jean, Fouilles de Karnak Nord. Neuvième et dixième campagnes (1975-1977), *BIFAO* 78 (1978), 41-52, with 1 folding plan and 8 pl.

Sequel to our number 76393.
After a survey of the preceding campaigns the author describes those of the 9th and 10th seasons during which the completion of the excavations has been attained. The monument of Tuthmosis I, called earlier a temple, appears on account of inscriptions to have been a treasury (*pr ḥḏ*). The chronology of the

layers is now generally clear: in the M.K. part of the town there was erected a structure at the S. side during the late XVIIth or early XVIIIth Dynasty. Then Tuthmosis I has built near it his Treasury, which was surrounded by a wall in the time of Hatshepsut and Tuthmosis III. Destroyed in the XIXth Dynasty, the area was partly covered by bakeries.

Various objects that have been found are described, among which a small statue of Renenutet (see pl. 14).

78390 JACQUET, J. et H. el-ACHIRIE, avec la collaboration de M. MEDIČE, J. VALOVIČ et de G. LECUYOT, Gerf Hussein. I. Architecture, Le Caire, Centre d' Études et de Documentation sur l'Ancienne Égypte, 1978 (21. 2 x 27.2 cm; portfolio containing III + 63 loose p., frontispiece, 3 + 57 + 40 loose pl. containing plans, map, ill. and fig.); at head of title: Collection scientifique.

This first volume in the Collection Scientifique on the rock temple of Gerf Hussein is devoted to its architecture.

The text part presents descriptions of the various architectural elements of the temple, first the outer, and then the inner parts.

The plates and the separately wrapped key plans conclude the volume.   L.Z.

JACQUET-GORDON, Helen, see our number 78136.

78391 JAMES, Frances, Chariot Fittings from Late Bronze Age Beth Shan, *in*: *Archaeology in the Levant*. Essays for Kathleen Kenyon. Edited by Roger Moorey and Peter Parr, Warminster, Aris & Phillips Ltd, [1978], 102-115, with 4 fig. and 5 pl.

The author studies the types and uses of a group of white-stone knobs in Beth Shan (Beisan), probably to be identified as fittings of the military chariots belonging to the Egyptian military installations in the city. She amply uses for comparison the Egyptian evidence, particularly that from Tutankhamon's chariots.   L.Z.

78392 JAMES, T.G.H., A Little Known Library in a Famous Museum, *PLA Report*, Greenvale, N.Y., 6, No.1 (Spring 1978), 16-20, with 7 ill. (1 on cover).

Article for the general reader about Egyptian texts on ostraca and papyri preserved in the British Museum.

JAMES, T.G.H., see also our numbers 78513 and 78514.

78393 JANSSEN, Jac. J., The Early State in Ancient Egypt, *in*: *The Early State*. Edited by Henri J.M. Claessen [and] Peter Shalník, The Hague-Paris-New York, Mouton Publishers, [1978], 213-234.

In this volume containing general articles as well as a number of case studies concerning the Early State, the author attempts to sketch its essential characteristics in Egypt up to the O.K., everywhere stressing the scanty knowledge about it and subsequently the utmost care with which hypotheses should be

put forward.
After a general introduction on the sources he discusses the birth of the Egyptian state; the conception of kingship, divine or sacral, and the role of the queen; the development of the administration and the people, and lastly the causes for the decline of the centralized state.  L.Z.

78394 JANSSEN, Jac. J., Year 8 of Ramesses VI Attested, *GM* Heft 29 (1978), 45-46.

Die Schlussfolgerung von Wente und van Siclen (vgl. unsere Nr. 76830), dass Ramses VI. etwa drei Monate in seinem 8. Jahr regierte, was allerdings bisher nicht beweisbar sei, kann nun exakt belegt werden. Die fragmentarische Transkription des unpublizierten O. IFAO 1425 in Černý's Notizen handelt von der zweimaligen Entlehnung eines Ochsen zum Pflügen. Die erste Entlehnung erfolgte im Jahr 7, I *prt* 18, die zweite im 8. Jahr, II *prt* 11. Die erste Leihdauer betrug 8, die zweite 7 Tage, die zu 15 Tagen zusammengezogen werden, so dass angenommen werden muss, dass beide Entlehnungen unmittelbar aufeinander folgten. Daher kann der Wechsel der Jahresdatierung zwischen dem I *prt* 18 und dem II *prt* 11 nur in die Regierungszeit Ramses' VI. gehören; die Reihenfolge von Ramses VI., VII. und VIII. ist somit korrekt.  *Inge Hofmann*

78395 JANSSENS, Yvonne, La Prôtennoia Trimorphe, (NH XIII, 1). Texte établi et présenté, Québec, Les Presses de l'Université Laval, 1978 (15.3 x 24 cm; X + 101 p.) = Bibliothèque copte de Nag Hammadi Section: textes, 4.

The text has been published before by the author in *Le Muséon*, Louvain 87 (1974), 351-413.
After a bibliography and a long introduction on the Nag Hammadi Codex XIII and the present text (Nag Hammadi Codex XIII, 1, 35-49), the author presents text and translation on opposite pages, followed by notes on the transcription and the translation, and the commentary.
Index of Greek and Coptic words, and of proper names at the end of the book.  L.Z.

JEFFREYS, D.G., see our number 78747.

78396 JENKINS, Nancy, Hatshepsut: the Female Pharaoh, *Aramco World Magazine*, New York 29, No. 4 (July-August 1978), 26-32, with 15 ill. (2 on inside covers).

Article for the general reader, with fine photographs by John D. Ross.  L.Z.

78397 JERNSTEDT, Peter, Zur Determination im Koptischen, *Wissenschaftliche Zeitschrift. Martin-Luther-Universität*, Gesellschafts- und sprachwissenschaftliche Reihe, Halle-Wittenberg 27, Heft 3 (1978), 95-106.

Original title: к детерминации в коптском языке, Советское Востоковедение 6 (1949), 52-62 (not in the AEB). Translated by P. Nagel, with some comments by W.-P. Funk.
Remarks on Shenutian usage. In a passage like ΟΥ-ϬΟΟΥ ΤЄ ЄΡЄ ΠЄΟΟΥ ΜΠΧΟЄΙC ϢΑ ЄΧⲰC 'she is a glorious person, over whom the glory of the Lord rises' (*Sinuthii Opera* [ed. Leipoldt], III, 58.17), resumption in the

virtual relative clause enlarging the binary non-verbal equative sentence is to its author pointer ⲦⲈ (fem.), not to its predicate ⲈⲞⲞⲨ (masc.). The generic discrepancy between these two here (and in other Shenutian passages adduced) disappears if ⲞⲨ is assumed to function as an indefinite substantive 'someone', with a subordinating, genitival relationship to the noun: 'a (female) person-of-glory' (cf. ⲦⲀ-ⲈⲞⲞⲨ), its gender-sensitivity being referential, no longer morphemic (as still in the non-bound correlative ⲞⲨⲀ/ⲞⲨⲈⲒ), the difference with the indefinite article having become neutralized.

Other substantival uses of ⲞⲨ (and ϨⲈⲚ) occur in associations with an abstract or interrogative noun, e.g. ⲞⲨ-ⲦⲈⲒ ⲘⲒⲚⲈ 'someone of this kind' or ⲞⲨ-ⲞⲨ 'what sort of person?', or with nouns indicating a material, like ϨⲈⲚ-ϨⲀⲦ 'silver pieces', or with de-concretized nouns, as in ϨⲈⲚ-ⲞⲨⲞⲈⲒⲚ 'lighting ones' (as persons, not 'lights').

Finally, the substantival hypothesis also explains such well-known adverbial formations like ϨⲚ ⲞⲨ-ⲘⲈ 'truly', lit. 'in something of truth' (not 'in a truth'). *J.F. Borghouts*

JOEL, Seth, see our number 78239.

JOHANNES, Dieter, see our number 78327.

78398 JOHNSON, Janet H., The Chicago Demotic Dictionary Project, *Enchoria* 8, Sonderband (1978), 11-13, with 1 fig.

Abstract of a paper read at the First International Colloquium of Demotists, held in Berlin, September 1977.
On the basis of Spiegelberg's files the Oriental Institute of Chicago announces the project of a comprehensive Demotic dictionary. The author presents some of its features and invites demotists to collaboration. *W. Brunsch*

78399 JOHNSON, Janet H., Remarks on Egyptian Verbal Sentences (20 p.) = *Afroasiatic Linguistics*, Malibu 5, Issue 5 (September 1978), 153-172.

The author presents a tentative set of Phrase Structure rules for ancient Egyptian, especially the stage known as Demotic, and shows that there were at most two kinds of sentences in Egyptian, those with nominal predicates and those with verbal predicates. She also shows how analysis in terms of Phrase Structure rules and Transformational rules may account for some specific changes of forms used in verbal sentences between different stages of the Egyptian language.
*Author's summary*

JOHNSON, Janet H., see also our number 78597.

78400 JOHNSON, Paul, The Civilization of Ancient Egypt, London, Weidenfeld and Nicolson, [1978] (16.9 x 25.2 cm; 240 p., 18 colour ill. [2 on cover], 2 ill. on endpapers, frontispiece, 2 maps, 88 ill., 1 fig.); rev. *BiOr* 37 (1980), 60 (anonymous). Pr. £ 6.25

In this valuable book for the interested reader by the former editor of the New Statesman the first three chapters deal in chronological order with the Pre- and

Protodynastic Period, the O.K., and the M.K., and N.K. The next four chapters are devoted to various aspects of ancient Egyptian life: to funerary customs and religion, to the hieroglyphic system, literature and the problem of literacy, and to the function and meaning of ancient Egyptian art, e.g. its relation to Maat and aspectivism. Then follow chapters on the decline of the civilization from Ramses III onward. The last chapter is devoted to the discovery of Egypt by science.
Select bibliography arranged after subjects, and an index at the end of the book.

*L.Z.*

78401 de JONG, W.J., De ingewanden van de egyptische dode, [Amsterdam], Egyptologische Vereniging Sjemsoethot, 1978 (21 x 29.6 cm; 22 p., 27 ill., 4 fig.) = Onderwerpen uit de Egyptologie, 1.

In this publication of an amateur Egyptological Society the author, being a chemist, discusses the history of the ancient Egyptian mummification process of the intestines of the dead. He explains the reasons for their removal and their treatment in the various periods with special attention for those of queen Hetepheres and Tutankhamon, and deals with the development of the canopic vessels, the chest and shrines, and the protective gods and goddesses related to them. At the end an English summary. The address of the editorial staff is: W.J. de Jong, Geinwijk 904, 1103 AP Amsterdam, The Netherlands. *L.Z.*

78402 JUNGE, Friedrich, "Emphasis by Anticipation" im mittelägyptischen Verbalsatz, *RdE* 30 (1978), 96-100.

La construction apeléé "inversion emphatique" (Sujet + *sḏm.f*) paraît être une structure adverbiale, dans laquelle le sujet mis en tête serait moins mis en évidence que le prédicat constitué par l'ensemble de la phrase qui le suit.

*Ph. Derchain*

78403 JUNGE, Friedrich, Syntax der mittelägyptischen Literatursprache. Grundlage einer Strukturtheorie, Mainz, Verlag Philipp von Zabern, [1978] (21 x 30 cm; 153 p.); at head of title: Deutsches Archäologisches Institut. Abteilung Kairo; rev. *BiOr* 37 (1980), 140-142 (Alessandro Roccati). Pr. DM 92

1. A transformational-generative analysis of the literary language of the M.K. whose (2.) point of issue is Polotsky's distinction between 'emphatic' and 'non-emphatic' forms. 3.Within the syntactic frame of an adverbial clause (S[entence] = N[oun] P[art] + A[dverbial] P[art]), the former are assigned a subject slot (whatever the verb form's own morphological associations with an agent, an object, and so on), complemented by a predicate. After a discussion of these concepts (taken in a 'logical' sense) the general scheme is [(Noun/emph. verb form)$_{NP}$ + (adverb/circumstantial verb form)$_{AP}$]$_S$. 4. One possible derivation from this is [(Noun)$_{NP}$ + (verb form)$_{AP}$]$_S$ where the NP is conventionally analyzed as anticipated; here, however, this position is considered normal, and exhibits Subject function. 5. In sentences of the type *ntf* (or *ỉn* + noun) *sḏm=f*, with a similarly anticipated element, the syntagm is interpreted as a noun-noun combination, reflecting a predicate-subject relationship (as logical terms, without positional constraints). All *pw*-clauses can be interpreted in a similar way.

6. In clauses with a frontally extraposed, *ir*-introduced element, a topic is offered for comment; these too are analyzed as [(*ir* A)$_{NP}$ + (rest)$_{AP}$]$_S$. 7. In *iw*-introduced clauses, *iw* (said to signalize syntactic independence throughout) actualizes what follows it. Thus *iw* is a subject to a predicate. The very fact of the distributional equality of the elements following *iw* (adverbial as well as nominal elements) blurs the distinction between nominal and adverbial categories. Also in other instances, nouns may function as adverbs; moreover, in a diachronic perspective, prepositions (the typical 'adverb-pointers') are really substantives. A similar historical argumentation would range the qualitative (another 'adverb') with nouns. Thus the so-called 'adverbial clause' is just a case of an 'unmarked nominal clause'. 8. *sdm=f*-like verb forms (prospective, circumstantial, etc.) can be argued to manifest semantic, but not syntactic, varieties of one and the same verb form with an essentially noun-like distribution, manifested by a broad range of syntactic positions. Also compound verb forms, such as the *sdm.in=f*, can be syntactically analyzed as internominal compoundings, *etwa* [(*sdm*)$_{NP}$ + (*in=f*)$_{NP}$]$_S$ which, in a slightly modified arrangement, may also be found as *etwa* [(*in*-N)$_{NP}$ + (*sdm=f*)$_{NP}$]$_S$. All this greatly helps to abolish the verbal clause as a syntactically operational concept. 9. After a summarization, there follows (10.) an appendix with practical rules for purposes of translation, as well as keys to the generative apparatus in the form of rules. 11. and 12. Register of places cited and literature.     *J.F. Borghouts*

78404   JUNGE, Friedrich, Wirklichkeit und Abbild. Zum innerägyptischen Synkretismus und zur Weltsicht der Hymnen des Neuen Reiches, *in*: *Synkretismusforschung*. Theorie und Praxis. Herausgegeben von Gernot Wiessner, Wiesbaden, Otto Harrassowitz, 1978 (= Göttinger Orientforschungen. Veröffentlichungen des Sonderforschungsbereiches Orientalistik an der Georg-August-Universität Göttingen. Reihe: Grundlagen und Ergebnisse, 1), 87-108.

After having introduced his terminology and his argument that the question of syncretism is only important as a historical process, the author first discusses the structure of the divine world, starting with remarks on names of gods as predicates of their qualities. He argues that the sharpness of the profile of a god depends on his belonging to constellations with various spheres, the number of which is conditioned by historical or religious-political reasons. He then deals with the gods and the real world. It is as parts of these constellations as structural elements that gods relate to the institutions and phenomena of the real world.
The third section is concerned with the world as an image. By playing the programs of the constellations man tries to obtain their results, but his actions cannot influence the course of the world. The play finds its perfection in the ritual which refers to the higher world as its image. In his conclusions the author draws parallels with neo-platonic conceptions.     *L.Z.*

78405   [KADISH, Gerald E.], Editorial Foreword, *JARCE* 15 (1978), 5-8.

The Foreword contains a list of topics (and their researchers) of the Research Fellowship of the American Research Center in Egypt for the year 1978-1979, and one of expeditions and projects for the year 1978-79.     *L.Z.*

78406   KADRI, Ahmed, Discovery of Limestone Blocks of the Late Period between Shebin el-Qantir and Bilbeis, *SAK* 6 (1978), 93-96, with 1 map and 2 pl.

Publication of five relief blocks found not far from Shibîn el-Qanâtir in the S. Delta. Two of them have a frieze of stars, the third one kheker-signs and what may have been a cartouche; the fourth bears the cartouches of a Ptolemy and may come from Hermopolis Parva, the fifth, with the Horus name of an unknown king, may come from Bubastis.

78407   KÁKOSY, L., Az alexandriai idő-isten, *Világosság*, Budapest 19 (1978), 613-620, with 2 ill.

"Der alexandrinische Zeitgott."
Osiris-Aion galt, wie Serapis-Aion, als Herr des Kosmos und der Zeit. In der alexandrinischen Verehrung des Aion sind auch ägyptische Elemente nachweisbar; diese verbinden sich mit dem Glauben an die Neugeburt.   *W. Wessetzky*

78408   KÁKOSY, László, Egyiptom és az Ószövetség, *Világosság*, Budapest 18 (1977), 418-426.

"Ägypten und das Alte Testament".
Viele Fäden verbinden Ägypten mit dem Nahen Osten. Über Israels "Gefangenschaft" berichtet keine ägyptische Quelle. Die Geschichte des goldenen Kalbes kann mit ägyptischen Tierkulten zusammenhängen. In der Geschichte wurde das Königreich Juda von Ägypten überrollt. Eine Wirkung auf die Literatur ist z.B. in der israelischen Weisheitsliteratur zu bemerken. Im Ps. 103 der LXX erinnern Bilder an Echnaton's Sonnenhymnus.   *W. Wessetzky*

78409   KÁKOSY, László, Egyiptomi és ántik czillaghit, Budapest, Akadémiai kiadó, 1978 (347 p., 36 ill.) = Apollo Könyvtár, 9.

"Der ägyptische und antike Sternglaube".
Die Kapitel sind: Der Himmel mit dem Auge der im Altertum Lebenden; Die Mythologie des Himmelgewölbes; Beginn der Astrologie in Ägypten; Sterne und Seelen (Sternglaube und Jenseitsglaube); Die klassische Astrologie; das Wiederlegen der Astrologie; Aus der Geschichte der Astrologie; Die Astrologie der Chaldäer und die hermeneutische Astrologie; Im Kampfe mit dem Schicksal.
*W. Wessetzky*

78410   KÁKOSY, László, Egyiptomi mitoszok a csillagok keletkezéséről, *in: Opuscula classica mediaevaliaque in honorem J. Horváth*, Budapest, 1978 (= Klasszika-Filológiai Tanulmanyok, 3), 237-248.

"Ägyptische Mythen über die Entstehung der Sterne".
Die Entstehung der Sterne verbindet sich im Glauben der Ägypter mit der Himmelsschöpfung. Nach dem Mythos der Himmelskuh begannen die Sterne erst nach der Schöpfung des Jenseits zu leuchten. Die Stelle P.T. 567 kann mit dem Volksglauben in Zusammenhang stehen, nach dem eine Göttin Steine, auch Türkise, über den Himmel streut. Nut gilt als Mutter der Sterne und Amun als ihr Schöpfer (Hymnus im Grab des Neferhotep). Nach dem Glauben der Spät-

zeit sind die Sternenbilder in einer früheren Phase der Schöpfung entstanden (Edfu VI, 182, 12). Wenn man im Sternbild des Grossen Bären einen Schenkel des Seth erblickt, wird dieses in den Horus-Seth-Mythos hineingezogen.

W. Wessetzky

78411 KÁKOSY, L., Einige Probleme des ägyptischen Zeitbegriffes, *Oikumene*, Budapest 2 (1978), 95-111, with 1 fig. and 1 ill.

The author discusses various aspects of the Egyptian conception of time; time in life and history (his argument is exclusively based on religious texts and representations); the words *nḥḥ* and *ḏt*; the phrase "years of *Tn*", indicating a period of extremely long duration; existence outside the time; and the god Ḥeḥ.

78412 KÁKOSY, L., The Fiery Aether in Egypt, *Acta antiqua academiae scientiarum hungaricae*, Budapest 25 (1977), 137-142, with 1 fig.

The author discusses the semicircle of flames around representations of gods in the latest period of the Pharaonic civilization. This concept of a fiery aether may have been borrowed from Iranian thought during the Persian domination and introduced into Late Period magic and mythology. *L.Z.*

78413 KÁKOSY, L., Zeus-Amun, in: *Jubilee Volume of the Oriental Collection 1951-1976. Papers Presented on the Occasion of the 25th Anniversary of the Oriental Collection of the Library of the Hungarian Academy of Sciences*, Edited by E. Apor, Budapest, MTAK, 1978, 111-114.

Remarks on Zeus-Amon identification in the Ptolemaic Period.

78414 KAMIL, Jill, Sakkara. A Guide to the Necropolis and Site of Memphis, London and New York, Longman, [1978] (12.2 x 18.4 cm; 172 p., 3 maps [1 on endpapers], 41 ill., 20 plans, 7 fig.); rev. *BiOr* 35 (1978), 147 (anonymous).
Pr. £ 2.40/ $ 5.50

The first introductory chapter gives a general historical survey from the Early Dynastic to the Islamic Period and a brief history of Memphis. Chapter 2 deals with the Early Dynastic Period: background, Mesopotamian influence, types of 1st Dynasty tombs and the most important tombs themselves, while chapter 3 is devoted to the monuments of the IIIrd Dynasty, particularly the Djoser complex. Chapter 4 is devoted to the most important tombs of the Vth Dynasty and the pyramid of Unas including some general information on the pyramids and the P.T. Chapter 5 describes the pyramids and the mastabas of the VIth Dynasty. Then the author jumps to the Late Period in chapter 6, dealing with more heterogeneous monuments such as the Serapeum, the Persian tombs and the Coptic Monastery. After a chapter (7) on the remains at Memphis, the last chapter (8) relates work in progress among which that on the tomb of Horemheb.
At the end of the booklet a chronological table mentioning the kings from the Early Dynastic Period to the O.K. *L.Z.*

KAMIR, Sid Ahmed Abd el Magid, see our numbers 78823 and 78824.

78415 KAPLONY, Peter, Zur Definition der Beschriftung-und Bebilderungstypen von Rollsiegeln, Skarabäen und anderen Stempelsiegeln, *GM* Heft 29 (1978), 47-60, with 67 fig. on 5 pl.

Es lassen sich neun verschiedene Siegeltypen unterscheiden (p. 54):
1. Königssiegel (Horusnamenssiegel, Ringnamenssiegel) mit und ohne Festnotiz. 2. Festsiegel mit Festnotiz (anonyme Königssiegel, sekundär auch anonyme Siegel von Privatleuten). 3. Figurensiegel (Glückssiegel, religiöse Symbole-Siegel, Ornamentsiegel) aus Festsiegeln degeneriert, die z. T. selbst aus Königs- und Amtssiegeln mit Festnotiz degeneriert sind. 4. Amtssiegel (Horusnamenssiegel) mit und ohne Festnotiz. 5. Verwaltungssiegel, gelegentlich mit einem Ringnamen, vereinzelt mit einem Horusnamen. 6. Beamtensiegel, z.T. Totensiegel, sekundär mit Festnotiz. 7. Privatsiegel, z.T. Totensiegel, sekundär mit Festnotiz. 8. Gottessiegel, sekundär, aus Fest- und Verwaltungssiegeln entstanden. 9. Produktensiegel, sekundär, aus Fest- und Verwaltungssiegeln entstanden.

*Inge Hofmann*

78416 KARKOWSKI, Janusz, Deir el-Bahari 1973-1974 (Travaux égyptologiques), *Études et Travaux* 10 (1978), 397-406, with 6 ill. and 3 fig.

Sequel to our number 76426.
A large part of the egyptological activities of the Polish mission at Deir el-Baḥri was devoted to the project of the reconstruction of the South Wall of the Upper Court. The author expresses some doubts about the reconstruction of the English Mission and presents some corrections to that reconstruction incorporated in Porter and Moss, II, 358, nos. 85, 1-6. The classification of the blocks in the lapidaria resulted in the localisation of numerous fragments in various parts of the temple. At the end the find of a wigmaker's workshop is briefly described (see our number 78469).
Compare also our number 78874. *L.Z.*

78417 KARKOWSKI, Janusz, Quelques remarques sur les temples de Buhen, *Études et Travaux* 10 (1978), 69-81, with 5 fig. and 6 ill.

The author makes 19 remarks with respect to details on the plates of our number 74117. *L.Z.*

78418 KASSER, Rodolphe, Un dictionnaire complet de la langue copte. Mots d'origine égyptienne et mots d'origine étrangère (grecque etc.), *Enchoria* 8, Sonderband (1978), 13* (159) -18* (64).

Abstract of a paper read at the First International Congress of Coptology, held in Cairo, December 1977.
The author presents the features of his new Coptic Dictionary that is to come out in the near future. *W. Brunsch*

KASSER, Rodolphe, see also our number 78269.

78419 KATS, A.F., W.D. van Wijngaarden, bibliografie van een Nederlands Egyptoloog, 's Gravenhage, P.A. Tiele Academie, 1978 (21.4 x 30 cm; 37 p.); series: Series Bibliographica.

The introduction contains a short biography, followed by a list of publications. Index at the end of the pamphlet. *L.Z.*

78420 KEEL, Othmar, Grundsätzliches und das Neumondemblem zwischen den Bäumen, *Biblische Notizen*, Bamberg Heft 6 (1978), 40-55, with 1 ill. and 1 fig.

In the first part of the article dealing with the connections between text and representation in the ancient Near East, the author discusses some ancient Egyptian examples. *L.Z.*

78421 KEEL, Othmar, Jahwes Entgegnung an Ijob. Eine Deutung von Ijob 38-41 vor dem Hintergrund der zeitgenössischen Bildkunst, Göttingen, Vandenhoeck & Ruprecht, 1978 (15.5 x 23.3 cm; 192 p., 102 fig., 7 pl.) = Forschungen zur Religion und Literatur des Alten und Neuen Testaments, 121. Pr. DM 48

Although mainly concerned with the chapters 38-41 of the Book of Job and their exegesis the author refers on several pages to representations from Ancient Egypt, e.g. where he discusses the animals of chapter 39 (p. 63-81). Of particular importance to Egyptologists are his studies on Behemot (40, 15) and Leviathan (41,1), resp. the hippopotamus and the crocodile (p. 127-156).

78422 KEEL, Othmar, The Symbolism of the Biblical World. Ancient Near Eastern Iconography and the Book of Psalms. Translated by Timothy J. Hallett, New York, The Seabury Press, [1978] (16 x 23.5 cm; 422 p., 480 fig., 24 pl.); rev. *BiOr* 36 (1979), 344-346 (Th. Booij). Pr. $24.50

English translation of our number 72370.
For the second edition, see our number 77405.

78423 KEIL, Volkmar, Zur Form der Regel des Schenute, *GM* Heft 30 (1978), 39-44.

Es wird untersucht, ob Schenute in den Zeiten, in denen er sich in die Einsamkeit zurückgezogen hatte, in Briefen die Regeln für seine Gemeinschaft an seine Mönche geschrieben habe. Bei den "Briefen" handelt es sich um Dokumente, die zum jährlichen Vorlesen bestimmt waren; die Regeltexte enthalten 1. das Verbots-/Gebotswort; 2. das Regelwort mit Straffolge; 3. das Fluchwort. Letztgenanntes stellt eine neue Gestalt der Regel dar, die auf der geistlichen Verpflichtung der Mönche basiert. *Inge Hofmann*

78424 KEMP, Barry J., The City of el-Amarna as a Source for the Study of Urban Society in Ancient Egypt, *World Archaeology*, London 9 (1977-1978), 123-139, with 1 map, 2 plans and 3 fig.

Studying the city of el-Amarna as a clear example of a single period site the author disputes that it was exceptional by an unusual degree of spaciousness. In Thebes too many-storeyed houses were probably rare, and other cities than el-

Amarna appear to spread down on the floodplain during the N.K. Hence the
evidence from el-Amarna has a wider relevance for the study of urban society
in Egypt.
Although the evidence from the excavations is not abundant the author points
out several methods to conclude from the architectural remains to the structure
of the society. He compares the areas of the houses with those in Deir el-Medîna
and Kahûn, and with those of the courtyard areas in el-Amarna itself. From the
plan of a group of houses in the North Suburb (square U. 38) he suggests that
it was inhabited by an extended family. There may also have existed a well established form of contact between owners and contractors for building houses
on new sites, and there was probably a sort of mature plan for the new city before the people moved into it.

78425   KEMP, Barry J., A Further Note on the Palace of Apries at Memphis, *GM* Heft
29 (1978), 61.

Zusatz zu unserer Nummer 77410.
Vor Petrie's Ausgrabungen in Memphis 1908 führte bereits Daninos Untersuchungen im gleichen Gelände durch, die er 1904 in *ASAE* 5 kurz beschrieb und
die hier referiert werden. Ausser einem wichtigen Bronzehort werden keine
weiteren Objekte genannt. Daressy lokalisierte den Fund in den Norden von
Kôm el-Nawa, was von Porter und Moss (III, 217) übernommen wurde. Doch
nach der klaren Angabe von Daninos wurde der Fund im Osten des Apries- Pa-
lastes getätigt.                                                *Inge Hofmann*

78426   KEMP, Barry J., The Harîm-Palace at Medinet el-Ghurab, *ZÄS* 105 (1978), 122-
133, with 2 maps and 1 plan.

Kemp discusses the principal building in Medînet el-Ghurab ("Gurob"). This
was not a temple, but the "harim of Mer-wer/She", a palace in its own right.
Immediately adjacent is a small temple dedicated to the (Ramesside) cult of
Tuthmosis III, founder of the N.K. settlement. The author stresses parallels
with Deir el-Medîna.                                      *M. Heerma van Voss*

78427   KEMP, B.J., Imperialism and Empire in New Kingdom Egypt (c. 1575-1087
B.C.), in: *Imperialism in the Ancient World*. The Cambridge University Research Seminar in Ancient History. Edited by P.D.A. Garnsey and C.R. Whit-
taker, Cambridge, Cambridge University Press, [1978], 7-57 and 284-297,
with 2 maps and 3 plans.

The paper consists of three parts: an introduction, a study on Nubia and one
on Western Asia under Egyptian domination.
First the author sets forth the specific character of formal texts dealing with
conquest, posing the question how their material can be interpreted in view of
actual events. Nearer to that level are the treaty with the Hittites and the Amarna
Letters, which show rational treatment of the international situation. On account of written and archaeological evidence the author then studies the patterns
of Egyptian activities abroad, pointing out two basic interests: economic returns
and the pursuit of "glory".
In the section on the Nubian area the author deals at length with its history during the N.K., the temples and towns, their distribution, and the system of Egyp-

tian activities. He discusses the character of Egyptian settlements in Nubia, the extent of Egyptianization of the local population, the penetration of Egyptian religion into the Nubian society, and the demographic developments in Nubia in this period, casting some doubt on the generally accepted idea of a dramatic decline of the population.

In Western Asia the Egyptians inherited an existing vassal system. Discussing the political, economic, cultural and religious aspects of the Egyptian domination, he stresses that it appears not to have brought prosperity and peace, but in how far the decline was general or was due to the Egyptians is uncertain.

78428 KEMP, Barry J., Preliminary Report on the El-'Amarna Survey, 1977, *JEA* 64 (1978), 22-34, with 4 maps, 3 fig. and 2 pl.

A 1:5000 scale map is being prepared of the whole area, and a 1:2500 map of the main city area. Two areas are noted for possible future excavation. Brick stamps were noted from an unexcavated building in square 0.43. Further work was done on the workmen's village and its extra-mural settlement, and an important discovery was made in the form of another stone village to the southeast, measuring 75 x 50 m. analagous to that of Deir el-Medîna. Another important identification was that of the so-called 'Roman camp' at Kôm el-Nana which appears to have been a palace or religious building of Akhenaten's reign. The enclosure measures c.225 x 210 m. and produced N.K. sherds and carved limestone fragments. A sandy depression in the north-east corner may indicate a well or pool. *E.P. Uphill*

KEMP, Barry J., see also our number 78320.

KENDALL, Timothy, see our number 78745.

78429 KENIK, Helen Ann, The Design for Kingship in I Kings 3:4-15: A Study in the Deuteronomistic Narrative Technique and the Theology of Kingship, *Dissertation Abstracts International*, Ann Arbor, Mich. 39, No. 4 (October 1978), 2365-A.

Abstract of a thesis Saint Louis University, 1978 (364 p.: order no. 7818703). Chapter 2 discusses i.a. the view of S. Herrmann that Israel borrowed the forms of an Egyptian literary genre, the Königsnovelle, and remodelled it. *L.Z.*

KENYON, Kathleen, see our number 78646.

78430 KERRN LILLESØ, Ebba, Four Late Egyptian Sculptures in Thorvaldsen's Museum, *SAK* 6 (1978), 97-106, with 6 pl.

The author discusses four sculptures from Thorvaldsen's museum in Copenhagen: the lower part of a naophorous kneeling figure (No. 356), representing the royal scribe *P3dpp*, from the Saite Period; a fragment of a libation bowl with a figure kneeling at the rim (No.357), according to the inscription an administrator of the Temples of Neith called *Ḥr-3ḥ-bỉt*, probably from Sais and from the XXVIth Dynasty; a grey granite head (No.358) from the Persian Period, and a black basalt head (No.359) from the 4th century B.C.

78431  KESTEMONT, Guy, La société internationale mitannienne et le royaume d'Amurru à l'époque amarnienne, *Orientalia Lovaniensia Periodica*, Leuven 9 (1978), 27-32.

The author demonstrates from the Armarna Letters that, before Aziru, the ruler of Amurru, allied himself with Egypt, Amurru was part of the international Mitanni society, and he points out that the animosity between the rulers of Byblos and Amurru was not an internal Egyptian, but an international conflict, that the Hittite empire took over after the collapse of the Mitanni power, and that the region of Nahr el-Kebir has always formed a frontier between political powers.
Compare also our number 77022.                                          *L.Z.*

KHALLOUF, L., see our number 78043.

78432  el-KHOULI, Ali, Egyptian Stone Vessels. Predynastic Period to Dynasty III. Typology and Analysis, 3 volumes, Mainz/Rhein, Philipp von Zabern, [1978] ([vol. I + II:] 15.5 x 22.5 cm; LXXXII + 862 p.;[vol. III:] 21 x 29.8 cm; 162 pl.); at head of title: Deutsches Archäologisches Institut. Abteilung Kairo; rev. *BiOr* 36 (1979), 174-175 (A.L. Kelley).

The text volume I begins with a historical introduction in which the excavations from which the basic material of the present study has come pass the review. Then the scheme of the work is explained, followed by a lengthy synopsis of the used classification.
The catalogue proper (p. 1-762) lists 6039 items (of which nos 5653-6039 unpublished and hence only briefly mentioned). They are divided into 36 classes, each of which consists of types and sub-types. The second principle of arrangement is the date of the vessels, the third one the sites where they come from. For each single piece are mentioned its provenance (where known), material, museum number and bibliography.
Two chapters deal with the origin of stone vase manufacture and date ranges of the various classes (763-788), and with the manufacture, ancient as well as modern, of the vessels (789-801).
At the end indexes of sites and tombs (802-843) and of materials (843-850), and various concordances as well as a bibliography.
The plate volume presents drawings of types and sub-types, some drawings and photographs illustrating the manufacture process, and photographs of selected vessels.

78433  el-KHOULY, Aly, Excavations at the Pyramid of Userkaf, 1976: Preliminary Report, *JEA* 64 (1978), 35-43, with 1 pl.and 1 fig.

The pyramid corresponds rather to the Fourth Dynasty type than to the Fifth. The north and west sides had never been cleared and this task was therefore undertaken, together with the restoration of the dangerous entrance. Three Ptolemaic burials were found to the north and a painted limestone slab from a Fifth Dynasty mastaba. A catalogue of 94 objects found during the work is included.                                          *E.P. Uphill*

78434 el-KHOULY, Aly, An Offering-Table of Sesostris I from El-Lisht, *JEA* 64 (1978), 44, with 1 pl.

This large table, 1.02 m wide and 0.51 m high, was discovered in 1976 during the clearance of the irrigation canal near the pyramids of Lisht, and must have come from either the upper or lower funerary temple of Sesostris I. It is of grey granite and invokes Geb. A translation of the inscription is given.
*E.P. Uphill*

78435 el-KHOULI, Ali, A Stela from Tura, *JSSEA* 8 (1977-1978), 46-47, with 1 pl.

Publication of a rectangular limestone offering stela, found in Tura, in Tomb No. 384, in 1964. After the style it can be dated to the M.K. It belonged to a man called *Dbs* and his wife *Gft*; other members of the family are also represented, while the woman's parents and siblings receive greater prominence than those of the man.

78436 KITCHEN, K.A., The Bible in its World. The Bible & Archaeology Today, Downers Grove, Illinois, InterVarsity Press, [1978] (14 x 21 cm; 168 p., 2 maps, 1 plan, colour ill. on cover).   Pr. $ 3.95

This book, intended for the general reader, mainly deals with biblical history and its background until Solomon, with at the end chapters on the Exile and Return to Palestine of the Israelites and on the time of the New Testament. A particular chapter is devoted to Ebla. Self-evidently ancient Egypt comes up for discussion on many pages, e.g. the Oppression and Exodus (p. 75-79), narratives in Egypt (61-62), instructions (106-107), Sheshonq (109-110). Notes and a select bibliography, maps and indexes at the end.
We did not see the original editon, Exeter, The Paternoster Press, 1977.

78437 KITCHEN, K.A., Documentation additionnelle sur Iouny (*RdE* 28, 156-8), *RdE* 30 (1978), 168.

Note additionelle sur notre no. 76443.
Trois nouveaux documents nommant le grand ritualiste Iouny.   *Ph. Derchain*

78438 KITCHEN, K.A., From the Brickfields of Egypt, *Tyndale Bulletin* 27 (1976), [1977], 137-147.

The author first outlines textual references to brick production in ancient Egypt, particularly those from the Louvre Leather Roll (*KRI* II, 789-799) and makes remarks on the organization and control of the work, as well as some others of a miscellaneous nature.   *L.Z.*

78439 KITCHEN, K.A., Ramesside Inscriptions. Historical and Biographical. III. Fascicle 1, Oxford, B.H. Blackwell Ltd, [1978] (20.4 x 29 cm; 32 p. [= III, 1-32]; rev. *BiOr* 37 (1980), 38 (W. Helck).

This fascicle is the first one in the series of volume III, the only one of which so far nothing had appeared, and which is concerned with the contemporaries of

Ramses II. It deals with the Private Monuments of Contemporaries of Ramses II, engaged in the Civil and Royal Administration, Category I: Viziers, and is completely devoted to inscriptions of the vizier Paser, mainly from his Theban tomb 106, and his other monuments in Western Thebes, particularly Deir el-Medîna. *L.Z.*

78440  KITCHEN, K.A., Ramesside Inscriptions. Historical and Biographical. III. Fascicle 2, Oxford, B.H. Blackwell Ltd, [1978] (20.4 x 29 cm; 32 p. [= III, 33-64]); rev. *BiOr* 37 (1980), 28 (W. Helck).

Sequel to our preceding number.
After the continuation of the inscriptions of the vizier Paser follow those of the viziers Khay, again mainly from Western Thebes, Neferronpet, the little-known Prahotep (called A) and the better known Prahotep (called B) who was buried in Sedment. *L.Z.*

78441  KITCHEN, K.A., Ramesside Inscriptions. Historical and Biographical. III: 3, Oxford, B.H. Blackwell Ltd, [1978] (20.4 x 29 cm; 32 p. [= III, 65-96]); rev. *BiOr* 37 (1980), 28 (W. Helck).

Sequel to our preceding number.
The first two pages continue the inscriptions of the vizier Prahotep, labelled B, the last of Kitchen's first category of viziers, in the section on civil and royal administration. The second category is devoted to the viceroys of Nubia: Heqanakht, Paser, and Huy, monuments of all of whom come from Nubia including Aswân. The many monuments of Setau are ordered geographically from Thebes and Upper Egypt up to Wadi Sebua, where this fascicle ends with twelve stelae of Setau and colleagues. *L.Z.*

78442  KITCHEN, K.A., Ramesside Inscriptions. Historical and Biographical. III: 4, Oxford, B.H. Blackwell Ltd, [1978] (20.4 x 29 cm; 32 p. [= III, 97-128]); rev. *BiOr* 37 (1980), 28 (W. Helck).

Sequel to our preceding number.
In this fascicle the monuments of Setau are continued in a geographical order from Wadi es-Sebua to Buhen and Sai. The next category of the private monuments of contemporaries of Ramses II in the civil and royal administration is that of colleagues and subordinates of viceroys of Nubia, which is subdivided into monuments of troop-commanders of Kush, deputies in Wawat and Kush, other high officials, lesser staff of the viceroy's administration, local governors, and local artists and craftsmen. *L.Z.*

78443  KITCHEN, K.A., Some Ramesside Friends of Mine, *JSSEA* 8 (1977-1978), 72.

Abstract of a paper.

78444  KLAKOWICZ, Beatrix, A Bohairic Translation of the Last Books of Daniel (PPalau Rib. inv. 61-inv. 65r), *Studia Papyrologica*, Roma 17 (1978), 7-33, with 2 pl.

The five fragments in Bohairic dialect preserve some passages of the last books of Daniel and the colophon. The texts are presented with textual notes only.
*L.Z.*

78445 KLASENS, A., Rijksmuseum van Oudheden, *Nederlandse Rijksmusea*, 's Gravenhage 98 (1976), [1978], 251-264.

Among the acquisitions of the year 1976 were a collection of Coptic manuscripts on parchment and papyrus, a bronze door-bolt from the XXVIth Dynasty and various shawabtis among which ones of Siptah, Hornakht son of Osorkon II and queen Tuy mother of Ramses II.
The collection of prehistoric artifacts, formerly in the possession of Edmond Vignard, Paris, and purchased in 1973, consisting of 4423 numbers, was incorporated into the inventory. At the end a short report on the second campaign of the Dutch-Anglo excavations at Saqqâra.
*L.Z.*

78446 KLEMM, Dankwart Dietrich, Gesteinsbestimmungen in der Archäologie, *in*: *Methoden der Archäologie*. Eine Einführung in ihre naturwissenschaftlichen Techniken. Herausgegeben von B. Hrouda, München, Verlag C.H. Beck, [1978], 327-346, with 8 ill., 1 fig. and 3 tables.

In this book on the application of the techniques of the natural sciences in archaeology, the author discusses the identification of stone. Some of the material is taken from Egyptian monuments
*L.Z.*

78447 KLICHOWSKA, Melania, Preliminary Results of Palaeoethnobotanical Studies on Plant Impressions on Potsherds from the Neolithic Settlement at Kadero, *Nyame Akuma*, Calgary No. 12 (May 1978), 42-43.

Ungefähr 150 Topfscherben von der neolithischen Siedlung Kadero (etwa 4000 v.Chr.) wurden hinsichtlich der Pflanzenabdrücke untersucht. Die meisten stammen von gezüchteten Zerealien: Sorghum vulgare, Sorghum sp., Eleusine coracana (Cynosurus coracana), Pennisetum sp. (= Panicum sp.), zwei Arten von Setaria sp., Digitaria sp., Eragrostis abissinica (Poa abissinica). Einige Kornabdrücke glichen denen von domestizierter Gerste (Hordeum sp). Ausserdem fanden sich Eindrücke von Samen wildwachsenden Grases. *Inge Hofmann*

78448 KOBYLINA, M.M., Изображения восточных божеств в севером причерноморье в первые века н. э , Москва, Издательство "Наука", 1978 (12.4 х 16.3 cm; 215 p., 2 fig., 139 ill., ill. on cover). Pr. 85 коп.

"Representations of Oriental Divinities on the North Coast of the Black Sea in the First Centuries A.D."
Slightly enlarged version of our number 76451.
The chapter on Egypt mentions now 29 instead of 25 objects (all illustrated).

78449 KOCHAVI, Moshe, Canaanite Aphek. Its Acropolis and Inscriptions, *Expedition*, Philadelphia, Penn. 20, No.4 (Summer 1978), 12-17, with 12 ill., 1 map and 1 plan.

Among the inscriptional finds from the necropolis of Tel Aphek-Antipatris were an Egyptian N.K. ring and a faience temple foundation deposit tablet, bearing the names of Ramses II and the goddess Isis.  *L.Z.*

78450  KOLTA, Kamal Sabri, Zur Geschichte der Diagnose der altägyptischen Augenkrankheit "Trachom", in: *Medizinische Diagnostik in Geschichte und Gegenwart*. Festschrift Heinz Goerke zum sechzigsten Geburtstag. Herausgegeben von Christa Habrich, Frank Margut und Jörn Henning Wolf unter Mitarbeit von Renate Wittern, München, Werner Fritsch, 1978, 41-50.

After few remarks on Egyptian oculists and ophtalmology the author deals with the symptoms of trachoma (e.g. *nḥ3t*, "unevenness" of the eyelids) as they are recorded in the Papyrus Ebers. He follows the references to this disease through Coptic, Greek and, particularly, Arabic medicine.

78451  KORNFELD, Walter, Onomastica aramaica aus Ägypten, Wien, Verlag der Österreichischen Akademie der Wissenschaften, 1978 (15.4 x 23.8 cm; 144 p.) = Sitzungsberichte. Österreichische Akademie der Wissenschaften. Philosophisch-historische Klasse, 333.

This onomasticon of Aramaic proper names from Egypt contains, apart from a list of Egyptian names on p. 77-97, other pertinent information in the introduction: additions to the Aramaic alphabet used for the transcription, the rendering of frequently occurring elements in the Egyptian proper names; names of gods and theophorous elements.
At the end of the book a retrograde index and an integrated one of all proper names.  *L.Z.*

78452  KOZLOFF, Arielle P., Ancient Art, *The Bulletin of the Cleveland Museum of Art*, Cleveland 65, No.6 (June 1978), 181, with 1 ill.

The only 1977 addition was a small ivory giraffe head from the time of Amenhotep III.  *L.Z.*

KRAMER, Samuel Noah, see our number 78264.

KRAUSE, Martin, see our number 78269.

78453  KRAUSS, Rolf, Das Ende der Amarnazeit. Beiträge zur Geschichte und Chronologie des Neuen Reiches, Hildesheim, Gerstenberg Verlag, 1978 (17 x 24 cm; XVI + 284 p., 2 pl.) = Hildesheimer Ägyptologische Beiträge herausgegeben von Arne Eggebrecht, 7; rev. *BiOr* 37 (1980), 319-321 (Robert Hari).

The book consists of two parts, one on the end of the Amarna Period, the other on the chronology of the N.K.
The major point in the first part is that ꜥnḫt-ḫprw-Rꜥ, that is, Meritaton, reigned independently after the death of Akhnaton and before her husband Smenkhkare. After presenting a survey of various reconstructions of the events at the end of the Amarna Period the author deals with the evidence of Manetho, particularly with Akencheres (= ꜥnḫ-n-Rꜥ), with some small objects (see the

plate) testifying the female royal name, with the identity of Niphururia and Akhnaton, and in a last section with the reigns of Smenkhkare and Tutankhamon in Amarna.

There follow ten excursuses, i.a. about the chronology of Šuppiluliumas' Syrian campaigns; the Amarna archive at the moment of Akhnaton's death; the names of Smenkhkare; chronology and status of Nefertiti; the marriage of Akhnaton with his daughter, which the author argues to have been actual (summary of the events on p. 118-121); the interpretation of the royal names in the form X-ḫpr(w)-Rᶜ, with a grammatical note to the difference of the plural ḫprw and the verbal substantive (summary p. 165).

Part 2, on the chronology of the N.K., begins with a survey of the problems. The dates of accession and durations of all reigns between Tuthmosis III and Ramses II are discussed, leading to the conclusion that the total is c. 200 years. The author then argues that the Sothis date of Pap. Ebers, based on observation on Elephantine, leads to the conclusion that the beginning of the N.K. falls probably in 1542/40 B.C. Some synchronisms with the history of the Near East confirm the year 1279 B.C. as year 1 of Ramses II. The results of this part are tabulated, with absolute dates, on p. 202-203.

An extensive excursus (204-263) is devoted to the XVIIIth Dynasty after the tradition of Manetho; two others to the era ἀπὸ Μενόφρεως and to Sethi I after Pseudo-Eratosthenes.

Indexes on p. 277-283.

78454  KRAUSS, Rolf, *Sō'*, König von Ägypten – ein Deutungsvorschlag, *Mitteilungen der Deutschen Orient-Gesellschaft zu Berlin*, Berlin 110 (1978), 49-54.

After having eliminated the possibilities for a personal identification with the Biblical name Sō' (II Kings 17, 4), the author attempts to explain the name from the Late Period pronunciation of the word (*ny-*)*swt*, "king".
Compare our numbers 73696 and 77275.                                       L.Z.

78455  KRIKORIAN, Abraham D., Vivi Laurent-Täckholm, *Nature*, London 275, No. 5680 (12 October 1978), 574.

Obituary notice.

78456  KROMER, Karl, Siedlungsfunde aus dem frühen Alten Reich in Giseh. Österreichische Ausgrabungen 1971-1975, Wien, Verlag der Österreichischen Akademie der Wissenschaften,1978 (21 x 29.2 cm; 130 p., 2 folding maps, 23 figs. [2 folding], 16 ill., 5 diagrams, 40 pl., ill. on cover) = Österreichische Akademie der Wissenschaften. Philosophisch-historische Klasse. Denkschriften, 136.

Final report on the Austrian excavations at Gîza E. of the Mycerinus Pyramid. (for preliminary reports, see our numbers 72394, 73418 and 74421). The first chapter describes the history of the excavations (summary p. 20-21) by which the dumped material of a settlement from the first dynasties was brought to light. This settlement will have been situated somewhere in the area of the pyramids and was entirely demolished, all material not taken away by its inhabitants being removed, houses included.

The long second chapter is devoted to a description of the various types of finds:

stone implements, mostly flintstone; ceramic vessels of several types, among which ceramic palettes; stone vessels; objects of faience; beads; copper implements; ship's models; seals and seal impressions, etc.
In the third chapter the architectural elements are studied, among which parts of painted plaster, while in a short last chapter type and duration of the original settlement are discussed. From the material it appears to have existed from the very beginning of the O.K. till the end of the reign of Chephren. Possibly it played a role in the festivals of Uniting the Kingdom, while artifacts from the IVth Dynasty seem to have been specially made for the tombs. The distribution of actual tools in the dump demonstrates that particular quarters were inhabited by artisans. After flourishing times first under Cheops and then under Chephren the settlement was destroyed at one time, obviously by order of the king.

KROMER, Karl, see also our number 78593.

78457 KRZYŻANIAK, L., New Data Concerning the Cultural Status of the Valley of the Upper (Main) Nile in Pre-Meroitic Times, in: *Études nubiennes*, 165-174, with 3 fig., and 4 ill. on 3 pl.

Es handelt sich um einen Bericht über die Ausgrabungen von Kadero, einer neolithischen Stätte nördlich von Khartûm; Überreste weisen daraufhin, dass die Bevölkerung eine aneignende Wirtschaftsform besass, wobei die Fischerei eine geringe Rolle gespielt zu haben scheint. Daneben besass sie bereits domestizierte Tiere (Rinder, Schafe, Ziegen, Hunde). Mahlsteine allein weisen aber noch nicht darauf hin, dass sie bereits kultiviertes Getreide hatte.
*Inge Hofmann*

78458 KRZYŻANIAK, Lech, New Light on Early Food Production in the Central Sudan, *Journal of African History*, Cambridge 19, 2 (1978), 159-172, with 4 fig.

Durch die Ausgrabungen der neolithischen Siedlung von Kadero wurde eine Anzahl von Skelettüberresten domestizierter Tiere zutage gefördert: Rinder, Schafe, Ziegen und Hunde. Die Rinderhaltung war von grosser wirtschaftlicher Bedeutung für die Siedlung und wurde ergänzt durch die Haltung von Ziegen und Schafen. Wahrscheinlich wurden auch die Hunde für diese Viehhaltung verwendet. Pflanzeneindrücke in Topfscherben zeigen, dass fast ausschliesslich Sorghum und zwei Arten von Hirse, die wahrscheinlich gleichfalls domestiziert waren, zum Lebensunterhalt dienten. Das erklärt auch die grosse Anzahl von Mahlsteinen, die in Kadero gefunden wurden. Dazu kam noch die Sammeltätigkeit, wobei das Sammeln von Mollusken die Hauptrolle spielte, während Jagen und Fischen wohl weniger betrieben wurde. Die prognathe Bevölkerung scheint eine autochthone am Nil gewesen zu sein, die durch Kontakt mit anderen und fremden Gruppen die domestizierten Tiere und kultivierten Pflanzen übernahm. *Inge Hofmann*

78459 KUCHMAN, Liza, Egyptian Clay Anthropoid Coffins, *Serapis* 4 (1977-1978), 11-22, with 2 pl.

The author presents a preliminary summary of her study of the clay anthropoid coffins found in Egypt and Nubia. The generally accepted idea that they are of non-Egyptian origin and that those found in Egypt belong to Philistines or other foreigners is certainly wrong. It is due to the fact that the objects are largely disregarded by the excavators. Actually, large numbers have come to light from all over Egypt, in about fifty cemeteries, so that clearly the home of this object is Egypt itself.
In three sections the author describes some instances from the earlier N.K., the late N.K. and the T.I.P., and the Ptolemaic-Roman Period.

78460 KUCHMAN, Lisa, Tell el-Maskhuta: First Season, Summer 1978, *Newsletter ARCE* No. 105 (Summer 1978), 12-13.

Short note to the excavations at Tell el-Maskhûta in the Eastern Delta, where apart from mainly Persian and Graeco-Roman material, MB II A/B burials were found similar to those found at Tell el-Dab'a. *L.Z.*

78461 KUHN, K.H., A Panegyric on Apollo, Archimandrite of the Monastery of Isaac by Stephen, Bishop of Heracleopolis Magna, Edited [and] Translated, Louvain, Secrétariat du CorpusSCO, 1978 (15.5 x 25.2 cm; XVI + 62 [and] III + 40 p.)= Scriptores Coptici, 39-40 = Corpus Scriptorum Christianorum Orientalium, 394-395.

In the introduction of the first volume, the edition of the text, the author lists his manuscript sources, discusses authorship, date and language and presents the contents in short. The text itself is presented after the complete version (Pierpont Morgan Library M 579), with three appendices containing the text of the minor manuscripts. Extensive indexes.
The second volume contains the translation and follows the same order. Here too indexes are added. *L.Z.*

78462 KULIKOVA, А.М., Неизданное письмо Ж.-Ф. Шампольона П. Л. Шиллингу; ВДИ 3 (145), 1978, 97-107, with 3 ill. and an English summary on p. 107.

Publication of a hitherto unknown letter of J.-F. Champollion to P.L. Schilling. *L.Z.*

78463 KURTH, Dieter, Zum Schriftsystem in den ägyptischen Tempeln der Spätzeit, *GM* Heft 29 (1978), 63-68.

Zu unserer Nr. 78206 werden einige weiterführende Überlegungen zum Schriftsystem der späten Tempelinschriften gemacht. In text Nr. 9° muss Chnum als Herr des Kataraktengebietes angesprochen werden. Als wesentlich werden zwei Probleme herausgestellt: 1. Wieviel Einsicht in die lebende Sprache der Zeit darf man sich aus den Inschriften der späten Tempel erhoffen? Es lassen sich hinter dem Schriftsystem Einblicke in die lebende Sprache gewinnen, aber mit anderer Erwartungshaltung und mit anderem Ausgangspunkt. 2. Das Problem der Akrophonie bei der Entwicklung neuer einkonsonantischer Lautwerte der Hieroglyphen, da zumindest in Esna zur Gewinnung neuer Lautwerte Konsonantenprinzip und akrophonisches Prinzip nebeneinander bestehen konnten.

*Inge Hofmann*

KVAS, I., see our number 78349.

LABROUSSE, Audran, see our number 78076.

LAFERRIÈRE, Pierre-Henri, see our number 78175.

78464 LAFFORGUE, Gilbert, L'Orient et la Grèce jusqu'à la conquête romaine, [Paris], Presses Universitaires de France, [1977] (12.6 x 18 cm; 272 p., 1 ill. on cover); series: Le Fil des Temps.

In this book on the ancient Near East and Greece before the Roman domination several short sections are devoted to Egypt in the first part dealing with the preponderant position of the Ancient Near East up to the 9th century B.C. We mention: Egypt in the fourth millennium B.C. (p. 15-17); Egypt: The O.K. and the F.I.P. during the flourishing of the Early Bronze Age in the third millennium (19-21); Egypt: The M.K. and the Hyksos during the Middle Bronze Age (20th to 16th centuries B.C.) (30-31); The N.K. during the Late Bronze Age (16th to 12th centuries B.C.) (44-47); and Egypt from 1166 to 716 B.C. during the Dark Period of the Early Iron Age. *L.Z.*

78465 LAMBELET, Edouard, Orbis terrae aegiptiae. Museum aegiptium. Illustrated guide to the Egyptian Museum. Guide illustrée du Musée Égyptien. Illustrierter Führer zum Aegyptischen Museum, Cairo, Lehnert & Landrock Succ. Publish., [1978] (17 x 25 cm; II + 301 p., numerous ill. [many in colour], fig. and plans).

This is a very useful guide for the visitor of the Egyptian Museum, with all explanations given in English, French and German. For objects of outstanding quality the catalogue number is underlined, while those of objects not illustrated are in brackets. The itinerary through the Museum follows for the lower galleries and rooms a clockwise order, beginning with the central hall and then left to the O.K. room, and is exactly indicated on the plans. Apart from the short descriptions to the objects and useful extra's such as cartouches in hieroglyphic print, there are very short introductions to the various periods, mainly indicating for the visitor what type of objects are conspicuous and typical for the period. The itinerary through the upper rooms and galleries presents a sharp selection, apart from musts as the Tutankhamun treasure, that of Hetepheres, the Jewellery Room and the Mummies Room. Many of the photographs are of mediocre quality, especially the coloured ones.
Glossary and chronological table at the end of the book. *L.Z.*

78466 LAMBREGHTS, Dominique, Les colosses osiriaques et dérivés, *Revue des archéologues et historiens d'art de Louvain*, Louvain 11 (1978), 187-188.

Abstract of a small thesis.

LANCEL, Serge, see our number 78210.

78467   LANDA, N., Ушебти Мутри, Сообщения Государственного Эрмитажа, Ленинград 43 (1978), 40-43, with 5 ill. and an English summary on p. 69.

"The Ushabti of Mutri".
Publication of a shawabti of a lady Mutri, who wears a wig of a shape so far not recorded for shawabtis (Ermitage Inv. No. 18515). The piece is dated to the reign of Tuthmosis I.                                                                                         L.Z.

78468   LANDENIUS, Hedvig, Two Spiral Snake Armbands, *Medelhavsmuseet Bulletin*, Stockholm 13(1978), 37-40, with 5 ill.

Publication of a pair of gold armbands (MM 1973:9 and 1973:10) of the spiral, snake type, usually connected with the Isis cult. The author discusses several examples and states that it is difficult to relate them to a specific date and geographical area.
In an appendix the results of an analysis of the gold are presented.

78469   LASKOWSKA-KUSZTAL, Ewa, Un atelier de perruquier à Deir el-Bahari, *Études et Travaux* 10 (1978), 82-120, with 6 ill.

Fairly deep under the surface in the area above the temple of Montuhotep at Deir el-Bahri, the Polish excavators found a wooden model head and four alabaster vessels, all enclosed by a piece of cloth. In the vessels were numerous bits of hair and wigs, fragments of ribbons, hair-nets and -pins, and suchlike. Obviously the objects came from the workshop of a wigmaker. The author presents a minute description of all items and a discussion of wigs in Egypt in general. On account of seal stamps and the type of some objects the find can roughly be dated in the period between the XIIth and the XVIIIth Dynasty.

LAUER, Jean-Philippe, see our number 78013.

78470   LAYTON, Bentley, Progress on the Coptic-English Dictionary of Gnostic Literature, *Enchoria* 8, Sonderband (1978), 19*(65)-20*(66).

Abstract of a paper read at the First International Congress of Coptology, held in Cairo, December 1976.
The author gives an account of the state of affairs of the Coptic-English Dictionary of Gnostic Literature that has been undertaken by T.O. Lambdin (Harvard) and himself (Yale). The dictionary will be modelled, as far as practical, on W. Bauer, "Griechisch-Deutsches Wörterbuch zu den Schriften des Neuen Testaments und der übrigen urchristlichen Literatur", Berlin, 1937.    *W. Brunsch*

78471   LAYTON, Bentley, The Soul as a Dirty Garment (Nag Hammadi Codex II, - Tractate 6, 131: 27-34), *Le Muséon*, Louvain 91 (1978), 155-169.

The author studies a difficult passage in the Exegetical Treatise concerning the Soul from the Nag Hammadi Codex II containing a comparison of the soul with garments. A translation of a magician's recipe for dyeing wool (P. Berlin Copt. 8316), from the 8th century A.D., is added.                                                L.Z.

78472  LEAHY, M.A., Excavations at Malkata and the Birket Habu 1971-1974 under the Direction of David B. O'Connor and Barry J. Kemp. The University Museum, University of Pennsylvania Egyptian Expedition. The Inscriptions, Warminster, Aris & Phillips Ltd., [1978] (21 x 29.5 cm; VI + 63 p., 24 pl., fig.on cover) = Egyptology Today. No. 2, Vol. IV.

After a preface by the editors of the series, of which this is the first published volume, the author presents in chapter 1 a general description of the material which consists of 177 hieratic jar labels (or dockets), 245 sealings, 10 painted labels and 2 wooden labels. Most of them came from site K, a temporary brick building erected for the first jubilee of Amenophis III in the years 29-30 and soon afterwards destroyed. The other inscriptions constitute a random sample similar to that published by Hayes in *JNES* 10 (1951); cfr our number 1826.
In chapter 2 the jar labels are discussed. First those in which a commodity is mentioned: *srmt*, here rendered as "ale" (by far the largest group), wine, meat products, oils etc. Then those mentioning only, because of their fragmentary state, royal estates, royal names, and other names and titles. There follow those of which only a phrase referring to the jubilee is preserved, and those of which only a few signs remain. At the end the wooden labels, and one ostracon with a few words from the Instruction of Amenemhat. On the plates each inscription is presented in facsimile and transcription; in the text in transliteration and translation, with comments.
Chapter 3 deals with the sealings. Since many are identical of each type only one is given. A particular group has various epithets of king Amenophis III. At the end short sections about the painted labels (always mentioning meat) and the brick stamps.
Indexes on p. 49-51. Concordances of objects and catalogue numbers on p. 52-56. A list of palaeographical forms on p. 58-63.
See also our number 78375, particularly the second part on the amphorae.

78473  LECLANT, Jean, L'exploration des côtes de la Mer Rouge. A la quête de Pount et des secrets de la Mer Erythrée, *Annales d'Ethiopie*, Paris 11 (1978), 69-73.

The author presents a survey of the Egyptian and classical evidence concerning Punt, arguing that it was reached over the Red Sea, but also through the wadis E. of Nubia. With other scholars he continues his research along the Red Sea shore which may result in more knowledge about the country.

78474  LECLANT, Jean, Fouilles et travaux en Égypte et au Soudan, 1976-1977, *Orientalia* 47 (1978), 266-320, with 37 ill. on 26 pl.

Sequel to our number 77464.
The survey of this year consists of 60 numbers for Egypt, 12 for Sudan and 10 for other countries. Among the sites in Egypt, apart from the regions of Memphis and Thebes, we mention: Tell ed-Dabʻa, Abûsîr, Dashûr, Medînet Mâdi, el-ʻAmarna, Aswân, the oases of Khârga and Dâkhla, and Philae; among those in Sudan: Meroe and Kadero. Indexes p. 317-320.

78475   LECLANT, Jean, Le grenouille d'éternité des pays du Nil ou monde méditerranéen, in: *Hommages Vermaseren*, 561-572, with 2 pl.

Proceeding from the decoration of a bronze bowl with frogs and lotus flowers, found in N. Ethiopia and clearly bearing a Meroitic motif, the author deals with the symbolism of the frog in Egypt and follows the representation from Egyptian to Meroitic and Graeco-Roman art, mentioning numerous examples.

78476   LECLANT, Jean, Histoire de la diffusion des cultes égyptiens, *Annuaire. École Pratique des Hautes Études.* Ve section – sciences religieuses, Paris 86 (1977-1978), 173-181.

Sequel to our number 77465.
The report deals with the diffusion of the Isis cults, Meroitic studies, and lists the publications of the director and the participants in the courses.          *L.Z.*

78477   LECLANT, Jean, International Association of Egyptologists, *Newsletter ARCE* No. 103 (Winter 1977/78), 3.

Announcement on the reorganization of the International Association of Egyptologists.          *L.Z.*

78478   LECLANT, J., Sedeinga (Nubie Soudanaise), *Nyame Akuma*, Calgary No. 13 (1978), 41.

Da sich Frau Giorgini vollständig der Publikation des Soleb-Tempels widmen will, wurde mit den Ausgrabungsarbeiten in Sedeinga ein neues Team unter der Leitung von Leclant betraut. Die ersten Forschungsarbeiten wurden in Nilwa, im Süden des Geländes, durchgeführt; ein Gebäudekomplex mit Resten von zwei Säulen erwies sich als eine Kirche des klassischen nubischen Typs mit einer abgerundeten Absis im Osten, die von zwei kleinen Zimmern flankiert ist. Das Dach wurde in der Mitte von den zwei Säulen gestützt. Zwei andere kleine Zimmer lagen auf der Westseite. Eine reichhaltige Sammlung von Keramik konnte zusammengestellt werden.          *Inge Hofmann*

78479   LECLANT, Jean, Titres et Travaux, [no publisher], 1978 (16 x 23.5 cm; 36 p.).

Enlarged and revised edition of our number 74438.
The list of publications is extended to 1978. Added is a paper called "Perspectives d'enseignement et orientation des recherches" in which the author presents his view on Egyptological studies.

LECLANT, Jean, see also our numbers 78008, 78013, 78076, 78119, 78338 and 78614.

LECUYOT, G., see our number 78390.

78480   LEE, Sandra L. and Frederick F. STENN, Characterization of Mummy Bone Ochronotic Pigment, *The Journal of the American Medical Association*, Chicago 240, No. 2 (July 14, 1978), 136-138, with 5 ill. (1 in colour on cover).

Short report of the radiological investigation of the N.K. mummy of a certain Harwa, which was lent to Northwestern University School by the Field Museum of Natural History in Chicago. It appeared that Harwa suffered from ochronosis.
*L.Z.*

78481 LEEK, F. Filce, *Eutropius Niloticus*, *JEA* 64 (1978), 121-122, with 3 pl.

Further examination (cfr our number 76490) revealed the prey of this fish to have been the small Barbus fish. The wrappings appeared to be derived from the flax plant. *E.P. Uphill*

78482 LELLO, Glenn †, Thutmose III's First Lunar Date, *JNES* 37 (1978), 327-330.

The writer disagrees with the view first put forward by Faulkner that the lunar date recorded at the time of the Megiddo campaign should be emended to read from 21st, 9th month, Year 23, to the 20th. Interpreting the change of day to the hour or two before dawn and after, the awkward extra day is got rid of and the true day of battle shown to be the 21st. *E.P. Uphill*

78483 LEMAIRE, André and Pascal VERNUS, L' origine égyptienne du signe 𓎯 des poids inscrits de l' époque royale Israélite, *Semitica*, Paris 28 (1978), 53-58.

The authors first point out the a priori probability of an Egyptian origin of the sign 𓎯 which occurs on inscribed weights of the Hebrew Kingdom. It is argued that the sign denotes the word "alabaster", which seems to have been used very often for the manufacture of weights. *L.Z.*

LEONARD, Jr., Albert, see our number 78184.

78484 LEOSPO, Enrica, La mensa isiaca di Torino, Leiden, E.J. Brill, 1978 (15.5 x 24.5 cm; XIV + 100 p., 32 pl. [5 folding]) = Catalogo del Museo Egizio di Torino. Serie prima – Monumenti e testi. Volume 4 = Édition spéciale des Études préliminaires aux réligions orientales dans l' empire romain à l' occasion du 60-ième anniversaire de Maarten J. Vermaseren publiée par Margreet B. de Boer et T.A. Edridge, 70; rev. *BiOr* 37 (1980), 175 (L. Castiglione); *CdE* LV, No. 109-110 (1980), 170-172 (Ph. Derchain). Pr. fl. 96

In the first chapter, on the history of the famous mensa isiaca at Turin, the author presents a long bibliography of the table, from 1572 till today, and a survey of its history. The second chapter is devoted, after remarks on the technical characteristics and composition, to a very detailed description of first the middle register with, in the centre, Isis in the chapel and the divinities accompanying her (Haroeris, Toth and two winged goddesses) and then the field goddesses, the Nile gods and the sacred bulls. Then follow the upper register bearing representations of the slaughtering of the antelope, offering scenes, and Amon and company, and the lower register showing offerings to Ptah, Hathor, Harsomtus and Sekhmet, while the last part of the chapter deals with the minor representations on the frame. The last pages of the chapter contain epigraphical remarks and a conclusion. The third chapter discusses the stilistic characteristics (i.a. horror vacui), the author, the provenance and the date of the table. No indexes are given. *L.Z.*

78485   LEPROHON, Ronald J., The Personnel of the Middle Kingdom Funerary Stelae, *JARCE* 15 (1978), 33-38.

An assessment of the relationships other than between familiars on the group of Abydene stelae where the well-known Overseer of the Treasure '*Iy-ḥr-nfr.t* is the protagonist (ANOC 1 in our number 74688). Such relationships concern subordinates (sometimes calling their patron *ı͗t*, 'father', and taking the occasion for listing their whole family on a stela where they occur themselves *qua- litate qua*) and working colleagues, either in '*Iy-ḥr-nfr.t*'s profession or from among the Abydene priests he met during a particular part of his career. Reasons for inclusion of names on a stela may have been (1) sharing costs (among colleagues), (2) lowering costs (where sculptor's names were included), (3) contracts (with Abydene priests), and, of course, (4) the general feeling that piety should be shared among acquaintances of whatever kind.     *J.F. Borghouts*

78486   LESKO, Barbara S., The Remarkable Women of Ancient Egypt, [Berkeley, California, B.C. Scribe Publications, 1978] (21.6 x 27.8 cm; [IX +] 34 p., colour ill. on cover, frontispiece, 11 fig., 22 ill. including 11 in colour).

This booklet on women in ancient Egypt is intended for the general public. It consists of two parts, dealing with royal wives and with the average women respectively.
In part one the author discusses the mythological basis of kingship from which the role of women in the royal family may stem, and some more important queens, e.g. Ahmose-Nofretari, Hatshepsut, Tiye, Nefertari, Twosre, and Cleopatra VII. Part 2 is devoted to working women, women in the cults, equality under the law, and the lady of the house.
There are many quotations in the text from various Egyptian sources, e.g. from love poems (p. 27).

78487   LETELLIER, Bernadette, La vie quotidienne chez les artisans de Pharaon, *Archéologia*, Paris No. 125 (décembre 1978), 26-37, with 21 ill. (7 in colour) and 2 maps.

On account of an exhibition on the workmen of Deir el-Medîna, which consisted of objects from the Louvre on loan to the Museums of Metz, end 1978 to beginning 1979, the author sketches a picture of Deir el-Medîna. She touches on subjects as the site itself, the social status of the workmen, their work for the royal tomb, the objects of daily life, their religious attitude, and the information coming from the tombs.
For the catalogue itself see our number 78821.     *L.Z.*

LETELLIER, Bernadette, see also our number 78821.

78488   Lexikon der Ägyptologie. Begründet von Wolfgang Helck und Eberhard Otto. Lieferung 18 [and] 19 (Band III, Lieferung 2-3). Herausgegeben von Wolfgang Helck und Wolfhart Westendorf unter Mitwirkung von Rosemarie Drenkhahn, Wiesbaden, Otto Harrassowitz, 1978 (20 x 28 cm; 320 col. [= col. 161-480], 1 map, 3 plans, 8 fig.).

Sequel to our number 77478.
Besides the usual range of smaller lemmata, on private names, toponyms, musical instruments, animals, concepts, etc. there occur a few larger ones. We mention, for instance, those on Isis, hunting (Jagd, Jagddarstellungen, Jagdmethoden, Jagdritual, Jagdtracht, Jagdzauber), the netherworld (Jenseitsführer, Jenseitsgericht, and, particularly, Jenseitsvorstellungen), *ka* (also Ka-Diener and Ka-Haus), canopic vessels and boxes, Karnak, ceramics, child, king and queen (Königin, with special lemmata on the Valley of the Queens and the titulary of queens, followed by compounds with "König", which are continued in fasc.20).

78489   LIEBOWITZ, Harold, The Impact of the Art of Egypt on the Art of Syria and Palestine, *in*: *Immortal Egypt*, 27-36, with 1 fig. and 7 ill. on 4 pl.

After a brief survey of Egypt's relations with Syria-Palestine through the ages the author deals with examples illustrating the enormity of the impact of Egyptian art on these regions: stelae from Ugarit, figurines from Byblos, strips of bone, ivory plaques, scarabs and scaraboids, etc. The iconographical similarities are discussed, but the author stresses that, although Syria and Palestine did adopt ready-made artistic languages, they did not necessarily adopt the underlying mythological associations.

78490   LINDBLAD, Ingegerd, Zwei Amarna Reliefblöcke in Stockholm, *Medelhavsmuseet Bulletin*, Stockholm 13 (1978), 19-22, with 2 ill.

Publication of two Amarna relief blocks, probably from Hermopolis, recently acquired by the Medelhavsmuseet, Stockholm. One bears part of a palanquin scene (MME 1975:27), the other the bent figure of a man (MME 1976:2).

78491   LIZANA SALAFRANCA, Joaquín G., Un fragmento de monumento funerario del Imperio Medio, *Boletin de la Asociacion Española de Orientalistas*, Madrid 14 (1978), 247-250, with 1 ill.

Short note on a fragment of the XIIIth Dynasty, containing an offering formula for the *sd3wty-bity*, *imy-r pr wr S-n-Wsrt* son of *S3-Ḥt-ḥr*.   L.Z.

78492   LLAGOSTERA CUENCA, Esteban, Estudio radiologico de las momias egipcias del Museo Arquelogico Nacional de Madrid. Radiological Examination of the Egyptian Mummies of the Archaeological Museum of Madrid, Madrid, 1978 (20.5 x 30 cm; 107 p., 19 colour ill. [1 on cover], 52 ill., 4 fig.).

This book on the radiological examination of the Egyptian mummies of the Archaeological Museum of Madrid has a Spanish text on the left hand and an English on the right hand pages.
After a foreword by the director, M. Almagro, and a short history of the collection, particularly the mummies, by M. Perez Díe, there follows the chapter on the radiological examination (the numbers and letters are not inventory numbers). The author first describes mummification in general and then presents the catalogue of the five human mummies and the wrapped animal mummies. The catalogue consists, for each mummy, of a photograph, a line drawing and

close-ups of X-rayed sections of the body, to which are added descriptions and remarks (one of the mummies is a recent falsification).
The book is concluded by a bibliography.
For another short study on the subject by the same author: Aplicación de la radiografia al estudio de momias egipcias, *Coloquios de la Cátedra de Paleontologia Universidad Complutense*, Madrid 32 (1977), 3-6, with 2 ill. *L.Z.*

78493 LLOYD, Alan B., Strabo and the Memphite Tauromachy, *in*: *Hommages Vermaseren*, 609-626.

Study of the bull-fight that according to Strabo took place in the dromos of the temple of Hephaestus/Ptah at Memphis. The author first deals with the classical references to the custom and then at some length with the Egyptian ones. They are divided into linguistic data: P.T. Spells 284 and 394, representations of the defeat of Chaos, and words for arenas and bulls (*mṯwn, b3wy, ptr/ptrt* and *twnw*); and iconographic data. A summary of the data on p. 623.
Lloyd then presents his interpretation. In the bull-fight the victor is the embodiment of Horus and the vanquished an incarnation of Seth. Who of the animals was Horus and who Seth became possibly manifest only by the result of the conquest.

78494 LLOYD, Alan B., Two Figured Ostraca from North Saqqâra, *JEA* 64 (1978), 107-112, with 1 fig. and 1 pl.

Found in the Sacred Animal Necropolis these consist of a brown-ware sherd showing a fighting cock and a limestone piece with a black ink drawing of an un-Egyptian ramming war-galley. The dates are Saite-Ptolemaic and Graeco-Roman. The latter is compared to the immense Nile ship of Ptolemy IV.
*E.P. Uphill*

78495 LOGAN, Thomas J., Varia Metropolitana II, *GM* Heft 27 (1978), 33-35, with 1 pl.

Ein Papyrus des Metropolitan Museum of Art (Acc. no. 35.9.20) beginnt ziemlich abrupt in der Mitte des Kapitels 1 des Totenbuches und enthält viele leere Stellen und Auslassungen. Es wird daran erinnert, dass die leeren Stellen hinweisen auf den Ausspruch des Shabako-Steines, der König habe das alte Dokument wurmzerfressen vorgefunden. Verfasser nimmt an, dass diese Worte verlässlich sind und dass das Dokument, auf das sich der Stein bezieht, vor der Regierungszeit des Shabako verfertigt wurde. *Inge Hofmann*

78496 LOGAN, Thomas J. and Bruce WILLIAMS, The Identity of the Meritamun Found by Winlock at Deir el-Bahri, *Serapis* 4 (1977-1978), 23-29, with 1 fig.

The authors argue that the Meritamun whose tomb was found by Winlock behind and below Hatshepsut's temple was Ahmes-Meritamun, daughter of Ahmosis and probably the wife of Amenophis I, while the Meritamun from the Royal Cache was the daughter of Tuthmosis III.

78497  LONG, Charlotte R., The Lasithi Dagger, *AJA* 82 (1978), 35-46, with 4 ill. and 1 fig.

The decoration of the so-called Lasithi dagger (Metr. Mus. of Art Inv. No. 26. 31.499), probably a Cretan product of the LM IB-IIIA periods, reflects contacts with Egypt by its similarity to an early New Kingdom archery case in the British Museum (Inv. No. 20648), decorated with a hunting scene and one of fighting bulls. *L.Z.*

78498  LÓPEZ, Jesús, Ostraca ieratici. N. 57001-57092, Milano, Istituto Editoriale Cisalpino - La Goliardica, 1978 (24.5 x 33 cm; 54 p., 50 double pl.) = Catalogo del Museo Egizio di Torino. Serie seconda - collezioni. Volume 3. Fascicolo 1; rev. *CdE* LV, No. 109-110 (1980), 117-118 (Marek Marciniak). Pr. L. 13.000

This first fascicle of the publication of ostraca preserved in the Egyptian Museum at Turin begins with a foreword by Silvio Curto and an introduction by the author. The latter relates the recent history of the pieces, nine of which (nos. 57001-'009) have already been part of the collection since A.D. 1824, while the others came through the excavations of Schiaparelli in 1900-1909. Most of them have never been published before. The author stresses how much he owes to Černý's transcriptions.
There follow descriptions of each separate text, with its bibliography, if available. The plates bear facsimiles and transcriptions on opposite pages, in a few instances a facsimile only.
Most texts are of a non-literary character, recording deliveries to the necropolis workmen (the "journal of the necropolis"), free and working days, various accounts, etc. Several were found by Schiaparelli in the Valley of the Queens and date from the years 22-26 of Ramses III.
A smaller part of the ostraca bears literary texts: the Hymn to the Nile (57064 and '067) and other hymns (57001-'003), the Instruction of Amenemhet (57066), the Instruction of a Man to his Son (57063), etc.
An index of names on p. 49-54.

78499  LORETZ, O., Die Stute in der Kavallerie des Pharao (Hl. 1,9), *Ugarit-Forschungen*, Kevelaer/Neukirchen-Vluyn 10 (1978), 440-441.

A note to our number 70435.

78500  LOWLE, D.A., A Suggestion Regarding the Identity of the Viceroy of Nubia Mentioned on Abu Simbel Rock Stela No. 15, *GM* Heft 30 (1978), 45-55.

Es wird der Frage nachgegangen, welchem Vizekönig von Kusch unter Ramses II. die Felsenstele Nr. 15 von Abu Simbel zugesprochen werden kann. Der Titel "Schwertträger" und eine Amtsstelle in der Kompanie "Herrscher der Beiden Länder" weist auf *Swty*, der dann in den späten zwanziger oder frühen dreissiger Jahren der Herrschaft Ramses' II. oder in dessem letzten Jahrzehnt als Vizekönig in Kusch tätig gewesen sein muss. *Inge Hofmann*

78501  LOYRETTE, Anne-Marie, Les animaux dans l' Égypte ancienne, *Archeologia*, Paris No. 114 (janvier 1978), 24-35, with 21 ill. (4 in colour).

On account of an exhibition having the theme animals in Ancient Egypt, which was held in the Museum of Natural History in Lyon and consisted of objects on loan from the Louvre, the author presents a picture of the exhibition. She touches upon subjects such as the Egyptian knowledge about animals, forbidden and benevolent animals, as symbols of divine power, as protectors of the king, their magical powers, and the sharp Egyptian eye for animal characteristics and the expression of humour in this respect.
The museum itself has a vast collection of mummified fauna, collected by Louis Lortet in the 19th century. *L.Z.*

78502 LUCCHESI, E., Deux feuilles coptes inédits de Shenouté (Paris, Copte 130$^2$, ff. 115, 122 et 131), *Le Muséon*, Louvain 91 (1978), 171-172.

The author presents the edition of two folios from the works of Shenoute which were omitted from Leipoldt's edition. They are: Paris, Bibl. Nat., Copte, volume 130$^2$, folios 122 and 115 + 131. *L.Z.*

78503 LUCCHESI, E., Un 'hapax' grec retrouvé en copte (shenoutien), *JEA* 64 (1978), 141-142.

Traces a link between a Greek word found in a Sicilian inscription and Sahidic Coptic as represented in Shenoute. *E.P. Uphill*

78504 LUCCHESI, Enzo, Remarque sur le lin "sardonique" d' Hérodote, Hist II 105, *Orientalia* 47 (1978), 109-111.

The author connects the word (λῶον) σαρδονικόν in this passage with Eg. s$^c$rt, "wool" (*WB.* IV, 49, 2).
In a postscriptum the author presents a different explanation: σαρδονικόν a corruption for σαρονικόν = Dem. s$^c$l, "wick".

78505 LUCCHESI, E., Un terme inconnu de l'Evangile de Vérité, *Orientalia* 47 (1978), 483-484.

The author proposes to derive the element ϢⲰⲦⲈ in ⲈⲚⲦⲀϢⲰⲦⲈ (Evangelium Veritatis XVII, v, p. 34, l. 21; Codex C.G. Jung) from ancient Egyptian $^c$d̲, ⲥⲉϥⲧⲉ , " to hack up, to hollow out" or generally "to destruct".
*L.Z.*

78506 LÜDDECKENS, Erich, Die demotischen Urkunden von Hawara. Ein Vorbericht, *in*: *Das ptolemäische Ägypten*, 221-226.

From Hawâra a large number of Demotic papyri have been published, dating from between years 365 and 67 B.C. They belong to people engaged in burial and the funerary cult. The author makes general remarks as regards these people, their occupations, family relations, etc.

78507 LÜDDECKENS, Erich, Stand und Aufgaben der Demotistik, *Enchoria* 8, Sonderband (1978), 15-23.

Abstract of a paper read at the First International Colloquium of Demotists, held in Berlin, September 1977.
The author gives an outline of the history and future of the studies of Demotic.
*W. Brunsch*

LÜDDECKENS, Erich, see also our number 78269.

78508 LUFT, Ulrich, Beiträge zur Historisierung der Götterwelt und Mythenschreibung, Budapest, 1978 (16.5 x 24 cm;[VIII +] 278 p. ) = Studia Aegyptiaca, 4 = Az Eötvös Loránd Tudományegyetem Ókori Történeti Transzékeinek Kiadványai, 22.

In the introduction the author deals with the concepts of history and myth, in ancient Egypt as well as with various Egyptologists, explaining his own points of view. He states i.a. that "die Historisierung der Götterwelt zu einem Teil der Religionspolitik der Priesterschaft (wird), der sich die Könige entweder beugten oder der sie versuchten auszuweichen".
The study proper consists of three parts. In the first the possibilities of the gods for directly influencing the state are studied. Various aspects such as decrees by the gods and oracles, orders given by gods, their thrones, the function of the king and royal titles such as *nb t3wy*. From this it appears that the power of the gods, that is, of priesthood, on politics and economy has increased during Egyptian history.
The second part is devoted to the connections between the gods and mythical events, and the historical time. In a long chapter (78-154) the "royal" gods pass the review: Osiris, Geb, Horus, Re, Thoth, Ptah and Seth, with the excursuses on C.T. Spell 313 and on the Shabaka stone.
There follow chapters on the phrase ". . . since the time of the god" (see already our number 76512) and on the years and the age of the gods, as well as on historical festivals on mythically established dates, on dynasties of gods and on dating after gods.
The third part discusses the influence of all this on particular myths, e.g. that of the divine begetting of the king, of Horus and Seth, the annihilation of mankind, Astarte daughter of Ptah, etc.
A summary of the conclusions on p. 240-244, followed by an index to the sources (245-246) and a bibliography.

78509 MACCOULL, L.S.B., Coptic Documentary Papyri in the Pierpont Morgan Library, *Enchoria* 8, Sonderband (1978), 21*(67)-23*(69).

Abstract of a paper read at the First International Congress of Coptology, held in Cairo, December 1976.
The author introduces some of the non-literary Coptic documents of the Pierpont Morgan Library to the public. She is going to publish them as a whole.
*W. Brunsch*

MACDERMOT, Violet, see our number 78724 and 78725.

MACDONALD, J., see our number 78126.

78510 von MACKENSEN, Ludolf, Neue Ergebnisse zur ägyptischen Zeitmessung. Die Inbetriebnahme und Berechnung der ältesten erhaltenen Wasseruhr, *Alte Uhren.  Zeitmessgeräte, Wissenschaftliche Instrumente und Automaten*, München 1 (Januar 1978), 13-18, with 5 fig. and 3 ill.

Experiments carried out during a whole year on a copy of the New Kingdom water clock from Thebes (now in the Cairo Museum), provided with a probable type of tap, make clear that its time indication is much more correct than so far assumed. *L.Z.*

78511 McNAUGHT, Lewis, Henry Salt. His Contribution to the Collections of Egyptian Sculpture in the British Museum, *Apollo*, London 108, No. 200 (October 1978), 224-231, with 14 ill.

In this article for the general reader the author sketches the importance of Henry Salt and his motives for the formation of his three separate collections which form a major part of the collection of Egyptian sculpture in the British Museum, and describes some of the most important pieces. *L.Z.*

78512 McNULTY, Ilene Beatty, A Hidden Beauty in the Monuments of Egypt, *Aramco World Magazine*, New York 29, No. 5 (September-October 1978), 4-11, with 25 colour ill. (2 on covers).

General article about various monuments, with fine photographs. *L.Z.*

78513 MacQUITTY, William, Ramesses The Great. Master of the World. Foreword by T.G.H. James, London, Mitchell Beazley Publishers Limited, [1978] (21.5 x 31 cm; 64 p., coloured frontispiece, 42 colour ill., 1 map, 5 fig.).

After a foreword by T.G.H. James the author tells the story of Ramses II. There are also touched upon subjects such as the religion, the architecture, Abu Simbel and Nefertari.
A chronological table and an explanation on the reading of the nomen and prenomen of Ramses II conclude this book intended for the general public. *L.Z.*

78514 MacQUITTY, William, The Wisdom of the Ancient Egyptians, London, Sheldon Press, [1978] (12.8 x 19.8 cm; IX + 85 p., ill. on cover). Pr. £1.75

After a foreword by T.G.H. James and an introduction dealing with a variety of subjects, the author presents a selection of sayings from the wisdom literature, and some stories. *L.Z.*

78515 MAHÉ, Jean-Pierre, Hermès en Haute-Égypte. Les textes hermétiques de Nag Hammadi et leur parallèles grecs et latins. Tome 1, Québec, Les Presses de l'Université Laval, 1978 (15.2 x 24.3 cm; XIX + 171 p.) = Bibliothèque copte de Nag Hammadi, Section: textes, 3.

Section I,2 of the general introduction contains short remarks on Thoth–Hermes Trismegistos, while in section III,2 the links of the Hermetica with Egyptian mythology and Greek philosophy are discussed.

The main part of the book, chapter 1, is devoted to the sixth treatise of Codex Nag Hammadi VI, which comprises p. VI, 52-63.
In the introduction the author i.a. discusses the Egyptian influences and then presents the Coptic text and the translation on opposite pages, followed by the commentary.
The seventh treatise, a prayer contained in Codex Nag Hammadi VI, 63,33 - 65,7 is presented in chapter 2, having the translation and Coptic text on one page and the Greek and Latin versions on the opposite. *L.Z.*

78516   el MAHI, A. Tigani, Some ecological effects of the introduction of cattle to the Central Sudan. El Kadero and el Zakyab sites, *Nyame Akuma*, Calgary No. 23 (1978), 36-38, with 2 fig.

Die Einführung domestizierter Rinder in den Sudan bedeutete die Umwälzung des gesamten Wirtschaftssystems, wie in zwei Modellen dargelegt wird. Das bis dorthin geführte Sammler- und Fischerleben wurde aber nicht völlig zugunsten der Viehwirtschaft aufgegeben. *Inge Hofmann*

78517   MAHMUD, Abdulla el-Sayed, A New Temple for Hathor at Memphis, Warminster, Aris & Phillips Ltd,[1978] (20.9 x 29.6 cm; IV + 22 p., 2 plans, 1 diagram, 2 fig.[1 on cover], 18 ill. on 9 unnumbered pl., 19 pl.) = Egyptology Today, 1.

In the introduction the author describes the discovery of a Hathor temple built by Ramses II at Memphis. After a description of the plan of the temple and its architectural elements and remarks on the history of the Hathor capitals follow the description and translation of the temple inscriptions, and a discussion of the objects consisting of pottery, obscene figurines, terracotta heads, moulds and faience and stone objects.
In this temple, possibly built at the occasion of a *sed*-festival of the king, a Heliopolitan sun-cult of Hathor *nbt ḥtpt* was founded by Ramses II for the first time at Memphis. In the conclusion the author raises the possibility of finding a temple for the Memphite Hathor *nbt nht* near this site. *L.Z.*

MAKKI, Bakhri Mirgani, see our numbers 78823 and 78824.

78518   MALAISE, Michel, Documents nouveaux et points de vue récents sur les cultes isiaques en Italie, *in*: *Hommages Vermaseren*, 627-717.

In the first section the author presents additions to his inventory of documents concerning the Isis cult in Italy (see our number 72459). The second section is devoted to the analysis of these new documents, dealing e.g. with their distribution over the peninsula and the Isis temples, and with the divinities with which Isis was related. In section 3 the author discusses recent studies on the subject and sets forth his points of view, e.g. on the question whether the syncretism already had begun in the Late Period and on the penetration of Egyptian cults in Italy.
At the end concordances between the author's inventory and the recent studies (p. 708-717).

78519   MALAISE, Michel, Nouvelle note sur les pendentifs cordiformes, *GM* Heft 29 (1978), 69-70.

Bezugnehmend auf unsere Nr. 75477 wird darauf aufmerksam gemacht, dass der herzförmige Anhänger nicht nur für den Verstorbenen oder das Gotteskind eine wesentliche Bedeutung hat, sondern aus den Darstellungen auf vier ramessidischen Ostraka aus Deir-el-Medîne geht hervor, dass der herzförmige Anhänger auch in profanem Kontext aufscheinen kann. Der Anhänger ist somit nicht mehr ein Ersatz für das Herz, sondern ein reiner Talisman. Die Schreibung des doppelten Herzens kann ḥ₃tj, aber auch ỉb.wj gelesen werden.   *Inge Hofmann*

78520   MALAISE, Michel, Les scarabées de coeur dans l'Égypte ancienne. Avec un appendice sur les scarabées de coeur des Musées Royaux d'Art et d'Histoire de Bruxelles, Bruxelles, Fondation Égyptologique Reine Élisabeth, 1978 (21.5 x 28 cm; 94 p., 9 pl.) = Monographies Reine Élisabeth, 4; rev. *Orientalia* 49 (1980), 421-422 (Alessandro Roccati).   Pr. F.B. 580

The study of the heart scarab consists of an introduction dealing with the importance of the heart according to Egyptian concepts, and seven chapters. In chapter 1 the funerary texts on the heart are discussed, particularly B.D. chapter 30 and 30 B, which are presented in hieroglyphs and translation with an extensive commentary.
In chapter 2 the author attempts to circumscribe the concept "heart scarab"; essential is the occurrence of the proper texts, although anepigraph scarabs of Amenophis IV may perhaps be included.
Chapter 3 deals with the origin and formal evolution of the heart scarab; chapter 4 with the materials they are made of and their stylistic development; chapter 5 with the outer appearance of the texts and the representations they bear; chapter 6 with the rituals with which they were placed on the mummy (anointment and Opening of the Mouth) and the places where they were put, which change through the ages.
Chapter 7 is devoted to the production of heart scarabs and their use during the ages and in various layers of the society. Their use has been widely spread, from the Pharaoh to the poor, and, in time, from the XVIIth to the XXVIth Dynasty. There follow a conclusion and, in an appendix, the publication of 12 heart scarabs from the collection of the Musées Royaux d'Art et d'Histoire at Brussels, each with all significant data (including scribal errors in the texts) and, for eight of them, a photograph on the plates.
Bibliography on p. 89-94; no indexes.

78521   MÁLEK, J., Imset (I) and Ḥepy (Ḥ) Canopic-Jars of Neferseshem-Psammethek, *JEA* 64 (1978), 138-140, with 1 fig.

Two jars formerly on loan to the Castle Museum Norwich provide a puzzle in identification, and five possible owners from a Memphite family are cited. Their dates cannot be fixed more precisely than Dynasties XXVI-XXX and their probable origin to a tomb, certainly at Saqqâra.   *E.P. Uphill*

78522   MÁLEK, Jaromír, A New Sculpture from *Mgbt*, the town of Mut, *GM* Heft 29 (1978), 71-77, with 1 fig.

Ein im Londoner Kunsthandel befindliches Statuen-Fragment, bestehend aus dem Kopf und den Schultern eines Mannes und etwa in die Zeit Amenophis' III. gehörend, enthält in der Inschrift eine Opferformel an Mut, Herrin von Megbet. Eine Liste der Varianten des Toponyms aus dem Mittleren und Neuen Reich wird zusammengestellt; das neue Statuenfragment verhilft zwar auch nicht zu einer tatsächlichen Lokalisierung von *Mgbt*. Es zeigt jedoch, dass die Ergänzung des Ortsnamens auf der Statue Cairo Mus. CG 585 durch Daressy möglich ist.

*Inge Hofmann*

78523 MÁLEK, Jaromír, *Spt* in *Urk*.IV,23,9 (+ Addendum), *RdE* 30 (1978), 168-171, with 2 fig. and 1 ill.

*spt*, repris au Wb.IV, 97,3 et 100,19, doit être un encenseur d'un type connu par plusieurs documents figurés. *Ph. Derchain*

MÁLEK, Jaromír, see also our number 78640.

78524 el MALLAKH, Kamal and Arnold C. BRACKMAN, The Gold of Tutankhamen. Preface by William Kelly Simpson, New York, Newsweek Books, [1978] (22.7 x 32 cm; 332 p., 24 ill., 155 colour pl.).

Apart from a preface by W.K. Simpson and an introduction by Kamal el-Mallakh, deputy editor-in-chief of el-Ahram, the main text is the same as that of our number 78114.
The value of this book lies in the many splendid colour pl. with captions divided into three sections containing the following subjects: tomb, gold mask and coffins, shrines; the young king, burial apparatus, keys to eternal life; hunting and war, ceremonial jewellery, objects of royal life.
Index at the end of the book. *L.Z.*

78525 MANNICHE, Lise, Amun ʿȝ šfyt in a Ramessid Tomb at Thebes, *GM* Heft 29 (1978), 79-84, with 1 ill.

Ein in der Ny Carlsberg Glyptotek in Kopenhagen befindliches Malereifragment (AEin 1073) stammt aus der Zeit Ramses' III. und kommt aus Theben. Die Darstellung zeigt einen tragbaren Schrein auf einem viereckigen Untersatz. Der Text legt dar, dass es sich bei dem Gott um Amun ʿȝ šfyt handelte, der eine Kapelle mit einer eigenen Verwaltung besass, wie aus dem P. Amiens hervorgeht. Der Gott kommt in einigen Privatgräbern der Ramessidenzeit vor. Das behandelte Fragment kommt gleichfalls aus einem solchen, dessen Eigentümer in einem besonderen Verhältnis zu dem Gott gestanden haben muss. Es könnte aus einem Grab in der Nachbarschaft von T.T. A 11 - A 25 stammen.

*Inge Hofmann*

78526 MANNICHE, Lise, Provenance of Louvre D 60, *GM* Heft 29 (1978), 85-88, with 1 ill.

Louvre D 60 ist das Fragment einer gemalten Bankettszene: drei Mädchen stehen vor einem Opfertisch, rechts werden in einem oberen Register die nicht mehr vorhandenen männlichen Gäste von einem männlichen Diener und die weiblichen Gäste von einem Mädchen bedient. Alle Figuren sind kahl, so dass angenommen wird, dass die schwarze Farbe der Haare verschwunden ist. Das Fragment ist identisch mit der Szene, die von Porter-Moss ($I^2$, 2, 819) für das Grab no. A 22 beschrieben wird. Die Szene wurde u.a. von Champollion beschrieben; danach kann nur ein Teil der Szene in den Louvre gelangt sein.

*Inge Hofmann*

78527 MANNICHE, Lise, Symbolic Blindness, *CdE* LIII, No.105 (1978), 13-21, with 4 fig.

La cécité de nombreux musiciens dans les reliefs amarniens n'est pas nécessairement une cécité réelle. L'auteur montre en effet des exemples où les chanteurs ou harpistes ont les yeux fermés ou bandés. En revanche, il n'existe pas de musiciennes privées de la vue.
On pourrait en conclure que le rituel interdisait aux hommes de voir le dieu ou le roi dans certains actes liturgiques. *Ph. Derchain*

78528 MARCINIAK, M., Création et développment du Centre des Recherches Nubiennes à Varsovie, *in*: *Études nubiennes*, 193-197.

Die reichen Funde von Faras veranlassten das Institut d'Archéologie Méditerranéenne de l'Académie Polonaise des Sciences ein Centre de Recherches Nubiennes zu gründen. Dieses beschäftigt sich nicht nur mit Material der christlichen Epoche, sondern umfasst die gesamte Kultur des alten Sudan wie z.B. die Ausgrabungsdokumentation des neolithischen Kadero. Für die Serie *Faras - Fouilles polonaises* sind 10 Bände geplant, von denen bereits einige erschienen sind. Eine neue Serie wird die Forschungsergebnisse aus Dongola vorlegen. Eine Zeitschrift mit dem Titel *Cahiers Nubiologiques* soll Artikel bringen, die sich mit Problemen Nubiens befassen. In der Zusammenarbeit mit auslandischen wissenschaftlichen Institutionen werden gleichfalls Werke publiziert.

*Inge Hofmann*

78529 MARCINIAK, Marek, Un reçu d' offrande de Deir el-Bahari, *BIFAO* 78 (1978), 165-170, with 1 pl.

Publication of an ostracon found in the ceiling of the sanctuary of Hatshepsut's temple and recording the receipt of an offering. Its provenance proves that the temple functioned already when still under construction. The name of Senenmut on the verso suggests a date between the regnal years 11 and 16 of the queen.

78530 MĂRGHITAN, Liviu et Constantin C. PETOLESCU, Les cultes orientaux à Micia (Dacia Superior), *in*: *Hommages Vermaseren*, 718-731, with 7 pl.

Archaeological researches in the Roman camp and civil settlement at Micia have brought to light several documents on oriental cults. Those of Egyptian divinities are discussed on p. 723-724.

78531 MARTIN, Geoffrey T., Excavations at the Memphite Tomb of Ḥoremḥeb, 1977: Preliminary Report, *JEA* 64 (1978), 5-9, with 4 pl.

Most of the season's work was carried out underground. Shaft I was excavated to a depth of 8 metres and a doorway leading to a corridor and the burial chambers found. Evidence showed these had been entered in the nineteenth century. In the chippings were found remains from the four burials, one of which was that of a Ramesside princess *B3kt - ʿnt*. Objects included shabtis, a heart scarab, an amulet and a canopic jar lid. Mycenaean L.H.IIIA2 pottery was also found. The burial chamber of an O.K. tomb was found at a lower level, the superstructure of which had evidently been removed by Horemheb when made his own tomb. It was later used as an anchorite's cell. Blocks from Djoser's complex were found reused in the building. Shaft IV was intended as the main burial place and contained objects of queen Mutnodjmet.

*E.P. Uphill*

78532 MARTIN, Geoffrey T., Mosaic Glass: a Correction, *JEA* 64 (1978), 141.

The writer defines the term more accurately with relation to his discussion of the Riefstahl catalogue (our number 68503; see the review *JEA* 56, 1970, 217-218). *E.P. Uphill*

78533 MARTIN, Geoffrey T., Some Private-Name and Stamp-Seals in Stockholm, *Medelhavsmuseet Bulletin*, Stockholm 13 (1978), 3-5, with 7 ill.

Publication of three scarabs of administrative officials (MM 19321 = MME 1962:47; MM 11348 and MM 11279) and two seal stamps (MM 11319; MM 14273). The scarabs date from the XIIth, the seals from the XIIth-XIIIth Dynasties. The stamps are in the form of a squatting nude boy, the first one bearing the hitherto unknown inscription "Seal of the fortresses of the Nubians Amenyseneb".

78534 MARTIN, Geoffrey T., The Tomb of Horemheb. Commander-in-Chief of Tutankhamun, *Archaeology* 31, No. 4 (July/August 1978), 14-23, with 1 plan, 1 map and 9 ill. (5 in colour).

Article for the general public on the discovery of the Saqqâra tomb of Horemheb, provided with particularly clear photographs of some of the reliefs and of a golden earring found in the courtyard.
Compare also our number 76700. *L.Z.*

78535 MARTIN, Geoffrey T., The Tomb-Chambers of Horemheb, *The Illustrated London News*, London 266, No. 6954 (January 1978), 50-51, with 4 ill.

Sequel to our numbers 75487 and 76524.
Description of the work done in the Memphite tomb of Horemheb during the 1977 excavation season. The work was concentrated upon the clearance of the underground tomb chambers. *L.Z.*

78536 MARTIN, Geoffrey T. and W.V. DAVIES, Current Research for Higher Degrees in Egyptology, Coptic and Related Studies in the United Kingdom, No. 3, *JEA* 64 (1978), 148-149.

Sequel to our number 74478 and the report in *JEA* 62 (1976), 188-189 (not included in the AEB).
*L.Z.*

MARTIN, Geoffrey Thorndike, see our numbers 78320 and 78537.

MARTIN, Karl, see our number 78179.

MARTIN-PARDEY, Eva, see our number 78180.

78537 MASSON, Olivier, Carian Inscriptions from North Saqqâra and Buhen. With Contributions by Geoffrey Thorndike Martin and Richard Vaughan Nicholls, London, Egypt Exploration Society, 1978 (25 x 31 cm; X + 102 p., 3 fig., 38 pl.) = Texts from Excavations. Fifth Memoir = Excavations at North Saqqâra. Documentary Series, 3; rev. *BiOr* 37 (1980), 33-37 (P. Meriggi); *Comptes rendus de l' Académie des Inscriptions et Belles-Lettres*, 1979, 553-554 (Jean Leclant).

In his foreword H.S. Smith describes the discovery of the Carian inscriptions in the catacombs of North Saqqâra and their archaeological context. They very probably came originally from a Caromemphite cemetery, the site of which is unknown. They may have been reused in the building works of the temple precincts between 380 and 343 B.C.
The first part of the volume, by Masson and written in French, contains the publication of 49 inscriptions, preceded by an introduction in which are discussed the supporting objects (38 stelae, 11 other pieces of stone), the Carian alphabet and its problems, and the contents of the inscriptions. Then each text is dealt with separately, with full technical details and a facsimile plus a tentative transcription. In a second chapter Masson discusses five Carian inscriptions discovered at Buhen; they may date from the expedition of Psammetichus II.
In part 2 Martin studies the fragmentary stela no. 2, made by an Egyptian or foreign craftsman and bearing hieroglyphic inscriptions, the Carian text having been added; and nos. 1 and 7, with contemporary Egyptian and Carian texts. Martin and Nicholls together deal with five other stelae bearing reliefs in Egyptianizing or provincial East Greek style and, with one exception, Carian inscriptions. Particular attention is paid to the (Greek) representations of the prothesis, or laying out, of a corpse.
In two appendices Masson deals with the texts on the Carian stela of Abûsîr (Berlin-East, Inv. No. 19553) and a similar one in Lausanne.
Concordances on p. 93-94; full indexes on p. 95-102.
On the plates all 55 inscriptions, and the Abûsîr stela, in photograph, as well as line drawings of the major stelae and Carian inscriptions.

78538 MATTHIAE, Gabriella Scandone, Una stele egiziana del Museo Nazionale di Palermo, *Bollettino d'Arte*, Roma, Serie 5, 61 (1976),[1978], 53-54, with 1 pl.

The author publishes a stela from the beginning of the XVIIIth Dynasty inscribed with an offering formula, preserved in the Museo Nazionale, Palermo.
*L.Z.*

78539  MATTHIAE, Paolo, Recherches archéologiques à Ebla, 1977: le quartier administratif du palais royal G,*Comptes rendus de l' Académie des Inscriptions & Belles-Lettres*, Paris, 1978, 204-235, with 20 fig., ill. and plans.

In the small central court of the administration centre of the royal palace at Ebla (Tell Mardikh) there were found sherds of vessels bearing the names of Chephren and Pepi I. *L.Z.*

78540  MATTHIAE, Paolo, Tell Mardikh: Ancient Ebla (Chronologies in Old World Archaeology, 1976-1977), *AJA* 82 (1978), 540-543, with 4 ill.

Mention is made of the find of vessels fragments bearing the name of Chephren and the alabaster lid of a jar with that of Pepi I. *L.Z.*

78541  MAZAR, A., מתקופת-הברונזה התיכונה והמאוחרת בארץ-ישראל חותמות-גליל , *Qadmoniot*, Jerusalem 11, No. 1 (=41) (1978), 6-14, with 35 ill.

"Cylinder Seals of the Middle and Late Bronze Age in Eretz-Israel".

MEDIČE, M., see our number 78390.

78542  Mednarodni znanstveni simposij "Problemi starega Egipta". Ljubljana/Zagreb, 29.9. – 1.10.1978. Zbornik l.del, Ljubljana, 1978 (17 x 23.5 cm; 118 p., 2 colour ill. on cover) = Orientalistika 2. Slovensko Orientalistično Društvo Ljubljana.

These are the proceedings of an International Scientific Symposium on "Problems of Ancient Egypt", held at Ljubljana/Zagreb from September 28th to October 1st, 1978.
The booklet contains abstracts, from one to three pages each, of 33 papers, arranged in alphabetical order after the names of the authors. Most of them are in English, French or German. Several deal with Egyptological studies in one particular country.

78543  MEGALLY, M., Hieroglyphic Palaeography and its Role in Egyptian Art and History,*in*: *Journal Faculty of Archaeology*, 105-107.

Description of a project to record and study the forms of hieroglyphic signs from O.K. monuments, beginning with Gîza and Saqqâra.

78544  MEINARDUS, Otto F.A., Zur Identifizierung ägyptischer Vogelmumien, *Armant*, Köln Heft 15 (1977), 3-17, with 4 fig. and 7 ill.

Der Verfasser beschreibt sieben Vogelarten die die alten Ägypter mumifiziert haben: Seeadler (haliaeetus albicilla); Wanderfalke (falco peregrinoides); Sperber oder Finkenhabicht (accipiter nisus); Zwergohreule oder Ohrkauz (otus scops); Turmfalke (falco tinnunculus); und heiliger Ibis (threskiornis aethiopica). Auch erwähnt er kurz die religiöse Rolle dieser Vögel. *L.Z.*

78545 MEINARDUS, Otto F., Zur Mumifizierung von Fiederbartwelsen, *Armant*, Köln Heft 14 (1976), 3-10, with 1 pl. and 2 fig.

Der Verfasser beschreibt die Mumie der Fiederbartwels (synodontis schall) und erörtert die Bedeutung des Fisches. Für eine Röntgenaufnahme siehe man unsere vorhergehende Nummer.
*L.Z.*

78546 Meisterwerke altägyptischer Keramik. 5000 Jahre Kunst und Kunsthandwerk aus Ton und Fayence, Höhr-Grenzhausen, Rastal-Haus, 16. September bis 30. November 1978 (21 x 20 cm; 264 p., coloured frontispiece, 2 maps, 17 fig., 139 ill., 16 colour ill., colour ill. on cover).

Catalogue of an exhibition in the Museum of Ceramics of the Westerwaldkreis at Höhr-Grenzhausen (near Coblenz), presenting an important and fairly complete survey of Egyptian ceramics.
There are four introductory chapters by specialists: Dorothea Arnold ("Why Egyptian Ceramics") deals i.a. with pottery in daily life, the "life" of a clay-vessel, the potter, the relation between ceramics and the great arts; Josef Riederer (Materials and Techniques), Walter Noll (Materials and Techniques of Painted Vessels), and Christine Strauss (Faience Production).
The catalogue, for which, besides these four, several other scholars are responsible, comprises 511 items. Each is carefully described, with mention of material, measurements, provenance, date and museum number. Several of them are represented by fine photographs, a few in colour.
The objects which came from various German museums are divided into 9 groups: materials and techniques; Prehistory and Early History; implements and objects of daily use; O. and M.K.; inscribed ceramics; N.K.; belief in the netherworld and burial customs; Late, Graeco-Roman and Coptic Periods; Nubia.
On p. 263-264 a bibliography to Ancient Egyptian Ceramics and one to Ancient Egypt in general.

78547 MELTZER, Edmund S., Mariette and *Aida* once again, *Antiquity* 52 (1978), 50-51.

In this reply to Fagan's article (our number 77224) the author suggests that Mariette's role in the production of "Aida" was more extensive than Fagan will allow.

78548 MELTZER, Edmund S., The Parentage of Tut'ankhamūn and Smenkhkare', *JEA* 64 (1978), 134-135.

The writer reaches no new conclusions about this but supports Ray's view (see our number 75617) rather than those expressed by the article in *JEA* 62 = our number 76156. He also draws attention to the recent identification of the middle-aged woman found in the tomb of Amenophis II as Queen Tiy.
*E.P. Uphill*

MELTZER, Edmund S., see also our number 78135.

78549 MERCATANTE, Anthony S., Who's who in Egyptian Mythology. Foreword by Dr. Robert S. Bianchi, New York, Clarkson N. Potter, Inc. Publishers, distributed by Crown Publishers, Inc., [1978] (14.7 x 22.2 cm; XXIII + 231 p., 61 fig., 1 coloured ill. on cover).

After a short foreword on the Egyptian religious world by R.S. Bianchi, the author's preface, a chronological table and an introduction to Egyptian religion, follows the glossary. It contains names of gods, of pharaohs, some Egyptologists, of geographical names, concepts and all kinds of other lemmata relating to the Egyptian religion in a wide sense. There are even translations of major Egyptian tales included.
Annotated bibliography at the end of the book. *L.Z.*

78550 MERKELBACH, Reinhold, Mythische Episoden im Alexanderroman, *in: Studien zur Religion und Kultur Kleinasiens.* Festschrift für Friedrich Karl Dörner zum 65. Geburtstag am 28. Februar 1976. Herausgegeben von Sencer Şahin, Elmar Schwertheim, Jörg Wagner. Zweiter Band, Leiden, E.J. Brill, 1978 (= Études préliminaires aux religions orientales dans l' Empire romain, 66), 602-618, with 3 ill. on 2 pl.

The author makes some remarks on the role of Nectanebos in the episode of the conception of Alexander in the Alexander novel. *L.Z.*

78551 MERRILLEES, R.S., El-Lisht and Tell el-Yahudiya Ware in the Archaeological Museum of the American University of Beirut, *Levant*, London 10 (1978), 75-98 with 2 pl.

The author first draws up a catalogue of the el-Lisht and Tell el-Yahûdîya wares (compare already our numbers 74496 and 74497) in the rich collection of the archaeological museum of the American University of Beirut. The catalogue is arranged under the headings el-Lisht ware, Transitional el-Lisht/Tell el-Yahûdîya wares, and Tell el-Yahûdîya wares, while the numerical sequence of the museum's accession numbers is followed so far as possible. The catalogue is provided with data such as accession numbers, provenance, source, description, illustration, and bibliographical references. Longer discussions are devoted to the difference between ichthyomorphic vases related to el-Lisht ware and the Tell el-Yahûdîya specimens, and to the vessels bearing bird motifs.
The following analysis is for some part devoted to the introduction of a clear and correct terminology for the black punctured fabrics of the el-Lisht and Tell el-Yahûdîya wares. The Cypriote evidence is amply discussed. As for the chronological implications, the author argues that it is hard to imagine that the el-Lisht ware lasted some 300 years during the S.I.P. without internal morphological or decorative development. *L.Z.*

MERTZ, Barbara S., see our number 78027.

78552 MERZ, Richard, Die numinose Mischgestalt. Urkundenkritische Untersuchungen zu tiermenschlichen Erscheinungen Altägyptens, der Eiszeit und der Aranda in Australien, Berlin–New York, Walter de Gruyter, 1978 (14.4 x 22 cm; XX + 306 p.) = Religionsgeschichtliche Versuche und Vorarbeiten. Herausgegeben von Walter Burkert und Carsten Colpe, 36; rev. *Mundus* 16 (1980), 28-29 (Otto Huth). Pr. DM 98

In this study of the origin and meaning of hybrid figures of deities the author discusses the subject on account of the data from three different civilizations, that of ancient Egypt, the Ice-age, and the Aranda (Australia), since he is interested in the problem in general.
Chapter 1 (p.3-69) is devoted to Egypt. Since the author is no Egyptologist he had to base his conclusions entirely on the study of secondary literature. After an introductory description of the hybrid figures in general and the pantheon of the P.T. he deals with theories about their origin: rationalistic (Erman), racial (Scharff), sociological (Otto), evolutionistic (Sethe) and typological (Morenz) explanations pass the review. A summary on p. 12-14, after which the problems left unsolved by these theories are discussed.
There follows a discussion of the representations from the Predynastic Period, animals, men and hybrid figures; first in general, e.g. the problem to what extent they belong to the religious sphere and that of dating the palettes, and then the representations themselves.
The last sections are devoted to the origin of the hybrid figure, in which the author shows himself sceptical as regards the mentioned explanations, and to its meaning: mask, symbol or reality.
After chapters on the two other civilizations the author presents the conclusions in part 2, of which one section (p. 255-266) is devoted to Egypt. Stressing the uncertainty of our knowledge about the way of thinking in the Predynastic and Archaic Periods, Merz argues that the distinction between man and animal was not absolute; the concept "animal" did not exist, no god was "purely human". There the explanation of the hybrid figure has to be sought.

METZEL, E., see our number 78095.

78553   de MEULENAERE, Herman, L'oeuvre architecturale de Tibère à Thèbes, *Orientalia Lovaniensia Periodica*, Leuven 9 (1978), 69-73, with 1 ill. and 1 pl.

The author presents an inventory, accompanied by short comments, of the documents of Tiberius concerning his building activities in the Mut temple and the Luxor temple.
Compare our number 76328. L.Z.

78554   de MEULENAERE, Herman, La statuette JE 37163 du Musée du Caire, *SAK* 6 (1978), 63-68, with 1 pl.

Publication of the granite block stela Cairo JE 37163, from the Karnak Cachette. Its owner, the lesōnis of the House of Amon of the second phyle Ankhnahebu, son of Wennofre and father of Djedamoniufankh, occurs also as a witness in Pap. Brooklyn 47.218.3 (see Parker, A Saite Oracle Papyrus = our number 62457), and the son also on the wooden stela Hildesheim No. 2127. The mention of a grandfather, first prophet and royal son Osorkon, presents a problem.

78555 de MEULENAERE, H. and W. CLARYSSE, Notes de prosopographie thébaine, *CdE* LIII, No. 106 (1978), 226-253.

Sous ce titre, la *CdE* se propose d' éditer à intervalles irréguliers des notes de prosopographie thébaine, pouvant concerner des personnages de toutes les époques, de l' Ancien Empire à la période romaine. Cette rubrique est en principe ouverte à tous. Pour l'inaugurer, Herman de Meulenaere (1-3) et Willy Clarysse (4-7) ont réuni sept notes dont voici les titres: 1. Les archivistes en chef de la trésorerie d'Amon; 2. La fin du "Troisième Prophète d'Amon" Pakhar; 3. Le Vizir Nespamedou; 4. *Ḥr-ḫtr*- Ἀρατρῆς; 5. Un groupe de tombes dans les Memnonia entre 227 et 175 av. J.C.; 6. Une famille de pastophores thébains; 7. Hurgonaphor et Chaonnophris, les derniers pharaons indigènes.

*Ph. Derchain*

78556 de MEVIUS, Sophie, Les trônes phéniciens flanqués de sphinx ailés, *Revue des archéologues et historiens d'art de Louvain*, Louvain 11 (1978), 185-187.

Abstract of a small thesis. Egyptian material is dealt with. *L.Z.*

78557 MICHAELIDOU-NICOLAOU, Ino, The Cult of Oriental Divinities in Cyprus. Archaic to Graeco-Roman Times, *in*: *Hommages Vermaseren*, 791-800, with 1 map and 4 pl.

On the first pages the author deals with the import in Cyprus of representations of Egyptian deities such as Bes, Ptah and Hathor in early periods. They are mostly terra cotta figurines or amulets, but Hathor heads occur on Archaic capitals and votive stelae. From the time of the Ptolemies, and particularly promoted by the Romans, Egyptian cults occur on the island, though they never seem to have been very important.

78558 MILLS, A.J., Approach to Third Millenium Nubia, *in*: *Études nubiennes*, 199-204.

Trotz unserer beachtlichen Kenntnisse über das 3. vorchristliche Jahrtausend in Unternubien, bestehen doch noch eine Reihe von Unklarheiten. Kulturell ist dieses Jahrtausend erfüllt von der A-Kultur und der ihr folgenden C-Kultur. Die Untersuchung legt die Problematik hinsichtlich der Beziehungen dieser beiden Kulturen dar, ihrer Herkunft, ihrer Übereinstimmungen und Divergenzen und der Verbindungen zu Kulturen im Westen und Osten des Niltales.

*Inge Hofmann*

78559 MILLS, A.J., The Dakhleh Oasis Project, *Nyame Akuma*, Calgary No. 12 (May 1978), 22-23.

Das Projekt soll die Siedlungsmuster, kulturelle Entwicklung, Aussenbeziehungen und Umweltveränderungen von Neolithikum bis zur römischen Epoche in der Oase Dachle erforschen. In der ersten Phase sollen archäologische Fundplätze lokalisiert und identifiziert sowie Umweltsgegebenheiten festgestellt werden. Es soll festgestellt werden, welche der libyschen Stämme dort siedelten und welche Verbindungen zwischen dieser südlichen Oase und dem nubischen

Niltal bestanden. Dem Problem eines trans- und sub-saharanischen Handels soll gleichfalls nachgegangen werden, da Dachle auf der Route nach Ennedi und dem Tschadsee liegt.
*Inge Hofmann*

MINK, Gerd, see our number 78269.

78560 MIOSI, Frank Ferry, Boats in the Pyramid Texts, *Dissertation Abstracts International*, Ann Arbor, Mich. 39, No. 3 (September 1978), 1647/8-A.

Abstract of a thesis University of Toronto, 1976 (No order no.).
The author discusses in detail 23 boat-names in the P.T., the already most intensively studied ones being left out. He concludes that the vast majority of boats are not solar. Two appendices supplement the material: the translation with notes of all P.T. spells pertaining to the discussed boats, and the form of all boats on account of boat determinatives.
*L.Z.*

MITTEN, David Gordon, see our number 78341.

78561 MIYAKE, Akiko, The Greek-Egyptian Mysteries in Pound's *"The Little Review* Calendar" and in Cantos 1-7, *Paideuma*, Orono, Maine 7 (1978), 73-111.

On the influence of the Osiris mysteries in some of the poetical works of Ezra Pound.
*L.Z.*

78562 MONTAGU, Jeremy, One of Tut'ankhamūn's Trumpets, *JEA* 64 (1978), 133-134, with 1 fig.

A detailed description of the bronze trumpet Cairo Cat. no. 69851.
*E.P. Uphill*

78563 MOORE, Albert C., Iconography of Religions. An Introduction, London, SCM Press Ltd,[1977] (22.5 x 25.5 cm;[V] + 337 p., 248 fig. and ill.); rev. *Biblical Archaeologist* 42 (1979), 61 (William J. Fulco).

In this book dealing with the iconography of various religions Egypt is discussed in chapter 3, "Polytheism in Ancient Religions". The section on Egypt, called "Egypt: Images and Eternity"(p. 66-76) rapidly surveys various aspects of the Egyptian religion.
There has also appeared an American edition: Philadelphia, Fortress Press, 1977.
*L.Z.*

78564 van MOORSEL, Paul et Jacques DEBERGH, Nubian Studies in Preparation. III, *Orientalia* 47 (1978), 321-331.

Sequel to our number 76566.
The list this time consists of 117 numbers (nos. 105-117 under "Addenda", p. 330), followed by indexes to authors and sites.

78565 MORET, Alexandre, Catalogue général des antiquités égyptiennes du Musée du Caire. Nos. 57001-57100. Denkmäler des Alten Reiches III. Monuments de l' ancien empire III. Autels, bassins et tables d' offrandes. Fasc. I: Nos. 57001-57023. Revisé et édité par Dia' Abou Ghazi, Le Caire, Service des Antiquités de l' Égypte, 1978 (30 x 39.5 cm; 25 p., 47 pl. [5 folding] ).

This continuation of the publication of O.K. monuments in the Cairo Museum (for the last preceding volume, see our number 64051) is based on a manuscript of Moret from 1908, revised and augmented by Mme Abou-Ghazi. The first fascicle deals with 23 objects: libation altars, basins and offering tables. Each of them is fully described, the technical data are given, and the objects are depicted on the plates in one or two drawings and in photographs. Preceding the catalogue are a preface and a short introduction in English.
See now also D. ABOU-GHAZI, Catalogue général des antiquités égyptiennes du Musée du Caire. Nos. 57001-57100. Denkmäler des Alten Reiches III. Altars and Offering Tables. Fasc. 2: Nos. 57024-57049, Le Caire, Service des Antiquités de l'Égypte. 1980.

MOSS, Rosalind L.B., see our number 78640.

78566  MRSICH, Tycho Q., Ein Beitrag zum "Hieroglyphischen Denken", *SAK* 6 (1978), 107-129.

After an introduction about the "hieroglyphic" character of Egyptian art the author deals with "hieroglyphic" and "non-hieroglyphic" thinking. In the latter he distinguishes empirical and speculative-metaphorical ways of thinking, both without a relation to the signs of the writing. However, objects that have received a hieroglyphic form will influence through it the way of thinking.
The author then discusses the relations between ideograms, phonograms, and determinatives, and in the next section he sets forth how the Egyptians understood their writing, dealing i.a. with the difference between word and sign and the meaning of names.
The article is continued in *SAK* 7 (1979), 163-225.

78567  MÜLLER, Christa, Zusammenstellung der Magisterarbeiten, Dissertationen und Habilitationsschriften in Göttingen, *GM* Heft 28 (1978), 21-23.

Es werden 1 Magisterarbeit, 17 Dissertationen und 4 Habilitationen aus dem Zeitraum 1884 bis 1976 zusammengestellt.  *Inge Hofmann*

78568  MUHLY, James D., Ancient Cartography. Man's Earliest Attempts to Represent his World, *Expedition*, Philadelphia, Penn. 20, No. 2 (Winter 1978), 26-31, with 6 fig. (2 on inside cover) and 4 ill.

In this brief survey of Western cartography down to Strabo there is also referred to the Map of the Goldmines.  *L.Z.*

78569  MUNRO, Peter, Der König als Kind (K.M. 1977.3), *SAK* 6 (1978), 131-137, with 1 pl.

Publication of a recent acquisition of the Kestner Museum, Hannover (K.M. 1977.3), a small royal head of a child showing the characteristics of the 'veiled' Amarna style. Probably the head belonged to a sphinx figure and represents Tutankhamon.

78570 MUSSIES, Gerard, Some Notes on the Name of Serapis, in: *Hommages Vermaseren*, 821-832.

The author studies first the exact sound of the name Osiris on account of Coptic and Greek writings, particularly the question whether the first sound was [o-] or [u-]. Then he discusses why this sound was dropped by the Greeks in the name Serapis, suggesting that it was a typical Greek abbreviation used right from the beginning of the cult. Perhaps it was interpreted as a vocative "oh Serapi". This loss of aspiration in ⲀⲠⲒ may be due to the Ionian dialect of the inhabitants of Naucratis (cfr *hby*>ἶβις and *hbny*>ἔβενος). At the end remarks on נפהץ in Jer. 46, 15, generally interpreted as נף פג , "Apis flew".

78571 MYŚLIWIEC, Karol, Le naos de Pithom, *BIFAO* 78 (1978), 171-195, with 8 fig. and 14 pl.

Publication of the remains of a monolithic naos of Ramses II called "naos Paponnot", found at Tell el-Maskhûta and of which one block is preserved in the Louvre Museum (E. 20572) and seven in Cairo. The author minutely describes the monument and the decorations of its walls representing scenes of the Sed festival, and those of its ceiling. He also deals with similar naoi that also bear representations of Ramses II crowned by Atum, one in the British Museum (No. 104) and another at present in Bristol (see Shorter, *JEA* 20 [1934], 18-19). They may all come from Pithom, or from one workshop in the Delta.

78572 MYŚLIWIEC, Karol, Studien zum Gott Atum. Band 1. Die heiligen Tiere des Atum, Hildesheim, Gerstenberg Verlag, 1978 (17 x 23.8 cm; [VI +] 290 p., 105 fig., 38 pl.[= p. 253-290]) = Hildesheimer Ägyptologische Beiträge herausgegeben von Arne Eggebrecht, 5; rev. *BiOr* 37 (1980), 143-147 (Jean-Claude Goyon); *Numen* 26 (1979), 277 (M. Heerma van Voss). Pr. DM 48

In the introduction the author states as the aim of the publication, of which this is the first volume: to establish the most significant conceptions concerning essence, figure and role of the god Atum. In this volume he presents and discusses the material about sacred animals connected with the god.
Myśliwiec successively deals in 14 chapters with: lion, bull, calf, ram, falcon, beatle, phoenix, pidgeon, monkey, ichneumon, snake, lizard, eel and crocodile, in their connections with Atum. Of these the chapters on lion, ram and snake take more space than the others. The chapters are well illustrated by drawings taken from sarcophagi, papyri, tomb and temple walls, etc., while the plates bear representations of unpublished objects among which bronze figures.
In chapter 15 the author deals with staffs, some in the form of a snake, with a ram's head, interpreting them as tools for the Opening of the Mouth ritual. The object is called Wer-hekau.
In the summary (p. 168-172) the author i.a. draws the following conclusions: the animals illustrate four essential aspects of Atum, primeval god, sun god,

Heliopolitan god and ruler of the netherworld. Originally each animal was connected with one aspect. Several animals are connected with one particular cult place, e.g. the eel with Sais and the phoenix with Heliopolis. Not all of them occur from the same period onward: snake, bull, lion, phoenix and beetle already in the O.K., the ram only from the N.K. (through Amon), eel and lizard from the XXVth Dynasty. Some became gods themselves, but the difference with symbols is hard to discern. The author stresses the intricacy of the syncretism and argues that the use of different animals may indicate different religious aspects of Atum.

There follows a catalogue (p. 174-204) of 42 (groups of) sources of various kinds which are still unpublished, the texts given in transcription and translation; all these are represented on the plates.

Indexes on p. 205-238.

Volume 2 has appeared in 1979 as No. 8 of the series.

78573   MYŚLIWIEC, Karol, Zwei Pyramidia der XIX. Dynastie aus Memphis, *SAK* 6 (1978), 139-155, with 8 fig. and 5 pl.

Publication of two pyramidia from Memphis, both dating from the reign of Ramses II (Cairo Temp. Nos. 7/11/24/3 and 7/11/24/1). The former belongs to an overseer of cattle called Ptahemwia, the latter to the Mayor of Memphis Amenhotep (or Ḥuy). The program of the latter is parallel to that of the four sides of the pillar-stela of Tjia (Cairo JE 89624; see also the exhibition Götter-Pharaonen, our number 78305, No. 54).

78574   MYSZOR, W., L'état actuel des études coptologiques en Pologne, *Enchoria* 8, Sonderband (1978), 25*(71) - 28*(74).

Abstract of a paper read at the First International Congress of Coptology, held in Cairo, December 1976.

A brief account of Coptic studies in Poland and an outlook on future plans.

W. Brunsch

78575   NAGEL, Peter, Bibliographie zur russischen und sowjetischen Koptologie, Halle/ Saale, Universitäts- und Landesbibliothek, 1978 (14.9 x 20.8 cm; XV + 103 p.) = Arbeiten aus der Universitäts- und Landesbibliothek Sachsen-Anhalt in Halle a.d. Saale, 23.

The bibliography of which the classification is presented on p. XIV-XV contains 403 nos.

L.Z.

78576   el NAGGAR, Salah, Étude préliminaire du plan du tombeau de Bocchoris à Saqqara, *Egitto e Vicino Oriente* 1 (1978), 41-59, with 14 plans, 1 fig. and 3 pl. (= p. 57-59).

Discussion of the plan of the tomb of Bakenrenef investigated by the mission of the University of Pisa (see our number 78118). Each part of it is described and at the end its architectural history is related.

78577 NASTER, P., Les articles du code de Hammurapi sur le dépiquage et parallèles iconographiques égyptiens, *Orientalia Lovaniensia Periodica*, Leuven 9 (1978), 21-26, with 1 fig.

The author compares an article from the Codex Hammurabi on the rent of oxen, donkeys and small cattle like goats or sheep for threshing purposes with a unique scene from the tomb of Mereruka in which three kinds of animals are shown on the threshing-floor. The sheep and ram in this scene were so far considered to be misplaced and borrowed from the scene of treading seed in the fields by those animals.
*L.Z.*

78578 NEEDLE, Bill, The Dennis Collection of Egyptian Antiquities. Ewing Museum of Nations. The University Museums Illinois State University, Normal, Illinois. September 2-30, 1978 (14 x 21.5 cm; 37 p., 59 ill., 1 map).

After a preface on the present whereabouts of this collection by R.A. Walker-Oni, director of the University Museum of Illinois State University , and an introduction on the person of the collector, James Teackle Dennis, follows the catalogue of the 57 pieces of the collection, which consists mainly of small objects such as scarabs, shawabtis and bronzes. Particularly worth mentioning is a group of small alabaster jars from the Hatshepsut temple at Deir el-Bahri. The author dates almost all objects to the XIIth and XVIIIth Dynasties.
Mr. Needle's eye is not always sharp since at least the painted relief purported to come from a tomb in the Valley of the Kings is obviously a very bad fake.
*L.Z.*

78579 NEEDLER, Winifred, Three Pieces of Unpatterned Linen from Ancient Egypt in the Royal Ontario Museum, *in*: *Studies in Textile History*. Published for the Royal Ontario Museum, Toronto, 1977, 237-251, with 5 ill. and 1 fig.

After an introduction on textiles the author studies three pieces of linen cloth at present in the Royal Ontario Museum (Acc. Nos. 910.85.223, 907.18.20, and 906.18.41) the first dating from the IIIrd or early IVth Dynasty and the other two from the XIth Dynasty.
*L.Z.*

78580 NEGBI, Ora, Cypriote Imitations of Tell el-Yahudiyeh Ware from Toumba tou Skourou, *AJA* 82 (1978), 137-149, with 10 ill. and 4 fig.

The author attempts to demonstrate that a series of Tell el-Yahûdîya juglets from Cyprus were not imported from the Levant or Egypt, but were locally manufactured in a later period after the imports to the island had ended.
*L.Z.*

78581 NELSON, Monique, avec la collaboration de Gisèle PIÉRINI, Catalogue des Antiquités Égyptiennes. Collection des Musées d' Archéologie de Marseille, [Marseille], 1978 (20.8 x 23.7 cm; 93 p., 58 ill. [23 in colour; 1 on cover], 1 map, 4 plans).

The introduction on the history of the Egyptian collection of the Musée Borely and its main contributor is by Simone Bourlard-Collin, keeper of the museums of archaeology in Marseille, while there is also one by Ch. Desroches Noblecourt. After a chronological table follows the catalogue of this most important Egyptian collection outside Paris. Room 1 contains mainly larger objects, such as statuary and sarcophagi, and 12 showcases displaying a variety of objects among which many bronzes; room 2, apart from two showcases, coffins, some stelae and offering tables. The third room is exclusively devoted to the four stelae of the royal scribe and great general of the army Kasa, from Saqqâra, XIXth Dynasty. The fourth room presents many smaller funerary objects, such as shawabtis, some mummies, and i.a. the particularly beautiful coffin lid of the chantress of Amon Tentamon, as well as objects from the Graeco-Roman and Coptic Periods.

Sometimes explanations for groups of objects are added. The descriptions of the more important objects are provided with the inv. nos.

General index at the end of the book. *L.Z.*

78582   NEUFELD, Edward, Apiculture in Ancient Palestine (Early and Middle Iron Age) within the Framework of the Ancient Near East, *Ugarit-Forschungen*, Kevelaer/Neukirchen-Vluyn 10 (1978), 219-247, with 17 ill. and 1 fig.

Although concentrating on an attempt to promote the possibility of apiculture in ancient Palestine, the author also offers a survey about honey hunting and beekeeping in Ancient Egypt. He devotes attention to the pictorial evidence in the Sun temple of Niuserre, and the tombs of Rekhmire and Pabasa at Thebes.

*L.Z.*

78583   NIBBI, Alessandra, The Hoe as the Symbol of Foundation in Some Early Egyptian Reliefs, *GM* Heft 29 (1978), 89-94, with 7 fig.

Entgegen der Auffassung Butzers (vgl. unsere Nr. 76132), der die Darstellung auf der Keule des Königs "Skorpion" fur eine Bewässerungsszene hält, wird Baumgartels These einer Gründungsszene verteidigt. Die primäre Verwendung einer Hacke gilt zwar dem Graben, aber es sollte dabei auch an das Aufhacken mit dem negativen Sinn einer Zerstörung gedacht werden. So interpretierte wenigstens Steindorff die Symbolik der hackenden Wesen auf der Städtezerstörungs-Palette, während die Verfasserin sie für Repräsentationen von Familien hält, die die Städte gründeten und sie beherrschten.   *Inge Höfmann*

78584   NIBBI, Alessandra, The Lake of Reeds of the Pyramid Texts and *Yam Ṣûph*, *GM* Heft 29 (1978), 95-100, with 1 fig. and 1 map.

Der Artikel behandelt die Übersetzungsschwierigkeiten von *yam*, das nicht nur Meer, sondern auch See und einfach Wasser bedeutet. So muss auch *yam ṣûph* ein binnenländisches Gewässer gewesen sein, da *ṣûph* als am Nil wachsend bekannt war. *ṣûph* scheint Papyrus gewesen zu sein. Der in den Pyramidentexten aufscheinenden "Schilfsee" im Osten Ägyptens und im Norden des Roten Meeres gelegen, könnte der Vorwurf zu dem *yam ṣûph* der biblischen Texte gewesen sein.   *Inge Hofmann*

78585   NIBBI, Alessandra, A Note on the Egyptian Collection in the Nicholson Museum, *GM* Heft 27 (1978), 7-10.

Es wird hingewiesen auf die ägyptische Sammlung des Nicholson-Museum der Universität Sydney, Australien. Sie geht zurück auf die Privatsammlung des Mediziners Nicholson, der 1856-57 Ägypten bereiste. 1860 gründete er das Museum und überliess der Universität etwa 400 ägyptische Gegenstände, gegen 100 griechische Vasen und einige prähistorische, römische und etruskische Objekte.
*Inge Hofmann*

78586  NIBBI, Alessandra, The *stt* Sign, *JEA* 64 (1978), 56-64, with 21 fig. and 1 pl.

This sign has often been identified as a shoulder-knot but is here shown to be more correctly the pack-saddle. The suggestion that the word would be better translated as 'imported' rather than 'Asiatic' is made, and the determinative for the goddess Satis is discussed.
*E.P. Uphill*

78587  NICCACCI, Alviero, Nuovi Scarabei Hyksos, *in: Studia Hierosolymitana*. Parte I: Studi Archeologici, Jerusalem, Franciscan Printing Press, 1976 (= Collectio Maior dello Studium Biblicum Franciscanum, No.22), 29-79, with 12 pl.

This is a catalogue of two collections of scarabs in Jerusalem, one of Fr. Godfrey Kloetzli and the other in the Museo della Flagellazione. The latter was brought together before the last World War in Alexandria, by Fra. Cleofa Steinhausen, and consists partly of pieces of known provenance; the former consists mainly of objects found in Palestine.
In three sections the author discusses the major problems (genuineness, date, material, classification, etc.); the general characteristics of the scarabs from the S.I.P.; and the classification system of the present catalogue (p. 35-44), in which he follows Olga Tufnell's system. Eight classes are distinguished after their motifs: royal names (Nos. 1-112); the formula $ˁn\ r\ ˁ$ (113-132); private names (133-138); religious and royal emblems (139-222); signs of good omen (223-241); animals (242-251); plants (252-262); geometrical motifs (263-317).
In the first group we find royal names from the XIIth to the XVIIth Dynasty, but also doubtful, probably fictitious names such as $W3ḥ-Rˁ$ and $Rˁ-ḫˁ$.
The last part contains the data of all 317 scarabs, which are all illustrated by a photograph and some also by a drawing.
The article is also published separately as a monograph, and in 1980 an English version has appeared: "Hyksos Scrarabs", Jerusalem, 1980 = Studium Biblicum Franciscanum Museum, 2.

78588  NICCACCI, Alviero, Sul detto 76 dei "Sarcofagi" (*CT* II, 1-17), *Liber Annuus. Studii Biblici Franciscani*, Jerusalem 28 (1978), 5-23.

The author studies C.T. Spell 76, particularly its second part (from 10b onwards), comparing its various versions. Although the structure is the same in all of them, the version of B2L seems to remain closest to the original.
The text consists of a double series of invocations to eight divinities *ḥḥ*, one on a mythological and one on a funerary level. Grammatical considerations strengthen this conclusion.

NICHOLLS, Richard Vaughan, see our number 78537.

NOLL, Walter, see our number 78546.

NOLLI, G., see our number 78101.

78589  NORTH, Robert, From Raamses to Ur: Excavators' Choices, *Orientalia* 47 (1978), 114-136.

Survey of recent publications in which also a number of egyptological studies from 1975 and 1977 are mentioned.

NUR EL-DIN, Mohamed Abd el-Halim Ahmed, see our number 78109.

78590  OBADÁLEK, Jiří, Ještě k záhadě médúmské pyramidy, *Nový Orient*, Praha 33, No. 10 (1978), 309-311, with 2 ill. and 2 fig.

"Once More the Riddle of the Pyramid of Maidûm".

OBENGA, Théophile, see our number 78614.

78591  [OCHSENSCHLAGER, Edward], Excavations of Nile Delta Cemetery, *Intellect*, New York 106, No. 2396 (May 1978), 443-444, with 2 ill.

Short note on the Mendes excavations. L.Z.

78592  O'CONNOR, Brendan, Zum Griffangelschwert von "el-Kantara" (Ägypten), *Archäologisches Korrespondenzblatt*, Mainz 8 (1978), 187-188, with 1 pl.

The author denies the possibility of an Eastern Mediterranean origin of a sword with a bent handle, found at el-Qantara, and consequently even doubts Qantara as its finding place. L.Z.

O'CONNOR, David B., see our number 78008.

78593  Die österreichischen Ausgrabungen in Sayala, Ägyptisch-Nubien, 1961-1966. Ausstellung Tiroler Landesmuseum Ferdinandeum Innsbruck, 28. April bis 27. August 1978, [Innsbruck, 1978] (20 x 22.5 cm; 48 p., 32 ill., 1 map, 1 plan).

After a preface by the curator of the museum, L. Zemmer-Plank, and an introduction Karl Kromer describes the archaeological results of the Austrian excavations at Sayala, Nubia. Then follows the catalogue proper containing short descriptions and inv. nos. of 270 exhibited pieces which are in some instances illustrated by a photograph. The catalogue is divided into five sections: the Pre- and Protodynastic A-group settlement; the tomb and settlement of the C-group and the Pan-graves culture; cemeteries and a drinking quarter from the Roman Period; Christian settlement. L.Z.

78594  OGDON, Jorge R., Estatuillas funerarias egipcias del tercer periodo intermedio, I. Inscriptas (Colección Ogdon-Buenos Aires), *Aegyptus Antiquus* 3, 1 (1978), 1-36, with 3 tables, 23 fig. and an English summary on p. 68-69.

After a short introduction on this collection of which the objects here described all come from the former collection of Henry M. Tudor, the author presents the catalogue of the shawabtis, all dating from the T.I.P. Full data such as Inv. no., materials, date, description, inscriptions and eventually parallels are given. The article is concluded by remarks on the names, genealogies and titles, which are resumed in a table.
*L.Z.*

78595 OGDON, Jorge R. and Lorenzo BAQUÉS, Escarabeos egipcios con inscripcion en las colecciones argentinas, *Boletin de la Asociacion Española de Orientalistas*, Madrid 14 (1978), 97-109, with 8 fig.

After remarks on the origin of the Egyptian scarabs in the Museo Arqueológico del Instituto de Egiptologia de la Argentina (MAIEA) and those from the private collection Ogdon, almost all originating from Petrie's excavations in 1911 and presented to Henry M. Tudor, the eight scarabs are described and briefly commented upon.
*L.Z.*

78596 ONASCH, Christian, Das meroitische Pantheon. Untersuchungen zur Religion in Kusch, Dissertation Berlin 1978 (14.7 x 29.7 cm; 221 p. in typescript).

Nach einer Übersicht zum Stand der meroitistischen Forschungen werden die Eigenschaften und der Werdegang der in Kusch vom Beginn der ägyptischen Herrschaft bis zum Ende des Reiches von Meroe auftretenden Gottheiten untersucht. Amun erlangte während des Neuen Reiches eine dominierende Position im Pantheon, die er seit dem 3. Jahrhundert v. Chr. mit Isis und Apedemak teilen musste. Die Religion der meroitischen Zeit war geprägt von den ägyptischen Traditionen aus dem Neuen Reich, den Einflüssen aus dem zeitgenössischen hellenistischen Ägypten und den einheimischen Kulten. Gegenüber der strukturbestimmenden Synthese ägyptischer und einheimischer Elemente traten alle anderen Einflüsse von aussen zurück. Im Totenkult waren die einheimischen Traditionen stärker wirksam als bei der Götterverehrung.
Ein Exemplar dieser Dissertation ist vorhanden in der Berliner Universitätsbibliothek (Humboldt-Universität) und für den internationalen Leihverkehr freigegeben.
*Ch. Onasch*

78597 The Oriental Institute Annual Report 1977/78, [Chicago, 1978] (15.2 x 22.8 cm; 143 p., 2 maps, 1 plan, 2 fig., 37 ill.).

As regards Egyptology, this volume contains reports on the following subjects: the season's work by the Epigraphic Survey at Luxor (Lanny Bell); the first season of investigations at the port of Quseir el-Qadîm (Janet H. Johnson and Donald Withcomb); the Demotic Dictionary Project (Janet H. Johnson). Moreover, there is a short note to the preparation of the publication of the excavation report to the Nubian Campaign, by Bruce Williams (p.26; see also p. 62), as well as brief information about individual research projects of the staff members.

78598 ORLANDI, Tito, Il *dossier* copto del Martire Psote. Testi copti con introduzione e traduzione, Milano, Cisalpino-Goliardica, 1978 (17.1 x 24.2 cm; 139 p. including 6 pl.) = Testi e documenti per lo studio dell' antichità, 61; rev. *Aegyp-*

tus 59 (1979), 293-295 (Sergio Pernigotti); *BiOr* 36 (1979), 181-182 (Gerald M. Browne); *CdE* LV, No. 109-110 (1980), 334-338 (A.I. Elanskaya); *Orientalia* 49 (1980), 128-132 (Hans Quecke). Pr. L. **13.000**

Continuing his publications of unpublished or partly published Coptic texts the author presents the dossier of Apa Psote. In the introduction the mss. are listed and discussed, particularly the Sahidic Pierpont Morgan Library M. 583, written A.D. 848, which contains the oldest version of the Passion of Psote. Other mss. came from the White Monastery and are now preserved in various collections.
The author then discusses the works themselves, the Passion in its older and its enlarged version, an encomium, a text dealing with the martyr's miracles, and an oration in honour of Psote. All texts are presented in Coptic with translations.
In an appendix (p. 93-115) the passion of Panine and Paneu in which the martyr Psote occurs. The texts also came from the White Monastery and are discussed in an introduction, followed by the Coptic text and its translation.
Indexes on p. 119-126.

78599   ORLANDI, Tito, La traduzione copta di Platone, Resp. IX, 588b-589b: problemi critici ed esegetici, *Atti della Academia nazionale dei Lincei*. Serie Ottava. *Rendiconti.* Classe di scienzi morali, storichi e filologiche 32 (1977), 1977, 45-62.

The author discusses some problems of the Coptic version of Plato's Republic IX, 588b-589b, in Nag Hammadi Codex VI, 48,16 - 50,24.    *L.Z.*

ORLANDI, Tito, see also our number 78269.

OSBORN, Dale J., see our number 78670.

78600   OSING, Jürgen, The Dialect of Oxyrhynchus, *Enchoria* 8, Sonderband (1978), 29*(75)-36*(82).

Abstract of a paper read at the First International Congress of Coptology, held in Cairo, December 1976.
The author shows that the Coptic dialect called Middle Egyptian (or Oxyrhynchite) is not identical with the dialect of Oxyrhynchus, but is closely related to it. The home area of Middle Egyptian is to be sought between the Faiyûm and Wâdi Sarga.
Compare our number 78711.    *W. Brunsch*

78601   OSING, Jürgen, Nochmals zur ägyptischen Nominalbildung, *GM* Heft 27 (1978), 59-74.

Verfasser setzt sich mit den Argumenten von Vergote (vgl. unsere Nr. 76798) auseinander, die dieser gegen seine Arbeit (vgl. unsere Nr. 76611) vorgebracht hat. Nach der Abhandlung methodischer Fragen (Erklärung des nicht-stammhaften -*w* im Auslaut ägyptischer Nomina; Vokalqualitäten und Silbenstruktur;

Feminina; Vergleich ägyptischer mit semitischer Bildungstypen für deverbal abgeleitete Nomina; Akzentvarianten; nicht-vollbetonte Wörter; methodische Grundlagen) wird auf einige Details eingegangen.  *Inge Hofmann*

78602   OSING, Jürgen, Zu einigen ägyptischen Namen in keilschriftlicher Umschreibung, *GM* Heft 27 (1978), 37-41.

Es werden Bedenken erhoben gegen einige von Zadok (vgl. unsere Nr. 77827) identifizierte ägyptische Personennamen in keilschriftlicher Umschreibung: ᵐhu-ut-na-aḫ-te nicht *Ḥ3.t-nḫt*, sondern *Ḥd-nḫt(w)*; ᵐbak-ki/e-e: es bieten sich zu viele äg. Namen für eine Bestimmung an, als dass eine Entscheidung möglich wäre; ᶠa-pi/e-' und ᵐa-ti-i mit ᵐa-te-e wohl nur als Nebenform: der Auslaut legt eine Verbindung zu äg. Namen mit der Koseendung *-j* nahe; ᶠa-pi/e-' ist vielleicht der gleiche Name wie ca. 700 Jahre vorher ᵐa-pi/e; bei den beiden anderen ist eine Entscheidung nicht möglich. Abschliessend wird die keilschriftliche Umschreibung aus der 18. Dynastie ᵐha-ti-ip aufgegriffen, für die die Interpretation der Wortform von äg. *\*ḥatip* weiterhelfen kann. Es kommt wohl nur die Gleichung mit dem äg. Personennamen *Ḥtp* in Frage.
*Inge Hofmann*

78603   OSING, Jürgen, Zum Namen des Tempels von Deir el-Hagar, *GM* Heft 30(1978), 57-59.

Die Neuaufnahme der Inschriften des Temples von Deir el-Hagar im Westen der Oase Dâchla zeigt eindeutig, dass sein Name *St-wḥʿ(t)* lautete und nicht *St-jʿḥ*.
*Inge Hofmann*

78604   OSING, Jürgen, Zur Wortbildung von A₂ ⲘⲎⲦ ⲀⲂⲀⲖ "Gegenwart", *GM* Heft 27 (1978), 43-44.

Verfasser sieht die Form der Ableitung vom ägyptischen Verbalstamm *\*mt3* < *mtr* "zugegen sein" als nicht zwingend an; man könnte auch eine Qualitativform sehen und eine spätere infinitivische Gebrauchsweise eines solchen Qualitativs annehmen.  *Inge Hofmann*

OTTE, M., see our number 78811.

OTTO, Eberhard, see our number 78488.

78605   PADRÓ I PARCERISA, Josep, El déu Bes: Introducció al seu estudi, *Fondaments*. Prehistoria i Mon Antic als Països Catalans, Barcelona 1 (1978), 19-41, with 8 fig. and 6 pl.

Dans le préambule, consacré à Bès et Ibiza, l'auteur analyse la théorie selon laquelle Ibiza sérait l'Île de Bès; cette théorie est basée sur la lecture de l'épigraphe punique inscrit sur les monnaies de l'île, et sur la réprésentation de l'image du dieu Bès sur ces mêmes monnaies. Cette théorie ne semble plus contestée jusqu'à maintenant par personne, et elle compte encore sur la faveur que ce dieu trouva parmi les Phéniciens dans tous les coins de la Méditerranée. Dans la première partie du travail, consacrée à l'origine et aux attributs de Bès, l'auteur rappelle la provenance africaine du dieu, attestée surtout par les textes de Dandara et de Philae. Il signale que de l'unique étymologie valable du nom du dieu on peut déduire sa relation avec le léopard. Il passe en revue les caractères nettement africains de Bès et il étudie notamment sa caractéristique essentielle, le fait qu'il soie un nain ethnique, danseur et musicien. La deuxième partie porte sur la diffusion et le caractère de son culte en Égypte. Ici on rappelle d'abord les antécédents de Bès en Égypte, les nains danseurs de l'Ancien Empire et le génie Aha des ivoires magiques du Moyen Empire. On énumère les apparitions de Bès au Nouvel Empire, depuis sa présence au temple de Hatchepsout à Deir-el-Bahari, déjà à côté de Thoueris. On le trouve comme protecteur des naissances et des femmes enceintes, des enfants, des dormants, des maisons et de ses habitants, de la reproduction et de l'amour, de la femme aussi bien en tant qu'objet de plaisir qu'en tant qu'épouse et mère, du sommeil enfin et, par là, du sommeil éternel. Dès la fin du Nouvel Empire Bès voit grandir énormément sa popularité, il devient un dieu protecteur par excellence, et encore sa conversion en divinité panthée lui permet dès cette époque de s'assimiler à Amon, à Min, à Sopdou, aux divinités solaires ou à Horus par exemple. Très caracteristique de cette époque est l'association constante de Bès aux stèles dites "d'Horus sur les crocodiles". Dès la XXVe Dynastie nous trouvons Bès aux temples nubiens de Naga et du Djebel Barkal; et parmi les innombrables témoignages des Périodes Saïte et Ptolémaïque, on peut signaler le Bès du Serapeum de Memphis, les chambres de Bès à Saqqara et sa présence habituelle aux mammisis des temples ptolémaïques. Au moment de la montée du christianisme, Bès devint l'un des principaux bastions du paganisme en Égypte, et il put faire face encore quelque temps à la suppression des cultes païens. Le travail finit avec une bibliographie très complète et avec un appendice sur la transcription des noms propres égyptiens en catalan. *Maria del Carmen Perez Díe*

78606 PADRÓ I PARCERISA, J. et E. SANMARTÍ-GREGO, Monuments relatifs aux cultes à l' époque romaine du Musée Archéologique de Barcelone, *in*: *Hommages Vermaseren*, 915-921, with 11 pl.

Catalogue of monuments belonging to Egyptian cults of the Roman Period that are preserved in the Archaeological Museum in Barcelona. Apart from a statue of Bes they are seven bronze objects and a lamp.

PAOLINI, Lucia, see our number 78122.

78607 PARDEE, Dennis, The Semitic Root *mrr* and the Etymology of Ugaritic *mr(r)* //*brk*, *Ugarit-Forschungen*, Kevelaer/Neukirchen-Vluyn 10 (1978), 249-288, with 2 tables.

Studying the Semitic root *mrr* in the Northwest Semitic languages, the author also shortly discusses the Egyptian word *mr*. Against Ward who favoured a meaning "to strengthen", "strong" in Wenamun 2, 67-68 and Sinuhe B 133 in our number 61724 he prefers a semantic content of "compassion, distress", "sick, displeasing, disagreeable". There is no trace of a sense "to strengthen" in any way comparable to Semitic *brk* "to bless". *L.Z.*

78608 PARKER, Harold M., Artaxerxes III Ochus and Psalm 44, *The Jewish Quarterly Review*, Philadelphia 68 (1977-1978), 152-168.

In connection with the cruelty of Artaxerxes III Ochus which may be referred to in Psalm 44, the author deals with his second successful campaign against Egypt which he humiliated. *L.Z.*

78609 PAULISCH, Gotthelf, Wie bauten die alten Ägypter ihre Pyramiden und grossen Tempel? Gedanken zur Bautechnologie, *Das Altertum*, Berlin 24 (1978), 242-246, with 1 ill. and 1 fig.

The author presents his hypothesis of how the ancient Egyptians have built their large buildings. *L.Z.*

PAULISSEN, E., see our number 78811.

78610 PAYSÁS, Javier M., Los medios de ascensión celeste en los Textos de las Pirámides (I), *Aegyptus Antiquus* 3,1 (1978), 37-67, with 2 fig. and an English summary on p. 70-71.

The author presents a classification of the utterances of the P.T. relating to the means for the king's ascension to heaven, which can be made along various ways. There follows an enumeration of the pertinent Spells in the C.T. and the B.D., after which the author draws his conclusions. *L.Z.*

78611 PECK, William H., Ancient Art in Detroit, *Archaeology* 31, No. 3 (May/June 1978), 14-18, with 5 ill. (2 in colour).

Short description of the collection of the department of ancient art in the Detroit Institute of Arts. Ancient Egypt is represented by sculpture and relief carvings, the decorative arts, mummies and mummy cases. Notable is the tomb chapel wall of Mery-nesut acquired from the Boston Museum of Fine Arts. *L.Z.*

78612 PECK, William H., Egyptian Drawings, Photographs by John G. Ross, New York, E.P. Dutton, [1978] (24.4 x 27.1 cm; 208 p., 3 ill. on title p., 18 + 132 ill., 16 colour pl.).

After a foreword by Cyril Aldred the author first studies the historical background of the Pre- and Protodynastic Periods and then discusses the artist's vision, dealing with i.a. the canon of proportions. After having described the materials and uses of Egyptian drawing and its connection with painting, writing and sculpture, he presents the subject-matter of Egyptian drawing: man, woman, royal image, god and sky, music and dance, fable and humour, hunting and combat, animal life, and architecture, while in the margin there is referred to the relevant plates and illustrations.
Then follow the captions to the colour plates and the monochrome ill., arranged after the above order. At the end of the book the bibliographical data to the illustrations and an index.
Another English edition has been published by Thames and Hudson, London, 1978. The German edition: Ägyptische Zeichnungen aus drei Jahrtausenden. Aus dem Englischen von J. Rehork, Bergisch-Gladbach, 1978 (?)(Pr. DM 58).

78613 PECK, William H., Two Seated Scribes of Dynasty Eighteen, *JEA* 64 (1978), 72-75, with 2 pl.

Two uninscribed statues, Detroit 31.70 and Berlin 22621, with the left knee raised, are dated stylistically to the reign of Amenophis III, this being supported by the fact that the Berlin one was found at Amarna and may thus just predate the move from the earlier capital. *E.P. Uphill*

PECK, William H., see also our number 78027.

78614 The Peopling of Ancient Egypt and the Deciphering of Meroitic Script. Proceedings of the Symposium held in Cairo from 28 January to 3 February 1974, [Paris], Unesco, [1978] (15.6 x 24.1 cm; 136 p., 1 map, 1 fig.) = The General History of Africa. Studies and Documents, 1.

Apart from a foreword on the preparation of a general history of Africa planned in eight volumes, the book consists of two parts: the peopling of ancient Egypt and the deciphering of Meroitic script.
The first article on the peopling of ancient Egypt, by Jean Vercoutter (p.15-36) sketches the present state of knowledge, the theories advanced and the topics for discussion and lines of research, followed by an extensive list of references and bibliography. Nicole Blanc then studies the peopling of the Nile Valley south of the twenty-third parallel (roughly Nubia and the Sudan) in an extensive way (37-63). In her conclusion she stresses the geographical approach to the history of the Nilotic peoples and the exhaustion of all possibilities of explanation by local conditions. References and bibliography at the end of the article. The last article of the first part, by Théophile Obenga, discusses the genetic linguistic relationship between Egyptian (ancient Egyptian and Coptic) and modern Negro-African languages. Looking for morphological (grammatical) correspondences he compares the gender categories, the formation of the plural and of abstract nouns through the prefix *bu-*, negative morphemes, and the explicit emphatic future by *n/na* and *k/ka*.
The first part is concluded by an extensive report on the discussions, in which various reputed Egyptologists took part (73-103). The general discussion dealt with the following subjects: chronological analysis of the results achieved; the problem of migration in different periods; results of the physical anthropology inquiry; the validity of iconographic inquiry; linguistic analyses; development of an interdisciplinary and pluridisciplinary methodology. Some recommendations in the fields of physical anthropology and the study of migrations were made.
Part 2 starts with Jean Leclant, "The present position in the deciphering of Meroitic script" (107-119), dealing with the following subjects: the discovery of the Meroitic texts, further investigation of the Nubian area, the inventory, interpretation and analysis of the texts, and present tasks. The bibliography is systematically arranged. The following report on the discussions contains also recommendations (121-125).
The book is concluded by three appendices: the system of analytical transcription of Meroitic texts, a list of the participants and the working paper for the symposium.
There is also a French edition: Le peuplement de l'Égypte ancienne et le déchiffrement de l'écriture méroïtique, 1978. *L.Z.*

78615   PERDU, Olivier, La préposition ḥft et les temporelles non-concomitantes, *RdE* 30 (1978), 101-114.

Les exemples de toutes époques réunis dans cet article se traduisent mieux si l'on admet pour la particule ḥft les sens "après que" ou "dès que" plutôt que "en même temps que" ainsi qu'on l'a fait jusqu'ici.    *Ph. Derchain*

78616   PEREMANS, W., Les indigènes égyptiens dans l'armée de terre des Lagides. Recherches anthroponymiques, *Ancient Society*, Leuven 9 (1978), 83-100.

The author investigates the occurrence of persons with Egyptian names in the Ptolemaic armed forces at land. They occur mostly among the common soldiers, notably the kalasirians (see our number 77813).    *L.Z.*

78617   PEREPELKIN, G., The Secret of the Gold Coffin, Moscow, "Nauka" Publishing House. Central Department of Oriental Literature, 1978 (12.5 x 20 cm; 167 p., 1 plan, 20 ill., 2 fig.); at head of title: USSR Academy of Sciences. Institute of Oriental Studies; rev. *CdE* LV, No.109-110 (1980), 136-140 (B. van de Walle).    Pr. 85 коп.

English version of our number 68460.

PEREZ DÍE, Maria del Carmen, see our number 78492.

78618   PERNIGOTTI, Sergio, Addendum a Ciennehebu, *Aegyptus* 58 (1978), 102-105, with 2 pl.

An addition to our number 77111.

78619   PERNIGOTTI, Sergio, A proposito del cono funerario Corpus n. 488, *Egitto e Vicino Oriente* 1 (1978), 119-123, with 6 fig.

Discussion of the inscription of funerary cone Corpus No. 488, which in the publication of the Corpus is fragmentary. From other examples the author states that it belonged to a secretary (?) of the Divine Consort called Ken-amon (not Amenhotep, as the Corpus has). The title remains uncertain. From the words Wsr ḥk3-ḏt the author concludes that the owner may have lived during the XXIIIrd Dynasty or slightly later.

78620   PERNIGOTTI, Sergio, A proposito di Sais e delle sue divinità, *Studi classici e orientali*, Pisa 28 (1978), 223-235, with 1 pl. and 4 fig.

Review article of our number 75660.

78621   PERNIGOTTI, Sergio, I "coni funerari" del Museo Civico Archeologico, *Il Carrobbio*, Bologna 3 (1977), 331-336, with 11 fig.

The Museo Civico of Bologna possesses 37 instances of funerary cones with 11 different impressions. These impressions are here published in facsimile with a description, translation and corpus number, preceded by a general introduction.

78622  PERNIGOTTI, Sergio, Un ostrakon demotico della collezione pisana, in: *Journal Faculty of Archaeology*, 35-42, with 2 pl. and an Arabic summary on p. 40-42.

Publication of a Demotic ostracon in the collection of Pisa (O.D. Pisa 464), measuring 22 x 15.5 cm and containing on one side an account of cereals, on the other an account of water. The author presents the text in photograph, transliteration and translation.

78623  PERNIGOTTI, Sergio, La statuaria egiziane nel Museo Civico di Bologna, *Annali della Scuola Normale Superiore di Pisa*. Serie III. Classe di lettere e filosofia, Pisa 8 (1978), 323-333.

Introductory article to the statuary in the Museo Civico, Bologna. See now S. Pernigotti, La statuaria egiziana nel Museo Civico Archeologico di Bologna, Istituto per la Storia di Bologna, 1980 = Cataloghi Nuova Serie, 2.   *L.Z.*

78624  PERNIGOTTI, Sergio, Le statue egiziane nel Museo Civico di Bologna (Due schede di catalogo), *Il Carrobbio*, Bologna 4 (1978), 385-392, with 2 fig., 3 ill. and 1 colour ill.

Stating that the publications by Curto (our number 61158) and Bresciani (our number 75093) do not present all pieces in the collection of the Museo Civico of Bologna in an adequate way, the author here publishes more fully two statues: 1. the family group of the sculptor of Amon Mai-nakhte, his wife and their three children (Inv. No. 1819), from the XVIIIth Dynasty; 2. the sitting dyad of the highpriest of Ptah at Thebes Amenhotep and his wife (Inv. No. 1814), with a daughter in high relief standing between the knees of the parents and three more daughters and four sons represented in sunk relief on the seat. This statue is dated to the late XVIIIth or early XIXth Dynasty. The pieces are carefully described, the inscriptions given in facsimile and translation.

78625  PERNIGOTTI, Sergio and Lucia CRISCUOLO, Testi demotici minori, *Enchoria* 8, Teil 1 (1978), 159-164, with 9 pl. [4 folding].

Publication of two Demotic stelae and five mummy-bandages of a private collection. All of them are from the Roman Period and were bought in Cairo.
*W. Brunsch*

PERNIGOTTI, Sergio, see also our numbers 78045 and 78123.

78626  PERSOONS, Annie, Les statues usurpées par Merneptah, XIXe dynastie, *Revue des archéologues et historiens d'art de Louvain*, Louvain 11 (1978), 188.

Abstract of a small thesis.

PESTMAN, P.W., see our number 78109.

78627  PETERSON, Bengt, A Sarcophagus Puzzle, *CdE* LIII, No. 106 (1978), 222-225, with 1 fig. and 1 ill.

Sous ce titre l'auteur publie un fragment du sarcophage intérieur d'Aménophis fils de Hapou, conservé dans une collection de Stockholm. *Ph. Derchain*

78628   PETERSON, Bengt, Steingefässe aus dem Neuen Reich, *Medelhavsmuseet Bulletin*, Stockholm 13 (1978), 6-13, with 1 fig. and 9 ill.

Publication of four vases with inscriptions.
1. A pear-shaped alabaster vase, probably from the tomb of the three wives of Tuthmosis III (MME 1957:2), with an inscription mentioning the king's name. For its contents, see our number 78835.
2. A limestone false vase (MM 10053) with an inscription mentioning the mayor of Thebes Sennefer and his wife. It possibly came from near tomb KV 42, the owner of which is unknown (see Hornung, our number 75349). Peterson suggests that Sennefer possessed a tomb in the Valley of the Kings.
3. A small alabaster vase (MM 11204) of a shape imitating a pomegranate, inscribed with the name of Tuthmosis III but probably of a later date.
4. A *nw*-shaped limestone vase (MM 10749) inscribed with the name of Ramses III.

78629   PETERSON, Bengt, Vier neue ägyptische Prinzessinnen, *Medelhavsmuseet Bulletin*, Stockholm 13 (1978), 23-24, with 2 ill.

Publication of a fragmentary male torso holding before him the figures of eight girls. The piece is in a private collection in Stockholm. According to three inscriptions the girls are princesses, but their names are unknown from elsewhere. The piece may date from the N.K.

78630   PETERSON, Bengt & Gunnel WERNER, Die Wiedergewinnung einer ägyptischen Situla, *Medelhavsmuseet Bulletin*, Stockholm 13 (1978), 32-36, with 5 ill.

The first author publishes a bronze situla in the Medelhavsmuseet (MM 10847). It is of a particular form, presenting a picture of the cosmos: a lotus flower bearing a naos. On its body four scenes are engraved, one with a woman adoring Hathor, the others with each one deity, namely Isis, Horus and Thoth. The second author discusses the manufacture and the restoration of the object.

PETOLESCU, Constantin C., see our number 78530.

78631   PETRI, Winfried, Astronomische Grundlagen der Ortung und Zeitbestimmung, in: *Methoden der Archäologie*. Eine Einführung in ihre naturwissenschaftlichen Techniken. Herausgegeben von B. Hrouda, München, Verlag C.H. Beck, [1978], 175-207, with 11 tables.

In this book on the application of the techniques of the natural sciences the author discusses astronomical aspects. In this connection Egypt is sometimes referred to.                                                                                          *L.Z.*

78632   PETROVSKY, N.S., Звуковые знаки египетского письма как система, Москва, Издательство "Наука". Главная редакция восточной литературы,

1978 (14.5 x 21.5 cm; 172 p., 24 fig., 10 tables); at head of title: Ленинградский государственный университет имени А. А. Жанова. Восточный факультет. Pr. 1 r. 40 k.

'The sound signs of the Egyptian script as a system'.
Chapter 1 (p. 15-58) reviews earlier descriptions of the writing system (of the O. and M.K.) from the classical period up till the present. Chapter 2 (59-66) prepares the ground for the author's own approach, along with a discussion of the notion 'system'; the main distinction made is between pronounced and non-pronounced ('mute') signs.
Chapter 3 (67-132) deals with internal systemic aspects. Bi- and triconsonantal signs are here more in focus than the monoconsonantal ('alphabetic') ones. In various grids phonetic components of pluriconsonantal signs occur in two-consonantal display: a vertical axis contains the first-occurring consonants, a horizontal the second radicals. Triconsonantal signs are analysed in a similar bidimensional way, and twice, thus, *nfr* as *n* +*fr* and *nf* +*r*. The intersections in the complete grid (with a maximum of 576 possible links) show the totality of phonetic combinations realised. Binary combinations realised within the bi- and triconsonantal subsystems amount to only 221, but the 'blank spots' are partly compensated by combinations of monoconsonantal signs (for their bidimensional display, zero second radicals are used), the latter giving 457 more. In Late Egyptian writing and in the rendering of foreign words, the number of unused combinations somewhat diminishes, but there remain many 'impossible' combinations. Biconsonantalism appears to be a leading principle in ancient Egyptian lexical organization (cfr our number 58321, here p. 130).
Chapter 4 (133-145) describes the character of the sound-signs as principally semantically oriented, just as the segmentations between the red 'verse points' are. Egyptian phonograms may be characterised as consonantal morphographemes, their semantics being attached to certain fixed complexes.
Extensive English summary on p. 150-171.  *J.F. Borghouts*

78633  PEZIN, Michel, Les Etiquettes de Momies du Musée de Picardie à Amiens, *Enchoria* 8, Teil 2 (1978), 9-12, with 2 pl.

Publication of four mummy-labels (one Greek, three Demotic-Greek) of the collection of the Musée de Picardie à Amiens with an excursus on the name Πετεμπετως (=*P3-ntj-m-p3-t3* [?]).  *W. Brunsch*

PEZIN, Michel, see also our number 78215.

PIÉRINI, Gisèle, see our number 78581.

78634  PINTORE, Franco, Il matrimonio interdinastico nel Vicino Oriente durante i secoli XV-XIII, Roma, Istituto per l'Oriente. Centro per le antichità e la storia dell' arte del Vicino Oriente, 1978 (20 x 28 cm; X + 207 p., 1 map, 1 folding table) = Orientis antiqui collectio, 14.

The subject of this study being interdynastic marriages in the Near East during the Late Bronze Age, by its very nature it contains extensive discussions of Egyptian evidence.  This is presented in chapters 2 and 3 (p. 11-67). The first one, after a section on Egyptian hypergamy, deals with the royal marriages with women from vassal states, from Mitanni, from the Kassite royal family, the Anatolian marriage of Amenophis III and those of Ramses II with Hittite princesses, as well as the difficult case of Daḫamunzu-Zannanza, that is, the negotiations concerning a marriage between a son of Shuppiluliumash and an Egyptian royal widow.

Chapter 3 is devoted to the form of the Egyptian-Asiatic royal marriages: proposal, negotiations, rhetorics of the wedding documents, etc.

After chapters on Asiatic interdynastic marriages the author discusses the general characteristics: pact and negotiations, bride wealth, the position of the royal consort. Chapter 7 contains general conclusions.

The author throughout uses sources in a large number of languages, including Egyptian, while the notes (145-193) refer to studies on the various areas. In an appendix a list of thirty interdynastic royal marriages, with references to the pages where they are dealt with. Indexes on p. 199-207.

78635 PLANTIKOW, Maria, Lexikon der Ägyptologie. Index zu Band II. Zusammengestellt, Wiesbaden, Otto Harrassowitz, 1978 (19.4 x 27.5 cm; VII + 97 p.).

Sequel to our number 76630.
Apart from the general index, there are others to topographical, royal and personal names, to gods, in the Latin alphabet as well as in Egyptian, to classical authors, to titles and functions, and to sources. *L.Z.*

78636 PLUMLEY, J.M., New Light on the Kingdom of Dotawo, in: *Études nubiennes*, 231-241, with 3 ill. on 2 pl.

In einem spätchristlichen Haus in Qasr Ibrîm wurde ein Krug gefunden, der 10 Lederrollen, 1 Papierrolle, 7 Briefe auf Pergament und 18 auf Papier enthielt. Sie stammen aus dem 12. Jahrhundert. Die Papierrolle ist in koptischer Sprache, alle anderen in mittelalterlichem Nubisch. Die Rollen nennen den oder die Namen von Königen und sind mit dem Königreich von Dotawo verbunden. Es wird die Frage aufgeworfen, ob der genannte Titel eines *Migin sonoj* dem des griechischen Eparchen entspricht. *Inge Hofmann*

78637 POMERANCE, L., Improbability of a Theran Collapse during the New Kingdom, 1503-1447 B.C., in: *Thera and the Aegean World*. I. Papers presented at the Second International Scientific Congress, Santorini, Greece, August 1978, London, Thera and the Aegean World, 1978, 797-803.

The author proceeds from a date of the reigns of Hatshepsut and Tuthmosis III between 1503 and 1447 B.C., though admitting that a slightly later date is also possible. Since from five Theban tombs from this period pictures of Aegean Keftiu testify to continuous contacts it looks impossible that the devastating cataclysm resulting from the eruption of the Thera volcano took place within these 54 years.

78638 POMERANTSEVA, N.A., Принцип композиции древнеегипетских памятников додинастического периода и эпохи первых двух династий, in: Искусство Востока и Античности, Москва, Издательство "Наука", 1977, 5-15, with 3 fig. and 4 ill.

"The Principles of Composition of Ancient Egyptian Monuments from the Predynastic Period and the Time of the First Two Dynasties".
The author describes the development of the characteristics of Egyptian art during the Predynastic and Archaic Periods.

78639 PONTE, E., Le semeiologia nella medicina dell' antico Egitto, *Minerva Medica*, Torino 69, No. 36 (28 Luglio 1978), 2443-2448.

General article.

78640 PORTER, the Late Bertha and Rosalind L.B. MOSS, Assisted by Ethel W. BURNEY, Topographical Bibliography of Ancient Egyptian Hieroglyphic Texts, Reliefs and Paintings. III². Memphis. Part II. Ṣaqqâra to Dashûr. Fascicle 1 (III². 393-574). Second Edition, Revised and Augmented by Jaromír Málek, Oxford, Griffith Institute, Ashmolean Museum, [1978] (18.8 x 27.3 cm; XXIV + 182 p. [=393-574], 1 map and 17 plans [nos. XLI-LVII] ).     Pr. £15

Sequel to our number 74583.
The fascicle begins with a list of abbreviations (p. XVII-XXXIII) and deals with the various pyramid complexes of Saqqâra, the necropolis North of the Step Pyramid (the Sacred Animal Complexes will be dealt with in fasc. 3) and the area around the Teti Pyramid.
Like in the preceding part I the additions compared with the first edition are so numerous as to make it a completely new book. We may point out, for example, the information about the Pyramid Enclosure of Sekhemkhet (p. 415-417) that was still entirely lacking in the first edition. That on the Zoser Pyramid Complex was enlarged from 4 to 16½ pages.
Another essential improvement is the information presented on the more important finds; for instance, the vessels inscribed in ink that were found in the galleries of the Zoser Pyramid (p.404-405) are recorded with their Cairo Museum numbers.
The plans at the end (only those pertaining to the present fascicle) are newly drawn, their number being much enlarged.
A few introductory remarks by the editor on the inner side of the cover; the introduction to the entire volume III² will appear with fasc. 3.
Fascicle 2 has appeared in 1979.

78641 POSENER, Georges, Catalogue des ostraca hiératiques littéraires de Deir el-Médineh. Tome III (fasc. 2) - Nos. 1410-1606, [Le Caire], Institut français d'Archéologie orientale, 1978 (25 x 32 cm; [IV +] 48 p. [= p. 33-80], 46 pl. [= pl. 23a-55a] ) = Documents de fouilles, 20.

Sequel to our number 77603.
The second fascicle contains the descriptions of nos. 1409 (continued) to 1606, and the texts, in most instances accompanied by facsimiles, of nos. 1435 rt. (facs.) to 1610.
The ostraca here published mainly belong to three groups, bearing lines of the "Enseignement loyaliste" (nos. 1413-1434), the Story of Sinuhe (1437-1440) and, particularly, the "Satire des métiers", Pap. Sall. II (1442-1590). Other texts are, e.g.: lists of private names (1410-1412), "Wishes of a Happy Survival"

(1441), the Story of Seth and Anat (1591-1592), a Praise of Thebes (1594; cfr *Hier. Ostr.* 8,3), magical texts (1436 and 1603), hymns (1435; 1503 + O. Michaelides 82), etc.

78642 POSENER, Georges, Le Papyrus Vandier, *Comptes rendus de l' Académie des Inscriptions et Belles-Lettres*, Paris, 1978, 746-755.

Pap. Vandier was named after the great scholar and his wife by the Institute of Papyrology and Egyptology at Lille, which acquired the papyrus recently. Although this papyrus from the 4th century B.C. bears on the recto a copy of the B.D., its verso contains a literary text, of which the beginning is well preserved. The story dates from the N.K., and is concerned with a Pharaoh Sisobk and the scribe-magician-general Meryra. The story relates how Meryra substitutes himself for the Pharaoh who is bound to die from an illness, but under certain conditions. Since these were broken, it is probable that the hero will have returned to earth in the broken part of the text. *L.Z.*

78643 POSENER, Georges, Philologie et archéologie égyptiennes, *Annuaire du College de France*, Paris 78 (1977-1978), 541-548.

Sequel to our number 77607.
On a fragmentary papyrus (early Ptolemaic at the latest), acquired by the Lille Egyptological Institute ('Papyrus Vandier'). Verso: some B.D. chapters; recto: an unknown story (written in advanced Late Egyptian) about an unknown king Sisobk and one Meryrē', a magician (ḥry-tp) and general. Both are perhaps attributable to the early N.K. (latter personage: cfr our number 2527, 119-120 [no. 60]). Once a certain prognostication has pointed out king Sisobk's death being near at hand, his court magicians prove to be unable to counteract this fate. They finally disclose the existence of Meryrē', who might perhaps save Pharaoh. Summoned to the court, Meryrē' explains that Pharaoh's life can only be prolonged at the cost of his own and reluctantly accepts to die for him. After certain settlements and ceremonies have been carried out, he departs for the Netherworld, meets the goddess Hathor and is taken before 'the great living god'. At this point the course of the story becomes obscure owing to the many lacunas. *J.F. Borghouts*

POSENER, Georges, see also our numbers 78161 and 78804.

78644 POSENER-KRIÉGER, Paule, A Letter to the Governor of Elephantine, *JEA* 64 (1978), 84-87, with 2 pl.

This papyrus Louvre E. 27151 found by Clédat in 1907 and measuring 21.3 cm x 22 cm. bears eleven lines on the recto and two lines and the address on the verso. The palaeographic evidence suggests a date of about the reign of Ramesses III or just after, and it is from Kh'ay of the house of Hor-Akhty to the governor Mentu-her. It concerns jars of honey, incense and logs of sycamore wood. *E.P. Uphill*

78645 POSMOWSKI, Pierrette, The Island of Isis Rises Again from the Nile, *Compressed Air Magazine*, Washington, N.J. 83, No. 11 (November 1978), 22-25, with 10 ill.

Short note on the transfer of the Philae temples to Agilkia, in which operation compressed air technology was a great help. *L.Z.*

78646 PRAG, Kay, Silver in the Levant in the Fourth Millennium B.C., *in*: *Archaeology in the Levant*. Essays for Kathleen Kenyon. Edited by Roger Moorey and Peter Parr, Warminster, Aris & Phillips Ltd, [1978], 36-45.

The author briefly surveys Egyptological literature on predynastic silver and lists the examples from the Naqâda II period. *L.Z.*

PRESEDO VELO, Francisco, see our number 78018.

PRIESE, Karl-Heinz, see our number 78008.

78647 PRIVATI, Béatrice, La poterie de la ville de Kerma. Premières observations, *Genava*, Genève 26 (1978), 128-134, with 41 fig. on 5 pl.

Die bei den Ausgrabungen in Kerma zutage geförderten Scherben werden klassifiziert und ausführlich beschrieben: sie verteilen sich auf die alte Kerma-Kultur (Ende des Alten Reiches und Erste Zwischenzeit), die mittlere Kerma-Kultur (Mittleres Reich) und klassische Kerma-Kultur (Zweite Zwischenzeit). Aus Ägypten importierte Ware ist relativ selten. *Inge Hofmann*

78648 PROMIŃSKA, E., Les ossements des tombes des églises de Dongola, *in*: *Études nubiennes*, 243-246, with 1 pl.

In oder bei den Kirchen von Dongola zwischen dem 8. und 13. Jahrhundert n.Chr. wurden 18 Gräber gefunden, die 11 Männer, 6 Frauen und 4 Kinder enthielten. Das Durchschnittsalter der Männer war 53, das der Frauen 44 Jahre. Die Schädel waren langkopfig; vier Männer waren 173,2 cm gross, zwei der Frauen 163,8 cm. Auffallend war die häufige Verletzung der Wirbelsäule und Arthrose; bei zwei Skeletten zeigten sich Spuren von Knochenbrüchen. Auch Kopfverletzungen wurden festgestellt. Die Funde zeigen, dass nicht nur Priester in den Kirchen bestattet wurden. *Inge Hofmann*

PROMIŃSKA, Elżbieta, see also our number 78233.

78649 QUAEGEBEUR, Jan, Egyptische goden die luisteren, *Alumni van de Universitaire Stichting*, Brussel 49 (December 1978), 9-19, with 1 ill. and 4 fig.

The author publishes a faience amulet in the Musées Royaux d' Art et d'Histoire in Brussels (No. E 3230) in the form of a small stela, inscribed in ink with the name of *Nfrt-iry* between two rows of three ears each. In this connection he mentions actual stelae decorated with ears and discusses the concept of the listening god. The Nefertari of the amulet is probably the deified Ahmose-Nefertari.

78650 QUAEGEBEUR, Jan, Les papyrus démotiques des Musées Royaux d'Art et d'Histoire à Bruxelles, *Enchoria* 8, Sonderband (1978), 25-28.

Abstract of a paper read at the First International Colloquium of Demotists held in Berlin, September 1977.
The author presents a list of the Demotic papyri of the collection in Brussels, which will be published or re-published by him in the near future. *W. Brunsch*

78651 QUAEGEBEUR, Jan, Reines ptolémaïques et traditions égyptiennes, in: *Das ptolemäische Ägypten*, 245-262, with 12 fig.

On account of Egyptian representations (reliefs and stelae), leaving aside Egyptian and Greek texts, the author investigates the position of the Ptolemaic queens. He deals with their iconography, presenting a choice of documents in chronological order, the positions in which the queens are represented, their headdresses, and some pharaonic parallels. One of his conclusions is that the queens were usually represented together with their husbands, either venerating the gods or being venerated themselves. It is only Arsinoe II who is adored alone, as a sovereign in her own right (cfr our numbers 71472 and 71474).

78652 QUAEGEBEUR, Jan and H. - J. THISSEN, Protokoll, *Enchoria* 8, Sonderband (1978), 4-6.

Protocol of the First International Colloquium of Demotists, held in Berlin, September 1977. *L.Z.*

QUAEGEBEUR, Jan, see also our number 78109.

78653 QUECKE, Hans, "...euch wie Weizen zu *mahlen*" (Lk 22,31 sahid.). Zu den koptischen Verben ϤⲰⲔ und ϬⲒⲔⲈ, *GM* Heft 29 (1978), 101-104.

Die Palau-Rib.-Handschrift gebraucht in Lk 22,31 das Verb "mahlen"; der sahidische Normaltext bietet ϬⲈⲔ, das bisher als Stat. nom. von ϤⲰⲔ angesehen und mit "sieben" übersetzt wurde. Der Verfasser wirft die Frage auf, ob das ϬⲈⲔ- nicht eher Stat. nom. von ϬⲒⲔⲈ sei und mit "mahlen" übersetzt werden müsse. *Inge Hofmann*

78654 QUECKE, Hans, Koptische "Hermeneiai"-Fragmente in Florenz, *Orientalia* 47 (1978), 215-219.

The author publishes two fragmentary sheets with Coptic Hermeneiai, that is, quotations from the Psalms that contain some catchword (e.g., in the first fragment, the word "kings"). The fragments are preserved in the Istituto Papirologico in Florence (Inv. CNR 8) and are here presented in transcription with a commentary.

78655 QUECKE, Hans, Das saïdische Jak-Fragment in Heidelberg und London (S 25), *Orientalia* 47 (1978), 238-251.

Discussion of a Sahidic fragment of the Gospel of St. James, numbered S 25 (see our number 75673); it is one sheet, of which part is in Heidelberg and another part in London (a third fragment, also in London, is of another sheet and here ignored). The author presents the text (p. 240) and various comments.

QUECKE, Hans, see also our number 78269.

78656 QUILLARD, Brigitte, Remarques sur un pendentif carthaginois en or en forme de Ptah-Patèque, *Karthago*, Paris 18 (1978), 139-143, with 1 pl.

Publication of a small golden pendant in a private collection, representing on one side the god Ptah as a dwarf standing on two crocodiles, on the other a winged Isis or Sakhmet, Isis, and Nepthys. The type of amulet is common in the Punic culture, but only one golden instance is known (from Cadiz; see the plate).

78657 QUINTENS, Werner, La vie du roi dans le Psaume 21, *Biblica*, Roma 59 (1978), 516-541.

Discussing the role of the life of the king in the Psalm 21 the author draws a comparison with the Poetical Stela of Tuthmosis III. He sees many common features in the phraseology, which are listed in a table, but points also out the differences (the stress on the king instead of god and the explicit role of the temple in the Poetical Stela). He pays particular attention to the divine gift of eternal kingship which is connected with the word "gold" in the Psalm. *L.Z.*

QUIVRON, Gonzague, see our numbers 78823 and 78824.

78658 RADWAN, Ali, Ramses II. und seine Mutter vor Osiris, *SAK* 6 (1978), 157-161, with 1 fig.

The author publishes a limestone relief block preserved in the Egyptian collection in Vienna (Inv. No. 5091) that occurs in the literature as "a stela from the Museum Miramar (No. 1152)". It represents Ramses II and his mother Tuia before Osiris (partly broken off).

78659 RAINEY, A.F., The Toponymics of Eretz-Israel, *BASOR* No. 231 (October 1978), 1-17, with 1 table.

When discussing the toponyms of Israel, the author also includes in a table, presenting the sound shifts of the Semitic alphabet in the various Semitic languages, their Egyptian transcriptions in initial, post-vocalic, post-consonantal and final positions. *L.Z.*

78660 RAMOND, Pierre, Un monument du héraut royal Nekhthorheb (Collection Pierre Ramond: 69-134), *Revue du Tarn*, Albi No. 90 (été 1978), 279-284, with 1 fig. and 5 ill.

Publication of the socle (5 x 3.5 x 3.5 cm) and small remains of a statuette recently acquired by the author. The statuette represents a man called *wḥm-nswt* Nekhthorheb holding before him a figure of Osiris. The piece dates from the Saite Period. To Nekhthorheb also belonged Cairo C. G. 39303.

78661 RANDI, James, King Tut's "Revenge", *The Humanist*, Buffalo, N.Y. 38, No.2 (March/April 1978), 44-47.

Demystifying remarks on the supposed curse of Tutankhamun. *L.Z.*

RAVASZ, Cs., see our number 78224.

78662  RAWSON, Jessica, Animals in Art, *Apollo*, London 107, No. 191 (January, 1978), 20-30, with 29 ill.

Short report on an exhibition for the catalogue of which see our number 77634.
*L.Z.*

78663  RAY, J.D., Nasal Vowels in Egyptian, *Enchoria* 8, Teil 2 (1978), 77-78.

On the evidence of the parallels $mn\text{-}r^c$: $m\jmath^c\text{-}r^c$ ($\mu\alpha\upsilon\rho\eta\varsigma$ : $\mu\alpha\rho\rho\eta\varsigma$) and $\check{s}\jmath^c\text{-}tw=f$ $stm$ : $\check{s}\jmath^c\text{-}mtw=f\,stm$ (ⲰⲀⲦ( Ⲉ ) ϤⲤⲰⲦⲘ : ⲰⲀⲚⲦ( Ⲉ ) ϤⲤⲰⲦⲘ ) the author concludes that a nasalisation of a vowel occurred before an 'ayin.   *W.Brunsch*

78664  RAY, J.D., The non-literary material from North Saqqâra: a short progress report, *Enchoria* 8, Sonderband (1978), 29-30.

Abstract of a paper read at the First International Colloquium of Demotists, held in Berlin, September 1977.
The author gives a brief summary of the different kinds of Demotic texts that have been found in Saqqâra in the years 1964 to 1975.   *W. Brunsch*

78665  RAY, J.D., Observations on the Archive of Ḥor, *JEA* 64 (1978), 113-120, with 1 pl.

Three new texts, additional nos. 66-68, found during the 1975 season at N. Saqqâra, and consisting of a sherd with thirteen lines of text joined from two fragments, as well as a third piece. The text mentions Antiochus and Alexandria but is not written in the hand of the 'Memphite' Ḥor. A translation and commentary are given, together with remarks on the birthday of Ptolemy VI Philometor and its equation with that of an Apis bull. The revised date for this is suggested as between Jan. and Oct. 186 B.C.   *E.P. Uphill*

78666  REDFORD, Donald B., The Razed Temple of Akhenaten, *Scientific American*, New York 239, No. 6 (December 1978), 100-110, with 1 map, 3 plans, 4 fig. and 3 ill.

The author discusses the temples built by Akhnaton at Karnak and the study of the talatat. He also presents a survey of the results of his excavations at Karnak-East. Apart from an urban settlement from the first millennium B.C. he had laid bare by the end of the 1977 season the entire South colonnade of the Gem-pa-aton temple. He discovered numerous relief fragments from which it was possible to determine the scenes on its south wall.

78667  REDFORD, D.B., Son of Sun-Disc, *Archaeological Newsletter. Royal Ontario Museum*, Toronto No. 154 (March 1978), 4 p., with 2 ill. and 1 fig.

Sequel to our number 76667.

The author briefly reports about the excavations at the Eastern quarter of Thebes from the Kushite through the Persian Periods, the debris of the XXIst Dynasty there, and the work done in the S.W. corner of the *Gm-p3-'Itn* of Akhnaton at Karnak. *L.Z.*

78668 REDFORD, Donald B., Two Notes on Talatat, *JSSEA* 8 (1977-1978), 81-83, with 2 fig.

The author first corrects his reading [*s*] *nkwt ḥm.[f]* in "The Akhenaten Temple Project" (our number 76737), 107, fig. 20: 28, since an adjoining block proves it to be *nḏt*, "dependents".
He then discusses a block with a scene where a girl has a thorn removed from her foot, a motif known from the tombs of Menna and Montemhat.

78669 REED, Bika, Rebel in the Soul. A Sacred Text of Ancient Egypt. Translation and Commentary, London, Wildwood House/Book Wise, Australia, 1978 (21.7 x 27.4 cm; 141 p., 93 fig. and ill. [1 on cover]).

This book, dedicated to Schwaller de Lubicz, is concerned with the Dispute of a Man with his Ba (Pap. Berlin 3024). The author presents a short history of the papyrus, a translation of the text, two excursuses on the rebel and the soul, and a commentary. She also compares her interpretation with Faulkner's translation by putting the two side by side. The book ends with the autographed transcription of the text. *L.Z.*

78670 REED, Charles A. and Dale J. OSBORN, Taxonomic Transgressions in Tutankhamun's Treasures, *AJA* 82 (1978), 273-283, with 14 ill. and 3 fig.

On account of representations of mammals and birds among the objects of the Tutankhamun exhibition the authors discuss some mistaken identifications by modern scholars: 1. The ostriches on the base of the ostrich feather fan belong to a species of large bustard; 2. the "bleating ibex" is a composite of Nubian ibex and dorcas gazelle, while its alleged genuine horn is made of wood; 3. the "recumbent ibex" on the side panel of the child's chair is an oryx; 4. the pattern of a "leopard's skin" on the model folding stool cannot be identified; 5. the duck's heads forming the ends of the legs of the folding stool are actually those of the Egyptian goose.
For a reply see I.E.S. Edwards, *AJA* 83 (1979), 205-206. *L.Z.*

78671 REEVES, C.N., A Further Occurrence of Nefertiti as *ḥmt nsw '3t*, *GM* Heft 30 (1978), 61-69, with 6 fig. on 3 pl.

Im Grab der Meryre II. in Amarna wird an zwei Stellen der Titel *ḥmt nsw ʿ3t* gleichbedeutend neben dem üblicheren *ḥmt nsw wrt* verwendet; in drei weiteren Szenen wird nur *ḥmt nsw ʿ3t* gebraucht. Außerdem findet sich der Titel auf zwei Architekturfragmenten aus dem Flusstempel von Amarna und auf zwei Bruchstücken einer Opfertafel, die ursprünglich zu einer Statue gehörte. *ḥmt nsw ʿ3t* wird nicht nur eine spätägyptische Variante des gebräuchlicheren *ḥmt nsw wrt* gewesen sein, aber die tatsächliche Bedeutung des Unterschiedes ist unsicher. *Inge Hofmann*

78672 REINEKE, Walter F., Gedanken zum vermutlichen Alter der mathematischen Kenntnisse im Alten Ägypten, *ZÄS* 105 (1978), 67-76.

Aus einer Vielzahl an Beobachtungen und Gedanken schliesst Verfasser, es habe zwei Phasen gegeben, in welchen die Mathematik sich entwickelte. Die Jahrhunderte unmittelbar vor der Reichseinigung, und die 3. und der Anfang der 4. Dynastie. Spätere Perioden haben nichts wesentliches mehr beigesteuert. Die Mathematik hat in Ägypten das empirische Stadium nicht verlassen, hatte auch keinen Anlass dazu. *M. Heerma van Voss*

78673 REINEKE, Walter F., 150 Jahre Ägyptologie–Entwicklung, Stand, Aufgaben. 1. Internationale Ägyptologenkongress, Kairo 1976, *Ethnographisch-archäologische Zeitschrift*, Berlin 19 (1978), 109-112.

Short report on the First International Congress of Egyptologists, held in Cairo, 1976. *L.Z.*

REINEKE, Walter F., see also our number 78265.

REISER-HASLAUER, Elfriede, see our number 78090.

78674 REYMOND, E.A.E., Demotic Literary Papyri in the Rainer Collection, Vienna; Ashmolean Demotic Papyri, *Enchoria* 8, Sonderband (1978), 31.

Abstract of a paper read at the First International Colloquium of Demotists, held in Berlin, September 1977.
The author gives a brief summary of Demotic literary papyri in Vienna and Oxford that she is going to publish. *W. Brunsch*

78675 REYMOND, E.A.E., On Some Hermetic Writings, *Enchoria* 8, Sonderband (1978), 31.

Abstract of a paper read at the First International Colloquium of Demotists, held in Berlin, September 1977.
Among the Demotic literary papyri in the Rainer Collection, Vienna, there are "fragments of four Egyptian learned books of late Ptolemaic and Roman date" which can be compared with the Greek $\beta i \beta \lambda o \iota\ \text{`E}\rho\mu o\tilde{\upsilon}$ and which the author is going to publish. *W. Brunsch*

78676 RIEDERER, Josef, Die Datierung ägyptischer Bronzehohlgüsse mit Hilfe der Thermolumineszenz-Analyse, *SAK* 6 (1978), 163-168.

By thermoluminescence analysis Egyptian bronzes can be dated absolutely, although at present the measure of incertainty is still 12% (that is, for the Late Period, c. 300 years).

RIEDERER, Josef, see also our number 78546.

78677 ROBERTS, P.M., Brazing in Antiquity, *Engelhard Europe*, Sutton, Surrey 12 (Winter 1978), 8-11, with 5 ill. (3 in colour).

The author discusses the technique of joining together metal components by brazing which appears to have been applied in Egypt from the third millennium B.C. onwards, but has been lost in the third or second century B.C. It was particularly used for golden jewellery, of which the ill. show examples.

78678 ROBERTSON, J.H. and R.J. BRADLEY, On the Presence of the Negro in the Nile Valley, *Current Anthropology*, New York 19 (1978), 177-178.

The author criticizes the methods employed in physical anthropology which are used to determine skeletal remains as belonging to negroes.
Compare our numbers 76469 and 78230.  *L.Z.*

78679 ROBINS, Gay, Amenhotpe I and the child Amenemhat, *GM* Heft 30 (1978), 71-75.

Als Frau von Amenhotpe I. wird eine Königin Ahhotpe angesehen, deren einer Titel *mwt nsw* (Sarg CG 61006) lautete. Demnach hätte sie Mutter eines Königs sein müssen; doch war die Mutter des Nachfolgers Thutmosis' I. Senisonb. Aufgrund eines Pektorals, das auf der Brust eines einjährigen Kindes in Deir el-Bahri gefunden wurde, wurde dieses, das Amenemhat hiess, als ein Sohn des Amenhotpe I. identifiziert. Es ergab sich aber, dass alle bisher beigebrachten Indizien dafür zu schwach sind und dass eine Koregentschaft nicht nachgewiesen werden kann. Die einzige *mwt nsw* Ahhotpe, die aus anderen Quellen bekannt ist, war die Mutter von Nebpehtire Ahmose, die als Eigentümerin des Sarges Kairo JE 28501 angesehen worden war. Sie gehört daher nicht zu Amenhotpe I. Da der Sarg JE 28501 nicht den Titel *mwt nsw*, sondern nur den einer *ḥmt nsw wrt* aufweist, ist anzunehmen, dass der Sarg CG 61006 der Mutter des Ahmose gehörte.
Vgl. unsere Nummer 78693.  *Inge Hofmann*

78680 ROBINSON, James M., The First International Congress of Coptology, *Newsletter ARCE* No. 106 (Fall 1978), 24-40.

Report on the First International Congress of Coptology, Cairo, December 8-18, 1976, consisting of two parts, the first of which was at the same time the second meeting of the International Committee for the Nag Hammadi Codices, while the second was devoted to the future of Coptic studies (see our number 78269). Both parts are extensively reported on. A list of the 106 registrants and the articles of the International Association for Coptic Studies, together with other information is also included.  *L.Z.*

ROBINSON, James M., see also our number 78269.

78681 ROCCATI, Alessandro, Nuove epigrafi greche e latine da File, *in: Hommages Vermaseren*, 988-996, with 9 pl.

Additions to our numbers 69068 and 69069.

78682 ROCCATI, Alessandro, L' offerta di Geb, *in: Atti del 1º convegno italiano sul Vicino Oriente Antico*, 101-108, with 8 pl. (1 folding).

The author assembles and discusses the evidence for a ritual "offering to Geb" occurring in a large number of texts from various periods. A copy has recently been discovered on the walls of the Saite Theban tomb No. 27 (see fig. 17), others in two Turin papyri (Nos CGT 54042 and 54043). From a number of texts the author has reconstructed the ritual; see fig. 19-24.

78683 ROCCATI, A., Le origine del medioegiziano, in: *Atti del Secondo Congresso Internazionale di Linguistica Camito-Semitica*. Firenze, 16-19 Aprile 1974, Raccolti da Pelio Fronzaroli, [Firenze], Istituto di Linguistica e di Lingue Orientali. Università di Firenze, 1978 (=Quaderni di Semitistica, 5), 287-289.

Discussing the transition from the O. to M.Eg. the author argues that it was a gradual development, the apparent differences being partly due to differences in material, in scribal practices, etc.

RODRIGUEZ, François, see our numbers 78823 and 78824.

RÖLLIG, Wolfgang, see our number 78131.

78684 ROESELER, Albrecht, Eine heilige Insel zieht um, *Armant*, Köln Heft 15 (1977), 18-22.

On the transfer of the Philae temples to the neighbouring island Agilkia.   *L.Z.*

78685 RÖSSLER-KÖHLER, Ursula, Zur Datierung des Falkenbildes von Hierakonpolis (*CGC* 14717), *MDAIK* 34 (1978), 117-125, with 1 plan and 2 fig.

Studying the famous copper falcon figure with its golden head with the plumed crown, found by Quibell in Hierakonpolis, that is usually dated in the VIth Dynasty, the author adduces arguments for a date in the XVIIIth Dynasty, possibly Tuthmosis III: the plumed crown does not occur with the falcon before the XVIIIth Dynasty; the form of the uraeus is that of that period; the temple in which the figure was found dates possibly from the time of Tuthmosis III; statues of a god in the shape of an animal with a figure of a king before it occur from this time onwards.

78686 ROQUET, Gérard, BHN et MN-, morphème du vétitif akhmimique dans les épitaphes d' Edfou, *BIFAO* 78 (1978), 525-532.

Studying vetitive formulae in epitaphs from Edfu and comparing them with those from other places the author found that in Edfu instead of MΠP- the Akhmimic form MN- was used, once even BHN, showing that Akhmimic was here the spoken language.

78687 ROQUET, Gérard, Un cas d' entrave stylistique à la palatalisation du [k] dans les *Textes des Pyramides*. - Poétique et phonétique historique, *BIFAO* 78 (1978), 477-485.

Proceeding from the couple *kbw:ṯbw* occurring in P.T. Spells 22b and 681c, and comparing it with Boh. ϩⲁ-ΤΟΥⲰ < Dem. *ḥr-tww* < P.T. Sp. 22: *ḥr-kbw(y)*, the author discusses instances of paronomasia in the P.T. He mentions several examples (e.g., *rn - nr, shm - hms*), some even showing indifference as regards the division in lexemes or morphemes (e.g., *tnm - n (i)tm*) and variations of the homorganic phonemes (*d3p - d3b, hnk - hkn*). This phenomenon may have caused once the choice of *kbw*, in the other case of *tbw*. Whether the non-palatalized form *kbw* was derived, for poetic reasons, from a dialect from the time of the redaction of the P.T. is uncertain. The author adds remarks on the connections between poetry, "oracular style" and phonetics.

78688   ROQUET, Gérard, Formes verbales à distribution équivalente. Modalité déprécative de la forme *j(w)=f r sdm*, ⲉ=ϥ ⲉ/ⲁ ⲥⲱⲧⲙ, *BIFAO* 78 (1978), 497-523.

The author attempts to determine the age of the specific shade of meaning which may in some contexts be expressed by ⲉ=ϥ ⲉ/ⲁ ⲥⲱⲧⲙ, *iw.f r sdm*. He lists 46 passages from Coptic epigraphic documents and 41 from Egyptian addresses to to the living or to passers-by, presenting each in transcription and translation with comments.
The results are tabulated on p. 520-521. It appears that, like in Coptic, the deprecative-hortative use of the *iw.f r sdm* occurs, until the early N.K., as frequently as the imperative and the optative, while the *mrr.f*, and the *sdm.k3.f* and *sdm.hr.f* occur less frequently.

78689   ROQUET, Gérard, Linteaux commémoratifs en dialecte fayoumique, *BIFAO* 78 (1978), 339-345, with 2 pl.

Publication of two wooden lintels with inscriptions in the Faiyumic dialect, preserved in private collections. The author lists eleven other lintels with similar texts.

78690   ROQUET, Gérard, Le morphème *(e)tah-* et les graffites coptes de Kalabcha, *BIFAO* 78 (1978), 533-538, with 1 fig.

The author draws attention to the use of the morpheme (ⲉ)ⲧⲁϩ in two graffiti from Kalabsha, which is of importance for the study of the geographic distribution of Coptic dialects.

78691   ROQUET, Gérard, *whm*, verbe plein et semi-auxiliaire. À propos d'une inscription d'Ancien Empire, *BIFAO* 78 (1978), 487-495, with 1 pl.

The author proceeds from a fragment of a Vth Dynasty tomb wall preserved in University College, London, which belonged to the tomb of a *D3d3 -m-ʿnh*. After translating its inscription, with extensive comments, he discusses the semi-auxiliary verb *whm*, its use and writings.

ROQUET, Gérard, see also our number 78705.

ROSS, John G., see our number 78612.

78692 ROSTRON, P.R., Glass from the Nile or Pharaoh's Pomade, *Glass*, London 55, No. 5 (May 1978), 252-255, with 2 ill.

The author relates some facts about Egyptian glass.  L.Z.

78693 ROTH, Ann Macy, Ahhotep I and Ahhotep II, *Serapis* 4 (1977-1978), 31-40.

The author discusses the evidence for a royal woman called Ahhotep in the late XVIIth and early XVIIIth Dynasties, concluding it probably all belongs to Queen Ahhotep, the wife of Tao II and mother of Kamosis and Ahmosis, except the Dra' Abu el-Naga' coffin which may be that of a wife of Kamosis. For a revised genealogy, see p. 37.
See also our number 78679.

78694 ROTTLÄNDER, Rolf C.A., On the Mathematical Connections of Ancient Measures of Length, *Acta Praehistorica et Archaeologica*, Berlin 7/8 (1976/7), 1978, 49-51, with 2 fig. and 7 tables.

Comparing measures of length in various ancient cultures, the author deals with the cubit and the *remen*.  L.Z.

ROUBET, Colette, see our number 78055.

78695 RUFFLE, John, A Staff of the Princess's Butler, Tuthmosis, *JEA* 64 (1978), 132, with 1 pl.

This staff in the City Museum, Birmingham (no. 474/52) is of hard wood and measures 1.3 m long. The inscription on it invokes Osiris and it may have belonged to the owner of Theban tomb no. 205.  *E.P. Uphill*

78696 RUSCH, William G., Coptic as a Resource in the Quest of the Historical Athanasius, *Enchoria* 8, Sonderband (1978), 37*(83)-42*(88).

Abstract of a paper read at the First International Congress of Coptology, held in Cairo, December 1976.
The author demonstrates that for the task of writing a biography of Athanasius of Alexandria the Coptic sources have also to be taken into account. *W.Brunsch*

RUSSMANN, Edna R., see our number 78027.

78697 RYHINER, M.-L., Un fragment d'inscription hiéroglyphique trouvé à Leptis Magna, *RdE* 30(1978), 172-174, with 1 ill.

Débris d'une stèle ou d'un naos avec quelques hiéroglyphes.  *Ph. Derchain*

78698 SALEH, Abd el-Aziz, Arabia and the Northern Arabs in Ancient Egyptian Records, in: *Journal Faculty of Archaeology*, 69-77.

The Egyptian name for Arabia occurs not earlier than in Demotic texts, where it is spelled 3rb3y, probably for 3rby3 = ʿrby3. Older texts mention the K3šw,

rather a collection of tribes in SW Transjordan than a state, and the territory of
Edom, while Arabia was also included under the term *t3-ntr*. Another term, extensively discussed by the author, is ʿ*3mw* by which the Egyptians indicated
Arabian tribalism.

78699   de SALVIA, Fulvio, Un ruolo apotropaico dello scarabeo egizio nel contesto
culturale greco-arcaico di Pithekoussai (Ischia), in: *Hommages Vermaseren*, 1003-1061.

The article not only discusses the apotropaic function of the scarab in the Archaic Greek civilization on Ischia, but also contains sections on the origin and
value of the cult of the scarab in Egypt and on its magical function of protecting children.

78700   SAMSON, Julia, Amarna. City of Akhenaten and Nefertiti. Nefertiti as Pharaoh.
With an Introduction by Professor H.S. Smith, Warminster, Aris & Phillips Ltd,
[1978] (21 x 29.5 cm; X + 144 p., 1 map, 1 plan, 6 fig., 85 ill.).

Revised and enlarged edition of our number 72619.
The introduction by H.S. Smith contains corrections, mainly with regard to the
position of Nefertiti. From p. 19 to p. 106 the book is exactly the same as the
first edition, except that the colour plates are replaced by plates in black and
white.
The main addition is, therefore, part 2 (p. 107-139), which discusses Nefertiti
as Pharaoh. Accepting Harris' suggestion that Nefernefruaton – Nefertiti and
Smenkhkare were the same person (see our numbers 73313, 73314 and 74291)
the author discusses more material from the Petrie and other collections with
regard to names and titles of the Queen, the crowns, and the King's Wife Kiya
(see Harris, our number 74290). The whole problem of Nefertiti's position is
re-studied, leading to the conclusion that she was first co-ruler and, after Akhnaton's death, actually the king. The author also rejects the idea that Meritaton
succeeded her mother as wife of the king and co-ruler.

78701   SANDARS, N.K., The Sea Peoples. Warriors of the Ancient Mediterranean 1250-1150 B.C., [London], Thames & Hudson, [1978] (16 x 24 cm; 224 p., 3 maps, 1 plan,
128 fig. and ill., 8 colour pl., frontispiece) = Ancient Peoples and Places, 89; rev.
*Antiquity* 52 (1978), 161-162 (A.M. Snodgrass).                    Pr. £ 7.50

This thorough study about the Sea Peoples, their origin and history, based on
material, both textual and archaeological, from the entire Eastern Mediterranean,
contains by its very nature many references and even entire sections and chapters on ancient Egypt.
After an introduction the first chapter presents a survey of the geographical
features of the Eastern Mediterranean. In chapter 2 the political situation in the
period before the invasions is sketched, with sections on the Hittites and their
allies in the battle of Kadesh, on commerce, and on mercenaries and outlaws.
Chapter 3 is devoted to the Aegean world in the 13th century B.C.; chapter 4
to the regions N. and W. of the Aegean: the Balkans and Italy with its islands.
In the chapters 5 to 8 the history of the invasions is discussed in a chronologically retrograde order, beginning with Egypt. Extensive study is made of the

enemies mentioned in the texts of Merenptah and Ramses III: Shardana, Lukka, Ekwesh, Teresh and Shekelesh, their dress and their land of origin. There follow sections on the wars of Ramses III, the land and the sea battles, discussing the evidence from Medînet Habu.

Chapters 6 and 7 describe the crisis in the Eastern Mediterranean: the fall of the Hittite Empire, Ugarit and Cyprus, and the new peoples in Syro-Palestine: Denyen, Philistines and Tjeker. Chapter 8 deals with the crisis in the Aegean.

In chapter 9 the author draws up the conclusions, stressing that no clear-cut solution to the problems is possible. A general economic and political crisis may be cause instead of result of the invasions, but the pattern is complicated. The invasions are partly continuation of endemic piracy and small-state warfare. On p. 199-202 a summary of the author's conceptions concerning each of the Sea Peoples.

The abundant illustration constitutes an integral part of the argument. Chronological tables on p. 203-207; notes on p. 208-213; index p. 220-224.

78702 SANDERS, Jack T., A Hellenistic Egyptian Parallel to Ben Sira, *Journal of Biblical Literature*, Missoula 97 (1978), 257-258.

The author briefly deals with the parallel between the Wisdom of Ben Sira (Ecclesiasticus ), 13:8-13 and Pap. Insinger, cols. 10-11.  *L.Z.*

SANMARTÍ-GREGO, E., see our number 78606.

SATZINGER, Heinz, see our number 78090.

78703 SATZINGER, Helmut, Der Leiter des Speicherwesens Si-êse Sohn des Qeni und seine Wiener Statue, *Jahrbuch der kunsthistorischen Sammlungen in Wien*, Wien 74 (1978), 7-28, with 13 ill.

The author studies a standard-bearing statue of the Chief of the Granary Si-ese, son of Qeni (Wien Inv. No. 34), of which he offers a minute description, and facsimile and translation with commentary of the inscriptions. He then deals with the career of this official from Asyût, of whom several other monuments have been preserved; with his father Qeni and his grandfather, also called Si-ese, who both occupied the same position as the Si-ese under discussion, and with a third Si-ese, son of Kha'ia, from the late XVIIIth Dynasty, who may or may not belong to the same family. Of all of these persons several monuments are discussed.

78704 SATZINGER, Helmut, Rund um die Form *sḏm.t.f*, *GM* Heft 27 (1978), 45-49.

Verfasser setzt sich mit den Argumenten von Junge (*GM* Heft 1, 1972, 32-34) auseinander, die dieser gegen einen seiner Artikel zu "schliesslich hörte er" (vgl. unsere Nr. 71497) vorgebracht hatte. Er kommt zu dem Ergebnis, dass zum einen die negative *t*-Form gesichert ist, zum anderen aber auch die *t*-Form nach Präpositionen. Die Grundbedeutung, die mit einem "schliesslich hörte er" charakterisiert werden kann, ist die einzige, die sich zugleich für beide *t*-Formen — die negierte indikativische und die affirmative subjunktivische — bewährt und sie somit auf semantischer Ebene verbindet.  *Inge Hofmann*

78705 SAUNERON, Serge, Dominique VALBELLE, Pascal VERNUS, J.P. CORTEG–GIANI, Michel VALLOGGIA, Jean GASCOU et Guy WAGNER, et G. ROQUET, Douch — Rapport préliminaire de la campagne de fouilles 1976, *BIFAO* 78 (1978), 1-33, with 5 plans (2 folding), 2 fig. (1 folding) and 8 pl.

Preliminary report on the first campaign at Qasr Dûsh, el-Khârga Oasis.
The site with as its main features a stone temple from the time of Domitian, an earlier fortress (from the 1st century A.D.) and a brick temple, is carefully described, together with later constructions covering part of the temple and the finds, among which Greek and Coptic ostraca.

78706 SAYED, Abdel Moneim A.H., The Recently Discovered Port on the Red Sea Shore, *JEA* 64 (1978), 69-71, with 1 pl.

Refutes the articles of Nibbi, our numbers 75551 and 76592, that the Egyptians were not seafarers and that they did not use any Red Sea ports. The discovery of the Twelfth Dynasty port at Mersa Gawâsîs and the finding of stelae with a reference to Bia-n-Punt indicated naval activity under Sesostris I, while a small shrine built by an official 'Ankhow actually had a pedestal built from four limestone anchors. Another stela here records an order by the king to his vizier Antefoker requiring him to build ships to be sent to the region of Bia-Punt. The port is probably that called Sawu on the stela of Khentekhtay-wer and the name *Sww* was found on the eastern jamb of the shrine. *E.P.Uphill*

el-SAYED, Abdulla Mahmud, see our number 78517.

78707 el-SAYED, Ramadan, À propos de l' activité d' un fonctionnaire du temps de Psammétique I à Karnak d'après la stèle du Caire 2747, *BIFAO* 78 (1978), 459-476, with 1 pl.

Study on a small, coloured, limestone stela (Cairo Cat. Gén. 2747) of a priest Besmut (IV), from the Saite Period. The piece is minutely described, the text given in hieroglyphs and translation with comments. The author also discusses the owner's functions (priest of Amon and Re in Thebes) and his family.

78708 el-SAYED, Ramadan, L' embaumement dans l' Égypte ancienne, *in: Journal Faculty of Archaeology*, 91-98.

The author presents a survey of our knowledge about mummification, describing the duration (70 days in total, in accordance with the period of invisibility of Sirius), the place, personnel and process of embalmment, the wrapping up of the mummy, the transport, and the final ceremonies near the tomb.

78709 el-SAYED, Ramadan, Piankhi, fils de Hérihor. Documents sur sa vie et sur son rôle, *BIFAO* 78 (1978), 197-218, with 2 fig. and 1 pl.

The author first discusses all mentions of Piankhi, the son of Herihor, either on his own monuments or on those of others. They are: stelae (particularly Cairo 3/4/17/1), inscriptions from the temples of Karnak, a statue (Cairo Cat. Gén. 42191), dockets on royal mummies and coffins, and some of the Late Ramesside Letters. In his conclusions (p. 213-218) he describes the functions that Piankhi held, what is known about his life, and his family.

SCARISBRICK, Diana, see our number 78777.

78710 SCHADEN, Otto John, The God's Father Ay, *Dissertation Abstracts International*, Ann Arbor, Mich. 39, No. 1 (July 1978), 400-A.

Abstract of a thesis University of Minnesota, 1977 (348 p.; order no. 7809739). Two major sections involve reports on the work of the University of Minnesota Egyptian Expeditions. In 1971 ca. 80 blocks bearing inscriptions and scenes from a temple of Tutankhamun and Eye in Karnak were copied and photographed. In 1972 the tomb of Eye in the Western Valley of the Kings was cleared. *L.Z.*

78711 SCHENKE, Hans-Martin, On the Middle Egyptian Dialect of the Coptic Language, *Enchoria* 8, Sonderband (1978), 43*(89)-58*(104).

Paper read at the First International Congress of Coptology, held in Cairo, December 1976.
The author discusses some of the main features of the Coptic dialect called Middle Egyptian or Oxyrhynchite, an exhaustive study of which still remains to be done.
Compare our number 78600. *W. Brunsch*

78712 SCHENKE, Hans-Martin, Zum sogenannten Tractatus Tripartitus des Codex Jung, *ZÄS* 105 (1978), 133-141.

A review article of our numbers 73388 and 75384.

78713 SCHENKEL, Wolfgang, Die Bewässerungsrevolution im Alten Ägypten, Mainz/Rhein, Verlag Philipp von Zabern,[1978] (21 x 29.7 cm; 87 p.); at head of title: Deutsches Archäologisches Institut. Abteilung Kairo; rev. *BiOr* 37 (1980), 317 (Alessandro Roccati). Pr. DM57

After a preface in which the author i.a. stresses the necessity of finding some way between collecting disconnected data and drawing up unverifiable theories, chapter 1 deals with the theoretical considerations that underly the present study. It e.g. discusses concepts such as Asiatic mode of production, the hydraulic hypothesis, and the irrigational revolution. As the main problems Schenkel indicates: the finiteness of expansion processes, lack of knowledge about the causes of present circumstances, the accidental character of events and their polycausality.
Chapter 2 is devoted to the techniques of Egyptian irrigation. Chapters 3 to 6 constitute the nucleus of the study. On account of 19 documents from the F.I.P. which are given in translation the author argues that artificial irrigation is mentioned during that period and that the main reason for its introduction is the repeated famines so often referred to in these texts. On the other hand, mentions of irrigation from the O.K. do not exist, those usually thought to be so being explained otherwise. Although the main reason for the famines may have been a

change in the climate resulting in lower inundations, other causes may have contributed to the revolution such as that the society had reached the limits of its possibilities of inner colonization and the growing pressure on the society by the expanding administration.

Chapter 6 discusses the expansion of the irrigation, dealing with terms for various categories of fields, e.g. k3yt (originally high lying land, hence not naturally irrigated; it gradually became the normal type of artificially flooded field), and its opposites iw and m3wt.

Chapter 7 presents a sketch of an anhydraulic origin of the bureaucratic administration in Egypt as has existed during the O.K.

A summary and a survey of the points requiring further research on p. 73-74, followed by an extensive bibliography and indexes.

78714 SCHENKEL, Wolfgang, Infinitiv und Qualitativ des Koptischen als Verbaladverbien oder die JERNSTEDTsche Regel und die Satzarten des Koptischen, *Enchoria* 8, Teil 2 (1978), 13-15.

Infinitive and Qualitative in the Coptic Bipartite Conjugation Pattern are nothing else than adverbial adjuncts. So this type of Coptic sentence can be determined as an adverbial phrase. *W. Brunsch*

78715 SCHENKEL, Wolfgang, Kritisches zur Textkritik: Die sogenannten Hörfehler, *GM* Heft 29 (1978), 119-126, with 1 fig.

Anhand eines Modelles werden die für die Textüberlieferungen relevanten Tätigkeiten des Menschen in ihrem Funktionszusammenhang: Hören, Sprechen, Lesen, Schreiben, Verarbeiten und Speichern aufgezeigt, ausserdem die externen Datenträger Vorlage und Kopie in iher Beziehung zueinander und zu den Tätigkeiten des Menschen. Im Verlaufe des Überlieferungsprozesses lassen sich drei Verlustarten an ursprünglicher Textsubstanz unterscheiden. Dabei ergab sich, dass "Hörfehler" nichts mit dem Hörvorgang zu tun haben, sondern Decodierungsvorgänge sind, mit deren Hilfe in der Verarbeitungstechnik im Endergebnis einer Lautfolge Bedeutungen zugeordnet werden. Angefügt werden noch Bemerkungen zu den "Lesefehlern" und den "Gedächtnisfehlern".

*Inge Hofmann*

78716 SCHENKEL, Wolfgang, Kultmythos und Märtyrerlegende, *in: Synkretismusforschung*. Theorie und Praxis. Herausgegeben von Gernot WIESSNER, Wiesbaden, Otto Harrassowitz, 1978 (=Göttinger Orientforschungen. Veröffentlichungen des Sonderforschungsbereiches Orientalistik an der Georg-August-Universität Göttingen. Reihe: Grundlagen und Ergebnisse, 1), 109-117.

Lecture based on our number 77679.

78717 SCHENKEL, Wolfgang, Das Stemma der altägyptischen Sonnenlitanei. Grundlegung der Textgeschichte nach der Methode der Textkritik, Wiesbaden, Otto Harrassowitz,1978 (17 x 23.9 cm; 71 p.) = Göttinger Orientforschungen. Veröffentlichungen des Sonderforschungsbereiches Orientalistik an der Georg-August-Universität Göttingen. IV. Reihe: Ägypten, 6.

After a preface and a general discussion of text criticism and text history in the first chapter the author discusses in the second chapter the general principles of the study of stemmas, namely the types of errors, external data, their value for the study, and the working procedure, which exists of four sets of rules, the problems of trial and error, and reality of the stemma. The third chapter is devoted to the principles of the traditions of texts, and is concerned with the significant differences among them. In the last chapter the author applies the methodological first part to the Sun Hymns (see our numbers 75347 and 76386), mainly of the N.K., and constructs a stemma of known versions, while he adds remarks on Late Period versions in connection with the N.K. stemma. The book ends with text historical conclusions and a register.   *L.Z.*

78718  SCHENKEL, Wolfgang, Eine Syntax des klassischen Ägyptisch ohne Verbalsatz, *GM* Heft 29 (1978), 105-117.

Die ägyptische Syntax kommt entgegen "europäischen" Sprachen ohne Verbalsatz aus; die Verbalformen der Suffixkonjugation sind nominale Formen. Im Laufe der ägyptisch-koptischen Sprachgeschichte entstand dann allerdings der Typ des Verbalsätzes. Von den semitischen Sprachen wurde die Aufteilung der Sätze in Verbalsätze und Nicht-Verbalsätze, d.h. Nominalsätze, übernommen. Polotsky konnte sodann nachweisen, dass bei den sog. Verbalsätzen einmal die Betonung auf dem finiten Verb liegt, zum anderen auf einer adverbialen Bestimmung.   Er bezeichnete sie als "emphatische" und nicht-"emphatische" Formen, doch hängt deren Unterschied nicht primär am Unterschied der Verbalformen, sondern an der Partikel *jw*. Die "emphatische" Konstruktion ist ein Adverbialsatz, dessen Übersetzung ins Deutsche kompliziert ist. Abschliessend wird vorgeführt, wie die wichtigsten Typen von Sätzen, die man bisher als Verbalsätze auffasste, als Nicht-Verbalsätze interpretiert werden können.   *Inge Hofmann*

78719  SCHENKEL, Wolfgang, Verbesserungsvorschläge zu A. Erman, Neuägyptische Grammatik, Catalogue of References, bearb. von G.E. Freeman und F.T. Miosi, *GM* Heft 30 (1978), 89-90.

Es handelt sich um 48 Verbesserungsvorschläge zu unserer Nr. 73249, die die Seiten 1-53 befreffen und sich meist auf falsche oder ungenaue Zitate beziehen.
*Inge Hofmann*

78720  SCHENKEL, Wolfgang, Zur herakleopolitanischen Tradition der Pyramidentexte, *GM* Heft 28 (1978), 35-44, with 1 fig. and 2 tables.

Der Sarg des *Nfr-j* von el-Berscha (Kairo CG 28088) gehört trotz des herakleopolitanischen Königsnamens *W3ḥ-k3-Rʿw-Ḥty* einem Privatmann. Auf Kopf und Fuss des Sargkastens sind Pyramidentexte angebracht, die übrigen Sargteile enthalten Sargtexte. Keiner dieser Pyramidentexte findet sich im ältesten, praktisch vollständig überlieferten Pyramidentextkorpus, dem des Unas. Es wird auf die Möglichkeit hingewiesen, dass Beziehungen der Herakleopoliten zur Grabanlage des Teti bestanden. Abschliessend wird auf drei Hauptgründe zur Gesamtveröffentlichung aller auf den Särgen überlieferten "eigentlichen" Pyramidentexte aufmerksam gemacht.   *Inge Hofmann*

SCHETELICH, Maria, see our number 78265.

78721   SCHIENERL, Peter, Erinnerungen an die Isisverehrung im traditionellen Schmuck Ägyptens, *Baessler-Archiv*, Berlin 25 (1977), 205-228, with 12 fig. and 3 ill.

The author connects the frequency of the red colour and the snake motif in the traditional jewellery of Upper Egypt with the legacy of the popularity of Isis. The documentation deals with finger rings and bracelets.   *L.Z.*

SCHIMMEL, Norbert, see our number 78832.

78722   SCHLICK-NOLTE, Birgit, Gläserne Raritäten aus der Sammlung Kiseleff, *SAK* 6 (1978), 169-175, with 1 colour ill.

The author discusses two glazed vessels and some fragments in the collection Kiseleff that are important by their shapes and/or colours (see colour pl.).

SCHLÖGL, Hermann, see our number 78275.

78723   SCHMANDT-BESSERAT, Denise, An Early Recording System in Egypt and the Ancient Near East, in: *Immortal Egypt*, 5-12, with 6 ill. on 4 pl. and 1 map.

The author discusses a pre-writing system with clay artifacts of geometric shapes that are found on numerous sites in the Near East, but also in Khartûm and Abydos. Their Akkadian name is *abnati* (sing. *abnu*). In some instances they were enclosed in a sealed hollow clay ball (bulla) or a clay tablet. Their shapes marked on the surface of the bullae may be a preceding stage to writing. Whether the shapes (disks, spheres, etc.) represented a type of goods (garments, oil, etc.) or had, as the author suggests, a numerical connotation is uncertain; it may not have been the same everywhere. The wide use of the *abnati* system may attest to early relations between the Nile Valley and the Near East.

78724   SCHMIDT, Carl and Violet MACDERMOT, The Books of Jeu and the Untitled Text in the Bruce Codex. Text edited [with] translation and notes, Leiden, E.J. Brill, 1978 (15.7 x 24.8 cm; XXVI + 345 p.) = Nag Hammadi Studies, 13 (volume editor: R. McL. Wilson); series: The Coptic Gnostic Library; rev. *Biblica* 60 (1979), 271-275 (Hans Quecke).   Pr. fl. 224

After an introduction on the Bruce Codex which contains the books of Jeu and an untitled text, a description and a summary of its contents, follow the text and the translation with notes on opposite pages. The book in concluded by a bibliography, a key index to words of Greek origin, and indexes of Greek and selected Coptic words, of proper names and source references.   *L.Z.*

78725   SCHMIDT, Carl and Violet MACDERMOT, Pistis Sophia. Text edited [with] translation and notes, Leiden, E.J. Brill, 1978 (15.7 x 24.8 cm; XX + 806 p.) = Nag Hammadi Studies, 9 (volume editor: R. McL. Wilson); series: The Coptic Gnostic Library; rev. *Biblica* 60 (1979), 271-275 (Hans Quecke).   Pr. fl. 224

After an introduction on the history of the Askew Codex which contains the texts of the Pistis Sophia, a description of the manuscript and a summary of its contents, follow the text and the translation with notes on opposite pages. The book is concluded by an extensive bibliography, a key index to words of Greek origin, and indexes of Greek and selected Coptic words, of proper names and source references. *L.Z.*

78726 SCHMITZ, Bettina, Untersuchungen zu zwei Königinnen der frühen 18. Dynastie, Ahhotep und Ahmose, *CdE* LIII, No. 106 (1978), 207-221.

Dans l'imbroglio familial de la fin de la 17e et du début de la 18e dynastie, l'auteur tente une nouvelle fois de voir clair. Selon elle, il n'y aurait en qu'une seule Ahhotep, grandmère d'Amenophis Ier (au contraire de l'opinion générale, qui en fait deux). En revanche, elle peuple son tableau généalogique d'une multitude d'Ahmose des deux sexes subtilement distingués les uns des autres. Thouthmosis Ier ne serait en aucune façon apparenté à son prédécesseur. Pourtant, la correction que cette constatation imposerait, de faire commencer la 18e dynastie après Aménophis Ier, n'est pas proposée. *Ph. Derchain*

78727 SCHMITZ, Franz-Jürgen, Amenophis I. Versuch einer Darstellung der Regierungszeit eines ägyptischen Herrschers der frühen 18. Dynastie, Hildesheim, Gerstenberg Verlag, 1978 (17 x 23.8 cm; XIV + 273 p., 2 maps [ 1 folding], 3 plans [ 1 folding], 1 fig.) = Hildesheimer Ägyptologische Beiträge, 6; rev. *BiOr* 37 (1980), 317-319 (M. Gitton).

This monograph on the second ruler of the XVIIIth Dynasty is mainly based on published sources. After the introduction chapter 1 deals with the titles, dated monuments and mummy of the pharaoh, with latter's vicissitudes at the end of the N.K. Since, as the author argues, Ahmose died about his 40th year Amenophis came to the throne at an age of about 20 years, which leaves no room for a regency by Ahmose-Nefertari.
Chapter 2 is devoted to the absolute chronology of the early XVIIIth Dynasty. The day of accession to the throne of Amenophis is discussed as well as that of his death and of his "Appearance". His first regnal year is fixed about 1525 B.C., 1550 B.C. being the date of the beginning of the dynasty.
Chapter 3 deals with the royal family, Amenophis' ancestors, the wives, sons and daughters of Ahmose (see also our number 77757). In chapter 4 Amenophis' construction works are enumerated: those in Karnak (with a discussion of the building standing there until Tuthmosis III), on the West Bank (a way station at Deir el-Bahri, and the *Mn-Ist*, which is not a mortuary temple but a temple of Amon together with the king and Ahmose-Nefertari), in Abydos, el-Kâb and elsewhere in Egypt, on Uronarti and Sai, and in the Sinai.
In chapter 5 the author studies the statues of the king and a few reliefs from his reign, stressing that they show a development from the M.K. style to the later one of the Tuthmosids. Chapter 6 deals with the few stelae of the period, royal monuments and those of contemporaries.
The next two chapters are devoted to the inner and the foreign policy, i.a. listing his viziers and other high officials, including priests, and the viceroys of Kush, and discussing the extension of the empire in Asia (for the Asiatic policy, see now Redford, *JAOS* 99 [1979], 270-287), activities in Libya, the oases and the Sinai, and in Nubia up to Sai.

In the last chapter the author discusses where to situate the royal tomb. Since neither Weigall's (KV 39) nor the usually accepted view of Carter (the tomb of Ahmose Nefertari) agree with the data of the Pap. Abbott, the author suggests that the king was buried in Inhapi's tomb (No. 320), the royal cache. The labels on some royal mummies may strengthen this conclusion that agrees with his translation of the relevant passage from the Pap. Abbott.
A summary on p. 233-239, followed by a catalogue of monuments (buildings, stelae, reliefs, inscriptions, etc.,) and a reconstructed complete titulary of the King (p. 263). Indexes on p. 265-270.

78728 SCHMITZ, Franz-Jürgen, Zur Lesung und Deutung von 𓄣 𓄣 und 𓎺, *GM* Heft 27 (1978), 51-58.

Es gibt Bezeichnungen, die eine spezielle Verehrungsform Amenophis' I. und Verbindung mit dem Reichsgott Amun zeigen. Es werden 20 Belege vorgestellt, von denen dreiviertel einen mit zwei Herz-Zeichen geschriebenen Begriff wiedergeben, der *ibib* gelesen wurde (Wb I, 63). Nun wird das Herz-Zeichen aber auch *ḥ3tj* gelesen, was im NR wohl oft als Dualform missverstanden wurde. Für die Schreibung 𓎺 gibt es 4 Belege; sie scheint eine neuägyptische Variante des Determinatives des Granittopfes darzustellen. Alle 20 Belege müssen *ḥ3tj* mit der Bedeutung "Abbild, Statue" gelesen werden; sie zeigen einen speziellen Statuentypus aus dem Kultbereich des vergöttlichten Königs.        *Inge Hofmann*

78729 SCHNABEL, D., Ägypten, *Das Altertum*, Berlin 24 (1978), 62.

Short note on the treatment of the mummy of Ramses II in Paris.        *L.Z.*

78730 SCHOTT, Erika, Das Goldhaus im Grab des Nefer-Renpet, *GM* Heft 29 (1978), 127-132, with 4 fig.

Der Inhaber des Grabes TT 178, Nefer-renpet, genannt Kel, war Schatzhausschreiber unter Ramses II., als der er sich zweimal in seinem Grab darstellen lässt. In einer Beischrift wird das "Goldhaus des Amon" genannt, das wahrscheinlich im Ramesseum lag. Es bestand aus zwei Häusern; neben dem Goldhaus lag das Schatzhaus. Das Goldhaus der Frühzeit gehörte zum Königspalast, dasjenige im Ramesseum zum Tempel. Das Ramesseum war keine Residenz, sondern das "Morgenhaus" des Königs, wenn er zu den grossen Festen nach Theben kam. Hier spielten sich die Reinigungs- und Bekleidungszeremonien ab, die seit dem A.R. eng mit dem Goldhaus zusammenhängen und als "Gottesgeburt" bezeichnet werden können. Priester der Gottesgeburt sind im Goldhaus beschäftigte Beamte. In Theben wird das Goldhaus ein Tempelmagazin, es gehört nicht zum "Morgenhaus" und zum Königsschmuck, aber in den Titeln der Beamten erinnert man sich noch an die "Gottesgeburt".        *Inge Hofmann*

78731 SCHULMAN, Alan R., 'Ankhesenamun, Nofretity, and the Amka Affair, *JARCE* 15 (1978), 43-48.

A chronological re-arrangement of certain facts, mainly from cuneiform sources, c. Šuppiluliumaš. (1) Two attacks on the Egyptian-dominated territory of Amka should be distinguished, under partly different Hittite commanders. (2) The year 16 recording an attack against Karkemish under Horemheb (our number 73596, if not actually a fake) may have been usurped from Akhnaton's counting, and thus be close to Akhnaton's probably planned attack against Canaan (compare our number 66501). (3) The request by a recently widowed Egyptian queen for a Hittite husband may safely remain associated with 'Ankhesenamun (not Nefertiti), and the deceased king (N/Bibkhupuriya) with Tutankhamun (= *Nb-ḫprw-rʿ*).

Egyptian evidence is adduced for warlike activities against the Hittites during the Amarna period (partly witnessed by Horemheb as a military commander) and afterwards (Horemheb as king, a status which retrospectively influenced the way some of the earlier campaigning was recorded). *J.F. Borghouts*

78732   SCHULMAN, Alan R., Aspects of Ramesside Diplomacy: The Treaty of Year 21, *JSSEA* 8 (1977-1978), 112-130.

Investigating some aspects of the treaty concluded in Ramses II's year 21 between him and Hattusilis the author stresses that both parties had to gain by it. After discussing the political events between the battle of Kadesh and the year 21 of Ramses II the author draws attention to the passage in the treaty affirming the succession of Hattusilis' son to the Hittite throne, with active military support of Egypt, if necessary. This he explains by pointing out that Urhi-Teshup, Hattusilis' nephew who had been deposed by him, had fled to Egypt and was there received at the court. The reason for Egypt to conclude the treaty is less clear; perhaps it was fear for an invasion of the Sea Peoples.
A summary of the paper in the same volume, p. 71.

78733   SCHULMAN, Alan R., Setau at Memphis, *JSSEA* 8 (1977-1978), 42-45, with 1 pl.

Publication of a limestone block preserved in the University Museum, Philadelphia (No. E 13655). It has been found during the Museum's excavations at Memphis, 1915-1925, and bears a representation of Setau and the names of Ramses II as well as a prayer to him. It is the right-hand part of a lintel, the other half probably bearing a similar text. The lintel may have belonged to a chapel of Ramses II in Memphis.

78734   SCHULMAN, Alan R., Two Scarab Impressions from Tel Michal, *Tel Aviv*, Tel Aviv 5 (1978), 148-151, with 1 fig., and 2 ill. on a pl.

The author discusses two scarab impressions from Tel Michal. Since they are impressed on small balls of clay (bulla) they serve as apotropaic talismans. The cryptographic inscription of one of the two is explained. *L.Z.*

78735   SEIDL, Erwin, Studien zu Urkunden aus der Satrapenzeit Ptolemaios' I., *SAK* 6 (1978), 177-184.

Studying the relations between the papyri Loeb the author argues that they constitute the archive of an official, possibly in Hermopolis, by whom the papers of a suspected *Wsjr-ḥʿ* were seized, among them one harmless document. The official, a *mr-3ḥ*, seems to be the oikonomos of the nome, while *Wsjr-ḥʿ*

may be the komogrammateus of Tehne. The author then gives a reconstruction of the matter dealt with in Pap. Loeb 4-6 and 22 concerning a field of 10 arourai, and of another field of 1 aroura.

SETTGAST, Jürgen, see our number 78832.

78736 SHEA, William H., The Inscribed Late Bronze Jar Handle from Tell Ḥalif, *BASOR* No. 232 (Fall 1978), 78-80. with 3 ill.

The shekel-sign on a bronze jar-handle from Late Bronze Age Tell Ḥalif, which was borrowed from the Egyptian hieratic, puts the evidence for the use of that Egyptian sign back to the 13th century B.C., i.e. the Canaanite period prior to the rise of the Hebrew monarchy. *L.Z.*

78737 SHINNIE, P.L., Trade in Medieval Nubia, *in*: *Études nubiennes*, 253-263.

Mit Ausnahme einiger noch unpublizierter Dokumente aus Qasr Ibrîm liefern die nubischen Texte wenig Material für die Darstellung der Wirtschaft im mittelalterlichen Nubien. Das Aussmass des Handels is unbekannt, auch über etwaige Zwischenhändler lassen sich keine Aussagen machen. Eine Geldwirtschaft fehlte weitgehend. Unsere hauptsächlichste Quelle sind arabische Berichte; archäologische Funde zeigen, dass aus dem Norden Keramik, Glas und Stoffe importiert wurden, desgleichen Bronzegegenstände, die wohl gegen Sklaven, Gold und Elfenbein eingetauscht wurden. *Inge Hofmann*

78738 SHINNIE, P.L. and Margaret SHINNIE, Debeira West. A Mediaeval Nubian Town. University of Ghana Expedition to Nubia, Warminster, Aris & Phillips, [1978] (21 x 29.5 cm; VIII + 107 p., 124 fig. [2 folding], 2 maps, 53 pl.); rev. *BiOr* 37 (1980), 58-59 (Bruce G. Trigger).

Es handelt sich um die von der Universität von Ghana in den Jahren 1961-64 durchgeführten Ausgrabungen in Debeira West, einer christlichen Niederlassung aus dem 8.- 11. Jahrhundert. Die Friedhöfe enthalten auch Gräber aus der C- und X- Kultur. Es wird die Architektur sakraler und profaner Bauten, die aufgefundene Keramik, die Kleinfunde unterschiedlichster Art beschrieben. Die Glaswaren werden von D.B. Harden, die Ostraka (griechisch, arabisch, koptisch) von J.W.B. Barns und zwei zerbrochene meroitische Stelen von dem verstorbenen B.G. Haycock beschrieben. Eine Zusammenfassung nimmt zu den Baumethoden, dem Ackerbau und der Ernährung Stellung. *Inge Hofmann*

78739 SHISHA-HALEVY, Ariel, A Coptic Proverb, *Aegyptus* 58 (1978), 174-176.

Short note on a Coptic proverb in the Bohairic *Acta Martyrum* I, 234, 19 ff. concerning the fool and the wise. *L.Z.*

78740 SHISHA-HALEVY, Ariel, An Early North-West Semitic Text in the Egyptian Hieratic Script, *Orientalia* 47 (1978), 145-162.

The author studies O. Cairo 25759 recto, published by Černý, conceiving the text to be in N.W. Semitic, although in hieratic writing. A tentative vocalized transcription and translation on p. 162.

78741 SHISHA-HALEVY, Ariel, Quelques thématisations marginales du verbe en néo-égyptien, *Orientalia Lovaniensia Periodica*, Leuven 9 (1978), 51-67.

In the author's opinion the bipartite character of a sentence where an emphasizing *sḏm=f* form occurs as the 'thème' (topic) and is being predicated over by an adverbial element is paralleled by other constructions. Such constructions where in a similar way various kinds of predication are made over a theme consist of (a) a circumstantial clause and (b) a nominalized clause. Category (a) consists of (1) *m-ḏr* + *sḏm=f*, (2) various constructions introduced by what is considered 'circumstantial' *iw* and (3) protatic clauses. (b) is represented by an agentive infinitive. Various observations follow. One of these deals with several uses of *iw*, and occasionally Coptic parallels are adduced. *J.F. Borghouts*

78742 SHISHA-HALEVY, Ariel, A Shenoutean Pun and the Preservation of a Precoptic Lexemic Distinction, *JEA* 64 (1978), 141.

The pun involves the use of the word deriving from the verbs *ḏbꜣ* 'block up' and *ḏbꜥ* 'seal', which in Coptic appear in similar form. *E.P. Uphill*

78743 van SICLEN, III, Charles Cornell, A Fragment of an Offering Table from el-Târif with a Ritual Text, *MDAIK* 34 (1978), 165-169, with 2 fig. and 1 pl.

During the excavations at el-Târif a fragmentary granite offering table has been discovered in a house near Saff el-Baqar. This block is here published, its texts translated with comments. It is an abridged version of episode 32 of the Ritual of Amenophis I, and may date from the early XXIst Dynasty. The original provenance is uncertain.

van SICLEN, III, Charles C., see also our number 78335.

SIDARUS, A.Y., see our number 78269.

SIJPESTEIJN, P.J., see our numbers 78772 and 78773.

SILVANO, Flora, see our number 78122.

78744 SIMPSON, William Kelly, Aspects of Egyptian Art: Function and Aesthetic, in: *Immortal Egypt*, 19-25, with 2 pl.

Stressing that an Egyptian work of art cannot be dissociated from its original use so that it can only be understood as an aspect of religion, the author first deals with types of statues (tomb, temple, and ex-voto statues) and their functions. Then several aspects of art are commented upon: the meaning of inscriptions on a statue, the measure of objectivity of portraits, the lack of expression of emotions, etc. As an example the author discusses O.K. offering chapels. At the end remarks about the individual qualities of artists expressed within the usual repertory.

78745 SIMPSON, William Kelly, The Mastabas of Kawab, Khafkhufu I and II. G 7110-20, 7130-40 and 7150 and Subsidiary Mastabas of Street G 7100. With drawings and contributions by Suzanne Chapman, Nicholas Thayer, Lynn Holden, and Timothy Kendall. Based upon the excavations and recordings of George A. Reisner, William Stevenson Smith, Alan Rowe, T.R.D. Greenless, Dows Dunham, and Nicholas Melnikoff of the Museum of Fine Arts, Boston – Harvard University Expedition. In collaboration with the Pennsylvania-Yale Archaeological Expedition to Egypt, Boston, Department of Egyptian and Ancient Near Eastern Art. Museum of Fine Arts, Boston, 1978 (26.5 x 33.7 cm; X + 34 p., 47 pl. with ill., 72 pl. with plans, sections and drawings [9 folding], frontispiece) = Giza Mastabas. Edited by William Kelly Simpson, 3; rev. *BiOr* 37 (1980), 158-160 (Hartwig Altenmüller).

Sequel to our number 76724 dealing with the tombs of Street G 7100, namely the double tombs of Kawab, Cheops' eldest son, and Khafkhufu I, the mastaba of Khafkhufu II, and the remains of some minor mastabas with their shafts and burial chambers. This group of tombs is situated just east of the three smaller pyramids of the Cheops complex.
The publication follows the same scheme as the preceding volumes: detailed description of all elements of each of the three main tombs, with transliteration and translation of the inscriptions, followed by a discussion of the finds and a list of the families of the owners.
From Kawab's tomb the reliefs have been largely destroyed, as have been the statues (some ten to twenty) originally standing in it. The decoration of the tombs of Khafkhufu I and II is far better preserved. The subsidiary mastabas contained a large number of vessels and two broken statues.
Like in the preceding volumes of the series the illustration, both in photograph and drawing, is abundant and clear.

SIMPSON, William Kelly, see also our numbers 78027 and 78524.

78746 SIST, Loredana, Una statua de scriba nel Museo Archeologico di Siracusa, *Vicino Oriente*, Roma 1 (1978), 133-140, with 2 pl.

Publication of the fragmentary granite statue of the Saite prophet Pedamenope (owner of Theban Tomb No. 33) preserved in the Archaeological Museum in Syracuse (Inv. No. 288), which frequently has been mentioned in the literature (cfr our number 73671, p. 172-173). The author describes the piece and gives the text on the "papyrus" lying on the scribe's knees in facsimile and translation with notes.

78747 SMITH, H.S. and D.G. JEFFREYS, The North Saqqâra Temple-Town Survey: Preliminary Report for 1976/77, *JEA* 64 (1978), 10-21, with 5 plans and fig., and 1 pl.

Work was undertaken in the vast walled enclosure 250 m sq. first discovered by Mariette at the east end of the Serapeum dromos. To the south lies an even more massive walled enclosure 325 x 275 m sq., in which cat burials were discovered in the nineteenth century. The area under discussion is connected with the Anubieion, the embalmers' quarter of Memphis, and the Asklepieion, the temple precinct of Imhotep. The footings for the Serapeum Way were discovered at the foot of the escarpment and a battered naophorous statue of XXVIth to XXXth Dynasty date showing that the site was in use in pre-Ptolemaic times. A relief of Ptolemy V Epiphanes offering incense to Anubis helped to identify the northern enclosure with the Anubieion. *E.P. Uphill*

SMITH, H.S., see also our numbers 78320, 78537 and 78700.

78748 SMITH, Mark, Remarks on the Orthography of Some Archaisms in Demotic Religious Texts, *Enchoria* 8, Teil 2 (1978), 17-27.

The author studies some of the grammatical archaisms that occur in Demotic religious texts, such as the masculine plural genitival adjective *nw*, the feminine singular genitival adjective *nt*, the preposition *mỉ*, the preposition *m*, the pseudoverbal construction *ḥr* + infinitive and the combination *ỉḫ* + *ỉs* + infinitive, which he explains as a double writing of *ḥr* + causative prefix + infinitive.
*W. Brunsch*

78749 SMITH, Mark, The Transliteration of Demotic, *Enchoria* 8, Sonderband (1978), 33-36.

Abstract of a paper read at the First International Colloquium of Demotists, held in Berlin, September 1977.
The author gives an outline of the difficulties and different methods of transliterating Demotic and suggests some changes. *W. Brunsch*

SOOTS, M., see our number 78349.

78750 SPALINGER, Anthony J., A Canaanite Ritual Found in Egyptian Reliefs, *JSSEA* 8 (1977-1978), 47-60, with 2 pl.

The author, studying several scenes of besieged Canaanite cities from N.K. temples, turns the attention to the scene in which a chief in the city holds a lit brazier in his hand. He connects it with the ritual of the child sacrifice (for that, see Keel's article, our number 75390; not quoted). From the text accompanying the scene in the temple of Beit el-Wâli Spalinger draws the conclusion that the enemy chief holding the brazier is extolling Ba'al. He adduces material from the Semitic world for the infant sacrifice and, particularly, the ritual of incense offering to Ba'al on the roof tops.

78751 SPALINGER, Anthony, The Concept of the Monarchy during the Saite Epoch — an Essay of Synthesis, *Orientalia* 47 (1978), 12-36.

The author presents an outline of the political history of the Saite Dynasty, concentrating upon the political aspect of the crown, particularly upon the "Realbild" as against the "Idealbild". He deals in turn with each of the reigns, summarizing the major traits on p. 28-29, e.g. that the rulers were no warrior-kings as those of the XVIIIth Dynasty, but rather diplomats, and regarded as mortals more than ever before, and that the deities of Sais did not benefit from the victories as Amon had during the earlier periods.

In the last part, on the so-called Saite Renaissance - about which Spalinger states in the beginning of the article that the term is not quite correct - the author i.a. argues that the choice of older elements was eclectic; in art particularly the Memphite tradition was revived, while in the literature elements from the F.I.P. are found.

78752 SPALINGER, Anthony J., The Date of the Death of Gyges and its Historical Implications, *JAOS* 98 (1978), 400-409.

Attempting to fix the date of the death of Gyges of Lydia at approximately 644 B.C. the author also discusses his sending troops to support Psammetichus I ca. 664/3 B.C. This military support was not directed against Assyria, but took place in connection with the unification of Egypt. The author also argues that the Scythian war with Psammetichus I must have taken place after 633 B.C.
*L.Z.*

78753 SPALINGER, Anthony, The Foreign Policy of Egypt Preceding the Assyrian Conquest, *CdE* LIII, No. 105 (1978), 22-47.

Un nouvel examen d'un certain nombre de monuments du règne de Taharqa montre que le règne de ce roi fut en réalité bien rempli d'activités politiques en direction de l'Asie. Dans les premières années il a dû même y exercer une certaine influence. Sa politique connut toutefois de gros déboires sur lesquels il s'explique dans une inscription où il cherche à se disculper, sans pour autant rejeter la responsabilité des désastres sur le dieu. On peut cependant reconnaître une analogie thématique avec certains textes du Moyen Empire, comme C.T. 1130 et le passage des Admonitions contenant les "reproches à la divinité". Un second chapitre concerne la politique occidentale des Assyriens, à partir de sources non égyptiennes, et la préparation de leur invasion de l'Égypte. L'article se termine par une liste des documents datés de Taharqa. *Ph. Derchain*

78754 SPALINGER, A.J., Hittite Strategy in North Syria and the Egyptian Reaction, *JSSEA* 8 (1977-1978), 69.

Abstract of a paper.
Through correct understanding of the events in the seventh regnal year of Mursilis II a better perspective on the Syrian wars of Sethi and Ramses II can be achieved.

78755 SPALINGER, Anthony, A New Reference to an Egyptian Campaign of Thutmose III in Asia, *JNES* 37 (1978), 35-41, with 1 ill. and 1 fig.

Gives an account of an unpublished fragmentary text, Philadelphia no. 1/31, carved on a limestone stela. It appears to have come from Thebes and has three lines remaining recounting the erection of a stela on the Euphrates bank. Translation and notes are provided. *E.P. Uphill*

78756 SPALINGER, Anthony, On the Bentresh Stela and Related Problems, *JSSEA* 8 (1977-1978), 11-18.

The author argues that the toponym *Bḫtn* in the text on the Bentresh stela does not mean Bactria, although it was so understood in later ages, as two passages in classical authors (Tacitus, Annals II, 60 and Diodorus I, 47, 5 ff.) prove. It was actually a mistake for Hatti, written e.g. 𓊪𓏏𓃀𓈉 , with 𓏌 for 𓈖 and 𓈘 for 𓈖. Various spellings of *Ḥt3* are quoted, among which particularly *P3-Ḥ3ty* in the letter of Amenophis II to the viceroy *Wsr-S3tt* (Urk. IV, 1344, 3), where the author also wants to read Hatti. That the *n* in *Bḫtn* was derived from cuneiform *=na*, a Hurrian suffix (Ḫatti=na), seems less likely.

78757   SPALINGER, Anthony J., Psammetichus, King of Egypt: II, *JARCE* 15 (1978), 49-57.

Sequel to our number 76741.
While in Herodotus II, 105 the encounter between Psammetichus I and the Scythians in Palestine is peaceful, it amounts to a true conflict in later classical traditions where it occurs as a part of the legends around king Sesostris (cfr our number 66399), with the Scythian king being called Idanthyrsos. Following contemporary sources, the Assyrians had withdrawn their troops to the east, and a treaty had been concluded with them. Neither was the Egyptian expansion into Western Asia which led to what can be reconstructed as a clash with the Scythians hindered by Josia of Judah. While the conflict must be pin-pointed somewhere between 621 and 616 B.C., the interval between 622 and 620 satisfies the Biblical and the Babylonian evidence as well as Herodotus' own chronology.
                                                                                                    *J.F. Borghouts*

78758   SPALINGER, Anthony, The Reign of King Chabbash: An Interpretation, *ZÄS* 105 (1978), 142-154, with 3 fig.

The reign of Chabbash, a native ruler, was a short one. It is to be placed before 338/337 B.C., and probably after July 5/6 343 B.C. He was defeated by the Persians, and ignored by the descendants of Nectanebo II and the later political, pro-Greek literature.
Addenda: *ZÄS* 107 (1980), 87, cfr 135-137.                    *M. Heerma van Voss*

SPALINGER, Anthony J., see also our number 78027.

78759   SPENCER,[A.] Jeffrey, Expedition to Saqqâra, *The British Museum Society Bulletin*, London No. 28 (July 1978), 13-15, with 6 ill.

Short report on the combined British Museum - Egypt Exploration Society expedition to record late O.K. tombs at Saqqâra.                    *L.Z.*

78760   SPENCER, A.J., Two Enigmatic Hieroglyphs and their Relation to the Sed-Festival, *JEA* 64 (1978), 52-55.

A discussion of the references to the boundary-markers used at the Heb-Sed and with links established for the half-heaven symbols also used in the broad court during running ceremonies.                    *E.P. Uphill*

78761  Spiel und Sport im alten Ägypten. Beiträge und Notizen zur Ausstellung im Schweizerischen Sportmuseum Basel. 1. September bis 30. Oktober 1978, [Basel, Schweizerisches Sportmuseum Basel, 1978] (21 x 19 cm; 53 p., 1 plan, 9 fig., 11 ill., ill. on cover).

The booklet accompanying an exhibition in the Swiss Sportmuseum in Basel consists, apart from a foreword and the greetings by President el-Sadât, of four chapters: an introduction to games and sport in ancient Egypt by the organiser, Max Triet; sport and kingship, with translations of significant passages, by Wolfgang Decker; the meaning of hunting, by Elisabeth Staehelin; and a survey of the themes of the exhibition (acrobatics, bows, children's games, wrestling, etc.), by Max Triet.
The exhibition mostly consisted of enlarged photographs and drawings, several of which here reproduced, a few accompanying advertisements.

78762  STADELMANN, Rainer, Tempel und Tempelnamen in Theben-Ost und -West, *MDAIK* 34 (1978), 171-180.

The author lists and discusses the names of the mortuary temples on the Theban West bank, first those of the XVIIIth Dynasty, then those of the XIXth Dynasty, particularly that of Sethi I. From the names and direction of the buildings he argues that there existed particular connections with the great hypostyle hall and the first court of the Luxor temple on the East bank and the mortuary temples, they all being way-stations and sanctuaries of the bark. These connections were the result of their functions during the processions that started on the one side and went to the other side of the river.

78763  STAEHELIN, Elisabeth, Zur Hathorsymbolik in der ägyptischen Kleinkunst, *ZÄS* 105 (1978), 76-84, with 1 pl. and 1 ill.

Über den Fischanhänger in *Pap. Westcar* V, 16, vgl. VI, 9. Es geht der Verfasserin um die Hathor-Ambiance in der Ruderinnengeschichte und in dem Grab des Gaufürsten Uchhotep in Meir. Die Göttin kann als Fruchtbarkeitsspenderin eng mit dem Gedanken der Wiedergeburt verbunden werden. Mehrere Begräbnisse, eine Halskette (Brit. Mus. 3077; Tafel IIa) und ein Schminkgefäss (Brit. Mus. 2572; IIb und c), erweisen diese Beziehung. Alle Belege weisen einen Fischanhänger auf und gehören (wohl) dem Mittleren Reich. Der Hathorfisch ist entweder ein Fiederbartwels oder ein Buntbarsch.   *M. Heerma van Voss*

STAEHELIN, Elisabeth, see also our number 78761.

78764  STEINMANN, Frank, Die gesellschaftliche Stellung der ägyptischen "Künstler" im Neuen Reich (1554-1085 v.u.Z.), *Das Altertum*, Berlin 24 (1978), 36-43, with 4 ill.

Defining "artists" in the widest possible sense as comprising all people connected with the production of art objects of various kinds the author distinguishes five groups of men involved: unskilled transport workers, skilled artisans, foremen, overseers (not physically engaged) and high officials. Tools and materials were property of the institutions, though the artisans also possessed some tools. The author compares the social status of the five groups.

STENN, Frederick F., see our number 78480.

78765 STERBETZ, Étienne, Documents dans les arts plastiques pour l' étude de la migration des bernaches à cou roux, *Bulletin du Musée Hongrois des Beaux-Arts,* Budapest 50 (1978), with 1 map and 3 ill.

The author studies the migration of the barnacle goose with reddish neck (Branta ruficollis Pall.) after the evidence of ancient paintings. One of them is the famous Meidum painting. The bird is now extremely rare in Egypt. Hungarian version on p. 173-175.

78766 STERNBERG, Heike, Die Grabstele des *Ḏmj* und der *Snb.t.* im Pelizaeus-Museum Hildesheim (Inv.-Nr. 4590), *GM* Heft 28 (1978), 55-61, with 1 fig. and 1 ill.

Die Stele wurde 1970 aus dem Kunsthandel erworben. Dargestellt sind der Grabherr und seine Frau vor Opfergaben und zwei kleinere Dienerfiguren in der rechten oberen Bildhälfte. Jede Person hat eine Beischrift, die direkt vor deren Gesicht angebracht ist. *Ḏmj* ist Truppenvorsteher und Vorsteher der Fremdsprachigen; die Herkunft der Stele ist wohl Gebelên. Aus stilistischen und paläographischen Gründen ist sie in die 1. Zwischenzeit zu datieren.

*Inge Hofmann*

78767 STERNBERG, Heike, Die Grabstele des *Šdj-jtj=f* und der *Nfr-ḫʿw-nb* im Pelizaeus-Museum Hildesheim (Inv.-Nr. 1884), *GM* Heft 28 (1978), 45-54, with 1 table, and 1 fig. and 1 ill.

Die Stele wurde vor 1914 aus dem Kunsthandel erworben. Das Relief ist eingeritzt und aufgemalt und zeigt Reste von rotbrauner und ockerfarbiger Bemalung. Dargestellt sind ein nach rechts gewandter, stehender Mann mit einem langen Stab und seine Ehefrau mit einem Spiegel. Beide blicken auf die Opfergaben. Das Inschriftenfeld enthält die Totenopferformel und, direkt über der Figur der Frau angebracht, eine Beischrift zur Ehefrau. Die Stele gehört unzweifelhaft zu den Stelen aus Nagʿ ed-Dêr und ist in die frühe 1. Zwischenzeit zu datieren.

*Inge Hofmann*

78768 STOOF, Magdalena, Die Darstellung des Kindes im alten Ägypten, *Wissenschaftliche Zeitschrift Martin-Luther-Universität.* Gesellschafts- und sprachwissenschaftliche Reihe, Halle-Wittenberg 27, Heft 1 (1978), 115-121, with 11 ill. on 3 pl.

The author deals with various aspects of the child in ancient Egypt, such as the relations to the parents and the family; its depiction; its education, especially for the son; the socio-economic position of children; exploitation and slavery; children and games; mortality rate.    *L.Z.*

STÓS-FERTNER, S., see our number 78270.

STRAUSS, Christine, see our number 78546.

78769 STRICKER, B.H., Architectonische monoliethen, Amsterdam-Oxford-New York, B.V. Noord-Hollandsche Uitgeversmaatschappij, 1978 (16 x 24 cm; 20 p., 1 fig., 3 ill.) = Mededelingen der Koninklijke Nederlandse Academie van Wetenschappen, Afd. Letterkunde. Nieuwe Reeks - Deel 41 - No. 5, 109-128.

The author first deals with monolithic shrines that represent the womb enclosing as the embryo the statue of the god, and then with the obelisk that represents a sun-ray descending from the zenith (*wpt*). The symbolism of impregnation by the divine word (the sun-ray) and connected concepts are discussed, while a section is devoted to a relief in the Leiden Museum (Inv. No. V 128; see p. 124) which represents a mummy beside an obelisk upon which the head of Osiris. A last section deals with the colossi standing in front of the temple on the place of the obelisks, symbolizing a human body.

STROMMENGER, Eva, see our number 78832.

78770 STROUHAL, E., Geschichte der anthropologischen Erforschung Ägyptens, *Homo*, Göttingen 29 (1978), 108-121.

The author discusses in this article the history of the anthropological research of ancient Egypt. We mention the titles of the various sections: the beginning of anthropological research in Egypt; the question of the original population compared with the historical Egyptians; attempts to describe the developments of the ancient Egyptian population and the beginnings of the anthropology of the modern Egyptians; the anthropological investigations of the anatomists of the Cairo medical school; the English biometric school; the contributions of the Italian anthropologists; other contributions to the racial history of Egypt; modern typological conceptions; modern contributions to the regional anthropology of the recent population; prospect. *L.Z.*

78771 SUTTON, Denys, The Robert and Lisa Sainsbury Collection, *Apollo*, London 107, No. 194 (April 1978), 332-344, with 42 ill. (2 in colour).

Short introduction and photographs of objects from the Sainsbury collection, which i.a. includes a M.K. hippopotamus statuette and a crouching male figure from the Gerzean Period. *L.Z.*

78772 SIJPESTEIJN, P.J., Copticisms in Greek Documents?, *Aegyptus* 58 (1978), 172-173.

Short note on possible Copticisms in two Greek documents in the Papyrussammlung in Vienna. *L.Z.*

78773 SIJPESTEIJN, P.J., Geneeskunst in het oude Egypte, *Organorama*, Oss 15, No. 2 (1978), 15-21, with 8 ill.

Slightly abbreviated version of our number 77705.

SZENTLÉLEKY, Tihamér, see our number 78157.

SZILÁGYI, Jean-Georges, see our number 78157.

78774 TAIT, W.J., Demotic Literary Texts, *Enchoria* 8, Sonderband (1978), 37-38.

Abstract of a paper read at the First International Colloquium of Demotists, held in Berlin, September 1977.
The author stresses the importance of the study of Demotic literary texts.

*W. Brunsch*

78775 TAWFIK, Sayed, Die Alabasterpaletten für die sieben Salböle im Alten Reich, *GM* Heft 30 (1978), 77-88, with 3 ill.

Alabasterpaletten mit Aufzeichnungen der sieben Salböle (sieben als heilige Zahl) sind seit der Mitte des Alten Reiches bekannt und kommen fast ausschliesslich in Privatgräbern vor; im Mittleren Reich sind sie sehr selten. Sie sind rechteckig und tragen meist am oberen oder unteren Rand kreisrunde Vertiefungen, die wohl tatsächlich als Näpfchen für die darüber oder darunter genannten Salböle dienten. Die Namen, nur zum Teil übersetzbar, lauten: Festduft, Lobpreis(?) Öl, Zederöl, *Ny-ḥnm*-Salböl, *Tw3wt*-Salböl, bestes Zederöl, bestes Libyeröl. Die Namen werden in den Opferlisten in Privatgräbern des Alten Reiches und in den P.T. genannt; im Mittleren Reich findet man in Sargkammern gelegentlich anstelle der Paletten sieben Gefässe für die Salböle dargestellt; im Neuen Reich werden die Salben im Ritual gebraucht.

*Inge Hofmann*

78776 TAWFIK, Sayed, A *wʿb* Priest Stela from Heliopolis, *GM* Heft 29 (1978), 133-138, with 2 fig. on 1 pl.

Die jetzt im Smithsonian-Institut in Washington aufbewahrte Stele wurde am 14. Juli 1976 im Weissen Haus dem Präsidenten Ford als Geschenk des ägyptischen Volkes überreicht. Die rechteckige, oben abgerundete Kalkstein-Stele wurde 1967 in Heliopolis ausgegraben. Der Text besteht aus 13 Kolumnen: der Schreiber *Nb-pḥt-Rʿ* opfert dem *k3* seines Vaters, dem *wʿb*-Priester der Hathor, der Herrin von Hetepet, *Nn* und seiner Frau, der Hausfrau *Tmt*(?). Die Darstellung zeigt in einem oberen Register *Nb-pḥt-Rʿ* vor seinen Eltern, in einem unteren Register zwei weitere Söhne, *P3sr* und *Mḥy*. Die Stele wird in die 18. Dynastie, wahrscheinlich in die Regierungszeit Amenophis' III. datiert.

*Inge Hofmann*

78777 TAYLOR, Gerald, Finger Rings from Ancient Egypt to the Present Day. Catalogue with an Introduction by Diana Scarisbrick, London, Lund Humphries for the Ashmolean Museum Oxford and the Worshipful Company of Goldsmiths, 1978 (21 x 19.8 cm; 100 p., 1 colour ill. on cover, many fig., 8 colour pl., 193 ill.).

After general information on rings, among which nine Egyptian types are described, follows the catalogue proper. For ancient Egypt 35 rings are described: scarabs, cartouche rings and various rings from the N.K. originating i.a. from Thebes, Abydos, el-Amarna and Gurob. The follow those of the Late Period and of the Greco-Roman Period, those showing Greek and Roman influences in Egypt, and the Meroitic one from Faras.

*L.Z.*

78778 TEICHMANN, Frank, Der Mensch und sein Tempel. Ägypten, [Stuttgart], Urachhaus, 1978 (21 x 25 cm; 205 p., 66 ill.[many in colour; 3 on cover], 45 fig. including plans).

The author deals with the pyramids and the N.K. temples from an anthroposophical point of view, although relying on trustworthy translations of pertinent ancient Egyptian texts. A summary, chronological table, a concise bibliography and an index conclude the volume. *L.Z.*

78779 THALMAN, Jean-Paul, Tell 'Arqa (Liban Nord). Campagne I-III (1972-1974). Chantier I. Rapport préliminaire, *Syria*, Paris 55 (1978), 1-151, with 56 fig., ill. and plans, and 4 pl.

In the section on chronology (p. 102-104) in this excavation report on Tell 'Arqa in the Northern Lebanon the author refers to its mention in the Annals of Tuthmosis III as Irqata-Arca during the campaign of year 42, which may have caused the destruction of stratum MB II B. *L.Z.*

THAYER, Nicholas, see our number 78745.

78780 THÉODORIDÈS, Aristide, Le testament à l' époque pharaonique, *Revue historique de droit français et étranger*, Paris 56 (1978), 698-699.

Abstract of a paper.

THIEME, M., see our number 78109.

78781 THIERRY, Solange, Le Musée Royal de Mariemont, *L' Œil*, Lausanne No. 278 (Septembre 1978), 38-45, with 17 ill. (2 in colour).

The author describes the collection of the Museum of Mariemont, which incorporates a small Egyptian collection. Some of the Egyptian objects are depicted. *L.Z.*

THILO, Thomas, see our number 78265.

78782 THISSEN, H.J., Demotische Texte der Kölner Sammlung, *Enchoria* 8, Sonderband (1978), 39-40.

Abstract of a paper read at the First International Colloquium of Demotists, held in Berlin, September 1977.
The author presents some of the Demotic texts of the collection of the Institut für Altertumskunde of Cologne which he is going to publish. *W. Brunsch*

THISSEN, Heinz-Josef, see also our number 78652.

78783 THOMAS, Elizabeth, The 'Well' in King's Tombs of Biban el-Molûk, *JEA* 64 (1978), 80-83.

The writer analyzes the purpose of the deep shafts in the royal tombs, as both

protection against thieves and water, in addition to any religious significance that they may have had.  
*E.P. Uphill*

TIGANI el MAHI, A., see our number 78516.

78784 TÖRÖK, L., Bemerkungen zum Problem der "römischen" Gräberfelder von Sayala (Nubien), *Acta archaeologica academiae scientiarum hungaricae*, Budapest 30 (1978), 431-435.

Review article of our number 76041.

78785 TÖRÖK, L., Money, Economy and Administration in Christian Nubia, *in*: *Études nubiennes*, 287-311.

Das meroitische Reich verfügte über keine eigene Geldwirtschaft; für die christlichen Reiche lässt sich archäologisch ebenfalls kein Geld nachweisen, wohl aber findet es sich in schriftlichen Quellen erwähnt, die sich jedoch alle auf das Nordreich Nobatia beziehen. Die Wirtschaftsbeziehungen zu Ägypten, die Bedeutung des Königs und des Eparchen, das Steuerwesen und die Verwaltung des Landes werden untersucht. Als Ergebnis wird gewonnen, dass die christlichen Reiche eine Reihe von Zügen ihrer Wirtschaftsstruktur dem meroitischen Reich entlehnt haben müssen, so u.a. den Eparchen als Nachfolger des *pešto*-Prinzen. In beiden Gestalten aber kann man nicht die Förderer der separatistischen Bewegungen sehen, wie es im allgemeinen geschieht.  
*Inge Hofmann*

78786 TÖRÖK, L., Remarks on the Meroitic Chamber in Philae, *in*: *Études nubiennes*, 313-316, with 1 folding pl.

Anhand der Personen von Manitawawi und Bekemete wird versucht, die Ausschmückung der sogenannten meroitischen Kammer in Philae zu datieren. Diese muss um 253 n.Chr. erfolgt sein, also zur Zeit des Teqorideamani. Die in der Kammer erwähnten königlichen Namen Laḫidamani und Maloqorebar werden als Mutter und Sohn nacheinander auf dem Thron folgend angesetzt und ihnen provisorisch die Pyramiden N 27 und N 26 zugewiesen. Auf sie sollen dann Yesboḫeamani mit der Regierungszeit 295-320? in N 24? und eine Königin mit der Regierungszeit 320-339? in N 25 folgen.  
*Inge Hofmann*

78787 TÖRÖK, L., Two Meroitic Studies: The Meroitic Chamber in Philae and the Administration of Nubia in the 1st to 3rd Centuries A.D., *Oikumene*, Budapest 2 (1978), 217-237, with 1 fig. and 2 tables.

Es wird versucht, die Inschriften und Szenen der sogenannten Meroitenkammer in Philae zu datieren und eine Beziehung herzustellen zwischen den gewonnenen Daten und unserer bisherigen Kenntnis der spätmeroitischen Verwaltung. Auf Teqorideamani (246-265?) folgt die Königin Laḫidamani (265-275?), dann (Maloqorebar)? (275-295?), Yesboḫeamani (295-320?) und eine Königin (320-339?)(Vgl. aber Hinkel, *Nyame Akuma*, Calgary No. 14 (May 1979), 56-59). Es folgt eine detaillierte Beschreibung der Meroitenkammer, in der die Namen Laḫidamani und Maloqorebar vorkommen, und die vier auftretenden Würdenträger vorgestellt: der nubische Vizekönig, der Flussgeneral (vgl. dazu aber unsere Nr. 76382), die römischen Gesandten und Delegierten und die Priesterschaft. Ihre Bedeutung für die spätmeroitische Verwaltung wird herausgearbeitet.

*Inge Hofmann*

78788 TOSI, Mario, Documenti di Deir el Medina (Scavi nel Museo di Torino, VIII), *Oriens Antiquus* 17 (1978), 31-34, with 3 pl.

The author publishes a column bearing the name of Hehnekhu, probably the son of Pashedu (Turin provisional No. 1005) and the upper part of a doorpost bearing a representation of Ptah, both coming from Schiaparelli's excavations at Deir el-Medîna. *L.Z.*

78789 TRAN TAM TINH, V., De nouveau Isis lactans (Supplement I), *in*: *Hommages Vermaseren*, 1231-1268, with 24 pl.

Additions to the inventory of representations of Isis lactans (see our number 73727).

TRIET, Max, see our number 78761.

78790 TRIGGER, B.G., Nubian Ethnicity: Some Historical Considerations, *in:Études nubiennes*, 317-323.

Die Bezeichnung "nubisch" einmal für ein bestimmtes Volk, dann für einen geographischen Raum, den dieses Volk bewohnt, kann erst ab dem 6. nachchristlichen Jahrhundert verwendet werden ohne Verwirrung zu stiften. Kulturelle Umwälzungen sind nicht an völkische Wanderungen gebunden, und wir wissen nicht, seit wann die Nubier tatsächlich im Niltal ansässig sind (Variationsbreite: Altes Reich und 4. nachchristliches Jahrhundert). Bei der Verwendung des Terminus "nubisch" muss geklärt werden, ob man ihn in einem geographischen oder ethnischen Sinn versteht. Wer sich mit der Kulturgeschichte Nubiens befasst, muss Rasse, Sprache und Kultur gesondert behandeln. Der ethnische Terminus "nubisch" sollte für die Gruppen reserviert bleiben, von denen wir sicher wissen, dass sie eine nilnubische Sprache gesprochen haben sowie für Kulturen, deren Mitglieder in allen Gesellschaftsschichten überwiegend Nubisch sprachen. *Inge Hofmann*

TRIGGER, Bruce G., see also our number 78008.

78791 Tübinger Atlas des Vorderen Orients. Herausgegeben vom Sonderforschungsbereich 19 "Tübinger Atlas des Vorderen Orients" der Universität Tübingen. 1. Lieferung, Wiesbaden, Dr. Ludwig Reichert Verlag, 1977 (large folio; 17 loose sheets).

This first fascicle of the Tübinger Atlas of the Near East contains the preliminary pages: title page, prefaces in German and English, a list of collaborators, the contents (with the basic division of geography and history).
Specifically to pharaonic Egypt pertains in this fascicle map B IV 2, The Nile

Delta (Egypt). Libyan Chiefdoms, by Farouk Gomaà.
See already our number 74251. *L.Z.*

78792 Tübinger Atlas des Vorderen Orients. Herausgegeben vom Sonderforschungs-bereich 19 "Tübinger Atlas des Vorderen Orients" der Universität Tübingen. 2. Lieferung, Wiesbaden, Dr. Ludwig Reichert Verlag, 1978 (large folio, 8 loose sheets).

Sequel to our preceding number.
To pharaonic Egypt pertains in this fascicle map B IV 4, Iberian Peninsula. Egyptian and Egyptianized finds, by Ingrid Gamer-Wallert (see also our number 78272). There is added a loose page containing corrections to map B IV 2, The Nile Delta (Egypt). Libyan Chiefdoms, which appeared in the previous fascicle.
*L.Z.*

78793 TUFNELL, Olga, Graves at Tell el-Yehudiyeh: Reviewed after a Life-Time, *in*: *Archaeology in the Levant*. Essays for Kathleen Kenyon. Edited by Roger Moorey and Peter Parr, Warminster, Aris & Phillips Ltd, [1978], 76-101, with 9 fig.

The author republishes the contents of a dozen graves found inside the camp and in the eastern cemetery of Tell el-Yahûdîya, and published by Petrie in "Hyksos and Israelite Cities" (1906). After a short description of the graves she first draws up a general classification of ten classes of scarab designs based on the above work and Naville, "Mound of the Jew and the City of Onias" (1891), and then compares them with the scarabs recovered in the graves. She draws the conclusion that the Hyksos camp was occupied from about 1700-1600 B.C. Then follow two lists, one on the scarabs from the graves at Tell el-Yahûdîya and the other on those in the above general publications, both according to design classes. After a description of other objects found in the graves such as pottery she draws her conclusions as to the people buried in the Tell el-Yahûdîya graves. The article ends with individual inventories of the discussed graves.
*L.Z.*

78794 TURNER, Eric G., The Terms Recto and Verso. The Anatomy of the Papyrus Roll (= Actes du XVe Congrès International de Papyrologie. Première Partie), Bruxelles, Fondation Égyptologique Reine Élisabeth, 1978 (17.1 x 24.2 cm; 71 p., 13 fig.) = Papyrologica Bruxellensia, 16.

Although mainly concerned with Greek papyrology this little monograph is of some interest to Egyptology since it deals with the recto-verso problem. *L.Z.*

78795 TUTUNDŽIĆ, Sava, Из рада Првог међународног конгреса египтолога у Каиру, Историјски гласник, Beograd 1-2 (1977), [1978], 199-200.

"From the Work of the First International Congress of Egyptology in Cairo".
A brief survey of the work of the Congress, stressing its significance.
(Correction of the press in: Историјски гласник 1-2 (1978), 200.)
*S. Tutundžić*

78796 UBERTI, Maria Luisa, Scarabeo punico del Museo Archeologico Nazionale di Cagliari, in: *Atti del 1º Convegno Italiano sul Vicino Oriente Antico*, 157-162, with 1 pl.

Short study of a Punic scarab originating from the Punic necropolis of Tharros, at present preserved in the Museo Archeologico Nazionale at Cagliari (Inv. No. 9450; former collection Spano). It may bear the name of pharaoh Achoris.
*L.Z.*

78797 USSISHKIN, David, Excavations at Tel Lachish–1973-1977, Preliminary Report = *Tel Aviv*, Tel Aviv 5, Nos 1-2 (1978), 97 p., with 30 fig. and plans, and 32 pl.

The Late Bronze Age temple at Tel Lachish (level 6, area P) is Egyptian in character. Also in level 6, near the city wall (area S) a scarab with the representation of a hunting pharaoh was found.
*L.Z.*

78798 USSISHKIN, David, Lachish. Renewed Archaeological Excavations, *Expedition*, Philadelphia, Penn. 20, No. 4 (Summer 1979), 18-28, with 20 ill. and 2 plans.

Three decorative columns from the Late Bronze Age temple form an indication of the Egyptian influence at Lachish during that period.
*L.Z.*

78799 VACHALA, Břetislav, Postavení egyptské královny ve Staré říši, *Nový Orient*, Praha 33, No. 7 (1979), 215-216, with 1 ill. and 2 pl.

Verfasser gibt eine Zusammenfassung eines Kapitels aus seiner Doktorarbeit "Sociální postavení ženy v Egyptě za Stare říše" (Die soziale Stellung der Frau in Ägypten zur Zeit des alten Reiches). Dabei benutzt er zeitgenössische Texte und analysiert im besonderen die Titel der Königinnen des A.R.   *B. Vachala*

78800 VACHALA, Břetislav, Die Stele des Sebekhotep, *Archív Orientální*, Praha 46 (1978), 36-37, with 1 pl.

The author publishes a late M.K. or XIIIth Dynasty stela of Sebekhotep son of Iku, which contains an offering formula. The stela was originally deposited in the castle of Zásmuky, Central Bohemia, but is at present in the collections of the state castle of Žleby, Central Bohemia.
*L.Z.*

78801 VALBELLE, Dominique, La porte de Tibère à Médamoud. L'histoire d'une publication, *BSFE* No. 81 (Mars 1978), 18-26, with 3 ill.

L'auteur fut chargée par Sauneron de publier le propylône ouvrant vers le grand temple de Médamoud. Elle rappelle le bon état de conservation du monument en 1743, lors du passage de Pococke, et son écroulement avant l'Expédition d'Égypte, puis les travaux du Service des Antiquités, le transport, l'apparition du soubassement.
Seul ce dernier avait fait l'objet d'articles, de la main de Drioton. Faute de restauration, et le soutènement moderne momentanément retiré, on a pu procéder à une copie sur place. La publication utilisera, outre les ancients croquis,

relevés et photos, des éléments recueillis par la suite: assemblage photographique des blocs par Robichon, puis dessins par Leïla Menassa et empreintes au latex des inscriptions plus difficiles ou inaccessibles à l'oeil. Un réseau d'allusions à l'essentiel des cultes locaux et voisins décorait le propylône, introduisant au temple lui-même. Vu le peu de hauteur conservée de celui-ci, il pourra nous apporter un appréciable complément d'information.  *J. Custers*

78802    VALBELLE, Dominique, Une tombe de la fin de l'ancien Empire à Balat, *BIFAO* 78 (1978), 53-63, with 5 fig. (1 folding) and 6 pl.

The most northern tomb at Balât (for the cemetery, see our number 78803), numbered Mt1 and being the best equipped from this modest group of tombs, is carefully described with its contents consisting of alabaster vessels, toilet equipment, amulets, and beads, and ceramic vases. It may date from the VIth Dynasty and belong to a person from the suite of the governor.

VALBELLE, Dominique, see also our number 78705.

78803    VALLOGGIA, Michel, Rapport préliminaire sur la première campagne de fouilles à Balat (Oasis de Dakhleh), *BIFAO* 78 (1978), 65-80, with 2 plans (1 folding) and 12 pl.

Report on the first campaign at Balât, at the eastern entrance to the Oasis el-Dâkhla, which was devoted to the necropolis of Qîla' el-Dâbba. The report deals exclusively with the mastaba MV (according to Fakhry's numbering) and its environment, where tombs from the O.K. are situated. First these burials are described (for tomb M1, see our number 78802), then the mastaba itself. An analysis of the painted fragments is in preparation.

VALLOGGIA, Michel, see also our number 78705.

VALOVIČ, J., see our number 78390.

78804    VANDIER †, J., Manuel d' archéologie égyptienne. Tome VI. Bas-reliefs et peintures. Scènes de la vie agricole à l'Ancien et au Moyen Empire, Paris, Éditions A. et J. Picard, 1978 (20.4 x 26.4 cm; VII + 355 p., 119 fig., 23 pl., 1 ill. on cover); rev. *Archeologia* No. 124 (Novembre 1978), 78 (A.L.); *BiOr* 36 (1979), 166-167 (William H. Peck); *CdE* LV, No. 109-110 (1980), 142-145 (Nadine Cherpion).

Sequel to our number 69620.
In the preface Posener explains that this sixth volume, the last one that will appear, deals only with part of the reliefs and paintings concerning agricultural life, those of the New Kingdom being absent, and that the seventh volume was intended to contain the scenes on temple walls.
In this volume, having the size of the previous plate volumes, the notes are placed opposite the relevant text passages and the drawings are executed on a larger scale. Also the plates are included in the volume.
The text consists of four chapters. Chapter 1 deals with the cultivating of land, and chapter 2 with flax reaping and corn harvest in the O.K., while chapter 3 is

devoted to all activities following the harvest in the O.K. The last chapter describes all agricultural scenes of the M.K., divided into those before and those of the XIIth Dynasty.
After a short bibliography there is an index to volumes IV-VI on p. 291-344.

L.Z.

78805 VARGA, Edith, Un cerceuil anthropoïde de la Basse Époque, *Bulletin du Musée Hongrois des Beaux-Arts*, Budapest 51 (1978), 41-54, with 1 fig. and 9 ill.

Publication of a wooden coffin preserved in the museum in Budapest (Inv. No. 51.2097/1-2). The object, of unknown provenance, belonged to a man called Dỉ-Ḥr-ỉ3wt and resembles the coffins of the Theban Montu priests. It is dated on account of its style to the XXIInd Dynasty.
Hungarian version of the article (Egy Késői Kori múmiakoporsó) on p.185-191.

78806 VERCOUTTER, J., Charles Kuentz (1895-1978), *BIFAO* 78 (1978), V.

Obituary article. Compare our number 78896.

78807 VERCOUTTER, Jean, Supports de meubles, éléments architectoniques, ou "établis"? (Inventaire: Balat 205-717 et 207-720), *BIFAO* 78 (1978), 81-100, with 9 fig., 2 pl. and 1 folding plan.

At the end of the first campaign at Balât a sondage was made in the settlement 'Ain Aseil at the eastern side of the oasis. Among other objects two small limestone truncated pyramids with a square hole in the top were found. Similar objects have been found at el-Amarna and Deir el-Medîna, and possibly elsewhere. They all came from houses. The author argues that they are supports for the feet of chairs and beds, studying the representations of the pieces of furniture and the few surviving actual objects and distinguishing six types of feet.
In an appendix Georges Castel presents notes to architectural elements found during the sondage in the settlement.

78808 VERCOUTTER, Jean, Les travaux de l' Institut français d' Archéologie orientale en 1977-1978, *BIFAO* 78 (1978), 565-587, with 2 folding maps, 1 folding plan and 10 pl.

Sequel to our number 77761.
Apart from an introduction to the history of the excavation program of the IFAO the report devotes most space to the first campaign in the Oasis el-Dâkhla (p. 570-576).

VERCOUTTER, Jean, see also our numbers 78013, 78136 and 78614.

78809 VERMEERSCH, P.M., Belgian Middle Egypt Prehistoric Project—1978, *Nyame Akuma*, Calgary No. 12 (May 1978), 20-22.

Ein Team des Belgian Middle Egypt Prehistoric Project der Universität Leuven hat einen Fundplatz aus dem mittleren Paläolithikum bei Nazlet Khâtir im

Nordwesten von Tahta ausgegraben. Die gefundenen Artefakte gehören der Levallois-Industrie an und können in die Zeit von 100.000 bis 40.000 vor der gegenwärtigen Zeit datiert werden. Es ist das erste Mal, dass die Levallois-Industrie mit Nil-Sedimenten des Oberen Pleistozän vergesellschaftet gefunden wurde.
*Inge Hofmann*

78810 VERMEERSCH, Pierre M., Elkab II. L' Elkabien, Épipaléolithique de la Vallée du Nil égyptien. Avec contributions de A. Gauthier, F. Gullentops, M.A. Demuynck, M. Couvert, Bruxelles, Fondation Égyptologique Reine Élisabeth/ Leuven, Universitaire Pers, 1978 (21.5 x 28 cm; VIII + 157 p., 2 maps, 10 plans, 15 tables [2 folding], 37 fig., 67 pl., and an English summary on p. 145-146); at head of title: Uitgaven van het Belgisch Comité voor opgravingen in Egypte. Publications du Comité des Fouilles Belges en Égypte; rev. *BiOr* 37 (1980), 45-46 (Fekri A. Hassan).

This is the second volume of a series; for vol. I see our number 71147.
The study is devoted to the Elkabian, a local variant of the Terminal Palaeolithic of Egypt. It consists of six chapters, dealing successively with: the geographical and geological situation of the area of Elkab; the sites (Elkab 1, 2, 3 and 4); the various types of lithic implements (with a summary of the technological and typological analyses on p. 95-100); three detailed investigations by specialists on the fauna, the C14 analyses, and the sediments of Elkab; a general survey of the Elkabian (p. 126-134), the ecological aspects and its place within the Epipalaeolithic of Egypt, and a report on the excavations in the SW part of Elkab in 1968-1969.
At the end an English summary and a bibliography.

78811 VERMEERSCH, P.-M., E. PAULISSEN, M. OTTE, G. GIJSELINGS and D. DRAPPIER, Middle Palaeolithic in the Egyptian Nile Valley, *Paléorient*, Paris 4 (1978), 245-252, with 4 fig.

Report on several middle Palaeolithic sites on the West Bank between Asyût and Nag' Hammadi: Beit Allam, Nazlet and el-Rîfa.
*L.Z.*

78812 VERNER, Miroslav, Československo-egyptská spolupráce v egyptologii, *Zprávy čs. společnosti orientalistické* 14, No. 2 (1977), 68-71.

"Die tsjechoslowakisch-ägyptische Zusammenarbeit in der Ägyptologie". Eine Übersicht über die archäologische Tätigkeit des Tschechoslowakischen Ägyptologischen Instituts in Ägypten (Teilnahme an der UNESCO-Aktion zur Rettung der Altertümer Nubiens in der ersten Hälfte der 60er Jahre und Ausgrabungen von 1960 bis heute) und über die Zusammenarbeit dieses Instituts mit der ägyptischen Altertümerverwaltung.
*B. Vachala*

78813 VERNER, Miroslav, Excavations at Abusir. Season 1976. Preliminary Report, *ZÄS* 105 (1978), 155-159, with 3 plans and 9 ill. on 6 pl.

The 11th Czechoslovak Egyptological Expedition started excavations in the "South Field" of Abûsîr on October 1st, 1976. They were dealing with a

large rectangular structure and with a group of limestone mastabas and brick tombs.
The excavators concluded that the structure had consisted of the pyramid and the mortuary temple of Queen Khentkaus, very probably the wife of Neferirkare. Discoveries included a ruined enclosure wall and a badly damaged sarcophagus chamber.
One mastaba was identified and investigated this year. It had sustained much damage owing to repeated robberies. The owner was a princess Khekeretnebty, "beloved of Isesi". Examination of her skull allowed the deduction that she died at the age of about 34. In a second building stage the tomb was enlarged, in all probability for the burial of a lady Tisethor whose false door was found in situ. Unfinished wall paintings show successive phases of execution. Next report in *ZÄS* 107 (1980), 158-169. *M.Heerma van Voss*

78814 VERNER, Miroslav, 11. egyptologická expedice, *Zprávy čs. společnosti orientalistické* 14, No. 1 (1977), 25-28.

"The 11th egyptological expedition". On the Czechoslovak excavations at Abûsîr. Compare our preceding number.

78815 VERNER, Miroslav, Umělé zavodňování ve starém Egyptě, *Nový Orient*, Praha 33, No. 9 (1978), 272-275, with 2 ill.

Ein populärwissenschaftlicher Artikel über die Problematik wasserwirtschaftlicher Arbeiten im alten Ägypten. *B. Vachala*

78816 VERNER, Miroslav, Záhady médúmske pyramidy, *Nový Orient*, Praha 33, No. 4 (1978), 110-114, with 1 ill. and 4 fig.

"Rätsel um die Pyramide von Medum".
Verfasser erörtert die Snofru-Pyramide in Medum, behandelt eingehend die Hypothese von K. Mendelssohn über die Katastrophe dieser Pyramide und verweist auf die Diskussionen zu dieser Hypothese in Ägyptologenkreisen.
*B. Vachala*

78817 VERNUS, Pascal, Athribis. Textes et documents relatifs à la géographie, aux cultes et à l' histoire d'une ville du Delta égyptien à l'époque pharaonique, [Le Caire], Institut français d' Archéologie orientale du Caire, 1978 (20.3 x 27.5 cm; XXIV + 505 p., 6 fig., 46 pl.) = Bibliothèque d'étude, 74.

The study discusses the available documentation to the city of Athribis and its region in Pharaonic times, later sources only being taken into consideration insofar as they throw light on that period.
The documents are presented in the first part (p. 1-329). They are divided into two groups: first, in a chronological order, 182 documents to the city and its surroundings (62 prior to the end of the N.K.), and then the religious texts in which Athribis or its divinities occur (Nos. 183-231). Each document is discussed, with a translation of the text and a bibliography; in several instances the text is given in printed hieroglyphs. Many less well known objects are represented by a photograph.

Part 2 discusses the results as well as the questions to which no answer is as yet possible. The first chapter deals with geographical problems: the site of Athribis, the meaning of its Egyptian name *Ḥwt-ḥry-ỉb*, its traditional name *Km-wr*, the geography of the city and the toponymy of its region.
Chapter 2 is devoted to the cults of the area, first of all that of *Ḫnty-ḫty*: his name, his iconography, his various functions and his relations to other gods, etc. Then the Osirian cults, i.a. *Km-wr* in the Osirian tradition, the Osirian relic at Athribis, the rite *ḥbs nṯr* and the goddess *Ḫwyt*, etc. (a survey of the Osirian cults in this region on p. 452-454). At the end minor divinities and goddesses venerated at Athribis. Summary of this chapter on p. 461-463.
The short chapter 3 lists the main points of the history of Athribis.
Some addenda on p. 473-474. Extensive indexes on p. 475-496.

78818   VERNUS, Pascal, Littérature et autobiographie. Les inscriptions de *S3-Mwt* surnommé *Kyky, RdE* 30 (1978), 115-146, with 5 fig.

L'auteur propose une nouvelle traduction accompagnée d'un important commentaire des inscriptions de la TT 409. L'article reprend les inscriptions en hiéroglyphes (voir notre No. 66449) et les traductions publiées antérieurement par Assmann, Brunner et Wilson. Celles-ci sont critiquées et améliorées quand il y a lieu, pour aboutir à une nouvelle traduction française donnée en fin de travail.
L'essentiel de cette étude est pourtant l'essai d'analyse littéraire du texte qui se révèle d'une grande originalité. En particulier, la distinction des différents niveaux de langue en rapport avec la diversité des contenus permet une nouvelle précision dans l'explication.                              *Ph. Derchain*

78819   VERNUS, Pascal, Une stèle archaïsante de la Basse Epoque, *GM* Heft 29 (1978), 139-143, with 1 ill.

Die hier vorgestellte Stele wurde unter den Antiquitäten bemerkt, die von der Galerie Uraeus in Paris ausgestellt waren. Vor einer Frau steht die Inschrift: "Gemacht von der Hausfrau *N3-nfr-ḥp*, Tochter des *Ḏd-Ptḥ-ỉ(w).f-ʿnḫ*", über dem ihr folgenden Mann: "Sein geliebter Sohn *Ḏd-Ptḥ-ỉ[(w).f-ʿnḫ]*". Gemäss der Namen gehört die Stele in die memphitische Gegend, nach der Epigraphie und Orthographie wahrscheinlich in die 26. Dynastie. Sie ist betont archaisierend und wirkt wie ein Denkmal aus dem Ende der 6. Dynastie und der 1. Zwischenzeit.                                            *Inge Hofmann*

78820   VERNUS, P., Un temoignage cultuel du conflict avec les Ethiopiens, *GM* Heft 29 (1978), 145-148.

In Edfu wird das Fest des Neumondtages im Verlaufe der elften Nacht von einer langen Zeremonie begleitet, während der religiöse Kompositionen verlesen werden. Eine davon ist das Ritual des "Zerstampfens der Fische" (*p3 dgdg rmw*). Dabei werden die Leichen der Rebellen von Napata erwähnt. Der Text scheint Ende der 25. oder Anfang der 26. Dynastie redigiert worden zu sein, als die *damnatio memoriae* der kuschitischen Herrscher ihren literarischen Niederschlag fand.                                          *Inge Hofmann*

VERNUS, Pascal, see also our numbers 78483 and 78705.

78821 La vie quotidienne chez les artisans de Pharaon. Le Louvre présente aux Musées de Metz. Du 12 novembre 1978 au 28 février 1979, [no place,1978] (19 x 22 cm; 107 p., 1 plan, 102 ill., colour ill. on cover).

Catalogue of an exhibition in Metz of objects from Deir el-Medîna preserved in the Louvre Museum.
After an introduction by Chr. Desroches Noblecourt and a brief description of the workmen's village by the author of the catalogue, Bernadette Letellier, the catalogue itself describes the 140 objects that were exhibited, each with technical data (but no bibliography) and the majority with a photograph. They range from coffins, stelae, reliefs and statues to baskets, tools, scarabs and ostraca, together presenting a clear picture of the workmen's community.
In a particular section (p. 84-87) Diane Harlé deals with the photographic reproduction of four pillars from the tomb of Nofretari.

VIERNEISEL, Klaus, see our number 78832.

78822 VILA, A., Quelques apports de la prospection archéologique au sud de la Cataracte de Dal, in: *Études nubiennes*, 347-358, with 10 ill. on 6 pl.

Das französisch-sudanesische Team erforschte das Gebiet zwischen dem Dal-Katarakt und der Insel Nilwatti auf beiden Ufern, und entdeckte mehr als 500 Fundplätze. Sie gehören in folgende Epochen: Paläolithikum, Mesolithikum, Neolithikum, altnubische Kultur (A-Gruppe), mittelnubische Kultur (C-Gruppe), Mittleres Reich, Kerma-Kultur, Neues Reich — dazu die Nekropole von Abri-Missiminia, die vor der 25. Dynastie angelegt und fortlaufend bis in die christliche Zeit verwendet wurde —, meroitische Kultur, X-Gruppe, christliche Kultur mit 13 Kirchen und 49 Friedhöfen. In einem Grab wurde eine Frau gefunden, die sitzend vergraben war, den Kopf auf dem Boden, und in dieser Haltung zu Tode gesteinigt worden war. Abschliessend werden die aufgefundenen Felsbilder beschrieben.  *Inge Hofmann*

78823 VILA, A., avec la collaboration de Alain FOUQUET, René FILLIOL, François RODRIGUEZ et Gonzague QUIVRON, Sid Ahmed Abd el Magid KAMIR, Bakhri Mirghani MAKKI et Osman Suleiman Mohammed ALI, La prospection archéologique de la Vallée du Nil, au Sud de la Cataracte de Dal (Nubie Soudanaise). Fascicule 9. L' île d' Arnyatta. Le district d' Abri (Est et Ouest). Le district de Tabaj (Est et Ouest), Paris, Centre National de la Recherche Scientifique, 1978 (21 x 27 cm; 137 p., 5 maps, numerous ill., fig. and plans); at head of title: Section française de Recherches Archéologiques/Sudan Antiquities Service. Khartoum National Museum; rev. *BiOr* 37 (1980), 329 (P.L. Shinnie); *CdE* LV, No. 109-110 (1980), 163-165 (Brigitte Gratien).

Sequel to our number 77771.
The volume deals with the island of Arnyatta and the districts of Abri and Tabaj on both riverbanks. First general sections on the geography and archaeology of the area, followed by an index of the sites arranged in chronological order. The major part of the volume consists of the sites' catalogue, each site be-

ing briefly described with its major finds, which are illustrated by photographs, drawings and plans of burials. Several of them date from the Christian Period, but other periods are present as well. We mention the Meroitic cemetery of Sheikh Amir Abdullah (Abri East; p. 68-85), where i.a. the head of a statue has been found (ill. 31, p. 73).

78824 VILA, A., avec la collaboration de Alain FOUQUET, René FILLIOL, François RODRIGUEZ et Gonzague QUIVRON, Sid Ahmed Abd el Magid KAMIR, Bakhri Mirghani MAKKI et Osman Suleiman Mohammed ALI, La prospection archéologique de la Vallée du Nil, au Sud de la Cataracte de Dal (Nubie Soudanaise). Fascicule 10. Le district de Koyekka (rive droite). Les districts de Morka et de Hamid (rive gauche). L' île de Nilwatti, Paris, Centre National de la Recherche Scientifique, 1978 (21 x 27 cm; 111 p., 5 maps, numerous ill., fig. and plans); at head of title: Section française de Recherches Archéologiques/Sudan Antiquities Service. Khartoum National Museum; rev. *BiOr* 37 (1980), 329 (P.L Shinnie); *CdE* LV, No. 109-110 (1980), 163-165 (Brigitte Gratien).

Sequel to our preceding number.
The volume is devoted to the area adjoining to the South that of the preceding one, situated on both riverbanks at the sides of the island of Sai. Remains from all periods have been discovered, particularly on the W. bank, where two Christian villages are found near Toshkei (p. 52-58) and Kayendi (81-85). On the island of Nilwatti in the South the remains of a Christian town with seven square towers (104-107).

78825 VITELLI, Karen D., Egyptian Artifacts Stolen from Aswan Museum, *Journal of Field Archaeology*, Boston 5, No. 1 (Spring 1978), 97.

Short description of 16 objects with their inventory numbers stolen from the museum at Aswân. L.Z.

78826 VITTMANN, Günther, Eine demotische Erwährung des Pabasa, *Enchoria* 8, Teil 2 (1978), 29-32.

In P. Louvre E 10935 there occurs a $ḥs$ $(n)$ $ḫn$-'$Imn$ $Mḥj$-$(m$-$)wsḫ$.$t$, daughter of a $r$-$p^ꜥ$.$t$ $ḥ3$.$t$-$p$-$ꜥ3$ $stm$-....,X, son of $P3$-$dj$-$b3st$.$t$. The name of $Mḥj$-$(m$-$)wsḫ$.$t$'s father was read $P3$-$rbj$ (?) or $P3j$-$bs$ (?) by Malinine. Vittmann shows, that $P3j$-$bs$ is the correct reading and that he is none other than the well-known Chief Steward Pabasa, the owner of the Theban Tomb No. 279. Furthermore he proves that the Demotic group after $stm$-$(ꜥš$ $)$- .... is to be read $dw3$-$ntr$.
W. Brunsch

78827 VITTMANN, Günther, Priester und Beamte im Theben der Spätzeit. Genealogische und prosopographische Untersuchungen zum thebanischen Priester- und Beamtentum der 25. und 26. Dynastie, Wien, [Afro-Pub], 1978 (14.5 x 20.8 cm; VI + 249 p., 12 pl.) = Veröffentlichungen der Institute für Afrikanistik und Ägyptologie der Universität Wien, 3 = Beiträge zur Ägyptologie, 1; rev. *BiOr* 36 (1979), 306-309 (M.L. Bierbrier). Pr. ÖS 215

This study of Theban priests and officials consists of an introduction, six chapters presenting and discussing the material, and a summary.
In the introduction the author explains his time-limits (c. 750-525) by stating that the great Theban families of the Saite Period disappeared at the beginning of the Persian domination. As regards the Theban area, this is the best documented at that time.
Chapter 2 deals with the family of Besenmut, mainly Montu-priests, and its lateral branches, with particular attention i.a. to its relation with the viziers, particularly Montuemhat (p. 36-39). Chapter 3 is devoted to the higher priesthood of Amon (first to fourth prophets) among which several of fairly low descent. Chapter 4 studies the families of the great stewards of the Divine Consort; chapter 5 the viziers, an incomplete series, possibly since in some periods the great stewards took over this function; chapter 6 the mayors of Thebes; chapter 7 the bearers of the (in some instances honorary) title "Overseer of Upper Egypt".
The abundantly documented study, illustrated by several genealogical tables, ends with extensive indexes to sources and private names (204-236) and an equally complete bibliography (237-249). On the plates some as yet unpublished pieces: five statues from Cairo, stelae from Heidelberg, Turin and Cairo, and a sarcophagus from Boston.

78828 VITTMANN, G., Zu den thebanischen Totelstelen der 25. und 26. Dynastie (Korrekturen und Ergänzungen zu P. Munro, *Die spätägyptischen Totenstelen* [ÄgFo. 25] 187-228), *Orientalia* 47 (1978), 1-11.

Corrections and addenda to our number 73523.

78829 VITTMANN, Günther, Zum Verständnis von Schiffbrüchiger 129 f., *GM* Heft 29 (1978), 149-152.

Untersucht wird die von Goedicke (unsere Nr. 74240) als "Belehrung" verstandene Interpretation der bisher als "Stern" übersetzten Einleitung der Erzählung der Schlange über das Unglück ihrer Angehörigen. Es wird versucht nachzuweisen, dass das bisherige Verständnis als eines Sternes, der von Himmel herabstürzt, das richtige war, zumal sich dieser Topos eines kosmischen Phänomens auch sonst in der ägyptischen Literatur nachweisen lässt. Ein "Sternwunder", das einen Kampf entscheidet, findet sich auch im Hethitischen. Hingewiesen wird auch auf eine ugaritische Parallele zur Erzählung der Schlange im "Schiffbrüchigen". *Inge Hofmann*

78830 VITTMANN, Günther, Zwei thebanische Totenstelen der 26. Dynastie im Seattle Art Museum, *WZKM* 70 (1978), 5-14, with 2 pl.

Of two hitherto unpublished wooden Late Period stelae from Deir el-Bahri, now in the Seattle Art Museum (Inv. Nos Eg. 32.1 = 48.223 and Eg. 32.2 = 48.224) the author presents a typology according to Munro (our number 73523), a description, the inscriptions in translation, a commentary and remarks on the genealogy. *L.Z.*

78831 VODOZ, Irene, Les scarabées gravés du Musée d'Art et d'Histoire de Genève. Mémoire de licence dirigé par Robert Hari, [Genève, Éditions de Belles-Lettres], 1978 (21 x 30 cm; 176 p., numerous fig., 36 pl.) = Aegyptiaca Helvetica. Herausgegeben von/publiée par Ägyptologisches Seminar der Universität Basel et Faculté des Lettres de l' Université de Genève, 6.

After a preface by Hari and an introduction about the scarab in general by the author the book contains a catalogue of 90 scarabs plus 35 of which the genuineness is doubtful. Each of the 90 major pieces is carefully described, with the technical data, a drawing of the underside (by Christiane Castioni) and three photographs, of the underside, back and one side (by Elisabeth Gaudin). The doubtful pieces are briefly treated, but with drawing and photographs.
The scarabs are divided into several groups, each preceded by general remarks. They are: scarabs with royal names (Nos 1-12); with $Mn\text{-}ḫpr\text{-}R^c$ (13-26); with representations of persons (27-34); of divinities (35-51); with phrases (52-54); representations of animals (55-64); symbols (65-79); ornamental and vegetal designs (80-88); names of officials (89-90).
Among the major pieces we mention: one of Shepseskaf (No. 1); one with the titles and names of Tuthmosis I (No. 4); a "Marriage Scarab" of Amenophis III (No. 7); one with a human head, possibly a negro, on its back (No. 50); one with name and titles of the chancellor $Snb\text{-}sw\text{-}m^c$ from the XIIth Dynasty (No. 90).
Bibliography, indexes and tables of concordances with the inventory numbers at the end.

VOIGT, K., see our number 78095.

78832 Von Troja bis Amarna. The Norbert Schimmel Collection New York. Herausgegeben von Jürgen Settgast unter Mitarbeit von Ulrich Gehrig, Eva Strommenger, Klaus Vierneisel, [Mainz, Philipp von Zabern, 1978] (21 x 23 cm; 219 [unnumbered] p., numerous ill. [many in colour], 2 maps, coloured frontispiece, colour ill. on cover); at head of title: Verein zur Förderung des ägyptischen Museums Berlin-Charlottenburg; rev. *Acta Archaeologica Academiae Scientiarum Hungaricae* 31 (1979), 420-421 (L. Castiglione).

This is the catalogue of an exhibition in Berlin, Hamburg and Munich of 310 objects from the Norbert Schimmel collection. For a catalogue of an earlier exhibition in Cleveland of objects from the same collection, see our number 74021.
The Egyptian items are numbered 191-310, of which the numbers 286-310 are talatat. They are preceded by an introduction by Settgast, while a few lines introduce the Amarna reliefs. The objects are all carefully described, with mention of their date, material and measurements, and of each one or more photographs. Several of them are the same as those in the older catalogue, which, however, comprises less numbers.

VOS, René L., see our number 78109.

78833 VYCICHL, Werner, Coptic Dialect Geography Based on Inscriptions, *Enchoria* 8, Sonderband (1978), 63[*] (109)-65[*] (111).

Abstract of a paper read at the First International Congress of Coptology, held in Cairo, December 1976.
An important and up to now often neglected source for localizing Coptic dialects are toponyms, personal names and remnants of Coptic words in local Egyptian (Arabic) dialects. This study is being undertaken by the author.

W. Brunsch

78834 VYCICHL, W., L'état actuel des études chamito-sémitiques, in: *Atti del Secondo Congresso Internazionale di Linguistica Camito-Semitica*. Firenze, 16-19 aprile 1974. Raccolti da Pelio Fronzaroli, [Firenze], Istituto di linguistica e di lingue orientali. Università di Firenze, 1978 (= Quaderni di Semitistica, 5), 63-76.

The author deals with two specific features of the Hamitic languages (Egyptian, Berber, Cushitic, Tchadic): the biliteral verbs and the "emphatic" verb form of the Egyptian and the geminated verb form in the other Hamitic languages. Then the author discusses various problems such as the question of the Hamitic group of languages as a unity, the close relationship between the Semitic and the Egyptian, a short discussion of the name of the god Kneph-Agathos Daimon (Eg. *km 3t.f*), studies on the vocalization of ancient Egyptian, and the word for statue (*twtw*).
The rest of the article is devoted to the other Hamitic languages. His conclusion is that the common features of the Hamito-Semitic languages go back to a common source and are not borrowed from the Semitic. L.Z.

78835 WADSTEN, Tommy, Characterization of the Solid Residue in an Ancient Egyptian Alabaster Jar, *Medelhavsmuseet Bulletin*, Stockholm 13 (1978), 14-18, with 5 fig.

Investigation of the contents of the vase MME 1957:2 (see our number 78628) proved the residue to consist of the proper ingredients for preparing soap.

WAGNER, Guy, see our number 78705.

78836 WAHBAH, Gamal, Two Ramesside Blocks Discovered on Philae, *MDAIK* 34 (1978), 181-183, with 2 fig. and 2 ill. on a pl.

The author publishes two inscribed blocks found on Philae, one mentioning the viceroy Setau and parallel to one found in Buhen, the other with the lower part of a scene and the words "the fortress of Ramses Meryamon".

WAHBA[H], Gamal, see also our number 78247.

78837 WALDBAUM, Jane C., From Bronze to Iron. The Transition from the Bronze Age to the Iron Age in the Eastern Mediterranean, Göteborg, Paul Åströms Förlag, 1978 (22.5 x 31 cm; 106 p., 15 fig., 36 tables) = Studies in Mediterranean Archaeology, 54.

In this book concerned with the introduction of iron in the Eastern Mediterranean between 1200-900 B.C. Egypt is dealt with in each chapter in a separate

section. After an introduction on the selection and distribution of the material, on the chronology, and remarks with respect to the pertinent countries, the author deals first with the distribution of iron in the Bronze Age. Then follows the period 1200-900 B.C. for which also a comparison with other metals is made.
The last chapter is devoted to the raw materials, mining and metallurgy in that time. Summaries at the end of each chapter.
Conclusions, bibliography and an index of place names at the end of the book.
L.Z.

WALKER- ONI, R.A., see our number 78578.

78838   van de WALLE, Baudouin, La chapelle funéraire de Neferirtenef, Bruxelles, 1978 (21.5 x 27 cm; 96 p., 2 plans, 3 fig., 23 pl.[6 folding]); at head of title: Musées Royaux d'Art et d'Histoire. Koninklijke Musea voor Kunst en Geschiedenis.                                            Pr. F.B. 950

This is the final publication of the tomb chapel of Neferirtenef in the museum at Brussels, on which the author has published already in 1930 a "Notice sommaire" (re-edited in an improved version in 1973; see also our number 74786). In the introduction the author relates the modern history of the mastaba that stood originally near the SE corner of the Step Pyramid and came to Brussels in 1907. The first chapter is devoted to the architecture of the building and the state of its conservation; the second to $Nfr$-$\overset{?}{\imath}r.t.n.f$, his functions and his family; the third to the decoration which, in view of the restricted space in the chapel, could only contain a choice of the usual scenes.
Then, in what is by far the longest chapter (p. 23-76), all scenes are described, with the texts in hieroglyphs and translation, followed by conclusions. The next short chapter argues that the decoration is to be dated to the second half of the Vth Dynasty.
In an appendix the two known statues of Neferirtenef, Cairo C.G. 21 and 157, are briefly dealt with.
A bibliography on p. 85-89, followed by the plates that bear drawings of the entire wall scenes with all inscriptions and photographs of chosen details.

78839   WARD, William A., The Egyptian Objects, *in*: Patricia Maynor Bikai, The Pottery of Tyre, Warminster, Aris & Phillips Ltd, [1978], 83-87, with 1 fig. in the text and 4 fig. on the pl.

The author publishes the Egyptian objects from the pottery of Tyre. They are an inscribed vase fragment of the XXVth to XXVIth Dynasties, an inscribed quartz cylinder seal from the beginning of the O.K., and some scarabs and an ovoid, mostly from the N.K.                                            L.Z.

78840   WARD, William A., The Four Egyptian Homographic Roots $b3$. Etymological and Egypto-Semitic Studies, Rome, Biblical Institute Press, 1978 (19.5 x 26.9 cm; VI + 196 p., 6 fig.[1 folding]) = Studia Pohl: Series Maior. Dissertationes scientificae de rebus orientis antiqui, 6; rev. *BiOr* 37 (1980), 139-140 (Jürgen Osing).                                            Pr. L. 9600/ $12

After an introduction on the purpose of the study and the consequences of its results for verification of other suggestions and conceptions, the author sets forth in chapter 1, on morphological questions, preliminary remarks on homonyms and homographs in Semitic and Egyptian, on the w-, n- and ḥ- prefixes and the loss of alef, and he discusses the problem of the biconsonantal root in Semitic and Egyptian.

The next four chapters are each devoted to one of the four roots b₃ he distinguishes and are subdivided into an introduction on the Semitic cognates, a discussion on the Egyptian terms, and a summary. In the second chapter the author discusses the first root, labelled b₃ I, meaning "to tremble, to flutter", which is a dialectical variant of p₃ = Sem. pr. Among the words studied there is the word sb₃, "star". The root has only a limited range. Chapter 3 is devoted to the root b₃ II, "to break earth, to open". The terms are subdivided into verbs meaning "to break, to smash", words for "hole", etc., among which a word b₃w/by, "a kind of ship" and bbwyt, "a kind of wig"; into objects which "dig" or "make holes"; and words derived from the meaning "to open up" (wb₃). The summary states that there are two major semantic bases: "to break earth", without w-prefix and with reduplicated forms, and "to drill open", with w-prefix and without reduplicated forms.

After a review of the scholarly opinions on the b₃ concept, the author discusses in chapter 4 the root b₃ III, which may, in origin at least, essentially mean "to possess supra-mundane power". No cognates of the root are known, the root indeed expressing uniquely Egyptian ideas. By far the longest chapter 5 is devoted to b₃ IV, "to pour out , to mix", which is familiar from the Semitic. After an excursus on Sem. wbl = Eg. wb₃, "to carry", the author discusses words derived from the sense "to pour out"; words indicating a "reservoir" for liquids; words for objects used to pour out; words derived from the sense "to pour out (semen)=to impregnate"; from the sense "to mix liquid and dry ingredients"; and words meaning "moist", etc. So far this root was unrecognised in Egyptological lexicographical studies.

Chapter 6 is concerned with the spellings of b₃, "ba" and b₃, "ram" in the P.T. and C.T., the results of which are summarized in a conclusion.

Index of Egyptian, Demotic, Coptic and Semitic words discussed at the end.

*L.Z.*

78841   WARD, William A., The $H\overset{\circ}{i}w$-Ass, the $H\overset{\circ}{i}w$-Serpent, and the God Seth, *JNES* 37 (1978), 23-24, with 1 fig. and 1 table.

Seth was associated with the ꜥ₃-ass as early as the M.K., whereas the term $h\overset{\circ}{i}w$ translated by the writer as "braying ass" appears as early as the P.T., and could therefore provide an earlier link with the god. The term can also be used to denote the serpent Apophis. The different traditions of North and South are discussed and the occurrences of the word on M. Eg. coffins tabulated.

*E. Uphill*

78842   WARD, William A., Scarabs from the Montet Jar. A Late Eleventh Dynasty Collection at Byblos, *Berytus*, Beirut 26 (1978), 37-53, with 4 fig. and 5 tables.

Proceeding from his earlier study together with Olga Tufnell in which they argued that the objects in the "Montet Jar" date from the Herakleopolitan Period (see our number 66588) the author here analyses the 68 scarabs from the jar, dealing with them as a group and attempting to indicate their place in the history of the early scarab style (see also our following number). He concludes that they are later than the standard F.I.P. scarabs, but earlier than those of the XIIth Dynasty, although sharing features of both periods.

78843   WARD, W.A., Studies on Scarab Seals. Volume I. Pre-12th Dynasty Scarab Amulets. With an Appendix on the Biology of Scarab Beetles by S.I. Bishara, [Warminster, Aris & Phillips Ltd, 1978] (21 x 29.6 cm; X + 116 p., 52 ill. and fig., 16 pl., frontispiece).  Pr. £12.50

In the introduction the author discusses earlier studies on scarabs (the book of Hornung and Staehelin, our number 76387, was not yet available to him) and the aims of the present work. The wide-spread occurrence of scarabs makes them useful for establishing the relative chronology in the Mediterranean world. For a correct typology and chronology the study of back and sides of the objects is essential, while, since the early instances do not bear names or titles, the typology is exclusively based, apart from the shape and dimensions, on the designs.

Chapter 1 presents the preliminaries: materials and method. The latter consist of establishing a sequence of the types on account of the finds from well dated contexts (220 items), supplemented by 171 items from a more vaguely dated origin. In chapter 2 this material is statistically analysed as regards the dimensions of the scarabs, their designs, the types of the heads, back and side, and the materials of which they consist. This leads to the distinction of four overlapping periods (period 4 mainly represented by the objects from the Montet Jar). The result is a historical description of the development of the scarab style until the early XIIth Dynasty.

Chapter 3 contains remarks on the design repertoire. First a discussion of the original meaning and use of the scarab, stating that it is an amulet and that there is no definite proof of sealing with it before the time of Amenemhet I. Ward then deals with the history of the designs, distinguishing seven classes (class 1, linear patterns, with 5 sub-classes), and with the interpretation of their meaning. He i.a. rejects for this period Drioton's cryptographic theory. There follow four appendices. Appendix A contains notes on the dating of some stylistic features, e.g. the *nbtỉ* design and the *smȝ* symbol. Appendix B discusses the early private-name scarabs, probably dating from the time of Amenemhet I. Appendix C deals with the use of amethyst before the XIIth Dynasty. In Appendix D Sadek Ibrahim Bishara discusses biology and identification of the scarab beetles.

At the end a chronological distribution list (p. 102-108) and an inventory (109-115) of the 391 objects on which the study has been based, and which all are represented by drawings (mostly three of each item; no. 390 not illustrated) on the plates, with on the opposite pages mention of their measurements, classification, material, bibliography and period.

78844   WEBB, Virginia, Archaic Greek Faience. Miniature Scent Bottles and Related Objects from East Greece, 650-500 B.C., Warminster, Aris & Phillips Ltd, [1978] (21 x 30 cm; XI + 176 p., map on endpapers, colour frontispiece, 27 fig., 5 maps, 2 plans, 22 pl., colour ill. on cover); rev. *Acta Archaeologica Academiae Scientiarum Hungaricae* 31 (1979), 429-430 (L. Castiglione); *CdE* LV, No. 109-110 (1980), 174 (Albert Leonard, Jr.). Pr. £17.50

By the very nature of this book on archaic Greek faience Egypt is dealt with very often.
After an introductory chapter discussing the history of the use of faience in Egypt and its composition and techniques on account of its influence on the archaic Greek faience, the next nine chapters are devoted to the various types. In each chapter the author particularly discusses the Egyptian types and motifs when dealing with origins and iconography, as well as in her conclusions, while also the detailed catalogues to the various types contain many references to Egypt. Among the types discussed are those of double vases with a kneeling figure and jar in front, of kneeling women with a baby on their back and an ibex in their lap, those with decorations of animals, human beings and plants, with animal and human shape, and with cartouches of XXVIth Dynasty kings. Detailed notes on p. 152-169 and an index on p. 171-174. L.Z.

78845 WEIGALL, Arthur E. P., A Report on the Antiquities of Lower Nubia (The First Cataract to the Sudanese Frontier) and Their Condition in 1906-7. A Photographic Reprint with Additions, Oxford, Printed at the University Press by Horace Hart, 1907 [Printed in Dar el-Maaref, 1978] (24 x 34 cm; XX + 142 p., 94 + 7 pl., 3 maps [one folding, in colour], 2 colour pl.). Pr. P.T.2450

Reprint of the original edition of 1907, to which have been added p. IX-XIV, with an alphabetical list of the monuments threatened by various building stages of dams, and an indication of what happened with each of them (by Dia' Abou-Ghazi). To it belongs a supplement to the plates, with two maps and 14 ill. of the reconstruction works on the temples and their present state.

78846 WEINFELD, Moshe, "ימן השמים נלחמו". בישראל ובמזרח הקדמון התערבות גרפים שמימיים בקרב עם האויב, *in*: *H.L. Ginsberg Volume*. Editor Menahem Haran, Jerusalem, The Israel Exploration Society, 1978 (= Eretz-Israel. Archaeological, Historical and Geographical Studies, 14), 23-30, with an English summary on p. 122-123, non Hebrew section.

" 'They Fought from Heaven' - Divine Intervention in War in Ancient Israel and in the Ancient Near East".

78847 WEINSTEIN, James, A New Shawabti of the Viceroy Nehy, *JARCE* 15 (1978), 39-42, with 1 pl.

The object (sandstone; l. 53 cm), now in Burlington, Vermont, Robert Hull Fleming Museum (Inv. No. 1910.6.1) was acquired in Egypt about 1851. The *dossier* of this XVIIIth Dynasty viceroy is drawn from 19 monuments.
J.F. Borghouts

WEINSTEIN, James M., see also our number 78151.

78848   WELCH, Eugene Douglas, The *Lebensmüde* and its Relationship to the Hedonistic Harpers' Song of the Middle-New Kingdoms, *Dissertation Abstracts International*, Ann Arbor, Mich. 39, No. 5 (November 1978), 2916-A.

Abstract of a thesis Brandeis University, 1978 (229 p.; Order no. 7819965). The author reworks the entire translation of the "Lebensmüde", avoiding the connotation of suicide. In his opinion, the *ba* is arguing for an escape into an irresponsible hedonism, but finally recognizes the validity of the man's more responsible approach.                                                           L.Z.

78849   WENIG, Steffen, Meroitische Kleinkunst, Leipzig, Insel Verlag, 1978 (12 x 18.2 cm; 56 p., 32 colour ill., ill. on cover) = Insel-Bücherei Nr. 1027.

Thirty-two full-page colour illustrations of small Meroitic objects of art (decorated vessels, jewellery, statuettes, etc.) are followed by a few pages on Meroitic art (p. 35-46). The catalogue of the objects with data and a short note to each of them on p. 47-55.

WENIG, Steffen, see also our number 78008.

WENTE, Edward F., see our number 78347.

78850   WERNER, Edward K., The Amarna Period of Eighteenth Dynasty Egypt. Bibliography Supplement 1977, *Newsletter ARCE* No. 106 (Fall 1978), 41-56.

Third annual supplement to the basic bibliography in our number 76831, again provided with author and title indexes. Sequel to our numbers 76832 and 77795.                                                                                                                       L.Z.

WERNER, Gunnel, see our number 78630.

78851   WERTIME, Theodore A., Tin and the Egyptian Bronze Age, *in*: *Immortal Egypt*, 37-42.

In December 1976 there have been found three mines of casserite in the Eastern desert of Egypt (see our number 76593), while the author discovered this ore a month afterwards near the sixth cataract. These discoveries may completely alter our ideas about the origin of tin in Egypt and the Near East. Neither Iran, Turkey, Greece nor Thailand appear to be its source, but there is at least a strong probability that it came from Egypt and Nubia.

78852   WESSEL, Klaus, Die Stillende Gottesmutter, *SAK* 6 (1978), 185-200, with 2 pl.

The author once more discusses the theme of the Galactrophusa in Coptic art.

78853   WESSETZKY, V., Ein Beitrag zur Geschichte der ägyptischen Kulte in Brigetio, *in*: *Hommages Vermaseren*, 1316-1319, with 1 pl.

In addition to his study of Egyptian cults in Hungary (our number 61733) the author discusses evidence for these cults from Brigetio (Ószöny), a Pannonian frontier town, particularly two Osiris statuettes.

78854 WESTENDORF, Wolfhart, Altes Ägypten, in: *Krankheit, Heilkunst, Heilung*. Herausgegeben von Heinrich Schipperges, Eduard Seidler, Paul M. Unschuld, Band 1, Freiburg i. Br., Verlag Karl Albert, 1978, 115-143.

In this valuable study of the meaning of health and disease in the Egyptian civilization the material is divided into three sections dealing with the sources, diseases, and healing.
The first section not only gives a survey of the medical texts but also a discussion of their nature and contents, various categories of diseases, etc. In the second section the concept disease is discussed in connection with the Egyptian ideas concerning life and death. Various subjects, such as the origins of diseases, social behaviour with regard to ill people, development of the concept during the ages, and contacts with other civilizations are dealt with. The last section is concerned with the activities of the doctor, his methods and their background, the social position of doctors, etc.

78855 WESTENDORF, Wolfhart, Beiträge zum Wörterbuch, *GM* Heft 29 (1978), 153-156.

Es werden die Wörter behandelt: 1. ꜥbj(.t) = "Zügel"; 2. *ḥśj = "verbrennen"; 3. mštpn = "Mäuse-Ohr" = Vergissmeinnicht? Bei letzerem kann es sich aber nicht um unsere Gartenblume "Vergissmeinnicht" handeln, sondern um ein zu derselben Familie gehörendes Bor(r)etschgewächs, das als Küchen- und Gewürzpflanze diente und dessen blaue Blüten als Kranzschmuck verwendet werden konnten.                                                                                   *Inge Hofmann*

78856 WESTENDORF, Wolfhart, Bemerkungen zum Abschluss des Koptischen Handwörterbuches, *Enchoria* 8, Sonderband (1978), 41-44.

Abstract of a paper read at the First International Colloquium of Demotists, held in Berlin, September 1977.
Since the last fascicle of the Koptisches Handwörterbuch (our number 77801) has come out now, the author gives an outline of the future tasks that remain to be done on the Coptic lexicon.                                                                         *W. Brunsch*

78857 WESTENDORF, Wolfhart, Geleitwort [Zu Hans Jakob Polotsky. Göttingen 25. Juli 1928], *GM* Heft 28 (1978), 9-10, with 1 pl.

Das vorliegende Heft ist Hans Jakob Polotsky gewidmet, der 1928 sein Studium der Ägyptologie an der Georg-August-Universität Göttingen beendete. Seine Dissertation "Zu den Inschriften der 11. Dynastie" eröffnete eine Reihe von Arbeiten, die zu den Standardwerken der Ägyptologie und Koptologie gehören. Die Beiträge, die nur von Mitgliedern des Ägyptologischen Seminars der Universität Göttingen stammen, sollen darlegen, dass Polotsky im Seminar seinen festen Platz hat.                                                                                    *Inge Hofmann*

78858 WESTENDORF, Wolfhart, Uräus und Sonnenscheibe, *SAK* 6 (1978), 201-225, with 22 fig.

After a short systematic survey of the relations between the uraeus and the sun-god the author discusses the historical development leading to this connection, from the Prehistoric Period onwards. He follows the motif of the sun-bearer from the giraffe with a sun-disk on its head through the snake-neck panthers to the snake, referring to other sun-bearing animals, to the hieroglyph $k\hat{\imath}s$ (in Cusae), to the replacement of the cat by the snake as sun-bearer, etc.

WESTENDORF, Wolfhart, see also our number 78488.

78859   WHITE, John Bradley, A Study of the Language of Love in the Song of Songs and Ancient Egyptian Poetry, [Missoula, Montana], Published by Scholars Press for the Society of Biblical Literature, [1978] (13.6 x 21.2 cm; 217 p., 2 tables) = Society of Biblical Literature Dissertation Series, 38; rev. *BiOr* 36 (1979), 164 (Ph. Derchain); *ZAW* 90 (1978), 458 ([G.Fohrer]).   Pr. $6

Since the author proceeds from the hypothesis that the language of love in Solomon's Song of Songs is reminiscent of that in Egyptian love poetry, a considerable part of the book is devoted to Egyptian love poetry. In chapter 2 he studies for that reason the cultural milieu of the O. and M.K., and particularly that of the XVIIIth Dynasty. The chapter is concluded by a discussion of the problem of popular or artistic poetry, elements both present in the ancient Egyptian love poetry. Chapter 3 analyses themes, fictions and genres in Egyptian love poetry, mainly on account of Hermann's Altägyptische Liebesdichtung (our number 59286). Chapter 4 is devoted to the place of the Song of Songs in relation to the Egyptian love poetry. The above hypothesis is confirmed in the retrospect of the conclusion in chapter 5, while in the prospect remarks follow on the structure, the setting, the genre and the meaning of the Song of Songs. The appendix presents a translation with notes of the Egyptian love poems.
The book is concluded by a selected bibliography arranged after texts, reference and general works, and an index to biblical references.   *L.Z.*

78860   WIERCIŃSKI, Andrzej, Pyramids and Ziggurats as the Architectonic Representations of the Archetype of the Cosmic Mountain. Part II, *Almogaren*, Graz 8 (1977), 1978, 167-187, with 7 fig., 5 ill. and 8 tables (1 folding).

Sequel to our number 77807.
Although the second part of the article is not concerned with Egyptian pyramids, the author states in his conclusion that the qualitative and numerical analysis of the architectonic structure of 28 Egyptian pyramids show in all probability that they represent the Cosmic Mountain.   *L.Z.*

78861   WILDUNG, Dietrich, Götter-Pharaonen, *Die Kunst und das schöne Heim* 90, Heft 6 (Juni 1978), 333-340, with 13 ill. (4 in colour).

Short article on the occasion of the exhibition "Götter-Pharaonen", travelling around Germany and Holland. Compare our number 78305.

78862   WILDUNG, Dietrich, Eine königliche Statuengruppe der Nachamarnazeit, *SAK* 6 (1978), 227-233, with 1 fig. and 2 pl.

The author demonstrates that the small female torso in the Hermitage (Inv. No. 18577) was originally part of a dyad of which a male torso in the Musée d'Art et d'Histoire, Genève (Inv. No. 12440) is the male figure. He also argues that the persons represented are Pharaoh Eye and his wife.

78863 WILDUNG, Dietrich, Staatliche Sammlung ägyptischer Kunst, *Münchner Jahrbuch der bildenden Kunst*, München 28 (1977), 219-224, with 5 ill.

The author publishes the recent acquisitions of the Egyptian collection in Munich. We mention: from the Protodynastic Period a cylindrical vessel (Inv. No. ÄS 6077); from the M.K. the golden figure with inlays of a king engaged in the cultic running (probably from Illâhûn; Inv. No. ÄS 6071); a sistrophorous kneeling statue of Senmut, probably from Armant (Inv. No. ÄS 6265; more extensive description); three small Bes figures, possibly from el-Amarna (Inv. No. ÄS 6266); eighteen moulds for amulets, N.K. (Inv. Nos ÄS 6267-6284); the head of a royal shawabti, from the post-Amarna Period (Inv. No. ÄS 6076); faience tiles with the name of Ramses II, possibly from Qantîr (Inv. No. ÄS 6074/75); a mummy mask being part of a coffin, from the late N.K. (Inv. No. ÄS 6072); and a heart scarab, probably from Thebes, XXIst Dynasty (Inv. No. ÄS 6073).
L.Z.

WILDUNG, Dietrich, see also our numbers 78006 and 78305.

WILLIAMS, Bruce, see our numbers 78496 and 78597.

78864 WILLIAMS, Ronald J., Piety and Ethics in the Ramessid Age, *JSSEA* 8 (1977-1978), 131-137.

The author deals with the heightened moral sensibility that appears from some texts from Deir el-Medîna, demonstrating that Breasted's description of the Ramesside Period as "the age of personal piety" is not incorrect. He discusses concepts such as $gr$, "the silent man", $mniw$, "shepherd" and $šd$, "saviour", as well as the Egyptian concept of sin, that is, offence against Maʿat. Besides this moral sensibility there existed the belief in the powers of magic expressed in the mortuary texts.
A summary of this paper in the same volume, p. 69.

WILSON, R. McLaurin, see our numbers 78267 and 78269.

78865 WINTER, Erich, Der Apiskult im alten Ägypten, [Mainz, no publisher, 1978] (22 x 23.5 cm; 35 p., 14 ill. [11 in colour]).

This booklet, printed on behalf of the Novo-Industrie, a pharmaceutical firm, by the Verlag Philipp von Zabern, is not for sale.
The text, in German and English, presents a survey of the Apis cult in Egypt, the life of the Apis bull, and the tombs of the Apis bulls. In the last two pages brief remarks as to the Apis in the Hellenistic world.
Although intended for the general public the text, based on Egyptian and classical evidence, contains valuable scientific remarks, while the splendid photographs enhance the value of the study.

78866 WINTER, Erich, Der Herrscherkult in den ägyptischen Ptolemäertempeln, *in*: *Das ptolemäische Ägypten*, 147-160.

The author discusses the cult of the deceased Ptolemaic rulers as occurring in the temples of the period. He presents a list of 23 instances of deified kings, in a chronological order from Ptolemy III to IX, in which the ruling king turns to his predecessor(s), and five more in which the deceased kings appear as θεοί σύνναοι. The texts speak of the transfer of power to the ruling king and of the cult to the dead ones. The Ptolemaic ancestors never were generally deified; they always remained god for specific aims. Moreover, living kings never received an offering.

78867 WINTER, Peter, "Von Troja bis Amarna". The Norbert Schimmel Collection New York, *Pantheon*, München 36 (1978), 360-362.

Short report on an exhibition. For the catalogue see our number 78832.

78868 de WIT, Constant, Égypte des Ptolémées. Luxor, Gaber Aly Hussein, [no date] (10.8 x 16.5 cm; 57 p., 3 plans, 2 ill. on cover).

Very brief guide book for travellers to Ptolemaic Egypt, consisting of a historical introduction, description of the major temples, and an alphabetical list of place-names, each with with a few remarks regarding its importance for that period.

78869 de WIT, Constant, Oud-Egyptische kunst. Een inleiding. 2e verbeterde druk, Luxor, Gaber Aly Hussein, [1978] (15 x 19.7 cm; 165 p., numerous plans and fig., 66 pl., 2 ill. on cover).

Reprint, with small corrections, of a history of Egyptian art, the first edition of which has appeared in 1946 (Antwerpen-Brussel-Gent-Leuven, Uitgeversmij. N.V. de Standaard-Boekhandel).
The present edition lacks the footnotes and the index of the first, as well as bibliographical references at the end of the chapters. The 149 ill. on the plates are the same (colour frontispiece is missing), but of less quality. The size of the present volume is smaller.

78870 de WIT, Constant. Oue voir en Égypte?, Luxor, Gaber Aly Hussein, [1978] (10.8 x 16.5 cm; [III +] 67 p., 2 colour ill. on cover).

In this small guide without ill., maps and plans, the author describes, after a short historical survey and a chronological table, in a very concise way, the antiquities in the Cairo Museum and the buildings from the Islamic and Coptic periods in Cairo, those of Giza-Saqqâra-Memphis, Thebes, Dendera, Abydos, Esna, Edfu, Kom Ombo, Aswân and surroundings (including the St. Simeon monastery and the mausoleum of the Aga Khan), the High Dam, and Abu Simbel. The last page is devoted to general information.                L.Z.

78871 de WIT, Constant, Le rôle et le sens du lion dans l'Égypte ancienne. 2ième édition avec nouveaux addenda et corrigenda, Luxor, Gaber Aly Hussein Éditeur,

1978 (14.8 x 19.7 cm; XXXVII + 481 p., ill. on cover).

Second, revised and augmented edition of our number 2107. Actually the book is a reprint, on a much reduced scale, with on p. 476-481 new corrigenda and addenda (the first edition of 1951 had already some on unnumbered pages).

WITHCOMB, Donald, see our number 78597.

78872 WOLF, George, A Historical Note on the Mode of Administration of Vitamin A for the Cure of Night Blindness, *The American Journal of Clinical Nutrition*, New York 31 (1978), 290-292.

The author discusses the Egyptian way of curing eye diseases as xerophtalmia and night blindness by applying liver extracts to the eye.   *L.Z.*

78873 WOOD, Wendy, A Reconstruction of the Reliefs of Hesy-re, *JARCE* 15 (1978), 9-24, with 10 fig. on 4 pl. and 2 tables.

A reconsideration of the relative order of the six surviving wooden panels of the Saqqâra tomb of Hesi-rēʿ (5 representing the owner standing, 1 sitting before his offering table) from the inner chapel-corridor (containing 11 niches in all, in S-N direction, along west wall). Position of one is known as last and northermost (certified find by Quibell); here the owner (standing) gives, and the objects in his hand (ḥs-vase, rc-disk) form a name anagram. He extends (offerings) to a painted sitting figure on adjoining wall (only feet preserved), perhaps the king (Djoser), a unique feature before the N.K. Relative order of five others (all from niches of the south part; Mariette find) can be determined by taking their informational status as a guideline. Thus, the one with the sitting owner (best piece, probably master sculptor's work) heralds the program; the others (standing) show an active-passive alternation in attitude, as a kind of metric flow. Rectangular apertures on upper part of all perhaps once meant for fastening emblems of geographical districts where owner served during life (and continued to do so now, in afterlife). Relief iconography can be correlated to typology of contemporary tomb statuary.   *J.F. Borghouts*

78874 WYSOCKI, Zygmunt, Deir el-Bahari 1973-1974, *Études et Travaux* 10 (1978), 387-395, with 4 ill. and 1 folding fig.

Sequel to our number 76850.
Report of the director of the Polish mission at Deir el-Bahri. As regards the research and documentation works, he deals i.a. with the lapidarium containing the various architectonic elements of the temple on the Middle Terrace, the fragments of protodoric columns from various parts of the temple, and the South wall of the Upper Court. Errors in previous reconstructions are pointed out, and the discovery of a wigmaker's workshop is mentioned (compare our number 78469). The most arduous task of the campaign was the reconstruction of the South Wall of the Upper Court.
Cfr. our number 78416.   *L.Z.*

78875 YADIN, Yigael, The Nature of the Settlements During the Middle Bronze IIA Period and the Problem of the Aphek Fortifications, *Zeitschrift des Deutschen*

*Palästina-Vereins*, Wiesbaden 94 (1978), 1-23, with 9 fig. and plans, and 1 pl.

Discussing the nature of the settlements of the MB IIA Period in Israel, which began at ca. 1950-1900 B.C. and is contemporary with the Egyptian XIIth Dynasty, the author argues that the settlements were open in the period on account of the Egyptian policy.
Palestine's agricultural products constituted its essential importance for Egypt, and therefore, Egypt's political-military interest was to ensure that the cities should not be fortified. This necessitated the establishment by Egypt of a few strongholds for Egyptian garrisons, fortified by the Egyptians themselves.
The decline of Egyptian strength after the first phase of the XIIIth Dynasty in Palestine enabled the petty rulers to establish independent regimes and to fortify their cities. *L.Z.*

78876  YELLIN, Janice Wynne, The Role and Iconography of Anubis in Meroitic Religion, *Dissertation Abstracts International*, Ann Arbor, Mich. 39, No. 5 (November 1978), 3078-A.

Abstract of a thesis Brandeis University, 1978 (289 p.; Order no. 7819968). This study on the significance and iconography of Anubis in Meroitic religion consists of three parts: comparative iconography, archaeology, statistics. The conclusion is that his worship developed from and was always closely related to his cult in Egypt. *L.Z.*

78877  YOYOTTE, Jean, Apopis et la montagne rouge, *RdE* 30 (1978), 147-150.

Les toponymes *'I3k* et *Mrkḥ* de quelques notices de temples tardifs désignent vraisemblablement un seul lieu proche du Gebel el-Ahmar. La couleur de la roche serait à l'origine du mythe étiologique qui situait à cet endroit l'anéantissement d'Apophis.
(Voir aussi notre No. 78892). *Ph. Derchain*

78878  YOYOTTE, Jean, Religion de l'Égypte ancienne, *Annuaire. École Pratique des Hautes Études*. Ve section - sciences religieuses, Paris 86 (1977-1978), 163-172.

Sequel to our number 77822.
The author deals in some detail with the texts on a pink granite tub dedicated during the reign of Pharaoh Harsiesis of the XXIInd Libyan Dynasty (Egyptian Museum Cairo J.E. 37516). The text which is a copy of a purely Busirite ritual testifies also to a flourishing cult at Coptos of Osiris of Abydos, who developed in a later period into Osiris-Gebtyouy.
A short note on the problems concerning Tanis follows. *L.Z.*

78879  YOYOTTE, Jean, Un souvenir d'un grand prêtre memphite en Cyrénaïque, *RdE* 30 (1978), 174-175, with 1 fig.

L'auteur identifie le propriétaire d'un fragment de statue trouvé à Ptolémaïs de Cyrène. C'était le grand prêtre de Ptah Harmakhis fils d'Anemho (seconde moitié du 3e s.a.C.). *Ph. Derchain*

78880   [YOYOTTE, Jean], Sujets de thèses II, *BSFE* No. 81 (Mars 1978), 27-29.

Sequel to our number 77825.
List of 33 theses, all from the École du Louvre.                                    *L.Z.*

78881   [YOYOTTE, Jean], Sujets de thèses III, *BSFE* No. 82 (Juin 1978), 34.

Sequel to our preceding number.
6 theses are mentioned, all but one from the Sorbonne.                              *L.Z.*

78882   [YOYOTTE, Jean], Sujets de thèses IV, *BSFE* No. 83 (Octobre 1978), 36-39.

Sequel to our preceding number.
First a list of theses defended since 1 January 1978, followed by the subjects announced in 1978-1979, and some modifications.                                                  *L.Z.*

78883   YOYOTTE, Jean et Philippe BRISSAUD, Mission française des fouilles de Tanis. Rapport sur les XXVe et XXVIe campagnes (1976-1977), *BIFAO* 78 (1978), 103-140, with 7 plans (4 folding), 7 fig. (2 folding) and 10 pl.

Sequel to our number 73811.
In the first section Yoyotte deals with the research program. Excavations were made in three areas: the temple of Khonsu-Neferhotep, the area with constructions between its eastern wall and the Sacred Lake, and the wall West of the latter.
Both authors together present a description of the 25th campaign, while Brissaud describes that of 1977. On p. 121-122 a general survey of the present condition of the entire site.

78884   YURCO, F., Merenptah's Palestinian Campaign, *JSSEA* 8 (1977-1978), 70.

Abstract of a paper.
The author argues that the battle and triumph sequence represented on the W. wall of the Cour de la Cachette belongs to Merenptah, not to Ramses II, as generally suggested. One scene may refer to a field battle with Israel. The campaign must have pre-dated year 5 of Merenptah.

78885   YURCO, Frank, Meryet-Amun: Wife of Ramesses II or Amenhotep I. A Review, *Serapis* 4 (1977-1978), 57-64.

The author studies the limestone fragment from the Fitzwilliam Museum, recently published by Anne Millard (our number 77533). While she attributed the figure on it to the daughter and later wife of Ramses II, the author argues from the pose of the figure and the orientation of the inscription that she is accompanying the (deified) Amenophis I, not worshipping him.
Hence she is probably his wife (see also our number 78496). The piece may date from the Amarna or the post-Amarna Period.

78886   ZANDEE, J., L'Authentikos Logos, *BiOr* 35 (1978), 3-21.

A review article of our number 77523.

78887 ZAUZICH, Karl-Theodor, Demotische Papyri aus den Staatlichen Museen zu Berlin. Lieferung I. Papyri von der Insel Elephantine, Berlin, Akademie-Verlag, 1978 (21 x 30 cm; portefolio containing X + 54 loose p. and 20 loose pl. [11 folding] ).

In a brief introduction the author relates that the Demotic Elephantine papyri have been found during the excavations of 1906-1908, and that publications were prepared and in some cases delivered by Spiegelberg and Erichsen (see list on p. IX).
To each separate text one to three pages are devoted, while the plates bear fine photographs of all of them. A brief description is given of the outer appearance, followed by a transliteration with comments, and a brief summary of the contents. The texts are letters and accounts.

78888 ZAUZICH, Karl-Th., Ein Index der demotischen Literatur (IDL), *Enchoria* 8, Sonderband (1978), 45-46.

Abstract of a paper read at the First International Colloquium of Demotists, held in Berlin, September 1977.
The author announces his plan of compiling an index of Demotic literary texts.
                                                              W. Brunsch

78889 ZAUZICH, Karl-Theodor, Neue literarische Texte in demotischer Schrift, *Enchoria* 8, Teil 2 (1978), 33-38.

This article, originally a paper read at the First International Congress of Egyptology in Cairo 1976, deals with new fragments of literary Demotic texts in the Papyrussammlung West-Berlin.             W. Brunsch

78890 ZAUZICH, Karl-Th., Neue Namen für die Könige Harmachis und Anchmachis, *GM* Heft 29 (1978), 157-158.

Die Lesung der Namen Harmachis und Anchmachis geht auf Revillout zurück, doch ist das Ende nicht -*m-3ḫ t* sondern -*wn-nfr* zu lesen. Die neuen Lesungen *Ḥr-wn-nfr* und *ʿnḫ-wn-nfr* sind hieroglyphisch gut belegt, ausserdem ist *Ḥr-wn-nfr* sicher mit dem aus einem Graffito in Abydos bekannten Hyrgonaphor identisch. Daher ist der vermutete Aufstand des Hyrogonaphor zu streichen, da er gleichbedeutend mit dem des Rebellen "Harmachis" ist.     Inge Hofmann

ZEMMER-PLANK, L., see our number 78593.

78891 ZIBELIUS, Karola, Ägyptische Siedlungen nach Texten des Alten Reiches, Wiesbaden, In Kommission bei Dr. Ludwig Reichert Verlag, 1978 (17 x 24 cm; XXII + 290 p.) = Beihefte zum Tübinger Atlas des Vorderen Orients. Reihe B (Geisteswissenschaften), 19; rev. *BiOr* 37 (1980), 315-317 (Hans Goedicke); *CdE* LV, No. 109-110 (1980), 133-136 (Alain-Pierre Zivie).      Pr. DM 76

This volume of the series is devoted to place-names from the O.K., that is, the period between Djoser and the end of the VIth Dynasty. The names are listed alphabetically, from *ȝwrt* to *ḏdt*, followed by a few partly or wholly ill-

legible names. For each item the O.K. sources are indicated, its possible or certain date and localization discussed, and remarks on the divinities connected with it, transliteration, meaning of the name, and suchlike questions discussed. Not included are sites which are merely archaeologically known. Hence the material here presented will lead to drawing one of the two maps of the O.K., and much material not localized will not find a place on it. Excluded are e.g. most names of domains, except those that developed later into places.
In her introduction the author deals with general problems. She points out the paucity of archaeological sources for some regions and the problems of co-ordinating our knowledge from philological and from archaeological material. She also remarks that several later place-names already occur in the O.K. epithets of divinities. Study of lexical, grammatical and other aspects of place-names is to be made in connection with toponyms of later periods.
Indexes on p. 283-290.

ZIEGLER, Christiane, see our number 78056.

78892 ZIVIE, Alain-Pierre, Les carrières et la butte de Yak, *RdE* 30 (1978), 151-162.

Le toponyme *'I3k* (discuté et identifié par Yoyotte, notre No. 78877) apparaît pour la première fois dans l'histoire de Sinouhé. L'auteur examine en détail l'itinéraire de ce dernier et propose de localiser *'I3k* quelque part à l'ouest du Gebel el-Ahmar.                              *Ph. Derchain*

78893 ZIVIE, Alain-Pierre, Une empreinte de sceau d'époque saïte, *RdE* 30 (1978), 175-177, with 1 ill.

Une empreinte de sceau au cartouche d'Apriès. Provenance inconnue.
                                                                *Ph. Derchain*

78894 ZUHDI, Omar, Benteshina and the *n‘rn* Division, *JSSEA* 8 (1977-1978), 141-

The author argues that the *n‘rn* division that saved Ramses II's life at Kadesh was a contingent sent by Benteshina, the King of Amurru. For reasons of national pride these foreigners were depicted as Egyptian regulars.

## NECROLOGIES

78895 Avdiev, V.I.: ВДИ 4 (146), 1978, 208 (anonymous).

78896 Kuentz, Charles: *Annuaire. Association amicale des anciens élèves de l'École Normale Supérieure*, Paris, 1979, 81-82 (Jean Leclant); *BIFAO* 78 (1978), V (J. Vercoutter); *BSFE* No. 82 (Juin 1978), 4-5 (anonymous).

78897 Maragioglio, Vito: *Aegyptus* 58 (1978), 222-224 (Silvio Curto).

78898 Omlin, Joseph A.: *Aegyptus* 58 (1978), 222-224 (Silvio Curto).

78899 Rinaldi, Celeste: *Aegyptus* 58 (1978), 222-224 (Silvio Curto).

78900 Schiff Giorgini, Michela: *Oriens Antiquus* 17 (1978), 299-300 (Sergio Donadoni); *Studi classici e orientali* 29 (1979), 13-14 (Edda Bresciani).